INTERSECTIONS

INTERSECTIONS

Essays in the Sciences and Humanities

Steven D. Scott
Don Perkins
Erika Rothwell

University of Alberta

Prentice Hall Allyn and Bacon Canada
Scarborough, Ontario

Canadian Cataloguing in Publication Data

Main entry under title:

Intersections : essays in the sciences and humanities

Includes indexes.
ISBN 0-13-680059-9

1. College readers. 2. Essays. 3. Readers—Science. 4. Readers—Humanities.
5. English language—Rhetoric. I. Scott, Steven D. (Steven Douglas).
II. Perkins, Don.   III. Rothwell, Erika.

PE1417.157 1999   808.4   C99-930623-2

Allyn and Bacon, Inc., Needham Heights, MA
Prentice-Hall, Inc., Upper Saddle River, New Jersey
Prentice-Hall International (UK) Limited, London
Prentice-Hall of Australia, Pty. Limited, Sydney
Prentice-Hall Hispanoamericana, S.A., Mexico City
Prentice-Hall of India Private Limited, New Delhi
Prentice-Hall of Japan, Inc., Tokyo
Simon & Schuster Southeast Asia Private Limited, Singapore
Editora Prentice-Hall do Brasil, Ltda., Rio de Janeiro

ISBN 0-13-680059-9

Vice President, Editorial Director: Laura Pearson
Acquisitions Editor: Nicole Lukach
Developmental Editor: Lisa Phillips
Production Editor: Avivah Wargon
Copy Editor: Marjan Farabaksh
Production Coordinator: Wendy Moran
Cover Design: Anne Goodes
Cover Image: PhotoDisc
Page Layout: Christine Velakis and Heidi Palfrey

1 2 3 4 5   WEB   03 02 01 00 99

Printed and bound in Canada.

Visit the Prentice Hall Canada Web site! Send us your comments, browse our catalogues, and more at **www.phcanada.com**. Or reach us through e-mail at **phabinfo_pubcanada@prenhall.com**.

Table of Contents

ALPHABETICAL BY AUTHOR

Preface   *xiii*

Honoré de Balzac   **1**
"The Pleasures and Pains of Coffee" (1830)

Wendell Berry   **6**
"Why I Am Not Going to Buy a Computer" (1990)

Roberta Bondar   **12**
"Liftoff!" (1994)

Rachel Carson   **20**
"A Fable for Tomorrow" (1962)

Samuel L. Clemens   **23**
"Political Economy" (1870)

John Haslett Cuff   **28**
"Eat Your Hearts Out Cinephiles, The Tube Is Where It's At" (1996)

Marie Curie   **31**
Introduction to *Radioactive Substances*

Charles Darwin   **34**
Excerpt from *The Origin of Species* (1859)

Paul Davies   **38**
"Doomsday" (1994)

Charles Dickens   **43**
"Frauds on the Fairies" (1853)

Annie Dillard   **50**
"Living Like Weasels" (1982)

Edward Dolnick   **54**
"The Ghost's Vocabulary" (1991)

Umberto Eco   **61**
"Letter to My Son" (1964)

Jan Furlong   **67**
"Straight Talk at the Parakeet Café" (1998)

Alan Goodman   **70**
"Bred in the Bone?" (1997)

Stephen Jay Gould   **78**
"The Monster's Human Nature" (1995)

O. B. Hardison, Jr.   **86**
"Charles Darwin's Tree of Life" (1989)

Werner Heisenberg   **94**
"What Is an Elementary Particle?" (1976)

Douglas Hofstadter   **105**
"A Person Paper on Purity in Language" (1983)

Sherida Houlihan and John H. Wotiz   **113**
"Women in Chemistry Before 1900" (1973)

Michael Ignatieff   **120**
"Myth and Malevolence" (1995)

Jay Ingram   **124**
"The Atom's Image Problem" (1996)

Axel Kahn   **128**
"Clone Mammals . . . Clone Man?" (1997)

Walter Karp   **132**
"Why Johnny Can't Think" (1985)

Perri Klass   **138**
"India" (1987)

Thomas S. Kuhn   **143**
"The Route to Normal Science" (1962)

Lewis H. Lapham   **153**
"Sense and Sensibility" (1991)

Stephen Leacock   **158**
"A, B, and C: The Human Element in Mathematics" (1911)

Robert W. Lucky   **162**
"Finger-Pointing" (1985)

Rick McConnell   **166**
"Beginning to Understand the Beginning" (1996)

Walter Russell Mead   **170**
"Why the Deficit Is a Godsend" (1993)

Jessica Mitford   **179**
"Behind the Formaldehyde Curtain" (1963)

William Morris   **186**
"The Revival of Handicraft" (1888)

Joyce Carol Oates   **194**
"'State-of-the-Art Car': The Ferrari Testarossa" (1985)

George Orwell   **199**
"Politics and the English Language" (1946)

Cynthia Ozick   **210**
"Crocodiled Moats in the Kingdom of Letters" (1989)

Henry Petroski   **215**
"Lessons from Play; Lessons from Life" (1992)

Heather Pringle   **226**
"The Way We Woo" (1993)

Hilary Rose   **236**
"Marie Curie and Mileva Einstein Marić" (1994)

Morton L. Ross   **243**
"Praise to the Albany" (1975)

John Ruskin   **250**
"The English Villa," from *The Poetry of Architecture* (1838)

Richard Selzer   **259**
"A Mask on the Face of Death" (1987)

David Suzuki   **269**
"The Road from Rio" (1992)

Jonathan Swift   **276**
"A Modest Proposal" (1729)

Henry David Thoreau   **283**
"The Ponds," from *Walden* (1854)

Sherry Turkle   **287**
"Ghosts in the Machine" (1995)

J. D. Watson and F. H. C. Crick   **293**
"Molecular Structure of Nucleic Acids:
A Structure for Deoxyribose Nucleic Acid" (1953)

Ian Wilmut et al.   **297**
"Viable Offspring Derived from Fetal and Adult Mammalian Cells" (1997)

Marie Winn   **305**
"Television and Reading" (1985)

Glenn Zorpette   **313**
"How Iraq Reverse-Engineered the Bomb" (1992)

Appendix A: Lisa Grekul   **327**
"Putting Self-Help 'Leviathans' and 'Oracles' to Sleep":
A Discussion of Anthony Robbins' *Awaken the Giant Within* and
James Redfield's *The Celestine Prophecy* (1998)

Appendix B: Cherina Sparks   **333**
Fishing for Coyote in Sheila Watson's *The Double Hook* (1998)

**Appendix C: Robert Gust, Chris Turner, Peter Karl,
and Scott Koehn**   **340**
Detection of Landmines: A Technical Report for a Course in
Mechanical Engineering (1998)

Glossary   *356*

Title Index   *359*

Date Index   *361*

Alternative Table of Contents

THEMATIC

Biology, Natural History, and Nature

Carson   20
Darwin   34
Dillard   50
Goodman   70
Gould   78
Hardison   86
Kahn   128
Suzuki   269
Thoreau   283
Watson and Crick   293
Wilmut et al.   297

Business and Economics

Clemens   23
Mead   170
Morris   186
Swift   276
Zorpette   313

Chemistry

Balzac   1
Carson   20
Houlihan and Wotiz   113
Ingram   124
Watson and Crick   293
Wilmut et al.   297

Computers

Berry   6
Dolnick   54
Turkle   287

Education

Karp   132
Petroski   215

Engineering

Lucky   162
Morris   186
Petroski   215

Humour

Clemens   23
Dickens   43
Hofstadter   105
Leacock   158

Language and Communication

Clemens   23
Cuff   28
Dolnick   54
Furlong   67
Hofstadter   105
Ignatieff   120
McConnell   166
Turkle   287

Manners and Morals

Berry   6
Eco   61
Ignatieff   120
Lapham   153
Mitford   179
Pringle   226

Medicine

Klass   138
Selzer   259
Watson and Crick   293

Myth and Story

Davies   38
Dickens   43
Gould   78
Ignatieff   120
Leacock   158

Physics

Curie   31
Heisenberg   94
Ingram   124
Zorpette   313

Places

Furlong 67
Klass 138
Ross 243
Ruskin 250
Selzer 259

Race and Racism

Goodman 70
Hofstadter 105

Science and Ethics/Culture

Cuff 28
Kahn 128
Klass 138
Lapham 153
Mitford 179
Morris 186
Selzer 259
Winn 305
Zorpette 313

Scientists

Carson 20
Curie 31
Darwin 34
Heisenberg 94

Technology and Inventions

Berry 6
Bondar 12
Cuff 28
Mitford 179
Morris 186
Ruskin 250
Turkle 287
Watson and Crick 293
Wilmut et al. 297
Winn 305
Zorpette 313

Women and Science

Bondar 12
Rose 236

Alternative Table of Contents

STYLISTIC/RHETORICAL

Analogy

Davies 38
Dillard 50
Ingram 124
Leacock 158
Suzuki 269

Argument/ Persuasion

Berry 6
Eco 61
Gould 78
Hardison 86
Kahn 128
Karp 132
Mead 170
Swift 276
Watson and Crick 293

Bullets and Lists

Berry 6
Orwell 199

Cause and Effect

Berry 6
Dolnick 54
Eco 61
Ignatieff 120
Karp 132
Swift 276
Zorpette 313

Classification

Carson 20
Darwin 34
Dolnick 54
Goodman 70
Heisenberg 94
Kuhn 143
Orwell 199

Collaboration

Houlihan and Wotiz 113
Watson and Crick 293
Wilmut et al. 297

Comparison– Contrast

Clemens 23
Cuff 28
Ignatieff 120
Ingram 124
Morris 186
Rose 236
Winn 305

Definition

Berry 6
Goodman 70
Heisenberg 94
Ingram 124
Morris 186
Ruskin 250

Description

Balzac 1
Dillard 50
Eco 61
Furlong 67
Goodman 70
Ingram 124
Mitford 179
Oates 194
Ross 243
Ruskin 250
Thoreau 283

Example

Dickens 43
Houlihan and Wotiz 113
Ignatieff 120
Ingram 124
Lapham 153
Lucky 162
McConnell 166
Mitford 179
Orwell 199
Petroski 215

Narration

Bondar 12
Clemens 23
Dickens 43
Furlong 67
Leacock 158
Lucky 162
Ross 243

Process Analysis

Bondar   12
Dolnick   54
Lapham   153
Mitford   179
Ozick   210
Pringle   226
Ruskin   250
Swift   276
Zorpette   313

Research

Dolnick   54
Goodman   70
Gould   78
Turkle   287
Watson and Crick   293
Wilmut et al.   297
Zorpette   313

Preface

This collection of essays began as a response to the limitations of the available textbooks used in writing courses that are taken typically by science and technology students, and taught by humanities instructors. We began this project with the premise that the essay is a variable and cross-disciplinary form, and with the awareness that most essay anthologies are collections of writings in either the humanities *or* the sciences. We wanted to question and cross that boundary. As we began to put this collection together, we proceeded from fairly simple desires. We are all experienced instructors of composition and literature classes, and we decided that we wanted to include essays that we would enjoy, or that we had enjoyed, teaching in the classroom—in particular, but not exclusively, to students whose interests or majors were in the sciences. We wanted a selection that would embrace the range of writing that reflects on technology, in both scientific and cultural fields; a selection that would demonstrate good, clear, emphatic, interesting writing on a variety of topics within those fields; a selection of essays that could serve as models of effective writing and that employed techniques that students could incorporate into their own writing.

We began by looking for essays by contemporary writers whose works we admire, in periodical publications that we enjoy reading. We searched our sources for appropriate essays and articles, then began to sort our initial choices and to seek out new pieces for representation across styles, subject matter, genders, and cultures. We collected essays that deal with biology, natural history, chemistry, computers, women's issues, engineering, business, economics, technology, scientific ethics, language, communication, and manners and morals. As our search continued, we began, inevitably, to consider some standard and classic essays by authors whose work has been tested successfully in many classrooms. Our collection soon acquired another characteristic: it spans a wide range of historical periods.

Keeping our mixed sciences/humanities audience in mind, we settled on five principles of selection. First, we have selected essays that provide some historical coverage of the essay as a literary form, without making *Intersections* into an anthology that is devoted solely to the history of the essay. We have included essays as early as Swift's from the beginning of the eighteenth century, but we have also included essays published as recently as 1998. Second, we have included essays that we find enjoyable to read. The quality of the writing itself was very important when we were making our choices. We have, therefore, selected essays by long-established writers, but we have also chosen essays by newer, sometimes relatively unknown, writers. The authors represented here have widely different backgrounds, training, and interests, and include scientists, journalists, artists, students, novelists, and sociologists. Third, we wanted this collection to have essays of varying length. Although it is true that students are often asked to write relatively short papers, we thought it was important to include some essays of significant length, to demonstrate that the art of extended exposition is not dead, and to show how to maintain an argument through several thousand words. Fourth, we wanted our collection to incorporate a significant number of Canadian essays without becoming an anthology only of Canadian writing; thus we have included

English essays by American, Canadian, and British authors, as well as a few pieces in translation. Finally, we wanted to collect science essays written by women—not only essays about women in science, but also good scientific writing by women.

Each essay we selected according to these criteria is listed alphabetically by its author's name, chronologically according to the date of its first publication, and alphabetically by its title, for easy access. We have also provided alternative indices, loosely arranged groupings distinguished by style, rhetoric, and theme. Each essay is followed by a brief commentary. These commentaries are meant to aid instructors in conducting classroom discussions of the essays, and to aid students in their reading of the essays. In addition, we have included questions for discussion and suggestions for writing. These questions address particular aspects and techniques of the individual essays, while making connections to other essays in the collection.

Finally, we have included several appendices: three samples of student writing, and a glossary of basic rhetorical terms to aid students in their comprehension of rhetorical devices and styles. The student writing includes an argumentative and comparative academic paper by a fourth-year English student on two best-selling pieces of popular culture; an academic research paper by a second-year English student on a famous (and famously difficult) piece of Canadian literature; and a technical report on the detection of land mines by a group of fourth-year Engineering students. These papers have been included for instructors to use as models for students, and to demonstrate explicitly many of the important features of good student writing: they demonstrate the effective development of a bibliography; the successful embedding of quotations from primary and secondary sources; the appropriate use of information from one field in another setting; and the use of "lively" prose, even in an "academic" assignment.

This is a collection that is designed to cross several boundaries and address several intersections: between genders, among countries, and between science and technology and the humanities. Our fondest hope is that readers, too, will cross boundaries in considering these essays—and that they will enjoy reading the essays collected here as much as we have enjoyed collecting them.

Acknowledgments

As is true of any project like this one, there are many people who deserve our thanks. First of all, we thank our long-suffering families for their encouragement and sacrifices. We would like to thank the English Department at the University of Alberta for their support in the form of a Graduate Research Assistant. We would also like to thank Sharon Dreger, who was that G.R.A.; Professors Dale Wilkie and Jon C. Stott, for their unflagging enthusiasm and technical advice; Dr. Paul Lumsden, who helped to shape the project into what it has become; and Leonard Swanson, Assistant to the Dean of Engineering, for his prompt, cheerful, and ready supply of Engineering perspectives and materials.

We are grateful to the following reviewers for their thoughtful comments and suggestions: Lorne Daniel, Red Deer College; Linda Dydyk, Dawson College; Amanda Goldrick-Jones, Centre for Academic Writing, University of Winnipeg; Philip Lanthier, Champlain College, Lennoxville Campus; Larry McKill, University of Alberta; Daphne Read, University of Alberta; Jack Robinson, Grant MacEwan Community College; and A.M. Robinson, University of Alberta.

INTERSECTIONS

THE PLEASURES AND PAINS OF COFFEE

Honoré de Balzac

BIOGRAPHICAL NOTE

Honoré de Balzac (1799–1850) is considered one of the great French writers. His master-work is a multi-volume novel entitled *La Comédie humaine* (1842–46). This essay appeared as part of an appendix (added after the first edition) to Anthelme Brillat-Savarin's *La Physiologie du goût* (1825). The full appendix deals with the effects of coffee, wine, and tobacco and is entitled *Traité des excitants modernes*. Balzac died while still quite young, probably in part due to the effects of drinking a good deal of very strong coffee.

1   On this subject Brillat-Savarin is far from complete. I can add something to what he has said because coffee is a great power in my life; I have observed its effects on an epic scale. Coffee roasts your insides. Many people claim coffee inspires them; but as everybody like-wise knows, coffee only makes boring people even more boring. Think about it: although more grocery stores are staying open in Paris until midnight, few writers are actually becoming more spiritual.

2   But as Brillat-Savarin has correctly observed, coffee sets the blood in motion and stim-ulates the muscles; it accelerates the digestive processes, chases away sleep, and gives us the capacity to engage a little longer in the exercise of our intellects. It is on this last point, in par-ticular, that I want to add my personal experience to Brillat-Savarin's observations, and to add some remarks about coffee from the great sages.

3   Coffee affects the diaphragm and the plexus of the stomach, from which it reaches the brain by barely perceptible radiations which escape complete analysis; that aside, we may surmise that our primary nervous flux conducts an electricity emitted by coffee when we drink

Translated from the French by Robert Onopa. First published in *The Michigan Quarterly Review*, Spring 1996. Robert Onopa teaches in the Creative Writing Program at the University of Hawaii.

it. Coffee's power changes over time. Rossini has personally experienced some of these effects, as, of course, have I.

4   "Coffee," Rossini told me, "is an affair of fifteen or twenty days; just the right amount of time, fortunately, to write an opera."

5   This is true. But the length of time during which one can enjoy the benefits of coffee *can* be extended. This knowledge is so useful to so many people that I cannot but confess the secrets of releasing the bean's precious essence.

6   All of you, then you illustrious Human Candles—you who consume your own brilliant selves with the heat and light of your minds—approach and listen to the Gospel of the Watch, of Wakefulness, of Intellectual Travail!

7   1. Coffee completely pulverized in the Turkish manner has a much richer flavor than coffee ground in a coffee mill.

8   In many of the mechanical aspects of pleasure, Orientals are far superior to Europeans. Their particular genius—to observe as carefully as do those toads who spend entire years squatting on their haunches, holding their unblinking eyes open like two suns—has revealed to them what our science has only recently been able to show us through analysis. The principal toxin in coffee is *tannin*, an evil substance which chemists have not yet studied sufficiently. When the stomach membranes have been "tanned," or when the action of the tannin particular to coffee has numbed them by overuse, the membranes become incapable of contracting properly. This becomes the source of the serious disorders affecting the coffee connoisseur. There is a man in London, for example, whose immoderate use of coffee has left him with a stomach twisted in knots. An engraver in Paris I know personally needed five years to recover from the physical state his love of coffee had put him in. Finally, an artist, Chenavard, was burned to death by coffee: all because he went to cafés excessively, as workers go to cabarets, on the flimsiest excuse. Connoisseurs pursue coffee drinking the way they pursue all their passions; they proceed by increments, and, like Nicolet, move from strong to stronger stuff, until consumption becomes abuse. Yet when you pulverize rather than grind coffee, you crush it into a unique form of molecule which retains the harmful tannin and releases only the aroma. That is why Italians, Venetians, Greeks, and Turks can drink coffee incessantly without harm, a coffee the French contemptuously call *cafiot*. Voltaire drank just such coffee.

9   Remember, then. Coffee is composed of two elements: one, the extractable matter, which hot water or cold water dissolves quickly and which conducts the aroma; the other element, the tannin, is less dissolvable in water, and emerges from the surrounding plant tissue only slowly and with more effort. From which follows this axiom: *To brew coffee by contact with boiling water, especially for a long time, is heresy; to brew coffee with water that has already passed through coffee grounds is to subject the stomach and other internal organs to tannin.*

10   2. Using as a benchmark coffee brewed in the immortal coffeepot of my secretary, Auguste de Belloy (the cousin of a Cardinal, and, like him, related to the ancient and illustrious Marquis de Belloy), the very best coffee is made by an infusion of cold rather than boiling water; controlling the water temperature, after pulverizing the beans completely, is a second method of managing its effects.

11   There are, as we have seen, two basic types of coffee which you might brew with hot or cold water: coffee pulverized in the Turkish manner, and coffee that is ground. As we also have seen, when you merely grind coffee in an ordinary grinder, you release the tannin along with the aroma; pulverized coffee flatters the taste even as it stimulates the plexus, which reacts on the thousands of capsules which form your brain.

12 3. The quantity of coffee in the upper receptacle, the way the beans have been crushed, and the amount of water passed through them, determine the strength of the coffee; this three-part formula constitutes the ultimate consideration in dealing with the beverage.

13   Thus, for a while—for a week or two at most—you can obtain the right amount of stimulation with one, then two, cups of coffee brewed from beans which have been crushed with gradually increasing force and infused with hot water.

14   For another week, by decreasing the amount of water in the upper receptacle, by pulverizing the coffee even more finely, and by infusing with cold water, you can continue to obtain the same cerebral power.

15   When you have produced the finest grind with the least water possible, you double the dose by drinking two cups at a time; particularly vigorous constitutions can tolerate three cups. One can continue working this way for several more days.

16   Finally, I have discovered a horrible, rather brutal method that I recommend only to men of excessive vigor, men with thick black hair and skin covered with liver spots, men with big square hands and with legs shaped like bowling pins. It is a question of using finely pulverized, dense coffee, cold and anhydrous (a chemical term meaning without water), consumed on an empty stomach. This coffee *falls* into your stomach, which, as you know from Brillat-Savarin, is a sack whose velvety interior is lined with tapestries of suckers and papillae. The coffee finds nothing else in the sack, and so it attacks these delicate and voluptuous linings; it acts like a food and demands digestive juices; it wrings and twists the stomach for these juices, appealing as a pythoness appeals to her god; it brutalizes these beautiful stomach linings as a wagon master abuses ponies; the plexus becomes inflamed; sparks shoot all the way up to the brain. From that moment on, everything becomes agitated. Ideas quick march into motion like battalions of a grand army to its legendary fighting ground, and the battle rages. Memories charge in, bright flags on high; the cavalry of metaphor deploys with a magnificent gallop; the artillery of logic rushes up with clattering wagons and cartridges; on imagination's orders, sharpshooters sight and fire; forms and shapes and characters rear up; the paper is spread with ink—for the nightly labor begins and ends with torrents of this black water, as a battle opens and concludes with black powder.

17   I recommended this way of drinking coffee to a friend of mine, who absolutely wanted to finish a job promised for the next day: he thought he'd been poisoned and took to his bed, which he guarded like a married man. He was tall, blonde, slender, and had thinning hair; he apparently had a stomach of papier-mâché. There had been, on my part, a failure of observation.

18   When you have reached the point of consuming this kind of coffee, then become exhausted and decide that you really must have more, even though you make it of the finest ingredients and take it perfectly fresh, you will fall into horrible sweats, suffer feebleness of the nerves, and undergo episodes of severe drowsiness. I don't know what would happen if you kept at it then: a sensible nature counseled me to stop at this point, seeing that immediate death was not otherwise my fate. To be restored one must begin with recipes made with milk, and a diet of chicken and other white meats; finally the tension on the harp strings eases, and one returns to the relaxed, meandering, simple-minded, and cryptogamous life of the retired bourgeoisie.

19   The state coffee puts one in when it is drunk on an empty stomach under these magisterial conditions produces a kind of animation that looks like anger: one's voice rises, one's gestures suggest unhealthy impatience; one wants everything to proceed with the speed of ideas; one becomes brusque, ill-tempered about nothing. One actually becomes that fickle character, The Poet, condemned by grocers and their like. One assumes that everyone is equally lucid. A man of spirit must therefore avoid going out in public. I discovered this singular state through a series of accidents which made me lose, without any effort, the ecstasy I had been feeling. Some friends, with whom I had gone out to the country, witnessed me arguing about everything, haranguing with monumental bad faith. The following day I recognized my wrongdoing and we searched the cause. My friends were wise men of the first rank and we found the problem soon enough: coffee wanted its victim.

20   The truth I set down here is subject only to the tiny variations we find among individuals; it is otherwise in complete harmony with the experience of a number of coffee's devotees, among them the celebrated Rossini, a man who has studied the laws of taste, a hero worthy of Brillat-Savarin.

21   OBSERVATION: Among certain weak natures, coffee produces only a kind of harmless congestion of the mind; instead of feeling animated, these people feel drowsy, and they say that coffee makes them sleep. Such individuals may have the legs of serfs and the stomachs of ostriches, but they are badly equipped for the work of thought. Two young travelers, Combes and Tamisier, found the Abyssinians almost universally impotent; the two travelers did not hesitate to regard the misuse of coffee, which the Abyssinians abuse to the last degree, as the cause of this disgrace. If these remarks make it to England, the English government is hereby petitioned to settle this question by experimenting on the first condemned soul at hand, provided that soul is neither female nor too elderly.

22   Tea also contains tannin, but since tea has narcotic qualities, it does not otherwise affect the mind; it stirs the plexus only while its narcotic substances are absorbed rapidly in the intestine. The manner of preparing tea, moreover, is absolute. I am not sure at what point the quantity of water that the tea drinkers pour into their stomachs should be computed in its effects. If the experience of the English is typical, heavy tea-drinking will produce English moral philosophy, a tendency toward a pale complexion, hypocrisy, and backbiting. This much is certain: tea-drinking will not spoil a woman any less morally than physically. Where women drink tea, romance is depraved on its principle; the women are pale, sickly, talkative, boring, and preachy. In certain powerful constitutions, strong tea taken in large doses induces an irritation which overturns the treasures of melancholy; it produces dreams, but less powerful dreams than those of opium, for tea's Phantasmagoria passes in a fog. The ideas are sweet, affable, bland. Your state is not the very deep sleep which distinguishes a noble constitution suffering from fatigue, but an inexpressible drowsiness, rather, which summons up only the daydreams of the morning. An excess of coffee, like that of tea, produces an extensive drying out of the skin, which becomes scorched. Coffee also often induces sweating and makes one violently thirsty. Among those who abuse the bean, saliva becomes as thick and as dry as paper on the tongue.

NOTES AND DISCUSSION

In *The Book of Coffee and Tea* (New York: St. Martin's Press, 1975), Joel, David, and Karl Schapira write that "since its beginning coffee drinking has been associated with scholars, wits, and artists," and that, furthermore, "coffee and coffee houses seem too much an expression of the French sensibility to ever disappear easily, since behind every Parisian there is a wit, a revolutionary, and a gourmand." While in Balzac's time coffee houses may not have been quite as plentiful as they are today, they were, nonetheless, very popular and very important social and political venues. Notice, for instance, the strong social and political distinctions that Balzac draws between himself and Englishmen, who drink tea.

Balzac's account of his coffee preparation and consumption can be summarized with one of his own sentences: "Connoisseurs pursue coffee drinking the way they pursue all their passions; they proceed by increments, and . . . move from strong to stronger stuff, until consumption becomes abuse." The essay is a personal account of an increasing addiction to caffeine, with precise and strikingly detailed descriptions. While acknowledging that his final suggestion for making coffee is a "horrible, rather brutal method" of extracting the caffeine, Balzac nonetheless seems to have experienced this kind of "coffee"; he once even "recommended this way of drinking coffee to a friend." Balzac describes in detail the physical vigour, on one hand, and accelerated intellectual activity, on the other, that can be derived from strong and frequent enough doses of coffee. Yet, ultimately, Balzac's attitude towards coffee is mixed: he relishes the "sparks [that] shoot all the way up to the brain," but is also aware that his use has become abuse, one side effect of which is rather unsavoury: "saliva becomes as thick and as dry as paper on the tongue."

STUDY QUESTIONS

For Discussion:

1. How would you characterize the tone of Balzac's essay? What is the effect of the rather confessional style? Of the name-dropping? Compare the way certain rules and rituals are associated with Balzac's account of coffee consumption.

2. According to Balzac, one of coffee's great benefits is its ability to stimulate intellectual activity, which may partly explain the number of coffee shops on present-day university campuses. In your experience, is Balzac's description of the physiological effects of caffeine accurate?

Suggestions For Writing:

1. Do some research into the physiological and mental benefits and potential dangers of caffeine. Construct a short essay comparing your scientific research with Balzac's personal experiments. Alternatively, observe a physical reaction in yourself—the stress of final exams, perhaps—and try to describe that reaction as it intensifies or weakens over time.

2. Notice the way coffee and tea are connected in Balzac's essay with very different kinds of personalities. Research the way media advertisements portray coffee and tea drinkers and write an analytical essay based on your findings. Do the advertisements match Balzac's observations?

WHY I AM NOT GOING TO BUY A COMPUTER

Wendell Berry

BIOGRAPHICAL NOTE

Wendell Berry teaches in the Department of English at the University of Kentucky. He is a prolific writer, with over thirty novels and collections of essays and poems. Two of his more significant books of essays are *The Long-Legged House* (1969) and *The Unsettling of America* (1977). The focus of much of his writing is his farm on the Kentucky River, which often serves as a microcosm for the interaction between humans and nature.

1   Like almost everybody else, I am hooked to the energy corporations, which I do not admire. I hope to become less hooked to them. In my work, I try to be as little hooked to them as possible. As a farmer, I do almost all of my work with horses. As a writer, I work with a pencil or a pen and a piece of paper.

2   My wife types my work on a Royal standard typewriter bought new in 1956 and as good now as it was then. As she types, she sees things that are wrong and marks them with small checks in the margins. She is my best critic because she is the one most familiar with my habitual errors and weaknesses. She also understands, sometimes better than I do, what *ought* to be said. We have, I think, a literary cottage industry that works well and pleasantly. I do not see anything wrong with it.

3   A number of people, by now, have told me that I could greatly improve things by buying a computer. My answer is that I am not going to do it. I have several reasons, and they are good ones.

4   The first is the one I mentioned at the beginning. I would hate to think that my work as a writer could not be done without a direct dependence on strip-mined coal. How could I write

conscientiously against the rape of nature if I were, in the act of writing, implicated in the rape? For the same reason, it matters to me that my writing is done in the daytime, without electric light.

5   I do not admire the computer manufacturers a great deal more than I admire the energy industries. I have seen their advertisements, attempting to seduce struggling or failing farmers into the belief that they can solve their problems by buying yet another piece of expensive equipment. I am familiar with their propaganda campaigns that have put computers into public schools in need of books. That computers are expected to become as common as TV sets in "the future" does not impress me or matter to me. I do not own a TV set. I do not see that computers are bringing us one step nearer to anything that does matter to me: peace, economic justice, ecological health, political honesty, family and community stability, good work.

6   What would a computer cost me? More money, for one thing, than I can afford, and more than I wish to pay to people whom I do not admire. But the cost would not be just monetary. It is well understood that technological innovation always requires the discarding of the "old model"—the "old model" in this case being not just our old Royal standard, but my wife, my critic, my closest reader, my fellow worker. Thus (and I think this is typical of present-day technological innovation), what would be superseded would be not only something, but somebody. In order to be technologically up-to-date as a writer, I would have to sacrifice an association that I am dependent upon and that I treasure.

7   My final and perhaps my best reason for not owning a computer is that I do not wish to fool myself. I disbelieve, and therefore strongly resent, the assertion that I or anybody else could write better or more easily with a computer than a pencil. I do not see why I should not be as scientific about this as the next fellow: when somebody has used a computer to write work that is demonstrably better than Dante's, and when this better is demonstrably attributable to the use of a computer, then I will speak of computers with a more respectful tone of voice, though I still will not buy one.

8   To make myself as plain as I can, I should give my standards for technological innovation in my own work. They are as follows:

1. The new tool should be cheaper than the one it replaces.

2. It should be at least as small in scale as the one it replaces.

3. It should do work that is clearly and demonstrably better than the one it replaces.

4. It should use less energy than the one it replaces.

5. If possible, it should use some form of solar energy, such as that of the body.

6. It should be repairable by a person of ordinary intelligence, provided that he or she has the necessary tools.

7. It should be purchasable and repairable as near to home as possible.

8. It should come from a small, privately owned shop or store that will take it back for maintenance and repair.

9. It should not replace or disrupt anything good that already exists, and this includes family and community relationships.

After the foregoing essay, first published in the New England Review *and* Bread Loaf Quarterly, *was reprinted in* Harper's, *the* Harper's *editors published the following letters in response and permitted me a reply.*

9   Wendell Berry provides writers enslaved by the computer with a handy alternative: Wife—a low-tech energy-saving device. Drop a pile of handwritten notes on Wife and you get back a finished manuscript, edited while it was typed. What computer can do that? Wife meets all of Berry's uncompromising standards for technological innovation: she's cheap, repairable near home, and good for the family structure. Best of all, Wife is politically correct because she breaks a writer's "direct dependence on strip-mined coal."

10   History teaches us that Wife can also be used to beat rugs and wash clothes by hand, thus eliminating the need for the vacuum cleaner and washing machine, two more nasty machines that threaten the act of writing.

GORDON INKELES *MIRANDA, CALIF.*

11   I have no quarrel with Berry because he prefers to write with pencil and paper; that is his choice. But he implies that I and others are somehow impure because we choose to write on a computer. I do not admire the energy corporations, either. Their shortcoming is not that they produce electricity but how they go about it. They are poorly managed because they are blind to long-term consequences. To solve this problem, wouldn't it make more sense to correct the precise error they are making rather than simply ignore their product? I would be happy to join Berry in a protest against strip mining, but I intend to keep plugging this computer into the wall with a clear conscience.

JAMES RHOADS *BATTLE CREEK, MICH.*

12   I enjoyed reading Berry's declaration of intent never to buy a personal computer in the same way that I enjoy reading about the belief systems of unfamiliar tribal cultures. I tried to imagine a tool that would meet Berry's criteria for superiority to his old manual typewriter. The clear winner is the quill pen. It is cheaper, smaller, more energy-efficient, human-powered, easily repaired, and nondisruptive of existing relationships.

13   Berry also requires that this tool must be "clearly and demonstrably better" than the one it replaces. But surely we all recognize by now that "better" is in the mind of the beholder. To the quill pen aficionado, the benefits obtained from elegant calligraphy might well outweigh all others.

14   I have no particular desire to see Berry use a word processor; if he doesn't like computers, that's fine with me. However, I do object to his portrayal of this reluctance as a moral virtue. Many of us have found that computers can be an invaluable tool in the fight to protect our environment. In addition to helping me write, my personal computer gives me access to up-to-the-minute reports on the workings of the EPA and the nuclear industry. I participate in electronic bulletin boards on which environmental activists discuss strategy and warn each other about urgent legislative issues. Perhaps Berry feels that the Sierra Club should eschew modern printing technology, which is highly wasteful of energy, in favor of having its members hand-copy the club's magazines and other mailings each month?

NATHANIEL S. BORENSTEIN *PITTSBURGH, PA.*

15   The value of a computer to a writer is that it is a tool not for generating ideas but for typing and editing words. It is cheaper than a secretary (or a wife!) and arguably more fuel-efficient. And it enables spouses who are not inclined to provide free labor more time to concentrate on *their* own work.

16   We should support alternatives both to coal-generated electricity and to IBM-style technology. But I am reluctant to entertain alternatives that presuppose the traditional subservience of one class to another. Let the PCs come and the wives and servants go seek more meaningful work.

Toby Koosman Knoxville, Tenn.

17   Berry asks how he could write conscientiously against the rape of nature if in the act of writing on a computer he was implicated in the rape. I find it ironic that a writer who sees the underlying connectedness of things would allow his diatribe against computers to be published in a magazine that carries ads for the National Rural Electric Cooperative Association, Marlboro, Phillips Petroleum, McDonnell Douglas, and yes, even Smith-Corona. If Berry rests comfortably at night, he must be using sleeping pills.

Bradley C. Johnson Grand Forks, N.D.

Wendell Berry replies:

18 The foregoing letters surprised me with the intensity of the feelings they expressed. According to the writers' testimony, there is nothing wrong with their computers; they are utterly satisfied with them and all that they stand for. My correspondents are certain that I am wrong and that I am, moreover, on the losing side, a side already relegated to the dustbin of history. And yet they grow huffy and condescending over my tiny dissent. What are they so anxious about?

19   I can only conclude that I have scratched the skin of a technological fundamentalism that, like other fundamentalisms, wishes to monopolize a whole society and, therefore, cannot tolerate the smallest difference of opinion. At the slightest hint of a threat to their complacency, they repeat, like a chorus of toads, the notes sounded by their leaders in industry. The past was gloomy, drudgery-ridden, servile, meaningless, and slow. The present, thanks only to purchasable products, is meaningful, bright, lively, centralized, and fast. The future, thanks only to more purchasable products, is going to be even better. Thus consumers become salesmen, and the world is made safer for corporations.

20   I am also surprised by the meanness with which two of these writers refer to my wife. In order to imply that I am a tyrant, they suggest by both direct statement and innuendo that she is subservient, characterless, and stupid—a mere "device" easily forced to provide meaningless "free labor." I understand that it is impossible to make an adequate public defense of one's private life, and so I will only point out that there are a number of kinder possibilities that my critics have disdained to imagine: that my wife may do this work because she wants to and likes to; that she may find some use and some meaning in it; that she may not work for nothing. These gentlemen obviously think themselves feminists of the most correct and principled sort, and yet they do not hesitate to stereotype and insult, on the basis of one fact, a woman they do not know. They are audacious and irresponsible gossips.

21   In his letter, Bradley C. Johnson rushes past the possibility of sense in what I said in my essay by implying that I am or ought to be a fanatic. That I am a person of this century and am implicated in many practices that I regret is fully acknowledged at the beginning of my essay. I did not say that I proposed to end forthwith all my involvement in harmful technology, for I do not know how to do that. I said merely that I want to limit such involvement, and to a certain extent I do know how to do that. If some technology does damage to the world—as two of the above letters seem to agree that it does—then why is it not reasonable, and indeed moral, to try to limit one's use of that technology? *Of course*, I think that I am right to do this.

22   I would not think so, obviously, if I agreed with Nathaniel S. Borenstein that "'better' is in the mind of the beholder." But if he truly believes this, I do not see why he bothers with his personal computer's "up-to-the-minute reports on the workings of the EPA and the nuclear industry" or why he wishes to be warned about "urgent legislative issues." According to his system, the "better" in a bureaucratic, industrial, or legislative mind is as good as the "better" in his. His mind apparently is being subverted by an objective standard of some sort, and he had better look out.

23   Borenstein does not say what he does after his computer has drummed him awake. I assume from his letter that he must send donations to conservation organizations and letters to officials. Like James Rhoads, at any rate, he has a clear conscience. But this is what is wrong with the conservation movement. It has a clear conscience. The guilty are always other people, and the wrong is always somewhere else. That is why Borenstein finds his "electronic bulletin board" so handy. To the conservation movement, it is only production that causes environmental degradation; the consumption that supports the production is rarely acknowledged to be at fault. The ideal of the run-of-the-mill conservationist is to impose restraints upon production without limiting consumption or burdening the consciences of consumers.

24   But virtually all of our consumption now is extravagant, and virtually all of it consumes the world. It is not beside the point that most electrical power comes from strip-mined coal. The history of the exploitation of the Appalachian coal fields is long, and it is available to readers. I do not see how anyone can read about it and plug in any appliance with a clear conscience. If Rhoads can do so, that does not mean that his conscience is clear; it means that his conscience is not working.

25   To the extent that we consume, in our present circumstances, we are guilty. To the extent that we guilty consumers are conservationists, we are absurd. But what can we do? Must we go on writing letters to politicians and donating to conservation organizations until the majority of our fellow citizens agree with us? Or can we do something directly to solve our share of the problem?

26   I am a conservationist. I believe wholeheartedly in putting pressure on the politicians and in maintaining the conservation organizations. But I wrote my little essay partly in distrust of centralization. I don't think that the government and the conservation organizations alone will ever make us a conserving society. Why do I need a centralized computer system to alert me to environmental crises? That I live every hour of every day in an environmental crisis I know from all my senses. Why then is not my first duty to reduce, so far as I can, my own consumption?

27   Finally, it seems to me that none of my correspondents recognizes the innovativeness of my essay. If the use of a computer is a new idea, then a newer idea is not to use one.

NOTES AND DISCUSSION

This straightforward essay announces its plan at the beginning and then follows it through. Berry opens with three short paragraphs that describe his present writing habits. He ends this opening section by stating that he is not going to buy a computer for what are good reasons. The rest of the essay supports and elaborates those reasons. Berry ends with a list of standards for technological innovation. He implies that computers would not pass the test, if it were based on this list.

On the surface, this essay appears to be nothing more than a list of one writer's reasons for not owning a computer. By implication, however, it is a general critique of computers and, in particular, of their use by writers in their work. In addition, the essay may be read as a critique of modern North American society. The responses to his essay, when it appeared in *Harper's Magazine*, clearly show that Berry touched a sensitive nerve with his stand. In his reply Berry notes the strenuous nature of the letters' arguments. You might consider the vehemence of the responses, and think about whether those responses seem appropriate, given the apparent simplicity of Berry's stance.

STUDY QUESTIONS

For Discussion:

1. Berry claims that he wrote an argument, a good and convincing one, but complains that people don't seem to want to pay any attention to that claim. Do you agree that the argument that Berry mounts is "good and convincing"?

2. What does Berry fail to take into account when he decides not to buy a computer because the purchase would support the energy industries? Why is the choice to buy or not to buy a computer so fundamental and moral? More generally, who is Berry's audience in this essay?

For Writing:

1. This essay has an unusual shape: a short essay is followed by responses, which are followed by a final response from the initial writer. Contribute further to its unusual shape by writing a response of your own, taking into account as much as possible of the exchange so far. Can you think of any substantial arguments against Berry's? Try to not fall into the "trap" that Berry claims most of his opponents have fallen into.

2. Examine some of the unsupported assumptions and claims that both Berry and his detractors make and write a short analytical essay based on your findings. Some of these inquiries will require research. Areas you might want to explore include these: Berry's "useful wife" and the responses to her and her role; Berry's claim that he and his wife have set up a smoothly operating "cottage industry," and what that phraseology implies; the claim that most electricity comes from strip-mined coal; the degree to which Berry does in fact rely on power companies, and computers, to be published and read; and the amount of energy required for, and the environmental impact of, using and wasting paper rather than power.

LIFTOFF!

Roberta Bondar

BIOGRAPHICAL NOTE

Roberta Bondar is best known as the first Canadian woman in space. She was one of the original six Canadians chosen to be astronauts in 1983, and she flew on the space shuttle *Discovery* in January 1992. Her studies at Guelph, Western Ontario, and Toronto led to a PhD in neurobiology; she also obtained an MD from McMaster University.

January 22, 1992

Commander/NTD: A/G One.

Go ahead.

As A heads up to you, I'm sure you copied, though, we've set a resume time of 14:42 GMT at T minus nine minutes, and counting. We're awaiting final clear to launch from RSO. All other systems are ready to proceed.
We copy.
Be advised that I talked to the RSO and he says that he will not give me a clear to launch before 14:46 Zulu. That gives him a 15-minute field mills reading.

1   Waiting for the countdown clock to resume, it's hard not to be impatient, especially with all this gear on. I can't look out the mid-deck window because it's covered on entry and reentry with a metal shield. I can't read a book in the eerie green light of the chemsticks, and my orange pressure gloves make it impossible to push the buttons on my microcassette recorder without fear of dropping it onto the cold steel floor. Retrieving it, or anything else that gravity traps in the darkness, is out of the question; the six other crew members and I are all locked in place on our backs with lap belts and connectors, which will prevent us from smashing into the floor during the ride "uphill." My helmet, secured onto the neck ring of the space suit by "dog teeth," seems overly large for my head. Its rigidity somewhat restricts my neck motion. Although I feel like a goldfish with an anchor, I welcome the luxury of time to think about my preparation for this moment. It's a comfort to reflect back and recall as much detail as possible, to keep my memory hot for the adventure ahead.

2   If I had viewed a film clip of this scene when I was eight years old, would I have believed it? Perhaps. The seeds of space exploration had been sown at an early age. Come to think of it, I spent all my free time dreaming about space, wondering how I would pull it off, never willing to give up on what I felt was my destiny. Every birthday, I asked for a plastic model-rocket kit, a chemistry set, or a doctor's bag. I had to wait three more weeks until Christmas for the hockey sticks, Meccano sets, or basketball equipment. Not that *Discovery* looks anything like those early model rockets, which kept me wrapped up in my personal dream of becoming a space explorer. Real spacecraft use bolts, special glass, and computers. So far, the "glue" looks better on the real thing.

3   I remember my first space helmet. It was 1953. The excitement mounted, even then, as my sister Barbara and I waited for the chewing gum company to send the space headgear we had ordered. "They'll arrive in a large box because they'll have an air hose and glass cover," I thought. The long-awaited day finally arrived. The postman came to the door with two flat brown envelopes in his weathered hands, one for each of us. I was running upstairs to check out my moon rocket plans when Mom called out, "Girls, they're here!" What, squashed up in those envelopes? I was a logical child and "flat" was not associated in my mind with a space helmet. However, big sisters have more knowledge about such things. "Let's put them on and go exploring," Barbara suggested with great enthusiasm.

4   The cardboard helmets were tall, rectangular, and white. Although they had no glass, each had a large square opening so that I could scratch my nose and eat—two activities that are impossible to do with the visor down and locked on the NASA launch/entry suit. The Dubble Bubble helmets were also much lighter and sat comfortably on the shoulders, dropping rakishly over the front and back. We two intrepid space heroes set forth on our first mission in proper gear, complete with one red and one green Flash-Gordon-style water pistol and enough provisions for the exploration of the planet bounded by McGregor Avenue, Edward's Lane, and Upton Road in Sault Ste. Marie, Ontario.

5   In those days, I assumed I was already trained in everything that was needed for space flight. After all, what science-fiction movie or book even mentioned training? I made up my own operational techniques because no one else understood the intricate workings of the pieces of painted plywood that were my spacecraft. I was trainer and trainee. I was commander and crew.

6   Now, however, on this, my first real space mission, I am Payload Specialist One (PS1), science detail, on the first flight of the International Microgravity Laboratory Mission (IML-1). I represent Canada on this international crew. In preparation for this moment, I've spent five years of high school, eighteen years of university, eight years in the Canadian Astronaut Program, and three years of book work and practice dedicated to this flight. I've studied science for the mission in Europe and North America so that I will be able to perform inflight experiments for scientists all over the world, and for a year I've practised how to live in the shuttle with my fellow crew members. But although I know I'm well trained and fit to fly, no one really feels prepared for space flight. Travelling at twenty-five times the speed of sound is a mental boundary as well as a physiological one, which astronauts can only experience once they are in space.

7   But years before all that formal training, I was hungry for this day. My preparation for space flight continued throughout my preadolescent and adolescent years. An uncle's gift of a crystal set each for Barbara and me added a tremendous level of fidelity to an earlier system of plastic toy radio receivers and wires. My parents helped us develop various life skills through camping and activities in church groups, the family YMCA, and Girl Guides of Canada. (They also practised survival training during this time, especially at bedtime as they negotiated their way around our space station to say goodnight.)

8   In those days it was fun to explore the surface of a pretend planet or asteroid, to look for specimens of plants and soil, and to make contact with a strange new life-form—usually an unsuspecting neighbour. We moved rapidly into the era of space photography with our Brownie cameras, which we were never without. "You have to document everything," instructed my sister. I nodded my head in the most knowing way possible. But black and white? How could I take black-and-white pictures of a planet and make it look real? Fortunately, my View-Master provided colour images. Its reels gave me my first training in planet observation. The "canals" and red soil of Mars, spaceship interiors, stars, the moon, aliens—they were right there on film whenever I wanted them.

9   On Sunday trips to the shores of Lake Superior, the family car became more crowded after I insisted on bringing all my space equipment along. By day, the trip was enchanting. By night, the stars were always there over the lake, beckoning me to leave my own planet. The trip home was filled with sleep and dreams of the next day's adventures and observations. Life was fascinating and very, very big. It was too much for one small explorer to record on film all by herself.

10   I have always had a great interest in both adventure and photography. Even when I was a child, I sensed that photography captures history. At home, "Saturday night at the movies" consisted of family fun preserved forever on standard 8-mm film and 35-mm slides. Some family members preferred the action of the movies, but I thought the slides were clearer and more colourful. It was never a hardship to set up the equipment for those wonderful evenings. As an adult, I developed a deep respect for the technological side of photography— the sharpness of an image, the contrast between light and shadow, and the potential of the equipment itself.

11   I had to wait until 1984 to see photographs of Earth observation from space. During astronaut training, I was able to watch the hundreds of photographs taken on shuttle flights projected onto a large screen. It was as though I had been suddenly transported back into the childhood world of my View-Master, but instead of drawings or cartoons, now I was seeing the real thing. "How did they do that?" frequently spilled into my conscious thoughts. My knowledge of viewing the Earth from the orbit of a spacecraft was severely limited by the small number of photographs that had been made available to the public through the print

media, together with too few sessions combining geography, geology, and photography in our Canadian Astronaut Program.

12   Although it will be a challenge to perform the science experiments successfully in a weightless environment where everything floats, for me the best thing about the voyage will be the unique opportunity to view the Earth from space. Throughout the years, astronauts have captured the light of our world and of worlds beyond through photography. Each frame is not only a historical record of the planet's features that can be catalogued, reviewed, and compared flight to flight, it is also a record of human endeavour. The fact that a human being is "up there" is evidenced by the return to Earth of film from many different camera types, all loaded by humans, and exposed by humans. The Earth is literally seen through the eyes of an astronaut. Before manned space flight, this was not possible.

13   Back in 1962, astronaut John Glenn began to record the awesome beauty of our planet from the *Mercury Friendship 7* capsule. Since that time, upwards of one hundred thousand photographs of the Earth from space have been entered into the NASA Earth Observation Databank. Recording the history of our planet by means of space photography is not a simple matter of packing a road map and a point-and-shoot camera after reading the instruction book on how to change the film. Good photographic results from Earth-viewing depend on three factors: a receptive, committed crew member; correct training, both in Earth observation and in Earth photography; and the equipment itself, which includes all the lenses, films, filters, spot meters, and any new, improved gadgetry flying on the mission.

14   All crew members who have time available away from the busy schedule of on-orbit activities are able to use any one of the wide assortment of cameras to capture the Earth at one moment in time. The training of crew members has changed significantly since the *Mercury* missions. Now astronauts take mandatory courses in flight-specific Earth observation and the use of cameras.

15   In the *Apollo* program, the focus was on observing the lunar landscape—in preparation for mankind's first steps on another planetary body—rather than on observing Earth. During the *Apollo 8* mission, for example, more than seven hundred photographs of the moon were taken compared to about one hundred fifty photographs of the planet. It was the first opportunity to study certain features of the lunar surface free from the atmospheric distortion that is inherent in telescopic photography from Earth.

16   By the time *Apollo 11* launched from Cape Kennedy on July 16, 1969, for its nine-day lunar landing mission, space photography had advanced even further. The prime photographic objective of *Apollo 11* was to photograph the lunar surface—specifically "targets of opportunity," or scientifically interesting sites, and potential *Apollo* landing sites. Mission planners also wanted photographs of various lunar activities after landing, including man's first step onto the surface of the moon. There was a limited quantity of photographic equipment that could be floated to the moon, however, and as a result, the photographic requirements could be achieved only through creative selection and preparation of both cameras and film. For instance, above-atmosphere photography must include consideration of fogging or premature exposure of film, because radiation in space is greater than it is on the Earth. *Apollo 11* returned with 1,359 frames of 70-mm photography, 17 pairs of lunar-surface stereoscopic photographs, and 58,134 frames of 16-mm photography.

17   Later *Apollo* missions incorporated recommendations made by earlier crew and ground support personnel to improve the quality of the pictures. *Apollo 17*, in particular, achieved a significant advance in Earth observation. For the first time, the Antarctic continent was cap-

tured in a full view of the globe. It probably would not have been too difficult to exhaust the on-board film supplies photographing the beautiful, vibrant colours reflected from structures such as the Great Barrier Reef in preference to the main target of opportunity, the black-and-white surface of the moon.

18   Earth observation and Earth photography were boosted aloft in the United States' first manned space station, *Skylab*. Compared to today's shuttle flights at an average altitude of 300 km (162 naut. mi.), its orbit was at a moderate-to-high altitude of 435 km (235 naut. mi.) above the equator, with its path varying between 50 degrees north and 50 degrees south. From the launch of the first *Skylab* crew on May 25, 1973, to the return of the third and final crew on February 8, 1974, a total of 35,704 frames of Earth photographs were acquired. In this time, *Skylab* orbited every ninety-three minutes, covering the band between 50 degrees north and 50 degrees south of the equator every five days. Although weather and crew-member schedules precluded continuous operation of the photographic equipment during daylight periods, *Skylab* provided a giant leap forward in the ability of human beings to capture images of the planet.

19   After a seven-year hiatus, the United States returned to space on April 12, 1981, on board the orbiter *Columbia* at an altitude of 268 km (145 naut. mi.) for thirty-six orbits at 40 degrees above and below the equator. This historic flight of the Space Transportation System (STS) and the next three shuttle flights acquired more than twenty-two hundred photographs of the Earth with 70-mm cameras. For these initial missions, preflight lectures to the crew were given by an *ad hoc* scientific investigative team. Today NASA's unique Space Shuttle Earth Observations Project (SSEOP) combines the two powerful fields of Earth observation and Earth photography from space. It provides coordinated crew training in the Earth sciences preflight, support during the missions, and cataloguing and distribution of the photographs and information postflight.

20   My preflight training, as for all astronauts aboard the space shuttle, included sessions with professional photographers at NASA as well as scientists in the Earth Observation Office. The academic backgrounds of these scientists include geology, geography, computer science, and environmental studies, to name a few. Each crew member is provided with a preflight training manual with extensive colour reproductions and captions as well as cartographic information on specific places to photograph on that particular mission. These targets of opportunity vary according to the altitude of the orbiter, the inclination or latitude flown above and below the equator, the season in which the mission is being flown, and specific scientific interests such as natural phenomena (volcanoes, for example) and man-made phenomena (burning oil wells). Particular areas that are photographed on each shuttle flight are also indicated in the manual.

21   The value of documenting the evolution of the Earth is emphasized to each astronaut team that flies. This requires many sessions on types of landforms, vegetation patterns, and dynamic features that occur on the outer crust of the planet. Although most shuttle flights are of fairly short duration compared to the *Skylab* program, weather patterns that preclude photographing certain areas of interest may dissipate towards the end of the mission, allowing completion of an Earth-observation photographic objective. I have to be ready for whatever opportunity presents itself.

22   Before the flight, the Earth-observation personnel presented a summary of the desired Earth sites and recommended techniques for obtaining the best possible pictures. This is not to rule out creative photography on the part of the astronauts, but rather to provide

guidance that will prove very helpful in the weightless environment of space, where just restraining ourselves to be able to photograph will entail a major expense in energy and concentration.

> Launch Director/Cape Weather: Are you still with me on 212?
>
> Go ahead.
>
> Sorry about the delay. OK. We're still good on the mills. We've got five more minutes to go on those, over.
>
> OK, and we're going to head down to T minus five and hold there for that clock to time out on the field mill. And given that, are you a Go to proceed?
>
> At this juncture, unless we see something new with this cloud, yes, we would be.
>
> OK, copy.
>
> Will get an update. And just a quick-steady state winds for launch would be from 040 degrees at 10 knots, over.
>
> T minus nine minutes and counting.

23   We're going to do it! I wonder briefly whether I'll have to use any of my bail-out training. Even in this modest amount of light, the bail-out cue card is visible, stuck on a mid-deck locker. It is awe-inspiring to be sitting here, looking at a checklist in this green glow. Just beyond my big black boots that will protect my feet if things get out of hand, the cue card details two bail-out sequences. The only thing left to think about now is keeping the differences in the two scenarios, or modes, clear in my mind. In the first one—that's *before* liftoff—I need to take *off* the chute before rolling out of the chair. If I have to use the "Mode 1 pad egress" to get out in an emergency situation on the launch pad, it will be unassisted and will take place in the next three minutes. One more time through the checklist:

> Visor down and locked.
> Pull the green apple.
> Pull the quick-disconnect/lap belts.
> Release chute.
> Evacuate.
> Slide wire.

In the second bail-out sequence, *after* the launch, I keep the parachute *on*. It's so automatic now. One glance at the cue card, and I'll plug into the right escape mode.

OTC: Flight crew, close and lock your visors and initiate 02 flow, and on behalf of STS-42, sorry to have kept you waiting. Have a good flight, and a safe landing.

Well, thanks very much. We look forward to coming back and telling you all about it. You've done a superb job.

One minute.
(Hope you're all having fun out there.)

GLS is Go for auto-sequence start.
Twenty-five . . .
Twenty . . .
Fifteen . . .
Ten . . .
GLS is Go for main engine start.
T zero.
SRB ignition.

As we leave the Earth, I sing to myself:
O Canada,
Our home and native land!
True patriot love . . .

NOTES AND DISCUSSION

Following the transcription of formal, official, and public NASA radio communication, which establishes context, Bondar opens her personal and informal essay with a detailed sensory description of the moments before take-off, providing the reader with her impressions of what most people will never experience. Having described her physical situation, she moves on to describe her thoughts. For the balance of the essay Bondar describes her "present" situation and meditates upon the moments and circumstances in her past that have led her to this moment. Through carefully planned transitions, the memories Bondar relates of her preparation for space flight shift between accounts of childhood memories and dreams and of formal studies, training, and evaluations. These units of discussion differ in style and content. While Bondar is very precise about her childhood, describing specific people, places, and circumstances, she is far more general about her formal training. Eventually, Bondar focuses her attention specifically on the photographic records of the earth attained by astronauts, exploring the history, technology, techniques, and ecological and meteorological importance of such photographs. Note that the essay's structure also creates an intersection between personal and public histories, ambitions, and achievements. The conclusion of Bondar's essay returns to its beginning, detailing the last-minute preparations for the take-off and the take-off itself, but also brings together the various threads of discussion and description developed in the essay, all of which lead to this precise moment in time.

STUDY QUESTIONS

For Discussion:

1. How does Bondar's sister's imperative, "You have to document everything," relate to the larger content and themes of the essay? In your answer, consider the types of documentation appearing in the essay.

2. How are the childhood experiences Bondar recounts relevant to her career achievements? What relationship do you see between Bondar's childhood activities and her presence in the space shuttle?

For Writing:

1. The high cost of space exploration and experimentation has often been criticized. Basing your answer on a close reading of this essay, explain why Bondar feels such activities are important.

2. Bondar's essay is structured around at least four intertwining narratives: her childhood dreams and lifelong ambitions; her own sense of historical and patriotic importance; the place of this flight in space flight history; and the flight day and take-off. Analyze the relative importance of each of these narratives and consider whether each deserves the weight that Bondar assigns it.

A FABLE FOR TOMORROW

Rachel Carson

BIOGRAPHICAL NOTE

After receiving a Master's degree in zoology from Johns Hopkins University in 1932, Rachel Carson (1907–64) worked as a marine biologist for the United States Fish and Wildlife Service from 1936–49. In 1951 she wrote *The Sea Around Us*, which warned of the increasing danger of marine pollution. It was followed by *Silent Spring* (1962), which successfully raised public concern over the problems in food chains caused by modern synthetic pesticides. Her work had a tremendous influence on pesticide control in the United States, as well as on the popularization of ecological and conservationist attitudes and activism during the 1970s.

1   There was once a town in the heart of America where all life seemed to live in harmony with its surroundings. The town lay in the midst of a checkerboard of prosperous farms, with fields of grain and hillsides of orchards where, in spring, white clouds of bloom drifted above the green fields. In autumn, oak and maple and birch set up a blaze of color that flamed and flickered across the backdrop of pines. The foxes barked in the hills and deer silently crossed the fields, half hidden in the mists of the fall mornings.

2   Along the roads, laurel, viburnum, and alder, great ferns and wildflowers delighted the traveler's eye through much of the year. Even in winter the roadsides were places of beauty, where countless birds came to feed on the berries and on the seed heads of the dried weeds rising above the snow. The countryside was, in fact, famous for the abundance and variety of its bird life, and when the flood of migrants was pouring through in spring and fall people traveled from great distances to observe them. Others came to fish the streams, which flowed clear and cold out of the hills and contained shady pools where trout lay. So it had

been from the days many years ago when the first settlers raised their houses, sank their wells, and built their barns.

3   Then a strange blight crept over the area and everything began to change. Some evil spell had settled on the community: mysterious maladies swept the flocks of chickens; the cattle and sheep sickened and died. Everywhere was a shadow of death. The farmers spoke of much illness among their families. In the town the doctors had become more and more puzzled by new kinds of sickness appearing among their patients. There had been several sudden and unexplained deaths, not only among adults but even among children, who would be stricken suddenly while at play and die within a few hours.

4   There was a strange stillness. The birds, for example—where had they gone? Many people spoke of them, puzzled and disturbed. The feeding stations in the backyards were deserted. The few birds seen anywhere were moribund; they trembled violently and could not fly. It was a spring without voices. On the mornings that had once throbbed with the dawn chorus of robins, catbirds, doves, jays, wrens, and scores of other bird voices there was no sound; only silence lay over the fields and woods and marsh.

5   On the farms the hens brooded, but no chicks hatched. The farmers complained that they were unable to raise any pigs—the litters were small and the young survived only a few days. The apple trees were coming into bloom but no bees droned among the blossoms, so there was no pollination and there would be no fruit.

6   The roadsides, once so attractive, were now lined with browned and withered vegetation as though swept by fire. These, too, were silent, deserted by all living things. Even the streams were now lifeless. Anglers no longer visited them, for all the fish had died.

7   In the gutters under the eaves and between the shingles of the roofs, a white granular powder still showed a few patches; some weeks before it had fallen like snow upon the roofs and the lawns, the fields and streams. No witchcraft, no enemy action had silenced the rebirth of new life in this stricken world. The people had done it themselves.

8   This town does not actually exist, but it might easily have a thousand counterparts in America or elsewhere in the world. I know of no community that has experienced all the misfortunes I describe. Yet every one of the disasters has actually happened somewhere, and many real communities have already suffered a substantial number of them. A grim specter has crept upon us almost unnoticed, and this imagined tragedy may easily become a stark reality we all shall know.

NOTES AND DISCUSSION

Carson's essay is in the form of a story. Her first line—"There was once a town in the heart of America"—recalls the "once-upon-a-time" opening of many fables and fairy tales. Carson also chooses the simple, easily understood language of such stories. Although she is discussing a modern chemical invention—DDT, or dichlorodiphenyltrichloroethane—and is herself a scientist, she avoids technical or scientific language.

Carson's essay compares and contrasts two scenarios: the town as it used to be, and as it is now. She describes each scenario carefully, detailing the passing of seasons and the interactions of people, landscape, and wildlife. Notice that only two paragraphs describe the town in its ideal state, while five paragraphs describe it after the change. Carson builds suspense by detailing the changes the town endures without revealing the cause until the end of the essay.

Traditionally, fairy tales end happily, but Carson does not disclose any magic remedies at the conclusion of this essay. However, the essay is not the end of Carson's argument, but the beginning. It is the introduction to *Silent Spring*; it is intended to pique readers' interest and draw them into the body of the text where Carson defines the unnamed "white granular powder" and suggests remedies for its use.

STUDY QUESTIONS

For Discussion:

1. Carson never identifies the "white granular powder." In your opinion, does this weaken or strengthen her essay and its purpose?

2. Compare and contrast Carson's conclusion with David Suzuki's in "The Road from Rio." How are they similar and dissimilar? What authorial intentions might account for these similarities and differences?

For Writing:

1. Identify and examine Carson's use of elements found in traditional fairy tales and myths. How do these elements strengthen or weaken her point?

2. Write an essay that makes its point by describing a person, place, or thing before and after a significant change.

POLITICAL ECONOMY

Samuel Langhorne Clemens

BIOGRAPHICAL NOTE

Samuel Langhorne Clemens (1835–1910) was a printer, a prospector, a journalist, an accomplished public speaker, and a riverboat pilot. He is better known under his pen name, Mark Twain, as one of the great American writers. His most widely read and respected work is his novel *Huckleberry Finn* (1884), but he was also a prolific essayist. This is an example of Samuel Clemens—Mark Twain—at his most humorous.

1   Political Economy is the basis of all good government. The wisest men of all ages have brought to bear upon this subject the—

2   [Here I was interrupted and informed that a stranger wished to see me down at the door. I went and confronted him, and asked to know his business, struggling all the time to keep a tight rein on my seething political economy ideas, and not let them break away from me or get tangled in their harness. And privately I wished the stranger was in the bottom of the canal with a cargo of wheat on top of him. I was all in a fever, but he was cool. He said he was sorry to disturb me, but as he was passing he noticed that I needed some lightning-rods. I said, "Yes, yes—go on—what about it?" He said there was nothing about it, in particular—nothing except that he would like to put them up for me. I am new to housekeeping; have been used to hotels and boardinghouses all my life. Like anybody else of similar experience, I try to appear (to strangers) to be an old housekeeper; consequently I said in an off-hand way that I had been intending for some time to have six or eight lightning-rods put up, but—The stranger started, and looked inquiringly at me, but I was serene. I thought that if I chanced to make any mistakes, he would not catch me by my countenance. He said he would rather have my custom than any man's in town. I said, "All right," and started off to

wrestle with my great subject again, when he called me back and said it would be necessary to know exactly how many "points" I wanted put up, what parts of the house I wanted them on, and what quality of rod I preferred. It was close quarters for a man not used to the exigencies of housekeeping; but I went through creditably, and he probably never suspected that I was a novice. I told him to put up eight "points," and put them all on the roof, and use the best quality of rod. He said he could furnish the "plain" article at 20 cents a foot; "coppered," 25 cents; "zinc-plated spiral-twist," at 30 cents, that would stop a streak of lightning any time, no matter where it was bound, and "render its errand harmless and its further progress apocryphal." I said apocryphal was no slouch of a word, emanating from the source it did, but, philology aside, I liked the spiral-twist and would take that brand. Then he said he *could* make two hundred and fifty feet answer; but to do it right, and make the best job in town of it, and attract the admiration of the just and the unjust alike, and compel all parties to say they never saw a more symmetrical and hypothetical display of lightning-rods since they were born, he supposed he really couldn't get along without four hundred, though he was not vindictive, and trusted he was willing to try. I said, go ahead and use four hundred, and make any kind of a job he pleased out of it, but let me get back to my work. So I got rid of him at last; and now, after half an hour spent in getting my train of political economy thoughts coupled together again, I am ready to go on once more.]

      richest treasures of their genius, their experience of life, and their learning. The great lights of commercial jurisprudence, international confraternity, and biological deviation, of all ages, all civilizations, and all nationalities, from Zoroaster down to Horace Greeley, have—

3   [Here I was interrupted again, and required to go down and confer further with that lightning-rod man. I hurried off, boiling and surging with prodigious thoughts wombed in words of such majesty that each one of them was in itself a straggling procession of syllables that might be fifteen minutes passing a given point, and once more I confronted him—he so calm and sweet, I so hot and frenzied. He was standing in the contemplative attitude of the Colossus of Rhodes, with one foot on my infant tuberose, and the other among my pansies, his hands on his hips, his hat-brim tilted forward, one eye shut and the other gazing critically and admiringly in the direction of my principal chimney. He said now *there* was a state of things to make a man glad to be alive; and added, "I leave it to *you* if you ever saw anything more deliriously picturesque than eight lightning-rods on one chimney?" I said I had no present recollection of anything that transcended it. He said that in his opinion nothing on earth but Niagara Falls was superior to it in the way of natural scenery. All that was needed now, he verily believed, to make my house a perfect balm to the eye, was to kind of touch up the other chimneys a little, and thus "add to the generous *coup d'oeil* a soothing uniformity of achievement which would allay the excitement naturally consequent upon the first *coup d'état*." I asked him if he learned to talk out of a book, and if I could borrow it anywhere? He smiled pleasantly, and said that his manner of speaking was not taught in books, and that nothing but familiarity with lightning could enable a man to handle his conversational style with impunity. He then figured up an estimate, and said that about eight more rods scattered about my roof would about fix me right, and he guessed five hundred feet of stuff would do it; and added that the first eight had got a little the start of him, so to speak, and used up a mere trifle of material more than he had calculated on—a hundred feet or along there. I said I was in a dreadful hurry, and I wished we could get this business permanently mapped out, so that I could go on with my work. He said, "I *could* have put up those eight rods, and marched off about my business—some men *would* have done it. But no; I said to my-

self, this man is a stranger to me, and I will die before I'll wrong him; there ain't lightning-rods enough on that house, and for one I'll never stir out of my tracks till I've done as I would be done by, and told him so. Stranger, my duty is accomplished; if the recalcitrant and dephlogistic messenger of heaven strikes your—" "There, now, there," I said, "put the other eight—add five hundred feet of spiral-twist—do anything and everything you want to do; but calm your sufferings, and try to keep your feelings where you can reach them with the dictionary. Meanwhile, if we understand each other now, I will go to work again."

4   I think I have been sitting here a full hour this time, trying to get back to where I was when my train of thought was broken up by the last interruption; but I believe I have accomplished it at last, and may venture to proceed again.]

> wrestled with this great subject, and the greatest among them have found it a worthy adversary, and one that always comes up fresh and smiling after every throw. The great Confucius said that he would rather be a profound political economist than chief of police. Cicero frequently said that political economy was the grandest consummation that the human mind was capable of consuming; and even our own Greeley has said vaguely but forcibly that *"Political—*

5   [Here the lightning-rod man sent up another call for me. I went down in a state of mind bordering on impatience. He said he would rather have died than interrupt me, but when he was employed to do a job, and that job was expected to be done in a clean, workmanlike manner, and when it was finished and fatigue urged him to seek the rest and recreation he stood so much in need of, and he was about to do it, but looked up and saw at a glance that all the calculations had been a little out, and if a thunder storm were to come up, and that house, which he felt a personal interest in, stood there with nothing on earth to protect it but sixteen lightning-rods—"let us have peace!" I shrieked. "Put up a hundred and fifty! Put some on the kitchen! Put a dozen on the barn! Put a couple on the cow!—Put one on the cook!—scatter them all over the persecuted place till it looks like a zinc-plated, spiral-twisted, silver-mounted cane-brake! Move! Use up all the material you can get your hands on, and when you run out of lightning-rods put up ram-rods, cam-rods, stair-rods, piston-rods—*anything* that will pander to your dismal appetite for artificial scenery, and bring respite to my raging brain and healing to my lacerated soul!" Wholly unmoved—further than to smile sweetly—this iron being simply turned back his wristbands daintily, and said he would now proceed to hump himself. Well, all that was nearly three hours ago. It is questionable whether I am calm enough yet to write on the noble theme of political economy, but I cannot resist the desire to try, for it is the one subject that is nearest to my heart and dearest to my brain of all this world's philosophy.]

> *"—economy is heaven's best boon to man."* When the loose but gifted Byron lay in his Venetian exile he observed that, if it could be granted him to go back and live his misspent life over again, he would give his lucid and unintoxicated intervals to the composition, not of frivolous rhymes, but of essays upon political economy. Washington loved this exquisite science; such names as Baker, Beckwith, Judson, Smith, are imperishably linked with it; and even imperial Homer, in the ninth book of the Iliad, has said:—
>
> Fiat justitia, ruat coelum,
> Post mortem unum, ante bellum,

Hic jacet hoc, ex-parte res,
Politicum e-conomico est.

The grandeur of these conceptions of the old poet, together with the felicity of the wording which clothes them, and the sublimity of the imagery whereby they are illustrated, have singled out that stanza, and made it more celebrated than any that ever—

6   ["Now, not a word out of you—not a single word. Just state your bill and relapse into impenetrable silence for ever and ever on these premises. Nine hundred dollars? Is that all? This check for the amount will be honored at any respectable bank in America. What is that multitude of people gathered in the street for? How?—'looking at the lightning-rods!' Bless my life, did they never see any lightning-rods before? Never saw 'such a stack of them on one establishment,' did I understand you to say? I will step down and critically observe this popular ebullition of ignorance."]

7   THREE DAYS LATER.—We are all about worn out. For four-and-twenty hours our bristling premises were the talk and wonder of the town. The theaters languished, for their happiest scenic inventions were tame and commonplace compared with my lightning-rods. Our street was blocked night and day with spectators, and among them were many who came from the country to see. It was a blessed relief on the second day when a thunder storm came up and the lightning began to "go for" my house, as the historian Josephus quaintly phrases it. It cleared the galleries, so to speak. In five minutes there was not a spectator within half a mile of my place; but all the high houses about that distance away were full, windows, roof, and all. And well they might be, for all the falling stars and Fourth of July fireworks of a generation, put together and rained down simultaneously out of heaven in one brilliant shower upon one helpless roof, would not have any advantage of the pyrotechnic display that was making my house so magnificently conspicuous in the general gloom of the storm. By actual count, the lightning struck at my establishment seven hundred and sixty-four times in forty minutes, but tripped on one of those faithful rods every time, and slid down the spiral-twist and shot into the earth before it probably had time to be surprised at the way the thing was done. And through all that bombardment only one patch of slates was ripped up, and that was because, for a single instant, the rods in the vicinity were transporting all the lightning they could possibly accommodate. Well, nothing was ever seen like it since the world began. For one whole day and night not a member of my family stuck his head out of the window but he got the hair snatched off it as smooth as a billiard-ball; and, if the reader will believe me, not one of us ever dreamt of stirring abroad. But at last the awful siege came to an end—because there was absolutely no more electricity left in the clouds above us within grappling distance of my insatiable rods. Then I sallied forth, and gathered daring workmen together, and not a bite or a nap did we take till the premises were utterly stripped of all their terrific armament except just three rods on the house, one on the kitchen, and one on the barn—and, behold, these remain there even unto this day. And then, and not till then, the people ventured to use our street again. I will remark here, in passing, that during that fearful time I did not continue my essay upon political economy. I am not even yet settled enough in nerve and brain to resume it.

8   TO WHOM IT MAY CONCERN.—Parties having need of three thousand two hundred and eleven feet of best quality zinc-plated, spiral-twist lightning-rod stuff, and sixteen hundred

and thirty-one silver-tipped points, all in tolerable repair (and, although much worn by use, still equal to any ordinary emergency), can hear of a bargain by addressing the publisher.

NOTES AND DISCUSSION

Twain establishes a topic for the essay with the title, yet the story of the lightning-rod salesman slowly takes over, until it overwhelms the essay altogether. Notice the way tone is also subverted: by the third installment, Confucius is avowing that he "would rather be a profound political economist than chief of police," a confession worthy of Huckleberry Finn himself.

Much of the humour in this essay derives from the juxtapositions that it sets up: the supposedly worldly and wise essayist with the "simple" salesman; the narrator's apparent sophistication of language and thought with the vastly more sophisticated language of the "stranger" who interrupts him at his work. The essay becomes a clash of a classic tall tale with academic discourse, and an account of the tall tale winning out, though the title of the piece remains "Political Economy." Even the narrator acknowledges the salesman's superior use of language: "I asked him if he learned to talk out of a book, and if I could borrow it anywhere?"

This is an outstanding example of an essay that implicitly attacks the notion that the "serious" is always more important than the humorous. The humorous obviously wins in this case. Indeed, given its title, the essay can be read showing political economy to be nothing more than hucksterism, and thus as a case of the humorous *becoming* the serious. Notice how the language of the piece hits its stride once the "essay" has been given up completely, in the section entitled "Three Days Later."

STUDY QUESTIONS

For Discussion:

1. To what extent is the narrator a victim of his own love for big words (such as apocryphal and dephlogistic)? Do you have a good sense of what the narrator is like? Is that sense important to the essay? Construct a character sketch of him. How is your response different from or similar to the narrator's? Based on "Politics and the English Language," how do you think George Orwell would have responded to the salesman? To the narrator and his essay?

2. Why has Twain chosen to use lightning-rods in his essay? What do they add to the piece that another item would not?

For Writing:

1. Construct a short essay in which you compare Walter Russell Mead's darkly humorous characterization of political economists with Clemens's. Alternatively, compare the techniques and effects of this essay with those of Leacock's "A, B, and C."

2. Isolate the "political economy" portion of this essay, and analyze it. Discuss the way the narrator's theories of "political economy" and his practice of household economics comment on and subvert each other.

EAT YOUR HEARTS OUT CINEPHILES, THE TUBE IS WHERE IT'S AT

John Haslett Cuff

BIOGRAPHICAL NOTE

John Haslett Cuff writes about television and popular culture for the newspaper *The Globe and Mail*. This essay is one of his columns.

---

1   Although film-festival fever is breaking out in Toronto this week, moving west from Montreal and eventually winding up in Vancouver, I could care less, because day in and day out, television is more important and more entertaining than the movies. Even watching summer reruns of *Law & Order, ER,* or *The Drew Carey Show* is more appealing to me than a trip to the Cineplex to see the latest megabuck Hollywood bombast, whether it's *Independence Day, The Fan,* or *Courage Under Fire*. But this has not always been the case.

2   Chronologically I am a TV baby. I was born a year after ABC became a "network" of four stations, and I was starting to take my first steps about the same time CBS abandoned its premature commitment to colour and signed the first television superstar, Jackie Gleason. But I was, at first, far more attached to movies, enthralled as a child by the big-screen spectacle of *Quo Vadis* and *War and Peace* and almost any 25-cent double bill that the local Famous Players would let me watch.

3   My passion for films grew, unabated, through the sixties and seventies as I discovered Ingmar Bergman, Akiro Kurosawa, Stanley Kubrick, Martin Scorsese, and Robert Altman. And then, somewhere around the mid-seventies when *Jaws* and *Star Wars* began establishing box office records, the movies began to nosedive into the irrelevance of special effects, even as television began maturing and offering viewers an unparalleled range of entertainments such as *I, Claudius*, and, at the other extreme, *All in the Family*.

4   With the exception of independent and foreign films, still the staple of film festivals and the diet of devoted urban cinephiles, the bloated products of mainstream Hollywood continue to run a poor second to television. The medium has grown up in my lifetime to become the most economical, varied, and influential source of information and entertainment.

5   The obvious advantage television has over movies is its accessibility and the familial intimacy it has established with its audience after decades in the home of virtually every class of person. Even without TV's unquestioned rule as the primary provider of news and information, the culture of television drama and comedy is clearly superior to most of the $30-million-plus (the budget of an average studio movie) offerings available in cinemas.

6   Any five episodes of *Seinfeld, Frasier,* or *Roseanne* are arguably funnier and more meticulously crafted than a Jim Carrey, Robin Williams, or Eddie Murphy blockbuster, not to mention more sophisticated and relevant. The same comparison can be made of a top-flight TV drama such as *NYPD Blue* or *ER*. On an ongoing basis, these fine shows deliver more emotional punch and subtlety, as well as character and plot development than almost any $100-million-grossing action flick.

7   While this is true even of some of the most commercial network shows, the quality gap is even more marked when imported and specialty television is brought into the mix. There is simply no equivalent in contemporary, mainstream moviemaking to the oeuvre of a Dennis Potter or Alan Bleasdale, British TV writers who make most movies look like puerile drivel.

8   But these are highly subjective, qualitative comparisons and television is also superior in other significant and quantifiable ways. Most obviously, network television produces more entertainment for much less money than the Hollywood studios. Carrey's payday for a 90-minute movie would almost finance a whole season (22 hours) of prime-time TV drama.

9   Culturally, television is richer in ideas and issues and in its representation of society. Just look at the number and range of roles for women in television, and compare them with the paucity of good parts for women of any age in the movies. There are no film-actress superstars who can open a film and command the money that such muscle-bound hacks as Sly Stallone or Arnold Schwarzenegger routinely earn.

10   Yet television abounds with women stars, young and middle-aged, fat and anorexic. Many of the most enduringly popular sitcoms, such as *Roseanne, Murphy Brown, Grace Under Fire, Ellen,* and *Caroline in the City* dominate the ratings, and TV shows employ award-winning movie actresses such as Christine Lahti, Madeline Kahn, and Mercedes Ruehl in increasing numbers.

11   Television engenders loyalty and empathy with its characters in a way that movies don't, because over the course of a season viewers develop relationships with TV characters, sharing in their development in a way that is impossible in one-off movie fare. Such characters as Dr. Frasier Crane have been visiting us in our homes for years, and we have watched them age through story lines that reflect changes in fashion, society, and even politics.

12   While television has produced a rich mix of exceptional dramas over the past decade, movies have all but abandoned them, preferring high-octane, live-action cartoons instead. Perhaps the most important difference is that TV writers are forced to be more creative with language, plot, and even sex than the creators of movies. Since TV writers are not allowed to use profanity, nudity, or violence with the graphic abandon of their movie peers, the resulting drama is often more powerful, suggestive, and complex.

13   In addition, due to the immediacy of television and the speed with which it is produced, it is more relevant than the movies, more rooted in the social and political news of the day, and better able to explore issues that affect the audience and are a vital part of the public dialogue.

14   So, despite the volume of dreck that marks the beginning of any new TV season, I must confess I'm looking forward to the 1996–97 offerings. As for the few movies I really want to see, I'll probably catch them on pay-TV or video. That's a win–win situation.

NOTES AND DISCUSSION

For some time, cultural industries have been rated informally on a scale of relevance and aesthetic and artistic merit. It is not difficult, for instance, to find literary critics who are also fond of and are expert in film studies. Television, however, is different: many people who profess an enduring fondness for literature do not watch (or do not admit to watching) television. See, for example, the essay by Wendell Berry, "Why I Am Not Going to Buy a Computer," in which Berry, an English instructor, announces proudly that he does not own a television set. Because television is inexpensive and available to most people in North America it is neither exotic nor elitist and, by implication, neither interesting nor sophisticated.

John Haslett Cuff takes a divergent approach in this essay, claiming that television is in fact consistently more "economical, varied, and influential" as well as "more sophisticated and relevant" than Hollywood films. He supplies an abundance of evidence to support his claim and compares and contrasts television with Hollywood films, with television clearly emerging as the superior choice. However, notice the terms on which Cuff constructs his debate: although the opening sentence addresses film festival devotees, Cuff does not single out the festivals' content for criticism. Instead, he compares the "best" of television (the work of Dennis Potter, for instance) with what he considers to be the worst of Hollywood, the big-budget, blockbuster, special-effects-filled movie (like *Independence Day*).

STUDY QUESTIONS

For Discussion:

1. Discuss Cuff's argument that the work of Dennis Potter or Alan Bleasdale makes "most movies look like puerile drivel." Do you agree, or has Cuff managed to convince you that most television is superior to most movies?

2. Compare Marie Winn's obvious fear of and dislike for television with Cuff's equally obvious celebration. What do you think Cuff thinks of reading? That is, what unspoken assumptions does Cuff make regarding the responses of television viewers?

For Writing:

1. Using some of Cuff's criteria, construct a comparison/contrast essay of your own that examines a recent film and your favourite television shows.

2. Analyze the second-last paragraph of Cuff's argument, which praises the social and political relevance of television over movies. Do you think Cuff's claim is true or justified?

INTRODUCTION TO *RADIOACTIVE SUBSTANCES*

Marie Curie

BIOGRAPHICAL NOTE

Marie Curie (originally Maria Sklodowska, 1867–1934) was born in Warsaw, Poland. In 1891, after being refused admission to the University of Warsaw because of her sex, Sklodowska moved to Paris to study at the Sorbonne. In 1895, she married her teacher, Pierre Curie, with whom she studied radioactivity and magnetism. The Curies shared the 1903 Nobel Prize for Physics with Antoine-Henri Becquerel. After Pierre's death in 1906, Marie Curie succeeded him as professor of physics at the Sorbonne and received the Nobel Prize in 1911 for isolating pure radium. She died of cancer in 1934, survived by two daughters, Irène, a nuclear physicist, and Ève, a writer and musician.

1   The object of the present work is the publication of researches which I have been carrying on for more than four years on radioactive bodies. I began these researches by a study of the phosphorescence of uranium, discovered by [Monsieur] Becquerel. The results to which I was led by this work promised to afford so interesting a field that [Monsieur] Curie put aside the work on which he was engaged, and joined me, our object being the extraction of new radioactive substances and the further study of their properties.

2   Since the commencement of our research we thought it well to hand over specimens of the substances, discovered and prepared by ourselves, to certain physicists, in the first place to [Monsieur] Becquerel, to whom is due the discovery of the uranium rays. In this way we ourselves facilitated the research by others besides ourselves on the new radioactive bodies. At the termination of our first publications, [Monsieur] Giesel, in Germany, also

began to prepare these substances, and passed on specimens of them to several German scientists. Finally, these substances were placed on sale in France and Germany, and the subject growing in importance gave rise to a scientific movement, such that numerous memoirs have appeared, and are constantly appearing on radioactive bodies, principally abroad. The results of the various French and foreign researches are necessarily confused, as is the case with all new subjects in course of investigation, the aspect of the question becoming modified from day to day.

3   From the chemical point of view, however, one point is definitely established: i.e., the existence of a new element, strongly radioactive, *viz.*, radium. The preparation of the pure chloride of radium and the determination of the atomic weight of radium form the chief part of my own work. Whilst this work adds to the elements actually known with certainty a new element with very curious properties, a new method of chemical research is at the same time established and justified. This method, based on the consideration of radio-activity as an atomic property of matter, is just that which enabled [Monsieur] Curie and myself to discover the existence of radium.

4   If, from the chemical point of view, the question that we undertook primarily may be looked upon as solved, the study of the physical properties of the radioactive bodies is in full evolution. Certain important points have been established, but a large number of the conclusions are still of a provisional character. This is not surprising when we consider the complexity of the phenomena due to radioactivity, and the differences existing between the various radioactive substances. The researches of physicists on these substances constantly meet and overlap. Whilst endeavouring to keep strictly to the limits of this work and to publish my individual research only, I have been obliged at the same time to mention results of other researches, the knowledge of which is indispensable.

5   I desired, moreover, to make this work an inclusive survey of the actual position of the question.

6   I indicate at the end the particular questions with which I am specially concerned, and those which I investigated in conjunction with [Monsieur] Curie.

7   I carried on the work in the laboratories of the School of Physics and Chemistry in Paris, with the permission of Schützenberger, late Director of the School, and [Monsieur] Lauth, actual Director. I take this opportunity of expressing my gratitude for the kind hospitality received in this school.

NOTES AND DISCUSSION

This is the introduction to Marie Curie's doctoral dissertation. Due to general interest in radioactivity and in Curie herself as a woman scientist, her dissertation was published shortly after its acceptance by the Sorbonne. Curie's brief and carefully structured text outlines and summarizes the content of her thesis, functioning as an abstract of her work as well as an introduction. It follows the basic structure used in lab reports: an introduction, a description of the materials, methods, observations, and results, and a conclusion. Curie first introduces the object of her present work and establishes her area of research and her time-line. She then orders chronologically the events leading up to her present research and outlines the manner in which she collaborated with Messieurs Curie and Becquerel, offering observations on the present confused state of the study of radioactive bodies. Curie then introduces the dual focus of her thesis: "the existence of a new element, strongly radioactive, *viz.*, radium" and the establishment of "a new method of chemical research" that allowed her to isolate radium. She considers these dual discoveries fully established and proved by her research, but acknowledges that much work is still to be done in the study of the physical properties of radioactive elements. She also states that in the conclusion of her work she considers questions related to this study and the work of other scientists on the subject.

STUDY QUESTIONS

For Discussion:

1. How does Curie's introduction resemble the introductions you have been taught to write in your essay assignments?
2. Female contemporaries of Curie often made apologetic references to their sex or to their atypical involvement in science. What sort of tone does Curie create and maintain? What audience expectations might she be trying to address?

For Writing:

1. Compare and contrast Curie's introduction with the formula of a typical lab report.
2. Research Curie's contribution to the fields of chemistry and physics. What are her lasting contributions to these fields?

EXCERPT FROM *THE ORIGIN OF SPECIES*

Charles Darwin

BIOGRAPHICAL NOTE

Charles Darwin (1809–92) served as a naturalist on HMS *Beagle* from 1831–36, collecting many natural specimens and obtaining an intimate knowledge of many different landscapes and formations, which he drew on throughout his later career. In 1859 he published his famous *The Origin of Species*, which was violently attacked and vigorously defended in a variety of intellectual circles. Although he was not the first to propose the theory of evolution, Darwin was the first to gain wide acceptance for the idea, through his concept of natural selection.

1   Looking to geographical distribution, if we admit that there has been during the long course of ages much migration from one part of the world to another, owing to former climatal and geographical changes and to the many occasional and unknown means of dispersal, then we can understand, on the theory of descent with modification, most of the great leading facts in Distribution. We can see why there should be so striking a parallelism in the distribution of organic beings throughout space, and in their geological succession throughout time; for in both cases the beings have been connected by the bond of ordinary generation, and the means of modification have been the same. We see the full meaning of the wonderful fact, which has struck every traveller, namely, that on the same continent, under the most diverse conditions, under heat and cold, on mountain and lowland, on deserts and marshes, most of the inhabitants within each great class are plainly related; for they are the descendants of the same progenitors and early colonists. On this same principle of former migration, combined in most cases with modification, we can understand, by the aid of the Glacial period, the identity of some few plants, and the close alliance of many others, on the most distant mountains, and in the northern and southern temperate zones; and likewise the close alliance of some of the inhabitants of the sea in the northern and southern temperate latitudes,

though separated by the whole intertropical ocean. Although two countries may present physical conditions as closely similar as the same species ever require, we need feel no surprise at their inhabitants being widely different, if they have been for a long period completely sundered from each other; for as the relation of organism to organism is the most important of all relations, and as the two countries will have received colonists at various periods and in different proportions, from some other country or from each other, the course of modification in the two areas will inevitably have been different.

2   On this view of migration, with subsequent modification, we see why oceanic islands are inhabited by only few species, but of these, why many are peculiar to endemic forms. We clearly see why species belonging to those groups of animals which cannot cross wide spaces of the ocean, as frogs and terrestrial mammals, do not inhabit oceanic islands; and why, on the other hand, new and peculiar species of bats, animals which can traverse the ocean, are found on islands far distant from any continent. Such cases as the presence of peculiar species of bats on oceanic islands and the absence of all other terrestrial mammals, are facts utterly inexplicable on the theory of independent acts of creation.

3   The existence of closely allied or representative species in any two areas, implies, on the theory of descent with modification, that the same parent-forms formerly inhabited both areas; and we almost invariably find that wherever many closely allied species inhabit two areas, some identical species are still common to both. Wherever many closely allied yet distinct species occur, doubtful forms and varieties belonging to the same groups likewise occur. It is a rule of high generality that the inhabitants of each area are related to the inhabitants of the nearest source whence immigrants might have been derived. We see this in the striking relation of nearly all plants and animals of the Galapagos archipelago, of Juan Fernandez, and of the other American islands, to the plants and animals of the neighbouring American mainland; and of those of the Cape de Verde Archipelago, and of the other African islands to the African mainland. It must be admitted that these facts receive no explanation on the theory of creation.

4   The fact, as we have seen, that all past and present organic beings can be arranged within a few great classes, in groups subordinate to groups, and with the extinct groups often falling in between the recent groups, is intelligible on the theory of natural selection with its contingencies of extinction and divergence of character. On these same principles we see how it is, that the mutual affinities of the forms within each class are so complex and circuitous. We see why certain characters are far more serviceable than others for classification; why adaptive characters, though of paramount importance to the beings, are of hardly any importance in classification; why characters derived from rudimentary parts, though of no service to the beings, are often of high classificatory value; and why embryological characters are often the most valuable of all. The real affinities of all organic beings, in contradistinction to their adaptive resemblances, are due to inheritance or community of descent. The Natural System is a genealogical arrangement, with the acquired grades of difference, marked by the terms, varieties, species, genera, families, [etc.]; and we have to discover the lines of descent by the most permanent characters whatever they may be and of however slight vital importance.

5   The similar framework of bones in the hand of a man, wing of a bat, fin of the porpoise, and leg of the horse—the same number of vertebrae forming the neck of the giraffe and of the elephant—and innumerable other such facts, at once explain themselves on the theory of descent with slow and slight successive modifications. The similarity of pattern

in the wing and in the leg of a bat, though used for such different purpose, in the jaws and legs of a crab, in the petals, stamens, and pistils of a flower, is likewise, to a large extent, intelligible on the view of the gradual modification of parts or organs, which were aboriginally alike in an early progenitor in each of these classes. On the principle of successive variations not always supervening at an early age, and being inherited at a corresponding not early period of life, we clearly see why the embryos of mammals, birds, reptiles, and fishes should be so closely similar, and so unlike the adult forms. We may cease marvelling at the embryo of an airbreathing mammal or bird having branchial slits and arteries running in loops, like those of a fish which has to breathe the air dissolved in water by the aid of well-developed branchiae.

6   Disuse, aided sometimes by natural selection, will often have reduced organs when rendered useless under changed habits or conditions of life; and we can understand on this view the meaning of rudimentary organs. But disuse and selection will generally act on each creature, when it has come to maturity and has to play its full part in the struggle for existence, and will thus have little power on an organ during early life; hence the organ will not be reduced or rendered rudimentary at this early age. The calf, for instance, has inherited teeth, which never cut through the gums of the upper jaw, from an early progenitor having well-developed teeth; and we may believe, that the teeth in the mature animal were formerly reduced by disuse, owing to the tongue and palate, or lips, having become excellently fitted through natural selection to browse without their aid; whereas in the calf, the teeth have been left unaffected, and on the principle of inheritance at corresponding ages have been inherited from a remote period to the present day. On the view of each organism with all its separate parts having been specially created, how utterly inexplicable is it that organs bearing the plain stamp of inutility, such as the teeth in the embryonic calf or the shrivelled wings under the soldered wing-covers of many beetles, should so frequently occur. Nature may be said to have taken pains to reveal her scheme of modification, by means of rudimentary organs, of embryological and homologous structures, but we are too blind to understand her meaning.

NOTES AND DISCUSSION

In this passage, excerpted from the fifteenth and final chapter of *The Origin of Species*, Darwin painstakingly recapitulates and summarizes the contents of his book, which he characterizes as "one long argument." The excerpt is typical of Darwin's prose style and rhetorical strategies. Readers will immediately notice that he does not conform to contemporary style conventions for scientific or technical writing. For example, note his use of the pronoun "we" throughout this passage: he includes the reader in his explorations, discoveries, and explanations, making the reader part of the advancing argument, rather than merely an on-looker.

Darwin does not suggest that his observations and ideas are strikingly original, but claims that they are part of humanity's common pursuit of knowledge. He not only carefully establishes a series of cause-and-effect relationships, but also provides some parallel occurrences and then analyzes their meaning. Using these strategies, Darwin argues that evolution and geographical distribution are responsible for the parallels he observes in nature. He draws his examples from a wide variety of biological organisms, creating surprising and interesting comparisons and contrasts. He also deals with locales that are on a global scale, thereby enhancing the scope and impact of his argument. By describing the organisms in near-photographic detail, Darwin also imparts a sense of immediacy and verity to his writing.

STUDY QUESTIONS

For Discussion:

1. O. B. Hardison, Jr., writes that Darwin disparaged his own literary style and believed that he was "writing dry scientific prose for scientists." Consider Darwin's audience and the care he takes to anticipate resistance to his argument. After reading this excerpt, what can you deduce about the nature and attitudes of Darwin's readers?

2. Darwin's last sentence begins, "Nature may be said to have taken pains to reveal her scheme of modification. . . ." What literary device is Darwin employing? What effect does this device have on the passage?

For Writing:

1. Identify and examine two cause-and-effect relationships that Darwin establishes in this passage. How does he support his contentions?

2. Read more of the *The Origin of Species* and then research some current developments in creation theory. How much has the debate between the two theories changed since the publication of *The Origin of Species* in 1859?

DOOMSDAY

Paul Davies

BIOGRAPHICAL NOTE

Paul Davies is a Professor of Natural History at the University of Adelaide, Australia, where he is also Associate Director of the University's Institute of Physics. He has published over one hundred research papers in specialist journals that deal with cosmology, gravitation, and quantum field theory, and over twenty books, including *God and the New Physics* (1983), *Superforce* (1984), *The Cosmic Blueprint* (1987), *The Matter Myth* (1991), and most recently, *About Time* (1995) and *Are We Alone?* (1995). He is also well known as a popular author, broadcaster, and public lecturer. This essay is taken from his 1994 book *The Last Three Minutes*.

1   *The date: August 21, 2126. Doomsday.*

2   *The place: Earth. Across the planet a despairing population attempts to hide. For billions there is nowhere to go. Some people flee deep underground, desperately seeking out caves and disused mine shafts, or take to the sea in submarines. Others go on the rampage, murderous and uncaring. Most just sit, sullen and bemused, waiting for the end.*

3   *High in the sky, a huge shaft of light is etched into the fabric of the heavens. What began as a slender pencil of softly radiating nebulosity has swollen day by day to form a maelstrom of gas boiling into the vacuum of space. At the apex of a vapor trail lies a dark, misshapen, menacing lump. The diminutive head of the comet belies its enormous destructive power. It is closing on planet Earth at a staggering 40,000 miles per hour, 10 miles every second— a trillion tons of ice and rock, destined to strike at seventy times the speed of sound.*

4   *Mankind can only watch and wait. The scientists, who have long since abandoned their telescopes in the face of the inevitable, quietly shut down the computers. The endless simu-*

From *The Last Three Minutes*. Reprinted by permission of the publisher, Weidenfeld & Nicolson.

lations of disaster are still too uncertain, and their conclusions are too alarming to release to the public anyway. Some scientists have prepared elaborate survival strategies, using their technical knowledge to gain advantage over their fellow citizens. Others plan to observe the cataclysm as carefully as possible, maintaining their role as true scientists to the very end, transmitting data to time capsules buried deep in the Earth. For posterity. . .

5   *The moment of impact approaches. All over the world, millions of people nervously check their watches. The last three minutes.*

6   *Directly above ground zero, the sky splits open. A thousand cubic miles of air are blasted aside. A finger of searing flames wider than a city arcs groundward and fifteen seconds later lances the Earth. The planet shudders with the force of ten thousand earthquakes. A shock wave of displaced air sweeps over the surface of the globe, flattening all structures, pulverizing everything in its path. The flat terrain around the impact site rises in a ring of liquid mountains several miles high, exposing the bowels of the Earth in a crater a hundred miles across. The wall of molten rock ripples outward, tossing the landscape about like a blanket flicked in slow motion.*

7   *Within the crater itself, trillions of tons of rock are vaporized. Much more is splashed aloft, some of it flung out into space. Still more is pitched across half a continent to rain down hundreds or even thousands of miles away, wreaking massive destruction on all beneath. Some of the molten ejecta falls into the ocean, raising huge tsunamis that add to the spreading turmoil. A vast column of dusty debris fans out into the atmosphere, blotting out the sun across the whole planet. Now the sunlight is replaced by the sinister, flickering glare of a billion meteors, roasting the ground below with their searing heat, as displaced material plunges back from space into the atmosphere.*

8   The preceding scenario is based on the prediction that comet Swift-Tuttle will hit the earth on August 21, 2126. If it were to, global devastation would undoubtedly follow, destroying human civilization. When this comet paid us a visit in 1993, early calculations suggested that a collision in 2126 was a distinct possibility. Since then, revised calculations indicate that the comet will in fact miss Earth by two weeks: a close shave, but we can breathe easily. However, the danger won't go away entirely. Sooner or later Swift-Tuttle, or an object like it, *will* hit the Earth. Estimates suggest that 10,000 objects half a kilometer or more in diameter move on Earth-intersecting orbits. These astronomical interlopers originate in the frigid outer reaches of the solar system. Some are the remains of comets that have become trapped by the gravitational fields of the planets, others come from the asteroid belt that lies between Mars and Jupiter. Orbital instability causes a continual traffic of these small but lethal bodies into and out of the inner solar system, constituting an ever-present menace to Earth and our sister planets.

9   Many of these objects are capable of causing more damage than all the world's nuclear weapons put together. It is only a matter of time before one strikes. When it does, it will be bad news for people. There will be an abrupt and unprecedented interruption in the history of our species. But for the Earth such an event is more or less routine. Cometary or asteroid impacts of this magnitude occur, on average, every few million years. It is widely believed that one or more such events caused the extinction of the dinosaurs sixty-five million years ago. It could be us next time.

10   Belief in Armageddon is deep-rooted in most religions and cultures. The biblical book of Revelation gives a vivid account of the death and destruction that lie in store for us:

Then there came flashes of lightning, rumblings, peals of thunder, and a severe earthquake. No earthquake like it has ever occurred since man has been on Earth, so tremendous was the quake. . . . The cities of the nations collapsed. . . . Every island fled away and the mountains could not be found. From the sky huge hailstones of about a hundred pounds each fell upon men. And they cursed God on account of the plague of hail, because the plague was so terrible.

11   There are certainly lots of nasty things that could happen to Earth, a puny object in a universe pervaded by violent forces, yet our planet has remained hospitable to life for at least three and a half billion years. The secret of our success on planet Earth is space. Lots of it. Our solar system is a tiny island of activity in an ocean of emptiness. The *nearest* star (after the sun) lies more than four light-years away. To get some idea of how far that is, consider that light traverses the ninety-three million miles from the sun in only eight and a half minutes. In four years, it travels more than twenty trillion miles.

12   The sun is a typical dwarf star, lying in a typical region of our galaxy, the Milky Way. The galaxy contains about a hundred billion stars, ranging in mass from a few percent to a hundred times the mass of the sun. These objects, together with a lot of gas clouds and dust and an uncertain number of comets, asteroids, planets, and black holes, slowly orbit the galactic center. Such a huge collection of bodies may give the impression that the galaxy is a very crowded system, until account is taken of the fact that the visible part of the Milky Way measures about a hundred thousand light-years across. It is shaped like a plate, with a central bulge; a few spiral arms made up of stars and gas are strung out around it. Our sun is located in one such spiral arm and is about thirty thousand light-years from the middle.

13   As far as we know, there is nothing very exceptional about the Milky Way. A similar galaxy, called Andromeda, lies about two million light-years away, in the direction of the constellation of that name. It can just be seen with the unaided eye as a fuzzy patch of light. Many billions of galaxies, some spiral, some elliptical, some irregular, adorn the observable universe. The scale of distance is vast. Powerful telescopes can image individual galaxies several *billion* light-years away. In some cases, it has taken their light longer than the age of the Earth (four and a half billion years) to reach us.

14   All this space means that cosmic collisions are rare. The greatest threat to Earth is probably from our own backyard. Asteroids do not normally orbit close to Earth; they are largely confined to the belt between Mars and Jupiter. But the huge mass of Jupiter can disturb the asteroids' orbits, occasionally sending one of them plunging in toward the sun, and thus menacing Earth.

15   Comets pose another threat. These spectacular bodies are believed to originate in an invisible cloud situated about a light year from the sun. Here the threat comes not from Jupiter but from passing stars. The galaxy is not static; it rotates slowly, as its stars orbit the galactic nucleus. The sun and its little retinue of planets take about two hundred million years to complete one circuit of the galaxy, and on the way they have many adventures. Nearby stars may brush the cloud of comets, displacing a few toward the sun. As the comets plunge through the inner solar system, the sun evaporates some of their volatile material, and the solar wind blows it out in a long streamer—the famous cometary tail. Very rarely, a comet will collide with the Earth during its sojourn in the inner solar system. The comet does the damage, but the passing star must bear the responsibility. Fortunately, the huge distances between the stars insulate us against too many such encounters.

16   Other objects can also pass our way on their journey around the galaxy. Giant clouds of gas drift slowly by, and though they are more tenuous even than a laboratory vacuum they can drastically alter the solar wind and may affect the heat flow from the sun. Other, more sinister objects may lurk in the inky depths of space: rogue planets, neutron stars, brown dwarfs, black holes—all these and more could come upon us unseen, without warning, and wreak havoc with the solar system.

17   Or the threat could be more insidious. Some astronomers believe that the sun may belong to a double-star system, in common with a great many other stars in the galaxy. If it exists, our companion star—dubbed Nemesis, or the Death Star—is too dim and too far away to have been discovered yet. But in its slow orbit around the sun it could still make its presence felt gravitationally, by periodically disturbing distant comets and sending some plunging Earthward to produce a series of devastating impacts. Geologists have found that wholesale ecological destruction does indeed occur periodically—about every thirty million years.

18   Looking farther afield, astronomers have observed entire galaxies in apparent collision. What chance is there that the Milky Way will be smashed by another galaxy? There is some evidence, in the very rapid movement of certain stars, that the Milky Way may have already been disrupted by collisions with small nearby galaxies. However, the collision of two galaxies does not necessarily spell disaster for their constituent stars. Galaxies are so sparsely populated that they can merge into one another without individual stellar collisions.

19   Most people are fascinated by the prospect of Doomsday—the sudden, spectacular destruction of the world. But violent death is less of a threat than slow decay. There are many ways in which Earth could gradually become inhospitable. Slow ecological degradation, climatic change, a small variation in the heat output of the sun—all these could threaten our comfort, if not survival, on our fragile planet. Such changes, however, will take place over thousands or even millions of years, and humanity may be able to combat them using advanced technology. The gradual onset of a new ice age, for example, would not spell total disaster for our species, given the time available to reorganize our activities. One can speculate that technology will continue to advance dramatically over the coming millennia; if so, it is tempting to believe that human beings, or their descendants, will gain control over ever-larger physical systems and may eventually be in a position to avert disasters even on an astronomical scale.

20   Can humanity, in principle, survive forever? Possibly. Be we shall see that immortality does not come easily and may yet prove to be impossible. The universe itself is subject to physical laws that impose upon it a life cycle of its own: birth, evolution, and—perhaps—death. Our own fate is entangled inextricably with the fate of the stars.

NOTES AND DISCUSSION

Davies begins his essay with a descriptive scenario portraying Doomsday—the end of the world. His evocation of Doomsday is detailed, precise, and compelling. It seems designed to make readers uneasy, like a ghost story told late at night. Consider what effect this opening is likely to have on readers, and think about the essay's appeal.

In the beginning of the essay proper, Davies offers readers only partial reassurance. Much of his essay speculates about how little humanity knows and all the possibilities that surround the unexplained. His specific scenario is based on early predictions that the Swift-Tuttle comet would collide with Earth. Further calculations have shown that Swift-Tuttle will *not* collide with Earth, but Davies argues that the laws of probability ensure that someday some object *will* do so. Next, Davies offers the reader an overview of Earth's position in relation to the sun, the other planets, the galaxy, and other galaxies. He then classifies and discusses the various threats to Earth contained in these schemata: comets, other objects in space, the stars, and galaxies themselves. In the close of his essay, Davies seems to undermine the threat of sudden destruction that he has spent so much time establishing by stating that slow decay is in fact a greater threat to humanity than cataclysmic events. In his conclusion, however, he declares that humanity's fate is entangled with that of the stars and that humanity, like the universe, must be subject to physical laws, which impose life cycles.

STUDY QUESTIONS

For Discussion:

1. This essay is about the possible collision of a comet with Earth, as well as the inevitable approach of Doomsday due to slow decline. How would you identify Davies's central topic of discussion? What is the thesis of his essay?

2. What principles and strategies of organization and classification does Davies use in presenting his information?

For Writing:

1. Write an alternate Doomsday scenario, based on some observable phenomena in science, as an introduction to an essay in which you agree or disagree with Davies's argument.

2. Write an essay that identifies and classifies technological advances that seem most likely to aid humans in achieving immortality. (You may wish to articulate your system of classification on a separate page.)

FRAUDS ON THE FAIRIES

Charles Dickens

BIOGRAPHICAL NOTE

Charles Dickens (1812–70) worked as a journalist and aspired to be an actor before beginning a career as one of the most popular and prolific novelists in Victorian Britain. His first novel, *Oliver Twist* (1837–39), was followed by such classics as *David Copperfield* (1849–50), *A Tale of Two Cities* (1859), and *Great Expectations* (1860–61). Dickens also published a popular periodical entitled *Household Words*, in which this essay first appeared in October 1853.

1   We may assume that we are not singular in entertaining a very great tenderness for the fairy literature of our childhood. What enchanted us then, and is captivating a million of young fancies now, has, at the same blessed time of life, enchanted vast hosts of men and women who have done their long day's work, and laid their grey heads down to rest. It would be hard to estimate the amount of gentleness and mercy that has made its way among us through these slight channels. Forbearance, courtesy, consideration for the poor and aged, kind treatment of animals, the love of nature, abhorrence of tyranny and brute force—many such good things have been first nourished in the child's heart by this powerful aid. It has greatly helped to keep us, in some sense, ever young, by preserving through our worldly ways one slender track not overgrown with weeds, where we may walk with children, sharing their delights.

Reprinted from *Miscellaneous Papers from "The Morning Chronicle," "The Daily News," "The Examiner," "Household Words," "All the Year Round,", and other sources*, by Charles Dickens (Chapman and Hall, 1908). The essay was first published in *Household Words*, October 1, 1853.

2   In an utilitarian age, of all other times, it is a matter of grave importance that Fairy tales should be respected. Our English red tape is too magnificently red ever to be employed in the tying up of such trifles, but every one who has considered the subject knows full well that a nation without fancy, without some romance, never did, never can, never will, hold a great place under the sun. The theatre, having done its worst to destroy these admirable fictions—and having in a most exemplary manner destroyed itself, its artists, and its audiences, in that perversion of its duty—it becomes doubly important that the little books themselves, nurseries of fancy as they are, should be preserved. To preserve them in their usefulness, they must be as much preserved in their simplicity, and purity, and innocent extravagance, as if they were actual fact. Whosoever alters them to suit his own opinions, whatever they are, is guilty, to our thinking, of an act of presumption, and appropriates to himself what does not belong to him.

3   We have lately observed, with pain, the intrusion of a Whole Hog of unwieldy dimensions into the fairy flower garden. The rooting of the animal among the roses would in itself have awakened in us nothing but indignation; our pain arises from his being violently driven in by a man of genius, our own beloved friend, Mr. George Cruikshank. That incomparable artist is, of all men, the last who should lay his exquisite hand on fairy text. In his own art he understands it so perfectly, and illustrates it so beautifully, so humorously, so wisely, that he should never lay down his etching needle to "edit" the Ogre, to whom with that little instrument he can render such extraordinary justice. But, to "editing" Ogres, and Hop-o'-my-thumbs, and their families, our dear moralist has in a rash moment taken, as a means of propagating the doctrines of Total Abstinence, Prohibition of the sale of spirituous liquors, Free Trade, and Popular Education. For the introduction of these topics, he has altered the text of a fairy story; and against his right to do any such thing we protest with all our might and main. Of his likewise altering it to advertise that excellent series of plates, "The Bottle," we say nothing more than that we foresee a new and improved edition of Goody Two Shoes, edited by E. Moses and Son; of the Dervish with the box of ointment, edited by Professor Holloway; and of Jack and the Beanstalk, edited by Mary Wedlake, the popular authoress of Do you bruise your oats yet.

4   Now, it makes not the least difference to our objection whether we agree or disagree with our worthy friend, Mr. Cruikshank, in the opinions he interpolates upon an old fairy story. Whether good or bad in themselves, they are, in that relation, like the famous definition of a weed; a thing growing up in a wrong place. He has no greater moral justification in altering the harmless little books than we should have in altering his best etchings. If such a precedent were followed we must soon become disgusted with the old stories into which modern personages so obtruded themselves, and the stories themselves must soon be lost. With seven Blue Beards in the field, each coming at a gallop from his own platform mounted on a foaming hobby, a generation or two hence would not know which was which, and the great original Blue Beard would be confounded with the counterfeits. Imagine a Total Abstinence edition of *Robinson Crusoe*, with the rum left out. Imagine a Peace edition, with the gunpowder left out, and the rum left in. Imagine a Vegetarian edition, with the goat's flesh left out. Imagine a Kentucky edition, to introduce a flogging of that 'tarnal old nigger Friday, twice a week. Imagine an Aborigines Protection Society edition, to deny the cannibalism and make Robinson embrace the amiable savages whenever they landed. Robinson Crusoe would be "edited" out of his island in a hundred years, and the island would be swallowed up in the editorial ocean.

5   Among the other learned professions we have now the Platform profession, chiefly exercised by a new and meritorious class of commercial travellers who go about to take the sense of meetings on various articles: some, of a very superior description: some, not quite so good. Let us write the story of Cinderella, "edited" by one of these gentlemen, doing a good stroke of business, and having a rather extensive mission.

6   Once upon a time, a rich man and his wife were the parents of a lovely daughter. She was a beautiful child, and became, at her own desire, a member of the Juvenile Bands of Hope when she was only four years of age. When this child was only nine years of age her mother died, and all the Juvenile Bands of Hope in her district—the Central district, number five hundred and twenty-seven—formed in a procession of two and two, amounting to fifteen hundred, and followed her to the grave, singing chorus Number forty-two, "O come," etc. This grave was outside the town, and under the direction of the Local Board of Health, which reported at certain stated intervals to the General Board of Health, Whitehall.

7   The motherless little girl was very sorrowful for the loss of her mother, and so was her father too, at first; but, after a year was over, he married again—a very cross widow lady, with two proud tyrannical daughters as cross as herself. He was aware that he could have made his marriage with this lady a civil process by simply making a declaration before a Registrar; but he was averse to this course on religious grounds, and, being a member of the Montgolfian persuasion, was married according to the ceremonies of that respectable church by the Reverend Jared Jocks, who improved the occasion.

8   He did not live long with his disagreeable wife. Having been shamefully accustomed to shave with warm water instead of cold, which he ought to have used (see Medical Appendix B. and C.), his undermined constitution could not bear up against her temper, and he soon died. Then, this orphan was cruelly treated by her stepmother and the two daughters, and was forced to do the dirtiest of the kitchen work; to scour the saucepans, wash the dishes, and light the fires—which did not consume their own smoke, but emitted a dark vapour prejudicial to the bronchial tubes. The only warm place in the house where she was free from ill-treatment was the kitchen chimney-corner; and as she used to sit down there, among the cinders, when her work was done, the proud fine sisters gave her the name of Cinderella.

9   About this time, the King of the land, who never made war against anybody, and allowed everybody to make war against him—which was the reason why his subjects were the greatest manufacturers on earth, and always lived in security and peace—gave a great feast, which was to last two days. This splendid banquet was to consist entirely of artichokes and gruel; and from among those who were invited to it, and to hear the delightful speeches after dinner, the King's son was to choose a bride for himself. The proud fine sisters were invited, but nobody knew anything about poor Cinderella, and she was to stay at home.

10   She was so sweet-tempered, however, that she assisted the haughty creatures to dress, and bestowed her admirable taste upon them as freely as if they had been kind to her. Neither did she laugh when they broke seventeen stay-laces in dressing; for, although she wore no stays herself, being sufficiently acquainted with the anatomy of the human figure to be aware of the destructive effects of tight-lacing, she always reserved her opinions on that subject for the Regenerative Record (price three halfpence in a neat wrapper), which all good people take in, and to which she was a Contributor.

11   At length the wished-for moment arrived, and the proud fine sisters swept away to the feast and speeches, leaving Cinderella in the chimney-corner. But, she could always occupy her mind with the general question of the Ocean Penny Postage, and she had in her pocket an unread Oration on the subject, made by the well-known Orator, Nehemiah Nicks. She was lost in the fervid eloquence of that talented Apostle when she became aware of the presence of one of those female relatives which (it may not be generally known) it is not lawful for a man to marry. I allude to her grandmother.

12   "Why so solitary, my child?" said the old lady to Cinderella.

13   "Alas, grandmother," returned the poor girl, "my sisters have gone to the feast and speeches, and here sit I in the ashes, Cinderella!"

14   "Never," cried the old lady with animation, "shall one of the Band of Hope despair! Run into the garden, my dear, and fetch me an American Pumpkin! American, because in some parts of that independent country, there are prohibitory laws against the sale of alcoholic drinks in any form. Also, because America produced (among many great pumpkins) the glory of her sex, Mrs. Colonel Bloomer. None but an American Pumpkin will do, my child!"

15   Cinderella ran into the garden, and brought the largest American Pumpkin she could find. This virtuously democratic vegetable her grandmother immediately changed into a splendid coach. Then, she sent her for six mice from the mouse-trap, which she changed into prancing horses, free from the obnoxious and oppressive post-horse duty. Then, to the rat-trap in the stable for a rat, which she changed to a state-coachman, not amenable to the iniquitous assessed taxes. Then, to look behind a watering-pot for six lizards, which she changed into six foot-men, each with a petition in his hand ready to present to the Prince, signed by fifty thousand persons, in favour of the early closing movement.

16   "But grandmother," said Cinderella, stopping in the midst of her delight, and looking at her clothes, "how can I go to the palace in these miserable rags?"

17   "Be not uneasy about that, my dear," returned her grandmother.

18   Upon which the old lady touched her with her wand, her rags disappeared, and she was beautifully dressed. Not in the present costume of the female sex, which has been proved to be at once grossly immodest and absurdly inconvenient, but in rich sky-blue satin pantaloons gathered at the ankle, a puce-coloured satin pelisse sprinkled with silver flowers, and a very broad Leghorn hat. The hat was chastely ornamented with a rainbow-coloured ribbon hanging in two bell-pulls down the back; the pantaloons were ornamented with a golden stripe; and the effect of the whole was unspeakably sensible, feminine, and retiring. Lastly, the old lady put on Cinderella's feet a pair of shoes made of glass: observing that but for the abolition of the duty on that article, it never could have been devoted to such a purpose; the effect of all such taxes being to cramp invention, and embarrass the producer, to the manifest injury of the consumer. When the old lady had made these wise remarks, she dismissed Cinderella to the feast and speeches, charging her by no means to remain after twelve o'clock at night.

19   The arrival of Cinderella at the Monster Gathering produced a great excitement. As a delegate from the United States had just moved that the King do take the chair, and as the motion had been seconded and carried unanimously, the King himself could not go forth to receive her. But His Royal Highness the Prince (who was to move the second resolution), went to the door to hand her from her carriage. This virtuous Prince, being completely covered from head to foot with Total Abstinence Medals, shone as if he were attired in complete armour; while the inspiring strains of the Peace Brass Band in the gallery (composed of the Lambkin Family, eighteen in number, who cannot be too much encouraged) awakened additional enthusiasm.

20   The King's son handed Cinderella to one of the reserved seats for pink tickets, on the platform, and fell in love with her immediately. His appetite deserted him; he scarcely tasted his artichokes, and merely trifled with his gruel. When the speeches began, and Cinderella, wrapped in the eloquence of the two inspired delegates who occupied the entire evening in speaking to the first Resolution, occasionally cried, "Hear, hear!" the sweetness of her voice completed her conquest of the Prince's heart. But, indeed the whole male portion of the assembly loved her—and doubtless would have done so, even if she had been less beautiful, in consequence of the contrast which her dress presented to the bold and ridiculous garments of the other ladies.

21   At a quarter before twelve the second inspired delegate having drunk all the water in the decanter, and fainted away, the King put the question, "That this meeting do now adjourn until tomorrow." Those who were of that opinion holding up their hands, and then those who were of the contrary, theirs, there appeared an immense majority in favour of the resolution, which was consequently carried. Cinderella got home in safety, and heard nothing all that night, or all next day, but the praises of the unknown lady with the sky-blue satin pantaloons.

22   When the time for the feast and speeches came round again, the cross stepmother and the proud fine daughters went out in good time to secure their places. As soon as they were gone, Cinderella's grandmother returned and changed her as before. Amid a blast of welcome from the Lambkin family, she was again handed to the pink seat on the platform by His Royal Highness.

23   This gifted Prince was a powerful speaker, and had the evening before him. He rose at precisely ten minutes before eight, and was greeted with tumultuous cheers and waving of handkerchiefs. When the excitement had in some degree subsided, he proceeded to address the meeting: who were never tired of listening to speeches, as no good people ever are. He held them enthralled for four hours and a quarter. Cinderella forgot the time, and hurried away when she heard the first stroke of twelve, [so] that her beautiful dress changed back to her old rags at the door, and she left one of her glass shoes behind. The Prince took it up, and vowed— that is, made a declaration before a magistrate; for he objected on principle to the multiplying of oaths—that he would only marry the charming creature to whom that shoe belonged.

24   He accordingly caused an advertisement to that effect to be inserted in all the newspapers; for the advertisement duty, an impost most unjust in principle and most unfair in operation, did not exist in that country; neither was the stamp on newspapers known in that land—which had as many newspapers as the United States, and got as much good out of them. Innumerable ladies answered the advertisement and pretended that the shoe was theirs; but, every one of them was unable to get her foot into it. The proud fine sisters answered it, and tried their feet with no greater success. Then, Cinderella, who had answered it too, came forward amidst their scornful jeers, and the shoe slipped on in a moment. It is a remarkable tribute to the improved and sensible fashion of the dress her grandmother had given her, that if she had not worn it the Prince would probably never have seen her feet.

25   The marriage was solemnised with great rejoicing. When the honeymoon was over, the King retired from public life, and was succeeded by the Prince. Cinderella, being now a queen, applied herself to the government of the country on enlightened, liberal, and free principles. All the people who ate anything she did not eat, or who drank anything she did not drink, were imprisoned for life. All the newspaper offices from which any doctrine proceeded that was not her doctrine, were burnt down. All the public speakers proved to demon-

stration that if there were any individual on the face of the earth who differed from them in anything, that individual was a designing ruffian and an abandoned monster. She also threw open the right of voting, and of being elected to public offices, and of making the laws, to the whole of her sex; who thus came to be always gloriously occupied with public life and whom nobody dared to love. And they all lived happily ever afterwards.

26   Frauds on the Fairies once permitted, we see little reason why they may not come to this, and great reason why they may. The Vicar of Wakefield was wisest when he was tired of being always wise. The world is too much with us, early and late. Leave this precious old escape from it, alone.

NOTES AND DISCUSSION

Dickens's essay is designed to convince readers of the importance of preserving fairy tales in their pure and traditional form. He is strongly opposed to adding contemporary settings, props, characters, and themes (whether moral, political, or religious) to traditional tales. He feels that such touches destroy the traditional quality and effect of fairy tales. He compares fairy tales to a rare and exquisite garden and those who attempt to alter them to hogs digging up and destroying the garden.

However, Dickens does not merely state his point through metaphor; instead, he provides an extended example of a modernized (that is, Victorianized) fairy tale. The bulk of the essay is a retelling of Cinderella, filled with contemporary moral, political, and religious references, which considerably alter the nature of the story. Dickens includes references to temperance, vegetarianism, various religious reforms, dress reform, utilitarianism, abolition, pacifism, censorship, and female suffrage. This story is the key to Dickens's argument. After the heavily ironic "they all lived happily ever afterwards," he brings the essay to a swift close by alluding to the call to maintain simplicity in Oliver Goldsmith's novel *The Vicar of Wakefield* and to Wordsworth's sonnet "The World Is Too Much with Us," and stating simply (but imperatively) that fairy tales must be left alone.

STUDY QUESTIONS

For Discussion:

1. Dickens obviously intends his version of Cinderella to amuse. How do you react to this version of the story? How does this reaction differ from your reaction to the "purer" forms of the story you are already familiar with?

2. Consider Dickens's title and his use of "Frauds on the Fairies" in his conclusion. What does Dickens mean by "fraud"? Which "fraudulent practices" does he himself use in this essay?

For Writing:

1. Critique Dickens's chain of cause-and-effect reasoning in the opening paragraph of the essay. Do you agree with Dickens's characterization of fairy tales and his call to maintain their purity and originality? Why or why not?

2. Write your own contemporary version of Cinderella in which you communicate a didactic theme, or compare and contrast the motifs and themes of several versions of the Cinderella story. (You might consider the Grimm Brothers' version, entitled *Ashputtle*, the Disney version, or James Finn Garner's treatment in his *Politically Correct Bedtime Stories*.)

LIVING LIKE

WEASELS

Annie Dillard

BIOGRAPHICAL NOTE

Annie Dillard won the 1974 Pulitzer Prize for nonfiction for *Pilgrim at Tinker Creek*. She has since written several well-received books of essays, a memoir, and a novel. Dillard is a keen observer of human nature and its connection with the natural world, especially of the ways this connection reflects on human spirituality.

---

1   A weasel is wild. Who knows what he thinks? He sleeps in his underground den, his tail draped over his nose. Sometimes he lives in his den for two days without leaving. Outside, he stalks rabbits, mice, muskrats, and birds, killing more bodies than he can eat warm, and often dragging the carcasses home. Obedient to instinct, he bites his prey at the neck, either splitting the jugular vein at the throat or crunching the brain at the base of the skull, and he does not let go. One naturalist refused to kill a weasel who was socketed into his hand deeply as a rattlesnake. The man could in no way pry the tiny weasel off, and he had to walk half a mile to water, the weasel dangling from his palm, and soak him off like a stubborn label.

2   And once, says Ernest Thompson Seton—once, a man shot an eagle out of the sky. He examined the eagle and found the dry skull of a weasel fixed by the jaws to his throat. The supposition is that the eagle had pounced on the weasel and the weasel swiveled and bit as instinct taught him, tooth to neck, and nearly won. I would like to have seen that eagle from the air a few weeks or months before he was shot: was the whole weasel still attached to his

feathered throat, a fur pendant? Or did the eagle eat what he could reach, gutting the living weasel with his talons before his breast, bending his beak, cleaning the beautiful airborne bones?

3   I have been reading about weasels because I saw one last week. I startled a weasel who startled me, and we exchanged a long glance.

4   Twenty minutes from my house, through the woods by the quarry and across the highway, is Hollins Pond, a remarkable piece of shallowness, where I like to go at sunset and sit on a tree trunk. Hollins Pond is also called Murray's Pond; it covers two acres of bottomland near Tinker Creek with six inches of water and six thousand lily pads. In winter, brown-and-white steers stand in the middle of it, merely dampening their hooves; from the distant shore they look like miracle itself, complete with miracle's nonchalance. Now, in summer, the steers are gone. The water lilies have blossomed and spread to a green horizontal plane that is terra firma to plodding blackbirds, and tremulous ceiling to black leeches, crayfish, and carp.

5   This is, mind you, suburbia. It is a five-minute walk in three directions to rows of houses, though none is visible here. There's a 55 mph highway at one end of the pond, and a nesting pair of wood ducks at the other. Under every bush is a muskrat hole or a beer can. The far end is an alternating series of fields and woods, fields and woods, threaded everywhere with motorcycle tracks—in whose bare clay wild turtles lay eggs.

6   So. I had crossed the highway, stepped over two low barbed-wire fences, and traced the motorcycle path in all gratitude through the wild rose and poison ivy of the pond's shoreline up into high grassy fields. Then I cut down through the woods to the mossy fallen tree where I sit. This tree is excellent. It makes a dry, upholstered bench at the upper, marshy end of the pond, a plush jetty raised from the thorny shore between a shallow blue body of water and a deep blue body of sky.

7   The sun had just set. I was relaxed on the tree trunk, ensconced in the lap of lichen, watching the lily pads at my feet tremble and part dreamily over the thrusting path of a carp. A yellow bird appeared to my right and flew behind me. It caught my eye; I swiveled around—and the next instant, inexplicably, I was looking down at a weasel, who was looking up at me.

8   Weasel! I'd never seen one wild before. He was ten inches long, thin as a curve, a muscled ribbon, brown as fruitwood, soft-furred, alert. His face was fierce, small and pointed as a lizard's; he would have made a good arrowhead. There was just a dot of chin, maybe two brown hairs' worth, and then the pure white fur began that spread down his underside. He had two black eyes I didn't see, any more than you see a window.

9   The weasel was stunned into stillness as he was emerging from beneath an enormous shaggy wild rose bush four feet away. I was stunned into stillness twisted backward on the tree trunk. Our eyes locked, and someone threw away the key.

10   Our look was as if two lovers, or deadly enemies, met unexpectedly on an overgrown path when each had been thinking of something else: a clearing blow to the gut. It was also a bright blow to the brain, or a sudden beating of brains, with all the charge and intimate grate of rubbed balloons. It emptied our lungs. It felled the forest, moved the fields, and drained the pond; the world dismantled and tumbled into that black hole of eyes. If you and I looked at each other that way, our skulls would split and drop to our shoulders. But we don't. We keep our skulls. So.

11   He disappeared. This was only last week, and already I don't remember what shattered the enchantment. I think I blinked, I think I retrieved my brain from the weasel's brain, and tried to memorize what I was seeing, and the weasel felt the yank of separation, the careening splash-down into real life and the urgent current of instinct. He vanished under the wild rose. I waited motionless, my mind suddenly full of data and my spirit with pleadings, but he didn't return.

12   Please do not tell me about "approach-avoidance conflicts." I tell you I've been in that weasel's brain for sixty seconds, and he was in mine. Brains are private places, muttering through unique and secret tapes—but the weasel and I both plugged into another tape simultaneously, for a sweet and shocking time. Can I help it if it was a blank?

13   What goes on in his brain the rest of the time? What does a weasel think about? He won't say. His journal is tracks in clay, a spray of feathers, mouse blood and bone: uncollected, unconnected, loose-leaf, and blown.

14   I would like to learn, or remember, how to live. I come to Hollins Pond not so much to learn how to live as, frankly, to forget about it. That is, I don't think I can learn from a wild animal how to live in particular—shall I suck warm blood, hold my tail high, walk with my footprints precisely over the prints of my hands?—but I might learn something of mindlessness, something of the purity of living in the physical senses and the dignity of living without bias or motive. The weasel lives in necessity and we live in choice, hating necessity and dying at the last ignobly in its talons. I would like to live as I should, as the weasel lives as he should. And I suspect that for me the way is like the weasel's: open to time and death painlessly, noticing everything, remembering nothing, choosing the given with a fierce and pointed will.

15   I missed my chance. I should have gone for the throat. I should have lunged for that streak of white under the weasel's chin and held on, held on through mud and into the wild rose, held on for a dearer life. We could live under the wild rose wild as weasels, mute and uncomprehending. I could very calmly go wild. I could live two days in the den, curled, leaning on mouse fur, sniffing bird bones, blinking, licking, breathing musk, my hair tangled in the roots of grasses. Down is a good place to go, where the mind is single. Down is out, out of your ever-loving mind and back to your careless senses. I remember muteness as a prolonged and giddy fast, where every moment is a feast of utterance received. Time and events are merely poured, unremarked, and ingested directly, like blood pulsed into my gut through a jugular vein. Could two live that way? Could two live under the wild rose, and explore by the pond, so that the smooth mind of each is as everywhere present to the other, and as received and as unchallenged, as falling snow?

16   We could, you know. We can live any way we want. People take vows of poverty, chastity, and obedience—even of silence—by choice. The thing is to stalk your calling in a certain skilled and supple way, to locate the most tender and live spot and plug into that pulse. This is yielding, not fighting. A weasel doesn't "attack" anything; a weasel lives as he's meant to, yielding at every moment to the perfect freedom of single necessity.

17   I think it would be well, and proper, and obedient, and pure, to grasp your one necessity and not let it go, to dangle from it limp wherever it takes you. Then even death, where you're going no matter how you live, cannot you part. Seize it and let it seize you up aloft even, till your eyes burn out and drop; let your musky flesh fall off in shreds, and let your very bones unhinge and scatter, loosened over fields, over fields and woods, lightly, thoughtless, from any height at all, from as high as eagles.

NOTES AND DISCUSSION

In an essay entitled "Push It," Dillard instructs novice writers to "examine all things with an intense, restless eye." Some of Dillard's own intensity is clearly evident in "Living Like Weasels." Dillard's writing, with its almost Romantic concern with what nature may teach us, has been compared with Thoreau's, especially to parts of his most famous work, *Walden*. In particular, critics have frequently compared Dillard's description of Hollins Pond, with its breadth of detail, with the passage from *Walden* included in this anthology as "The Ponds."

In another essay, titled "Transfiguration," Dillard portrays the life of the writer as an all-or-nothing endeavour. In "Living Like Weasels" she seems to develop in the weasel's image, reputation, and character a metaphor for the writer's life. Dillard mixes myths about weasels with her own specific encounter, and speculates on what it might be like to live the way she assumes a weasel does. As she wrestles with similes, tone, and images to shape and communicate her observations, there is no denying or avoiding her desire to grasp and to impart the essence of the experience, as well as to share in the essence of "weasel."

Note Dillard's language in this essay, as she seeks to lift this event out of the ordinary. She uses many one-syllable words with precise effect: in the opening three sentences, only three words are more than one syllable, and only one is longer than two. Dillard develops a seductive rhythm in phrases such as "obedient to instinct," or in the alliterative phrase, "I like to go at sunset and sit on a tree trunk." Also effective are her sudden shifts to short, explosive phrases: "We could, you know. We can live any way we want."

STUDY QUESTIONS

For Discussion:

1. Dillard uses numerous similes and other comparisons in this essay. See, for example, the attempt to "soak him off like a stubborn label"; the steers "look like miracle itself"; "our look was as if two lovers, or deadly enemies, met unexpectedly on an overgrown path"; and "he would have made a good arrowhead." How are these comparisons related to the specific things described, and to the overall pattern of Dillard's imagery?

2. Does it matter that Dillard "genders" weasels "male" in this essay? What cultural associations does the word weasel have that this essay extends or challenges. Would "to weasel," for example, be a positive or a negative term to Dillard? How do you know?

For Writing:

1. Find a description of a weasel in a natural history text or similar source. Contrast the "scientific" description of the animal and its hunting and living habits with Dillard's more "poetic" description, and account for the differences.

2. Examine and explain Dillard's repetition of words and images in this essay. See, for example, her references to the jugular, the throat, and the skull; to the eagle; to images of softness, or to sharpness and pointiness/pointedness.

THE GHOST'S VOCABULARY

Edward Dolnick

BIOGRAPHICAL NOTE

Edward Dolnick first wrote this article for *The Atlantic Monthly*, where it was published in October 1991. *The Atlantic Monthly* is now available on-line, suggesting that the marriage of computers and literature *can* be successful. Dr. Donald Foster's work can also be found on-line.

---

1   In 1842 literature and science met with a thud. Alfred Tennyson had just published his poem "The Vision of Sin." Among the appreciative letters he received was one from Charles Babbage, the mathematician and inventor who is known today as the father of the computer. Babbage wrote to suggest a correction to Tennyson's "otherwise beautiful" poem—in particular to the lines "Every moment dies a man,/Every moment one is born."

2   "It must be manifest," Babbage pointed out, "that, were this true, the population of the world would be at a standstill." Since the population was in fact growing slightly, Babbage continued, "I would suggest that in the next edition of your poem you have it read: 'Every moment dies a man,/Every moment 1-1/16 is born.'" Even this was not strictly correct, Babbage conceded, "but I believe 1-1/16 will be sufficiently accurate for poetry."

3   Today computers are standard tools for amateur and professional literary investigators alike. Shakespeare is both the most celebrated object of this effort and the most common. At Claremont McKenna College, in California, for example, two highly regarded faculty members have devoted years of their lives to a computer-based attempt to find out whether Shakespeare, rather than Francis Bacon or the Earl of Oxford or any of a myriad of others, wrote the plays and poems we associate with his name.

First published in *The Atlantic Monthly*, vol. 268, no. 4, pp. 82–6 (October 1991). Reprinted by permission of the author.

4   As Babbage's venture into criticism foreshadowed, the marriage of computers and literature has been an uneasy one. At the mention of computers or statistics, many Shakespeareans and others in the literary establishment wrinkle their noses in distaste. To approach the glories of literature in this plodding way is misguided, they say, and misses the point in the same way as does the oft-cited remark that the human body is worth just a few dollars—the market value of the various chemicals of which it is composed. "This is just madness," says Ricardo Quinones, the chairman of the literature department at Claremont McKenna. "Why don't they simply read the plays?"

5   Rather than read, these literary sleuths prefer to count. Their strategy is straightforward. Most are in search of a statistical fingerprint, a reliable and objective mark of identity unique to a given author. Every writer will sooner or later reveal himself, they contend, by quirks of style that may be too subtle for the eye to note but are well within the computer's power to identify.

6   For a University of Chicago statistician named Ronald Thisted, the call to enter this quasi-literary enterprise came on a Sunday morning in December of 1985. Thisted had settled down with *The New York Times Book Review* and an article by Gary Taylor, a Shakespeare scholar, caught his eye. Taylor claimed that he had found a new poem by Shakespeare at Oxford's Bodleian Library. Among the many reasons Taylor advanced for believing in the authenticity of the poem, called "Shall I Die?," Thisted focused on one. "One of his arguments," Thisted says, "was that several words in the poem don't appear previously in Shakespeare. And that was evidence that Shakespeare wrote it. One's first reaction is, that's dumb. If Shakespeare *didn't* use these words, why would that be evidence that he wrote the poem?" But Taylor's article went on to explain that in practically everything he wrote, Shakespeare used words he hadn't used elsewhere. Thisted conceded the point in his own mind, but raised another objection. "If *all* the words in there were ones that Shakespeare had never used," he thought, "if it were in Sanskrit or something, you'd say, 'No way Shakespeare could have written this.' So there had to be about the right number of new words." That question—how many new words an authentic Shakespeare text should contain—was similar to one that Thisted himself had taken on a decade before. Together with the Stanford statistician Bradley Efron, then his graduate adviser, Thisted had published a paper that proposed a precise answer to the question "How many words did Shakespeare know but never use?" The question sounds ludicrous, like "How many New Year's resolutions have I not yet made?" Nonetheless, Efron and Thisted managed to answer it. They found the crucial insight in a generation-old story, perhaps apocryphal, about an encounter between a mathematician and a butterfly collector.

7   R. A. Fisher, the statistical guru of his day, had been consulted by a butterfly hunter newly back from Malaysia. The naturalist had caught members of some species once or twice, other species several times, and some species time and time again. Was it worth the expense, the butterfly collector asked, to go back to Malaysia for another season's trapping? Fisher recast the question as a mathematical problem. The collector knew how many species he had seen exactly once, exactly twice, and so on. Now, how many species were out there that he had yet to see? If the collector had many butterflies from each species he had seen, Fisher reasoned, then quite likely he had sampled all the species that were out there. Another hunting trip would be superfluous. But if he had only one or two representatives of most species, then there might be many species yet to find. It would be worth returning to Malaysia. Fisher devised a mathematical way to make that rough idea precise (and reportedly suggested another collecting trip). Efron and Thisted's question was essentially the same. Where the naturalist had tramped through the rain forest in search of exotic butterflies, the mathematicians could scan Shakespeare in search of unusual words. By counting how many words he used exactly once, exactly twice, and so on, they would attempt to calculate how many words he knew but had yet to use.

8   Neither Efron nor Thisted had imagined that their statistical sleight of hand could ever be put to a live test. No new work of Shakespeare's had been unearthed for decades. Now Taylor had given them their chance. A new Shakespeare poem, like a new butterfly-collecting trip to the jungle, should yield a certain number of new words, a certain number that Shakespeare had used once before, and so on. If Shakespeare did write "Shall I Die?," which has 429 words, according to the mathematicians' calculations it should have about seven words he never used elsewhere; it has nine. To Efron and Thisted's surprise, the number of words in the poem which Shakespeare had used once before also came close to matching their predictions, as did the number of twice-used words, all the way through to words he had used ninety-nine times before. The poem, which sounds nothing like Shakespeare, fit Shakespeare like a glove.

9   This is work that can suck up lives. One Defoe scholar, trying to pick out true Defoe from a slew of anonymous and pseudonymous works, has pursued his quarry for twenty years, with no end in sight. A team trying to determine if the Book of Mormon was composed by ancient authors or by the nineteenth-century American Joseph Smith took 10,000 hours to produce a single essay. (The largely Mormon team of researchers concluded that Smith had not written the Book of Mormon. Confirmed samples of Smith's prose, the researchers argued, showed patterns of word usage different from those in the Book of Mormon.) Paper after paper begins with a trumpet fanfare and ends with a plaintive bleat. One writer, for instance, decided to determine whether Jonathan Swift or one of his contemporaries had written a particular article, by pigeonholing his words according to what part of speech they were. "The only positive conclusion from over a year of effort and the coding of over 40,000 words," she lamented, "is that a great deal of further study will be needed." (Swift himself had satirized, in *Gulliver's Travels*, a professor who had "employed all his Thoughts from his Youth" in making "the strictest Computation of the general Proportion there is in Books between the Numbers of Particles, Nouns, and Verbs, and other Parts of Speech.")

10   Despite the shortage of triumphs the field is growing, because more and more of the work can be assigned to electronic drudges. Scholars once had to count words by hand. Later they had the option of typing entire books into a computer, so that the machine could do the counting. Today computers are everywhere, and whole libraries of machine-readable texts are available. Software to do deluxe slicing and dicing is easy to obtain.

11   As a result, everything imaginable is being counted somewhere. Someone at this moment is tallying up commas or meticulously computing adjective-to-adverb ratios. But sophisticated tools don't automatically produce good work. A future Academy of Statistics and Style might take as its motto the warning that the Nobel laureate P. B. Medawar issued to his fellow scientists: "An experiment not worth doing is not worth doing well."

12   Among those least likely to be fazed by such pronouncements is a professor of political science at Claremont McKenna College named Ward Elliott. Elliott is an authority on voting rights, a cheerful eccentric, and, like his father before him, inclined to view the Earl of Oxford as the true author of Shakespeare's works. Four years ago Elliott recruited Robert

Valenza, an expert programmer also on the Claremont McKenna faculty, and the two set to work on the authorship question.

13   This time the model would be not butterfly hunting but radar. Valenza had spent considerable time devising mathematical procedures to find the patterns obscured by noisy and jumbled electronic signals. Adapted to Shakespeare, the idea was to go beyond counting various words, as many others had done, and see whether consistent patterns could be found in the way certain key words were used together. Two writers might use the words "blue" and "green" equally often throughout a text, for example, but the writers could be distinguished if one always used them on the same page while the other never used them together.

14   This pattern-finding mathematics is widely used in physics and engineering, in deciphering television and radar signals, for example. Given a long list of words—not simply the "blue" and "green" of the example, but dozens more—the computer can quickly tell how Shakespeare typically balanced those words. "You might have a pattern," Valenza says, "with a lot of 'love,' very little 'hate,' and a good deal of 'woe.'" A different writer might use the same words, and even use them at the same rates as Shakespeare, but the configurations might be different. The result is that a given list of words produces a kind of voiceprint for each author.

15   Valenza and Elliott examined "common but not too common" words that Shakespeare used. To examine rare words, Valenza had reasoned, would be like trying to identify a voice from a whisper, and to examine common words would be to let the writer shout into your ear. The final, fifty-two-word list—with such miscellaneous entries as "about," "death," "desire," "secret," and "set"—was assembled by trial and error. It consisted of words with two key properties. In various works of Shakespeare's those words are used in patterns that yield the same voiceprint each time. And when other writers are tested, the same words yield voiceprints that are different from Shakespeare's.

16   The machinery in place, Valenza and Elliott began by testing Shakespeare's poetry against that of thirty other writers. Exciting results came quickly: The disputed "Shall I Die?" poem seemed not to be Shakespeare's after all. Three of the leading claimants to Shakespeare's work—Francis Bacon, Christopher Marlowe, and Sir Edward Dyer—were decisively ruled out. To Elliott's good-humored consternation, the test dealt just as harshly with the claims put forward on behalf of the Earl of Oxford. Worse was to follow. For even as this first round of tests ruled out the best-known Shakespeare candidates, it left a few surprising contenders. One possibility for the "real" Shakespeare: Queen Elizabeth I. "That did it for our chance of appearing in *Science*," Elliott laments, "but it vastly increased our chance of getting into the *National Enquirer*." (To his dismay, Elliott did find himself in *Science*, not as the co-author of a weighty research paper but as the subject of a skeptical news brief with the headline "Did Queen Write Shakespeare's Sonnets?")

17   Valenza and Elliott have since conducted more-extensive tests that have ruled out Queen Elizabeth. But the mishap highlights a risk that is shared by all the number-crunching methods. "If the glass slipper doesn't fit, it's pretty good evidence that you're not Cinderella," Elliott points out. "But if it does fit, that doesn't prove that you are."

18   The risk of being fooled is least for someone who combines a deep knowledge of literature with some statistical insight. Donald Foster, a professor of English at Vassar College, fits that bill. Foster's scholarship is highly regarded. Soon after "Shall I Die?" was presented to the world, for example, he wrote a long debunking essay that persuaded many

readers that the poem was not Shakespeare's. In a more recent essay he consigned whole libraries of research to the scrap heap. Hundreds or thousands of articles have been written to explain the epigraph to *Shakespeare's Sonnets*, which begins, "To the onlie begetter of these insuing sonnets, Master W.H." Who was W.H.? Foster's solution to the mystery, which won him the Modern Language Association's Parker Prize, is that W.H. was . . . a typo. The publisher, who wrote the epigraph as a bit of flowery praise to honor Shakespeare, had intended to print "W.SH."

19   Those essays had nothing to do with statistics, but Foster has done some statistical sleuthing of his own, and he is well aware of the hazards. One scholar compared Shakespeare's plays with someone else's poems, for example, and concluded that Shakespeare used the present tense more than other writers do. Another compared Shakespeare with later writers and concluded that he used many four-letter words, whereas other writers used shorter words—forgetting that archaic words like "thou" and "hath" drive Shakespeare's average up. "There are strong and compelling reasons for avoiding this kind of research," Foster says, "because it's so difficult to anticipate all the pitfalls." But Foster himself has often given way to temptation. Like many Shakespeareans, he steers clear of the "authorship question," but he has looked into a pertinent mystery.

20   Shakespeare acted in his plays. But with two exceptions, we don't know what roles he took. Foster believes he has found a statistical way to gather that long-vanished knowledge. "It occurred to me," he says, "that Shakespeare may have been influenced in his writing by the parts he had memorized for performances and was reciting on a more or less daily basis." Last year Foster figured out a way to test that hunch. "The results," he says, "have been absolutely stunning."

21   "We started by using a concordance to type in all the words that Shakespeare used ten times or fewer," Foster says. These aren't exotic words, necessarily, just ones that don't crop up often in Shakespeare. Scholars have known for some time that these "rare" words tend to be clustered chronologically. Foster found that if two plays shared a considerable number of rare words, in the later play those words were scattered randomly among all the characters. In the earlier play, the shared words were not scattered. "In one role," Foster says, "there would be two to six times the expected number of rare words." There stood Shakespeare: the words that Shakespeare the writer had at the tip of his pen were the ones he had been reciting as Shakespeare the actor.

22   If Foster is right, Shakespeare played Theseus in *A Midsummer Night's Dream* and "Chorus" in *Henry V* and *Romeo and Juliet*. In play after play the first character to come on stage and speak is the one that Foster's test identifies as Shakespeare: John Gower in *Pericles*, Bedford in *Henry VI*, Part I, Suffolk in *Henry VI*, Part II, and Warwick in *Henry VI*, Part III. And Foster's test picks out as Shakespeare's the two roles that we have seventeenth-century evidence he played: the ghost in *Hamlet* and Adam in *As You Like It*.

23   The theory can be tested in other ways. It never assigns to Shakespeare a role we know another actor took. The roles it does label as Shakespeare's all seem plausible—male characters rather than women or children. The test never runs in the wrong direction, with the unusual words scattered randomly in an early play and clustered in one role in a later play. On those occasions when Foster's test indicates that Shakespeare played *two* roles in a given play—Gaunt and a gardener in *Richard II*, for example—the characters are never onstage together. Foster's theory passes another test. When Foster looks at the rare words that *Hamlet* shares with *Macbeth*, written a few years later, those words point to the ghost in

Hamlet as Shakespeare's role. And if Foster looks at rare words that *Hamlet* shares with a different play also written a few years later—*King Lear*, for example—*those* shared words also pick out the ghost as Shakespeare's role.

24   Additional evidence has been uncovered. After *Hamlet*, the ghost's vocabulary exerted a strong influence on Shakespeare's writing and then tapered off. But Shakespeare's plays went in and out of production. When *Hamlet* was revived several years after its first staging, and Shakespeare was again playing the ghost, he began again to recycle the ghost's vocabulary.

25   It is a strange image, a computer fingering a ghost. But it is a sign of things to come. Eventually the prejudice against computers in literary studies will give way. "The walls are sure to crumble," Ward Elliott says, "just as they did in baseball and popular music. . . . Some high-tech Jackie Robinson will score a lot of runs, and thereafter all the teams in the league will pursue the newest touch as ardently and piously as they now shrink from it."

NOTES AND DISCUSSION

This paper explores a specific partnership between the sciences and the arts, freely crossing borders generally considered to be restrictive. Dolnick opens his essay with a humorous anecdote about the overall relationship of science and the arts, and then introduces the specific topic his essay deals with: the relationship between computers and literature. He then further narrows the category of "literature" to "Shakespeare." Dolnick quotes many different sources and authorities to give his paper substance; this is, in fact, a research paper. Examine the essay carefully, identifying all the passages where Dolnick quotes (both directly and indirectly) external material. What proportion of the paper is actually Dolnick's original writing? Notice the way in which he introduces and identifies the sources he quotes to the reader. He never expresses his own opinion directly, nor does he use the first person ("I"). Instead, he uses the detached, third person point of view throughout, taking on the role of an objective reporter and providing contrasting views of his subject. Nevertheless, readers may doubt his objectivity, due to sentences such as these: "Rather than read, these literary sleuths prefer to count"; and "This is work that can suck up lives."

The paper's second half offers an in-depth analysis of the work of Dr. Donald Foster, who approaches literary computing with what Dolnick portrays as good scientific methodology: Foster develops a hypothesis based on history and logic and then devises an experiment to test it, complete with checks against prejudiced results. Insightful and scientifically rigorous work such as Foster's, Dolnick concludes, is part of the future of literary studies — a future that links science and art more closely and comfortably than they have been linked in the past.

STUDY QUESTIONS

For Discussion:

1. Does the existence of a "statistical fingerprint" that identifies authors seem valid? Why, or why not? How valid are the analogies Dolnick draws between R. A. Fisher and the butterfly hunter, and Shakespeare and the computer critics?

2. Analyze the structure of Dolnick's essay, considering what rhetorical strategies govern the ordering of his examples of computer-assisted literary criticism. Why does Dolnick end with an account of Foster's research? Do these strategies ultimately convince you that "prejudice against computers in literary studies will give way"?

For Writing:

1. What do you think Dolnick's final opinion concerning computer-assisted studies of literature is? What specific passage supports and/or creates the reader's final impression? Do you agree with Dolnick's final opinion? Why, or why not?

2. Look for another article on computer-assisted literary studies. How does it compare and contrast with Dolnick's opinions? Does it change the opinion that you formed from reading Dolnick?

LETTER TO MY SON

Umberto Eco

BIOGRAPHICAL NOTE

Umberto Eco is a professor of semiotics (the study of signs in all aspects of culture) at the University of Bologna in Italy. He is also a novelist, philosopher, and literary critic. His first novel, *The Name of the Rose* (1981), was an international bestseller and has been made into a film starring Sean Connery. His second novel, *Foucault's Pendulum*, appeared in 1989 with a jacket blurb declaring that his studies "range from St. Thomas Aquinas to James Joyce to Superman." Eco's most recent publications include *The Island of the Day Before* (1995) and *The Search for the Perfect Language* (1995).

1   Dear Stefano,

Christmas is marching upon us, and soon the big stores downtown will be packed with excited fathers acting out their annual scenario of hypocritical generosity, having joyfully awaited this moment when they can buy for themselves—pretending it's for their sons—their cherished electric trains, the puppet theater, the target with bow and arrows, and the family Ping-Pong set. But I will still be an observer, because this year my turn hasn't yet come, you are too little, and Montessori-approved infant toys don't give me any great pleasure, probably because I don't enjoy sticking them in my mouth, even if the manufacturer's label assures me that they cannot be swallowed whole. No, I must wait, two years, or three, or four. Then it will be my turn; the phase of mother-dominated education will pass, the rule of the teddy bear will decline and fall, and the moment will come when with the sweet and sacrosanct violence of paternal authority I can begin to mold your civic conscience. And then, Stefano . . .

2   Then your presents will be guns. Double-barreled shotguns. Repeaters. Submachine guns. Cannons. Bazookas. Sabers. Armies of lead soldiers in full battle dress. Castles with drawbridges. Fortresses to besiege. Casemates, powder magazines, destroyers, jets. Machine guns, daggers, revolvers. Colts and Winchesters. Chassepots, 91's, Garands, shells, arquebuses, culverins, slingshots, crossbows, lead balls, catapults, firebrands, grenades, ballistas, swords, pikes, battering rams, halberds, and grappling hooks. And pieces of eight, just like Captain Flint's (in memory of Long John Silver and Ben Gunn), and dirks, the kind that Don Barrejo so liked, and Toledo blades to knock aside three pistols at once and fell the Marquis of Montelimar, or using the Neapolitan feint with which the Baron de Sigognac slayed the evil ruffian who tried to steal his Isabelle. And there will be battle-axes, partisans, misericords, krises, javelins, scimitars, darts, and sword-sticks like the one John Carradine held when he was electrocuted on the third rail, and if nobody remembers that, it's their tough luck. And pirate cutlasses to make Carmaux and Van Stiller blanch, and damascened pistols like none Sir James Brook ever saw (otherwise he wouldn't have given up in the face of the sardonic, umpteenth cigarette of the Portuguese); and stilettos with triangular blades, like the one with which Sir William's disciple, as the day was gently dying at Clignancourt, killed the assassin Zampa, who killed his own mother, the old and sordid Fipart; and pères d'angoisse, like those inserted into the mouth of the jailer La Ramée while the Duke of Beaufort, the hairs of his coppery beard made even more fascinating thanks to the constant attention of a leaden comb, rode off, anticipating with joy the wrath of Mazarin; and muzzles loaded with nails, to be fired by men whose teeth are red with betel stains; and guns with mother-of-pearl stocks, to be grasped on Arab chargers with glistening coats; and lightning-fast bows, to turn the sheriff of Nottingham green with envy; and scalping knives, such as Minnehaha might have had, or (as you are bilingual) Winnetou. A small, flat pistol to tuck into a waistcoat under a frock coat, for the feats of a gentleman thief, or a ponderous Luger weighing down a pocket or filling an armpit à la Michael Shayne. And shotguns worthy of Jesse James and Wild Bill Hickok, or Sambigliong, muzzle-loading. In other words, weapons. Many weapons. These, my boy, will be the highlight of all your Christmases.

3   Sir, I am amazed—some will say—you, a member of a committee for nuclear disarmament and a supporter of the peace movement; you who join in marches on the capital and cultivate an Aldermaston mystique on occasion.

4   Do I contradict myself? Well, I contradict myself (as Walt Whitman put it).

5   One morning, when I had promised a present to a friend's son, I went into a department store in Frankfurt and asked for a nice revolver. Everyone looked at me, shocked. We do not carry warlike toys, sir. Enough to make your blood run cold. Mortified, I left, and ran straight into two Bundeswehr men who were passing on the sidewalk. I was brought back to reality. I wouldn't let anybody fool me. From now on I would rely solely on personal experience and to hell with pedagogues.

6   My childhood was chiefly if not exclusively bellicose. I used blowpipes improvised at the last minute among the bushes; I crouched behind the few parked cars, firing my repeater rifle; I led attacks with fixed bayonets. I was absorbed in extremely bloody battles. At home it was toy soldiers. Whole armies engaged in nerve-racking strategies, operations that went on for weeks, long campaigns in which I mobilized even the remains of my plush teddy bear and my sister's dolls. I organized bands of soldiers of fortune and made my few but faithful followers call me "the terror of Piazza Genova" (now Piazza Mateotti). I dissolved

a group of Black Lions to merge with another, stronger outfit, then, once in it, I uttered a pronunciamento that proved disastrous. Resettled in the Monferrato area, I was recruited forcibly in the Band of the Road and was subjected to an initiation ceremony that consisted of a hundred kicks in the behind and a three-hour imprisonment in a chicken coop. We fought against the Band of Nizza Creek, who were filthy dirty and awesome. The first time, I took fright and ran off; the second time, a stone hit my lips, and I still have a little knot there I can feel with my tongue. (Then the real war arrived. The partisans let us hold their Stens for two seconds, and we saw some friends lying dead with a hole in their brow. But by now we were becoming adults, and we went along the banks of the Belbo River to catch the eighteen-year-olds making love, unless, in the grip of adolescent mystical crises, we had renounced all pleasures of the flesh.)

7   This orgy of war games produced a man who managed to do eighteen months of military service without touching a gun, devoting his long hours in the barracks to the grave study of medieval philosophy. A man of many iniquities but one who has always been innocent of the squalid crime of loving weapons and believing in the holiness and efficacy of warrior values. A man who appreciates an army only when he sees soldiers slogging through the muck after the Vajont disaster, engaged in a peaceful and noble civic purpose. A man who absolutely does not believe in just wars, who believes wars are unjust and damned and you fight always with reluctance, dragged into the conflict, hoping it will end quickly, and risking everything because it is a matter of honor and you can't evade it. And I believe I owe my profound, systematic, cultivated, and documented horror of war to the healthy, innocent, platonically bloody releases granted me in childhood, just as when you leave a Western movie (after a furious brawl, the kind where the balcony of the saloon collapses, tables and big mirrors are broken, someone shoots at the piano player, and the plate-glass window shatters) cleaner, kinder, relaxed, ready to smile at the passerby who jostles you and to succor the sparrow fallen from its nest—as Aristotle was well aware, when he demanded of tragedy that it wave the blood-red flag before our eyes and purge us totally with the divine Epsom salts of catharsis.

8   Then I imagine the boyhood of Eichmann. Lying on his stomach, with that death's bookkeeper expression on his face as he studies the Meccano pieces and dutifully follows the instructions in the booklet; eager also to open the bright box of his new chemistry set; sadistic in laying out the tiny tools of The Little Carpenter, the plane the width of his hand and the twenty-centimeter saw, on a piece of plywood. Beware of boys who build miniature cranes! In their cold and distorted minds these little mathematicians are repressing the horrid complexes that will motivate their mature years. In every little monster who operates the switches of his toy railway lies a future director of death camps! Watch out, if they are fond of those matchbox cars that the cynical toy industry produces for them, perfect facsimiles, with a trunk that really opens and windows that can be rolled up and down—terrifying! A terrifying pastime for the future commanders of an electronic army who, lacking all passions, will coldly press the red button of an atomic war!

9   You can identify them already. The big real-estate speculators, the slumlords who enforce evictions in the dead of winter; they have revealed their personality in the infamous game of Monopoly, becoming accustomed to the idea of buying and selling property and dealing relentlessly in stock portfolios. The Père Grandets of today, who have acquired with their mother's milk the taste of acquisition and learned insider trading with bingo cards. The

bureaucrats of death trained on Lego blocks, the zombies of bureaucracy whose spiritual decease began with the rubber stamps and scales of the Little Post Office.

10   And tomorrow? What will develop from a childhood in which industrialized Christmases bring out American dolls that talk and sing and move, Japanese robots that jump and dance thanks to an inexhaustible battery, and radio-controlled automobiles whose mechanism will always be a mystery? . . .

11   Stefano, my boy, I will give you guns. Because a gun isn't a game. It is the inspiration for play. With it you will have to invent a situation, a series of relationships, a dialectic of events. You will have to shout boom, and you will discover that the game has only the value you give it, not what is built into it. As you imagine you are destroying enemies, you will be satisfying an ancestral impulse that boring civilization will never be able to extinguish, unless it turns you into a neurotic always taking Rorschach tests administered by the company psychologist. But you will find that destroying enemies is a convention of play, a game like so many others, and thus you will learn that it is outside reality, and as you play, you will be aware of the game's limits. You will work off anger and repressions, and then be ready to receive other messages, which contemplate neither death nor destruction. Indeed, it is important that death and destruction always appear to you as elements of fantasy, like Red Riding Hood's wolf, whom we all hated, to be sure, but without subsequently harboring an irrational hatred of Alsatians.

12   But this may not be the whole story, and I will not make it the whole story. I will not allow you to fire your Colts only for nervous release, in ludic purgation of primordial instincts, postponing until later, after catharsis, the *pars construens*, the communication of values. I will try to give you ideas while you are still hiding behind the armchair, shooting.

13   First of all, I will teach you to shoot not at the Indians but at the arms dealers and liquor salesmen who are destroying the Indian reservations. I will teach you to shoot at the Southern slave owners, to shoot in support of Lincoln. To shoot not at the Congo cannibals but at the ivory traders, and in a weak moment I may even teach you to stew Dr. Livingstone, I presume, in a big pot. We will play Arabs against Lawrence, and if we play ancient Romans, we'll be on the side of the Gauls, who were Celts like us Piedmontese and a lot cleaner than that Julius Caesar whom you will soon have to learn to regard with suspicion, because it is wrong to deprive a democratic community of its freedom, leaving as a tip, posthumously, gardens where the citizens can stroll. We'll be on the side of Sitting Bull against that repulsive General Custer. And on the side of the Boxers, naturally. With Fantomas rather than with Juve, who is too much a slave of duty to refuse, when required, to club an Algerian. But now I am joking: I will teach you, of course, that Fantomas was a bad guy, but I won't tell you, not in complicity with the corrupt Baroness Orczy, that the Scarlet Pimpernel was a hero. He was a dirty Vendéen who caused trouble for the good guy Danton and the pure Robespierre, and if we play French Revolution, you'll participate in the taking of the Bastille.

14   These will be stupendous games. Imagine! And we'll play them together. Ah, so you wanted to let us eat cake, eh? All right, [Monsieur] Santerre, let the drums roll! Tricoteuses of the world, unite and let your knitting needles do their worst! Today we'll play the beheading of Marie Antoinette!

15   You call this perverse pedagogy? And you, sir, antifascist practically since birth, have you ever played partisans with your son? Have you ever crouched behind the bed, pretending to be in the Langhe valleys, crying, Watch out, the Fascist Black Brigades are coming on the right! It's a roundup, they're shooting, return the Nazis' fire! No, you give your son building blocks and have the maid take him to some racist movie that glorifies the extinction of native Americans.

16   And so, dear Stefano, I will give you guns. And I will teach you to play extremely complicated wars, where the truth will never be entirely on one side. You will release a lot of energy in your young years, and your ideas may be a bit confused, but slowly you will develop some convictions. Then, when you are grown up, you will believe that it was all a fairy tale: little Red Riding Hood, Cinderella, the guns, the cannons, single combat, the witch and the seven dwarfs, armies against armies. But if by chance, when you are grown up, the monstrous characters of your childish dreams persist, witches, trolls, armies, bombs, compulsory military service, perhaps, having gained a critical attitude toward fairy tales, you will learn to live and criticize reality.

NOTES AND DISCUSSION

Eco writes his essay in the form of a letter, using both essay and letter conventions. He opens with an ironic and witty generalization about father–son relationships that sets the tone for the rest of the essay. He then creates an immense list of the weapons he intends to give his son as gifts. The essay's range of allusions suggests that Eco knows the art, history, film, and economics of a variety of countries and cultures.

Eco's essay is built on a cause-and-effect relationship: that childhood games determine adult personality. However, his version reverses the popular conception about children's (specifically boys') play: Eco tells us his own childhood was "chiefly bellicose," but his adult self is the opposite. Notice how carefully he anticipates and disarms the reader's potential objections by including the information that he is "a member of a committee for nuclear disarmament and a supporter of the peace movement." He invokes the Aristotelian notion of catharsis while he sketches out the games that he will teach Stefano to play with his guns, games that reenact specific historical situations. Finally, he blurs the distinctions between fairy tale and fact, suggesting that wars, weapons, many pre-established hero-villain relationships, and perhaps even violence itself, belong to the realm of fantasy.

STUDY QUESTIONS

For Discussion:

1. How does Eco combine the conventions of an essay and a letter? How do you distinguish between these two forms? What is the thesis of Eco's essay—the true essence of Stefano's education?

2. Eco's essay is heavily allusive. How many allusions can you identify in the opening paragraphs? What assumptions do authors make and what risks do they take when they include allusions in their writing?

For Writing:

1. Write a response that refutes and opposes Eco's arguments. Since Eco's essay is largely based on personal experience, you may also wish to draw upon personal experience and include an account of how childhood toys and games have influenced your tastes and direction as an adult.

2. Do you think that Eco would endorse this method of education if his child were a girl? How would a letter to Stefana be different? Based on the use of reverse psychology and catharsis, write a letter that outlines an educational program for a daughter, rather than a son. Be sure to indicate clearly which qualities the educational program is designed to develop.

STRAIGHT TALK AT THE PARAKEET CAFÉ

Jan Furlong

BIOGRAPHICAL NOTE

A native Australian and long-time resident of Edmonton, Alberta, Jan Furlong is currently a graduate student at the University of Chicago.

---

1   The Parakeet Café was packed that night. Diners filled the small room and spilled out onto the pavement and under the frangipane trees along the curb-side. We crushed the fallen flowers underfoot as we entered and carried with us their waxen, sugary scent. The chorus of Van Morrison's "Into the Mystic" filtered through the voices of the crowd: cool-looking people, hip-looking people, in oversized clothing and tethered in leather jewelry. A redhead with a single braid in overalls and velvet slippers tossed something brandied in a pan behind the counter, while the neon parrot flashed on and off even more brightly as evening deepened. Definitely not my sort of place.

2   "No hope of a table, I s'pose?" I ask fatalistically. The redhead turns to face us. He's flushed. Wisps have escaped the braid and straggle forlornly over his face. His overalls are spotted with grease and generously powdered with flour. He is nursing what appears to be an opened vein in his left palm. He looks us up and down, cocks an eyebrow at a pile of fold-up metal furniture propped in a corner, then juts his chin in the direction of the street. With his good hand he thrusts a menu under my arm as I bash and rattle my table through the doorway. BYOB and self-seating, evidently.

3   Wedged between a mailbox and a telephone booth, I scan the menu and brush away moths while Margaret arranges to have our wine chilled. Through the parrot-lit storefront I can see Red give her more of the eyebrow treatment. I brace myself: Margaret is a big woman, even bigger when her feathers are ruffled. But I feel no chill in the air, hear no

sound of breaking glass; with amazing docility she steps behind the counter and lays the bottle harmlessly in the 'fridge. She comes back toward me wiping her hands on a tissue, her nostrils flared. "What this place needs," she snorts, "is a firm hand."

4   Margaret is my best friend. We met fifteen years ago when we were public servants together in Queensland. We agree on most things, and on others—well, I usually come around to her way of thinking eventually. Indeed, the goat cheese and the calamari are better than I'd expected. She expends great time and thought on choosing my dessert, running a critical finger down the list of tortes, regaling me with her culinary triumphs in this field, extolling the virtues of fresh ingredients over packaged, reliving the great dessert experiences of her youth. We love desserts. I raised a toast to her once in one of Sydney's better brasseries: that we would gladly drink our own urine, given the assurance that dessert was to follow.

5   "Not bad plonk, whatd'yer reckon?" I enquire solicitously. I'm a beer drinker myself, but I've chosen a little white that has set me back $6.50 and has come with an actual cork. True, the first gulp gripped one's jaw with an authority amounting to savagery while the second touched off shudders over one's entire frame, but then this was a chablis. Margaret smiles— or is it a tic?—and pats my hand. "Well, of course, you're a beer drinker, aren't you? Let's see, I think you'd probably like the pumpkin cheesecake."

6   We kill the bottle in record time, chewing over Margaret's trips to Africa and the Far East, her job as a technical writer, her pottery classes at Canberra's National University, her tragic affair with a Brisbane chemist. We both know she deserves better. Margaret was a ravishing, voluptuous creature as a girl and even now, despite her bulk, there are resonances of that beauty: in the graceful gestures of her well-kept hands, in the slow and deliberate way she crosses her legs, how she swings her glossy hair in its sleek bob. She speaks clearly and well, choosing her words with that same finicky care that Westerners use eating with chopsticks. And she listens carefully, cradling her chin in one hand, twisting the stem of her wine glass with the other, her narrow green eyes looking deep into mine. I enjoy her immensely; bringing our cheesecakes back to the table I sneak my maraschino cherry onto her plate.

7   We eat in absorbed silence, always a good idea given the texture of pumpkin and cream cheese. We are smiling conspiratorially as we spoon up the froth from our cappuccinos when there is a shrill cry from the next table. I glance across, and find myself unable to look away. He couldn't have been more than seventeen. Slight, tanned, he wore a faded pink sarong knotted at the waist—in front, North Coast style. His lips looked flaked and dry. He had the shoulder-length, white-gold hair that only surfers on the dole can afford. A moth had landed and entangled itself there; he raked his fingers through and through and turned down the corners of his mouth. His companion, a dark, heavy man in a safari jacket, leaned across, picked the moth out by its furry body and threw it onto the road. He had the silky, silvery powder from its wings on his hands; the boy's hair would feel like that, I thought.

8   Margaret leans across the table at me. "Nothing but a bum-boy," she hisses. Where Margaret spits, tall trees wither and die. It's not a gay word, a prison word; it's pure public school—something abject, pimply, furtive. I feel as though I have been bitten by a snake. I see now, yes, he is on the defensive: leaning ever so slightly away from the man at his side, hunching his near shoulder self-protectively, clasping and unclasping his hands between his knees. I catch his eye and try to smile. Maybe he's broke and hungry. The little bastard

winks and shows me the underside of his tongue. I've had about enough of the Parakeet Café. I throw a couple of twenties on the table and as we leave I give the Red the finger.

NOTES AND DISCUSSION

It is difficult to write English—indeed, any language—and remain strictly gender-neutral. This essay is a personal narrative that confronts the difficulties with gender and language. Notice the author's strategy in the construction of the essay's persona: there are many apparently conflicting messages about who the main character is, and what he or she is like. You might want to make a list of characteristics that you know for sure about the main character, and then see how many of those characteristics, even if accurate, are stereotypes. Notice, for instance, that it is impossible to tell the narrator's gender. On the one hand, he could be male: he prefers to drink beer, wrestles tables into place, pays for the meal, and "give[s] the Red the finger" when he and Margaret leave. On the other hand, she could be female: she eats cheesecake (and "love[s] desserts" in general), is Margaret's best friend, defers to Margaret's opinion on "most things," and lets Margaret choose everything they eat from the menu. The essay apparently takes place in Australia, and the narrator is apparently Australian, but examine closely the evidence that tells you even this much. Finally, notice how stereotypes are used in this essay, not only about the main character, but also about the less important characters. For example: think about the picture that is created in your mind when you read about "a redhead with a single braid in overalls and velvet slippers," or about the Brisbane chemist mentioned in paragraph six who had an affair with Margaret. For another interesting example of an essay that is centrally concerned with gender stereotypes in language, read Douglas Hofstadter's "A Person Paper on Purity in Language."

STUDY QUESTIONS

For Discussion:

1. Note the way that language is used in this essay. How would you respond to the suggestion that all language is always already loaded with markers, some referring to gender, some to other cultural considerations, and that those markers often exist at such an unconscious level that we notice them only when they are mentioned specifically or used inappropriately?

2. Compare Furlong's use of gender and stereotypes to Hofstadter's use of pronouns in "A Person Paper on Purity in Language." While the two essays have some concerns in common, their strategies are very different from each other. Explain those differences.

For Writing:

1. Choose a social situation that you have recently experienced and try to describe that situation in a completely gender-neutral paragraph. Alternatively, write that same paragraph in a way that avoids any gender or cultural stereotypes.

2. Stereotypes are invoked and indirectly critiqued in "Straight Talk." Write a plan for a scientific paper on the dangers of stereotypes. How would your paper's strategy differ from that of "Straight Talk"?

BRED IN THE BONE?

BIOGRAPHICAL NOTE

Alan H. Goodman is a professor of anthropology at Hampshire College in Amherst, Massachusetts. He delivered a talk on the topic of this essay to the Anthropology Section of the New York Academy of Science on October 28, 1996.

1   On the morning of May 30, 1995, rescue workers in Oklahoma City made a final, melancholy sweep through the ruins of the Alfred P. Murrah Federal Building. In the weeks after the building was bombed, 165 victims had been discovered and removed, but three more bodies had been lodged in places too unstable to reach. Rather than risk more lives in a futile rescue—any survivors of the blast would have long since died of starvation or suffocation—workers simply had marked the three locations with Day-Glo orange paint, before bringing down the rest of the building with dynamite. Now they picked methodically through the rubble, searching for glimpses of orange.

2   Clyde Snow, a forensic anthropologist with a long history of identifying victims of war crimes, was stationed in the state morgue at the time, listening to reports from the bomb site. "Everything was going swimmingly," he later recalled. "When they got down to level zero, people could hear them talking on their mobile phones: 'Okay, we have one, two, three bodies. . . . Fine, wrap it up, we can all go home.'" The rescue team, events soon showed, was jumping the gun just a bit. Two or three minutes after the third body had been found, a voice suddenly broke back over the airwaves: "Hey wait a minute! We've got a leg down here. A left leg."

This article is reprinted by permission of *The Sciences* and is from the March/April 1997 issue. Individual subscriptions are US$28 per year. Write to: The Sciences, 2 East 63rd Street, New York, NY 10021.

3   During the explosion and its aftermath, about twenty-five of the victims had been dismembered. Snow assumed, at first, that the leg must belong to one of those. "In all the confusion, with bodies going back and forth for X rays, I thought somebody just overlooked that one body had a left leg missing," he said. "So we'll just match it up." But one recount after another yielded the same number: 168 right legs, 168 left legs; none of the survivors was missing a leg. "We went through autopsy records, pathology reports, body diagrams, and photographs. I did it twice, the pathologist did it twice," Snow said. "It was just a mathematical paradox."

4   Baffled, Snow took a closer look at the leg itself. Sheared off just above the knee by the blast, it still wore the remains of a black, military-style boot, two socks and an olive-drab blousing strap. Its skin, Snow said, suggested "a darkly complected Caucasoid." By measuring the lower leg and plugging the numbers into computer programs that categorize bones by race and sex, Snow confirmed his hunch: the leg probably came from a white male. An attorney for the prime suspect in the bombing, Timothy J. McVeigh, pounced on the news, suggesting that the leg belonged to the "real bomber." Snow wondered if it might belong to one of the transients who hung out on the first floor of the building. Fred B. Jordan, the Chief Medical Examiner for the state of Oklahoma, guessed that the leg belonged to a person walking alongside the truck carrying explosives.

5   As it turned out, the leg belonged to none of the above. Its owner was one Lakesha R. Levy of New Orleans, an Airman First Class, stationed at Tinker Air Force Base in Midwest City, Oklahoma. On April 19 Levy had gone to the Murrah building to get a Social Security card and gotten caught near the epicenter of the blast. Levy was five feet, five inches tall, twenty-one years old and female. She was also, in the words of one forensics expert, "obviously black." With that disclosure, McVeigh's attorney declared, "no one can have confidence in any of the forensic work in this case."

6   Just a few weeks before the leg was found, in the pages of [*The Sciences*] magazine, Snow had said that he could accurately discern a victim's race from its skull 90 percent of the time. True, a skull provides more clues to its owner's identity than a leg does, and Levy's leg was discovered and examined under extremely trying conditions. But the leg was still covered in skin, only partly decomposed, and skin is the most common indicator of "race."

7   In fact, numerous examples suggest that mistakes like the one in Oklahoma City are common. They are common not because forensics experts do shoddy work—they don't, the errors in Oklahoma City notwithstanding—but because their conclusions are based on a deeply flawed premise. As long as race is used as a shorthand to describe human biological variations—variations that blur from one race into the next, and are greatest *within* so-called races rather than among them—misidentifications are inevitable. Whether it is used in police work, medical studies, or countless everyday situations where people are grouped biologically, the answer is the same: race science is bad science.

8   Thirty years ago, the American paleontologist George Gaylord Simpson declared all pre-Darwinian definitions of humanity worthless. "We will be better off," he wrote, "if we ignore them completely." The scientific concept of race—an outgrowth of the Greek idea of a great chain of being and the Platonic notion of ideal types—is anti-evolutionary to its core. It should therefore have been the first relic consigned to the scrap heap.

9   Race should have been discarded at the turn of the century, when the American anthropologist Franz Boas showed that race, language, and culture do not go hand-in-hand, as

raciologists had contended. But race persisted. It should have vanished in the 1930s, when the "new evolutionary synthesis" helped explain subtle human variations. Yet between 1899, when William Z. Ripley published *Races of Europe*, and 1939, when the American anthropologist Carleton S. Coon published a book by the same name, the concept of race as type persisted almost unchanged. (Coon, on the eve of the Second World War, went to some lengths to ponder the essence of Jewishness. "There is a quality of looking Jewish," he wrote, "and its existence cannot be denied.") Race should have disappeared in the 1950s and 1960s, when physical anthropologists switched from studying types to studying variations as responses to evolutionary forces. But race lived on. To Coon, for instance, races just became populations with distinct adaptive problems.

10   Most anthropologists today acknowledge that biological races are a myth. Yet the idea survives, in a variety of forms. A crude typology of world views goes something like this. At one end of the spectrum are the true believers: at the University of Western Ontario in London, for example, the psychologist J. Philippe Rushton asserts that there are three main races—Mongoloid, Negroid, and Caucasoid—and he ranks them according to intelligence and procreative ability. Here, sure enough, the old racial stereotypes leak out: the two traits allegedly appear in inverse proportion. You can have either a large brain or a large . . . (insert sexual organ of choice). Rushton's Mongoloids rank as the most intelligent; Negroids allegedly have the strongest sexual drive; Caucasoids fit into the comfortable middle.

11   At the other end of the spectrum are two groups who agree that races are a myth, but draw radically different conclusions from that premise. The politically conservative group, known for proclaiming a "color-free society," argues that if races do not exist, sociopolitical policies such as affirmative action ought not to be based on race. Social constructionists, on the other hand, realize that race-as-bad-biology has nothing to do with race-as-lived-experience. Social policy does not need a biological basis, especially when a dark-skinned American is still roughly twice as likely to be denied a mortgage as is a light-skinned person with an equivalent income. True races may not exist, but racism does.

12   A fourth group, the confused, occupies the middle ground. Some do not understand why race biology is such bad science, yet they avoid any appeal to race because they do not want to be politically incorrect. Others apply race as a quasi-biological, quasi-genetic category and cannot figure out what is wrong with it. Still others think the stance against racial biology is political rather than scientific.

13   That middle category of the confused is huge. It includes nearly all public health and medical professionals, as well as most physical anthropologists. Moreover, the continued "soft" use of race by that well-meaning group acts to legitimize the "hard" use by true believers and scientific racists.

14   And if most professionals are confused about race, most of the public is both dazed and confused. There is no single, stable, or monolithic public perception about race, but races are generally thought to be about genes (or blood) and (only slightly less permanent) cultural ties. Regardless, race is considered to be deep, primordial, and constant: in short, indistinguishable from its nineteenth-century definition.

15   In 1992 the forensic anthropologist Norman J. Sauer of Michigan State University in East Lansing published an article in the journal *Social Science and Medicine* provocatively titled, "Forensic Anthropology and the Concept of Race: If Races Don't Exist, Why Are Forensic Anthropologists So Good at Identifying Them?" Race may be unscientific, Sauer argued, but people of one socially constructed racial category still tend to look alike—and different

from the people of another "race." The biological anthropologist C. Loring Brace of the University of Michigan in Ann Arbor explains Sauer's paradox in a slightly different way. Forensic scientists are good at estimating race, Brace says, because so-called racial variations are statistically confounded with real regional differences. People do vary in a systematic way depending on their environment.

16   Both arguments make sense, and forensic anthropologists do important work. But how good are they, really, at identifying race? Like Snow, the authors of forensic texts and review articles typically maintain that the race of a skull can be correctly identified between 85 and 90 percent of the time. The scientific reference for those estimates—if cited as anything other than common knowledge—is a single, groundbreaking study by the physical anthropologists Eugene Giles, at the University of Illinois in Urbana-Champaign, and Orville S. Elliot, at the University of Victoria in British Columbia. In the early 1960s Giles and Elliot measured the skulls of modern, adult blacks and whites who had died in Missouri and Ohio, many of them at the turn of the century, as well as Native American skulls from a prehistoric site in Indian Knoll, Kentucky. Using a statistical equation known as a discriminant function, they then identified a combination of eight measurements that could determine a skull's "race" once its sex was known.

17   When Giles and Elliot applied the formula to additional skulls from the same collections, it agreed with the race assigned to the deceased at death between 80 and 90 percent of the time. To be useful, however, the formula has to work in place other than Missouri, Ohio, and prehistoric Kentucky. I have found four retests of the Giles and Elliot method, and their results do not inspire confidence. Two of the retests restricted themselves to Native American skulls: in one of them almost two-thirds of the skulls were correctly classified as Native Americans; in the second, only 31 percent were correctly classified. For the two other studies, in which the skulls were of mixed race, skulls were correctly identified as Native American just 18.2 percent and 14.3 percent of the time. Thus in three of the four tests, the formula proved less accurate than a random assignment of races to skulls—not even good enough for government work.

18   Contemporary Native American skulls may be particularly hard to classify because the formula is based on a very old sample. But the four retests were carried out on complete crania that had already been sexed, a necessary prerequisite to determining race. Forensic anthropologists often have much less to go on. Moreover, Native Americans are easier to classify than Hispanics or Southeast Asians, not to mention infants, children, or adolescents of any race. At best, in other words, racial identifications are depressingly inaccurate. At worst, they are completely haphazard. How many bodies and body parts, like Lakesha Levy's leg, are sending investigators down wrong paths because the wrong box was checked off?

19   Forensic anthropologists usually blame such mistakes on the melting pot. Yet distinct racial types have never existed. What changes are social definitions of race—the color line—and human biology. Whites in Cleveland in 1897 were different from whites in Amarillo, Texas, in 1997. Science 101: generalizations ought not be based on an ill-defined, constantly changing, and contextually loaded variable.

20   Skulls and corpses, one could argue, have ceased to care to which race they belong—though their families and friends might disagree. But when physicians base their actions on perceived racial categories, their patients ought to care a great deal. Does race, however imperfect a category, help physicians diagnose, treat, prevent, or understand the etiology of a disease?

21   Before the Second World War, physicians were often blinded by the conviction that certain races suffered from certain diseases. People who had sickle-cell anemia, for instance, were assumed to have "African blood." In 1927 the American physician J. S. Lawrence discovered a case of the disease in a "white" person. "Special attention was paid to the question of racial admixture of negro blood in the family but no evidence could be obtained," Lawrence wrote in the *Journal of Clinical Investigation.* "There must be some caution in calling this sickle-cell anemia because no evidence of negro blood could be found."

22   Evelynn M. Hammonds, a historian of science at the Massachusetts Institute of Technology, has brought to my attention some early diagnoses of ovarian cysts that express the same logic. In 1899 the American physician Thomas R. Brown reported that he often heard surgeons say that tumors found in black women had all the features of ovarian cysts, "but inasmuch as the patient is a negress it is certainly not so, as multilocular cysts are unknown in the negress." The following year Daniel H. Williams, the eminent African-American physician and the first American to perform successful heart surgery, quoted a physician from Alabama speculating that: "Possibly the Alabama negro has not evolved to the cyst-bearing age." Williams went on to show unambiguously, in a study, that ovarian cysts are common in black women including women from Alabama. He noted that white physicians have a history of ignoring black women, then offered examples of black women whose cysts swelled to 100 pounds or more before they were diagnosed.

23   Today the paradigm of racially distinct diseases has been replaced by the more flexible idea of a race as disease risk factor. Yet the medical effects are the same. Some 25 million Americans are said to suffer from osteoporosis, a progressive loss of bone mass that leads to 1.5 million fractures a year. Since the nineteenth century, blacks have been thought to have thicker bones than whites have and to lose bone mass more slowly with age. (A few years ago, when a dentist visited my laboratory, he was shocked to find that neither one of us could tell a black jaw from a white one.) In the journal *Seminars in Nuclear Medicine*, a review titled "Osteoporosis: The State of the Art in 1987" listed race as a major risk factor. The section on race begins: "It is a well-known fact that blacks do not suffer from osteoporosis."

24   That "fact" is backed by a single reference, a seminal paper by the American physical anthropologist Mildred Trotter and her colleagues titled "Densities of Bones of White and Negro Skeletons." Trotter and her colleagues evaluated the bone densities of skeletons from forty adult blacks and forty adult whites. They excluded skeletons with obvious bone diseases, but they did not describe how they chose the cadavers or whether the samples were matched for causes of death, diet, or other known risk factors for osteoporosis. Of the ten bones they studied in each skeleton, Trotter and her colleagues found that six tended to be denser in blacks than in whites; the other four showed no differences by race. Furthermore, the authors wrote, the decline in density took place at "approximately the same rate" for each sex-race group.

25   Trotter and her colleagues may have realized that their data could be overinterpreted. In later publications they present scatterplots with age on one axis and bone density on the other. The scatterplots confirm that bone densities tend to decline with age: the clusters of data points slope downward. It is a challenge, however, to discern any difference between the densities of bones from blacks and those from whites. The six lowest radius densities, for example, were found in bones of blacks.

26   Let me be clear: I am only following citations to see if the data say what the references say they say. But my conclusion is dismaying. If the "well-known fact that blacks do not suffer from osteoporosis" is based on poorly interpreted data, then black women may not be getting enough preventive care, are not targeted in the media, and are underdiagnosed as osteoporotic.

27 In every instance I have cited, a double leap of scientific faith seems to have taken place. First, a serious medical condition (sickle-cell anemia, ovarian cysts, osteoporosis) is regarded as genetic, even though environmental factors have not been adequately examined. Second, anything genetic is assumed to imply a panracial phenomenon. Thus, what might be true in a statistical sense is assumed true for all members of a so-called race. All blacks are protected from osteoporosis. All blacks are less prone to heart disease. By the same logic, Native Americans have some special predisposition to obesity and diabetes, though, in truth, rates vary wildly among groups and regions.

28 Why are my findings more than idiosyncratic examples? Why does race not work as a shorthand for biological variation? The answer lies in the structure of human variation and in the chameleon-like concept of race.

29 • Most traits vary in small increments, or clines, across geographic areas. Imagine a merchant walking from Stockholm, Sweden, to Cape Town, South Africa, in the year 1400. He would notice that the skin colors of local people darkened until he reached the equator, then slowly turned lighter again. If he took a different route, perhaps starting in Siberia and wandering all the way to Singapore, he would observe the same phenomenon, though none of the people he passed on this second route would be classified as white or black today: all of them would be "Asian." Race, in other words, does not determine skin color, nor does skin color determine race. As Frank B. Livingstone, an anthropological geneticist at the University of Michigan in Ann Arbor, put it more than thirty years ago: "There are no races, there are only clines."

30 • Most traits are nonconcordant. That is, traits tend to vary in different and entirely independent ways. If you know a person's height, you can guess weight and shoe size because tall people tend to be heavier and have bigger feet than short people. Those traits are concordant. By the same token, however, you could guess nothing about the person's skin color, facial features, or most genes. Height is nonconcordant with nearly every other trait. If you know skin color, you might be able to guess eye color and perhaps (but surprisingly inaccurately) hair color and form. But that is all. Race, for that reason, is only skin deep.

31 • As I mentioned earlier, nearly all variations in genetic traits occur within so-called races rather than among them. Some thirty years ago the population geneticist Richard C. Lewontin of Harvard University conducted a statistical study of blood groups with two of the more common forms. On average, he found about 94 percent of the variation in blood forms occurred within perceived races; fewer than 6 percent could be explained by variations among races. Extrapolating from race to individuals is hardly more accurate than extrapolating from the human species to an individual.

32 One could argue that such classifications, however crude, are still useful as first approximations. Here is where one needs to see race as something more that the equivalent of shoe size.

33 • Racial differences are interpreted differently. Sometimes people consider them genetic, sometimes ethnic or cultural, and sometimes they use the term "race" to mean differences in lived experience. When race is assigned as a risk factor, the meaning is often unclear, and that ambiguity dramatically affects medical treatment. Sometimes race is a proxy for socioeconomic status or even for the effects of racism. If so, a particular racial classification suggests a possible set of actions. But if a racial classification is intended to signal a panracial

genetic difference, as in osteoporosis, an entirely different set of actions should be undertaken. The conflation of genetics with culture, class, and lived experience may be the most serious flaw in racial analysis.

34   • Race is impossible to define in a stable, repeatable way because, to repeat, race as biology varies with time and place, as do social classifications. Color lines change. When the skeletons studied by Giles and Elliot began to be collected in Cleveland at the turn of the century, the United States Census Bureau classified people not only as white or black, but as mulatto, quadroon, or octoroon. Europe at the time was thought to be home to a dozen or so distinct races. One cannot do predictive science based on a changing and undefinable cause.

35   In studies such as those on osteoporosis—or any other disease—race is either undefined or assigned on the basis of the patient's own self-identification. "Since self-assignments to racial categories are commonly used," the authors of a review of race and nutritional status wrote in 1976, "the problem of racial identification is minimal." Compare that statement with the finding of a recent infant-mortality study by Robert A. Hahn, a medical anthropologist at the Center for Disease Control and Prevention in Atlanta, Georgia. Thirty-seven percent of the babies described as Native American on their birth certificates, Hahn discovered, were described as some other race on their death certificates.

36   When I started out in anthropology in the 1970s, I thought anthropologists would stop using race by the 1990s. Why does it persist? At the very least, on a scientific level, it violates the first law of medicine: Do no harm. For every instance in which knowing race helps an investigator, there is probably another instance in which it leads to a missed diagnosis or the premature closing of a police file. At best, it is a proxy for something else. Why not study that something else?

37   There are good, simple alternatives to classifying by race. In biological studies, from forensics to epidemiology, investigators could focus on traits specific to the problem at hand. If the problem is describing human remains, simply describe those remains as well as possible. In Oklahoma City, for example, the police would have been better off looking for anyone with a dark complexion rather than searching for a "darkly complected Caucasoid." Police officers are used to searching for people with specific traits ("suspect has a smiley-face tattoo on his left bicep"). Why not be equally specific about skin color and other "racial" traits? Epidemiologists, for their part, could focus on likely causal traits. If skin color is a risk factor, classify people by skin color alone. If the risk factor is a genetic trait, such as type A blood, compare individuals with and without type A blood.

38   I do not for a moment think that knowing race is a myth eliminates racism. But as long as well-meaning investigators continue to use the concept of race without clearly defining it, they reify race as biology. In so doing, they mislead the public and encourage racist notions. According to the American sociologist Donal E. Muir, those who continue to see race in biology but mean no harm by it are nothing more than "kind racists." By continuing to legitimize race, they inadvertently aid the "mean racists" who wish to do harm. Far too many scientists, unfortunately, still belong to both categories.

NOTES AND DISCUSSION

In "Bred in the Bone?" Alan Goodman argues that "true races may not exist, but racism does." This essay is an argument against institutional racism, and a hope that, if science moves beyond racism, the rest of society can also get over something that is only a culturally constructed category.

Goodman begins his paper with a striking example of a forensic misdiagnosis, and then continues to build his essay around examples and assumptions concerning race. He shows that, biologically, race is skin deep: it is a cultural myth and has no hard scientific basis or usefulness. It therefore needs finally to be expunged from scientific investigation: "As long as race is used as a shorthand to describe human biological variations—variations that blur from one race into the next, and are greatest *within* so-called races rather than among them—misidentifications are inevitable." Notice the way Goodman acknowledges, only to dismiss, scientists who support "race" as a useful or productive scientific category. If scientists continue to pretend that "race" is a useful category, though all the evidence indicates that it is nothing more than a myth, then they are in fact supporting institutionalized racism. And if scientists continue to be racist, one cannot expect society at large to get over racism.

Goodman's strategy is sound throughout, but the essay is especially striking in its treatment of the opening materials. It begins with a vivid anecdote that most of Goodman's audience will have some familiarity with. The Oklahoma City bombing is also likely to have some significant emotional and intellectual impact. It certainly has metaphoric and symbolic resonance.

STUDY QUESTIONS

For Discussion:

1. Discuss Goodman's argument that science and scientists have an important social and cultural responsibility to lead the rest of society in battling racism. Do you agree with Goodman? Why, or why not?

2. Goodman claims that race is culturally constructed, not biologically based—it is founded, in fact, on bias—and that colour is only skin deep: "Distinct racial types have never existed. What changes are social definitions of race—the color line—and human biology." Discuss this claim, and Goodman's support of it.

For Writing:

1. Compare the fundamental assumptions and strategies of Goodman's essay, which argues against racism in science, to Hofstadter's "A Person Paper on Purity in Language," which argues against sexism in language. As part of your paper, compile a list of racist tendencies that you detect in language.

2. Write a persuasive paper in which you argue for or against this proposition: since science and reason did not invent racism, though they implicitly supported it for years, science and reason cannot rid society of racism merely by proving that race is a myth.

THE MONSTER'S HUMAN NATURE

Stephen Jay Gould

BIOGRAPHICAL NOTE

Stephen Jay Gould is a paleontologist and educator at Harvard University. He is known for writing that makes science and scientific concepts entertaining and approachable to a non-specialized public. His essays are collected in several volumes, including *The Flamingo's Smile* (1985), *Bully for Brontosaurus* (1991), and *Eight Little Piggies* (1993). This essay is from his recent collection *Dinosaur in a Haystack: Reflections in Natural History* (1995).

1   An old Latin proverb tells us to "beware the man of one book"—*cave ab homine unius libri*. Yet Hollywood knows only one theme in making monster movies, from the archetypal *Frankenstein* of 1931 to the recent mega-hit *Jurassic Park*. Human technology must not go beyond an intended order decreed by God or set by nature's laws. No matter how benevolent the purposes of the transgressor, such cosmic arrogance can only lead to killer tomatoes, very large rabbits with sharp teeth, giant ants in the Los Angeles sewers, or even larger blobs that swallow entire cities as they grow. Yet these films often use far more subtle books as their sources and, in so doing, distort the originals beyond all thematic recognition.

2   The trend began in 1931 with *Frankenstein*, Hollywood's first great monster "talkie" (though Mr. Karloff only grunted, while Colin Clive, as Henry Frankenstein, emoted). Hollywood decreed its chosen theme by the most "up front" of all conceivable strategies. The film begins with a prologue (even before the titles roll) featuring a well-dressed man standing on stage before a curtain, both to issue a warning about potential fright, and to announce the film's deeper theme as the story of "a man of science who sought to create a man after his own image without reckoning upon God."

3   In the movie, Dr. Waldman, Henry's old medical school professor, speaks of his pupil's "insane ambition to create life," a diagnosis supported by Frankenstein's own feverish words of enthusiasm: "I created it. I made it with my own hands from the bodies I took from graves, from the gallows, from anywhere."

4   The best of a cartload of sequels, *The Bride of Frankenstein* (1935), makes the favored theme even more explicit in a prologue featuring Mary Wollstonecraft Shelley, who published *Frankenstein* in 1818 when she was only nineteen years old, in conversation with her husband Percy and their buddy Lord Byron. She states: "My purpose was to write a moral lesson of the punishment that befell a mortal man who dared to emulate God."

5   Shelley's original *Frankenstein* is a rich book of many themes, but I can find little therein to support the Hollywood reading. The text is neither a diatribe on the dangers of technology nor a warning about overextended ambition against a natural order. We find no passages about disobeying God—an unlikely subject for Mary Shelley and her free-thinking friends (Percy had been expelled from Oxford in 1811 for publishing a defense of atheism). Victor Frankenstein (I do not know why Hollywood changed him to Henry) is guilty of a great moral failing, as we shall see later, but his crime is not technological transgression against a natural or divine order.

6   We can find a few passages about the awesome power of science, but these words are not negative. Professor Waldman, a sympathetic character in the book, states, for example, "They [scientists] penetrate into the recesses of nature, and show how she works in her hiding places. They ascend into the heavens; they have discovered how the blood circulates, and the nature of the air we breathe. They have acquired new and almost unlimited powers." We do learn that ardor without compassion or moral consideration can lead to trouble, but Shelley applies this argument to any endeavor, not especially to scientific discovery (her examples are, in fact, all political). Victor Frankenstein says:

> A human being in perfection ought always to preserve a calm and peaceful mind, and never to allow passion or a transitory desire to disturb his tranquility. I do not think that the pursuit of knowledge is an exception to this rule. If the study to which you apply yourself has a tendency to weaken your affections . . . then that study is certainly unlawful, that is to say, not befitting the human mind. If this rule were always observed . . . Greece had not been enslaved; Caesar would have spared his country; America would have been discovered more gradually, and the empires of Mexico and Peru had not been destroyed.

7   Victor's own motivations are entirely idealistic: "I thought, that if I could bestow animation upon lifeless matter, I might in process of time (although I now found it impossible) renew life where death had apparently devoted the body to corruption." Finally, as Victor lies dying in the Arctic, he makes his most forceful statement on the dangers of scientific ambition, but he only berates himself and his own failures, while stating that others might well succeed. Victor says his dying words to the ship's captain who found him on the polar ice: "Farewell, Walton! Seek happiness in tranquility, and avoid ambition, even if it be only the apparently innocent one of distinguishing yourself in science and discoveries. Yet why do I say this? I have myself been blasted in these hopes, yet another may succeed."

8   But Hollywood dumbed these subtleties down to the easy formula—"man must not go beyond what God and nature intended" (you almost have to use the old gender-biased language for such a simplistic archaicism [*sic*])—and has been treading in its own footsteps ever since. The latest incarnation, *Jurassic Park*, substitutes a *Velociraptor* re-created from old

DNA for Karloff cobbled together from bits and pieces of corpses, but hardly alters the argument an iota.

9   Karloff's *Frankenstein* contains an even more serious and equally prominent distortion of a theme that I regard as the primary lesson of Mary Shelley's book—another lamentable example of Hollywood's sense that the American public cannot tolerate even the slightest exercise in intellectual complexity. Why is the monster evil? Shelley provides a nuanced and subtle answer that, to me, sets the central theme of her book. But Hollywood opted for a simplistic solution, so precisely opposite to Shelley's intent that the movie can no longer claim to be telling a moral fable (despite protestations of the man in front of the curtain, or Mary Shelley herself in the sequel), and becomes instead, as I suppose the makers intended all along, a pure horror film.

10   James Whale, director of the 1931 *Frankenstein*, devoted the movie's long and striking opening scenes to this inversion of Shelley's intent—so the filmmakers obviously viewed this alteration as crucial. The movie opens with a burial at a graveyard. The mourners depart, and Henry with his obedient servant, the evil hunchbacked Fritz, digs up the body and carts it away. They then cut down another dead man from the gallows, but Henry exclaims, "The neck's broken. The brain is useless; we must find another brain."

11   The scene now switches to Goldstadt Medical College, where Professor Waldman is lecturing on cranial anatomy and comparing "one of the most perfect specimens of the normal brain" with "the abnormal brain of a typical criminal." Waldman firmly locates the criminal's depravity in the inherited malformations of his brain; anatomy is destiny. Note, Waldman says, "the scarcity of convolutions on the frontal lobes and the distinct degeneration of the middle frontal lobes. All of these degenerate characteristics check amazingly with the case history of the dead man before us, whose life was one of brutality, of violence, and of murder."

12   Fritz breaks in after the students leave and steals the normal brain, but the sound of a gong startles him and he drops the precious object, shattering its container. Fritz then has to take the criminal brain instead, but he never tells Henry. The monster is evil because Henry unwittingly makes him of evil stuff. Later in the film, Henry expresses his puzzlement at the monster's nasty temperament, for he made his creature of the best materials. But Waldman, finally realizing the source of the monster's behavior, tells Henry, "The brain that was stolen from my laboratory was a criminal brain." Henry then counters with one of cinema's greatest double takes, and finally manages a feeble retort: "Oh, well, after all, it's only a piece of dead tissue." "Only evil will come from it," Waldman replies. "You have created a monster and it will destroy you." True enough, at least until the sequel.

13   Karloff's intrinsically evil monster stands condemned by the same biological determinism that has so tragically, and falsely, restricted the lives of millions who committed no transgression besides membership in a despised race, sex, or social class. Karloff's actions record his internal state. He manages a few grunts and, in *The Bride of Frankenstein*, even learns some words from a blind man who cannot perceive his ugliness, though the monster never gets much beyond "eat," "smoke," "friend," and "good." Shelley's monster, by contrast, is a most remarkably literate fellow. He learns French by assimilation after hiding, for several months, in the hovel of a noble family temporarily in straitened circumstances. His three favorite books would bring joy to the heart of any college English professor who could persuade students to read and enjoy even one: Plutarch's *Lives*, Goethe's *Sorrows of Young Werther*, and Milton's *Paradise Lost* (of which Shelley's novel is an evident par-

ody). The original monster's thundering threat certainly packs more oomph than Karloff's pitiable grunts: "I will glut the maw of death, until it be satiated with the blood of your remaining friends."

14   Shelley's monster is not evil by inherent constitution. He is born unformed—carrying the predispositions of human nature, but without the specific behaviors that can only be set by upbringing and education. He is the Enlightenment's man of hope, whom learning and compassion might model to goodness and wisdom. But he is also a victim of post-Enlightenment pessimism as the cruel rejection of his natural fellows drives him to fury and revenge. (Even as a murderer, the monster remains fastidious and purposive. Victor Frankenstein is the source of his anger, and he kills only the friends and lovers whose deaths will bring Victor most grief; he does not, like Godzilla or the Blob, rampage through cities.)

15   Mary Shelley chose her words carefully to take a properly nuanced position at a fruitfully intermediate point between nature and nurture—whereas Hollywood opted for nature alone to explain the monster's evil deeds. Frankenstein's creature is not inherently good by internal construction—a benevolent theory of "nature alone," but no different in mode of explanation from Hollywood's opposite version. He is, rather, born *capable* of goodness, even with an *inclination* toward kindness, should circumstances of his upbringing call forth this favored response. In his final confession to Captain Walton, before heading north to immolate himself at the Pole, the monster says:

> My heart was fashioned to be *susceptible of love and sympathy*; and, when wrenched by misery to vice and hatred, it did not endure the violence of the change without torture, such as you cannot even imagine. [My italics to note Shelley's careful phrasing in terms of potentiality or inclination, rather than determinism.]

16   He then adds:

> Once my fancy was soothed with dreams of virtue, of fame, and of enjoyment. Once I falsely hoped to meet with beings who, pardoning my outward form, would love me for the excellent qualities which I was *capable of bringing forth*. I was nourished with high thoughts of honor and devotion. But now vice has degraded me beneath the meanest animal . . . When I call over the frightful catalogue of my deeds, I cannot believe that I am he whose thoughts were once filled with sublime and transcendent visions of the beauty and the majesty of goodness. But it is even so; the fallen angel becomes a malignant devil.

17   Why, then, does the monster turn to evil against an inherent inclination to goodness? Shelley gives us an interesting answer that seems almost trivial in invoking such a superficial reason, but that emerges as profound when we grasp her general theory of human nature. He becomes evil, of course, because humans reject him so violently and so unjustly. His resulting loneliness becomes unbearable. He states:

> And what was I? Of my creation and creator I was absolutely ignorant; but I knew that I possessed no money, no friends, no kind of property. I was, besides, endowed with a figure hideously deformed and loathsome . . . When I looked around, I saw and heard none like me. Was I then a monster, a blot upon the earth, from which all men fled, and whom all men disowned?

18   But why is the monster so rejected, if his feelings incline toward benevolence, and his acts to evident goodness? He certainly tries to act kindly, in helping (albeit secretly) the family in the hovel that serves as his hiding place:

I had been accustomed during the night, to steal a part of their store for my own consumption; but when I found that in doing this I inflicted pain on the cottagers, I abstained, and satisfied myself with berries, nuts, and roots, which I gathered from a neighboring wood. I discovered also another means through which I was enabled to assist their labors. I found that the youth spent a great part of each day in collecting wood for the family fire; and, during the night, I often took his tools, the use of which I quickly discovered, and brought home firing sufficient for the consumption of several days.

19   Shelley tells us that all humans reject and even loathe the monster for a visceral reason of literal superficiality: his truly terrifying ugliness—a reason both heartrending in its deep injustice, and profound in its biological accuracy and philosophical insight about the meaning of human nature.

20   The monster, by Shelley's description, could scarcely have been less attractive in appearance. Victor Frankenstein describes the first sight of his creature alive:

How can I describe my emotions at this catastrophe, or how delineate the wretch whom with such infinite pains and care I had endeavored to form? His limbs were in proportion, and I had selected his features as beautiful. Beautiful!—Great God! His yellow skin scarcely covered the work of muscles and arteries beneath; his hair was lustrous black, and flowing; his teeth of a pearly whiteness; but these luxuriances only formed a more horrid contrast with his watery eyes, that seemed almost of the same color as the dun white sockets in which they were set, his shriveled complexion, and straight black lips.

21   Moreover, at his hyper-NBA height of eight feet, the monster scares the bejeezus out of all who cast eyes upon him.

22   The monster quickly grasps this unfair source of human fear and plans a strategy to overcome initial reactions, and to prevail by goodness of soul. He presents himself first to the blind old father in the hovel above his hiding place and makes a good impression. He hopes to win the man's confidence, and thus gain a favorable introduction to the world of sighted people. But, in his joy at acceptance, he stays too long. The man's son returns and drives the monster away—as fear and loathing overwhelm any inclination to hear about inner decency.

23   The monster finally acknowledges his inability to overcome visceral fear at his ugliness; his resulting despair and loneliness drive him to evil deeds:

I am malicious because I am miserable; am I not shunned and hated by all mankind? . . . Shall I respect man when he condemns me? Let him live with me in the interchange of kindness, and, instead of injury, I would bestow every benefit upon him with tears of gratitude at his acceptance. But that cannot be; the human senses are insurmountable barriers to our union.

24   Our struggle to formulate a humane and accurate idea of human nature focuses on proper positions between the false and sterile poles of nature and nurture. Pure nativism—as in the Hollywood version of the monster's depravity—leads to a cruel and inaccurate theory of biological determinism, the source of so much misery and such pervasive suppression of hope in millions belonging to unfavored races, sexes, or social classes. But pure "nurturism" can be just as cruel, and just as wrong—as in the blame, once heaped upon loving parents in bygone days of rampant Freudianism, for failures in rearing as putative sources of mental illness or retardation that we can now identify as genetically based—for all organs, including brains, are subject to inborn illness.

25   The solution, as all thoughtful people recognize, must lie in properly melding the themes of inborn predisposition and shaping through life's experiences. This fruitful joining cannot take the false form of percentages adding to 100—as in "intelligence is 80 percent nature and 20 percent nurture," or "homosexuality is 50 percent inborn and 50 percent learned," and a hundred other harmful statements in this foolish format. When two ends of such a spectrum are commingled, the result is not a separable amalgam (like shuffling two decks of cards with different backs), but an entirely new and higher entity that cannot be decomposed (just as adults cannot be separated into maternal and paternal contributions to their totality).

26   The best guide to a proper integration lies in recognizing that nature supplies general ordering rules and predispositions—often strong, to be sure—while nurture shapes specific manifestations over a wide range of potential outcomes. We make classical "category mistakes" when we attribute too much specificity to nature—as in the pop sociobiology of supposed genes for complexly social phenomena like rape and racism; or when we view deep structures as purely social constructs—as in earlier claims that even the most general rules of grammar must be learned contingencies without any universality across cultures. Noam Chomsky's linguistic theories represent the paradigm for modern concepts of proper integration between nature and nurture—principles of universal grammar as inborn learning rules, with peculiarities of any particular language as a product of cultural circumstances and place of upbringing.

27   Frankenstein's creature becomes a monster because he is cruelly ensnared by one of the deepest predispositions of our biological inheritance—our instinctive aversion toward seriously malformed individuals. (Konrad Lorenz, the most famous ethologist of the last generation, based much of his theory on the primacy of this inborn rule.) We are now appalled by the injustice of such a predisposition, but this proper moral feeling is an evolutionary latecomer, imposed by human consciousness upon a much older mammalian pattern.

28   We almost surely inherit such an instinctive aversion to serious malformation, but remember that nature can only supply a predisposition, while culture shapes specific results. And now we can grasp—for Mary Shelley presented the issue to us so wisely—the true tragedy of Frankenstein's monster, and the moral dereliction of Victor himself. The predisposition for aversion toward ugliness can be overcome by learning and understanding. I trust that we have all trained ourselves in this essential form of compassion, and that we all work hard to suppress that frisson of rejection (which in honest moments we all admit we feel), and to judge people by their qualities of soul, not by their external appearances.

29   Frankenstein's monster was a good man in an appallingly ugly body. His countrymen could have been educated to accept him, but the person responsible for that instruction—his creator, Victor Frankenstein—ran away from his foremost duty, and abandoned his creation at first sight. Victor's sin does not lie in misuse of technology, or hubris in emulating God; we cannot find these themes in Mary Shelley's account. Victor failed because he followed a predisposition of human nature—visceral disgust at the monster's appearance— and did not undertake the duty of any creator or parent: to teach his own charge and to educate others in acceptability.

30   He could have schooled his creature (and not left the monster to learn language by eavesdropping and by scrounging for books in a hiding place under a hovel). He could have told the world what he had done. He could have introduced his benevolent and educated monster to people prepared to judge him on merit. But he took one look at his handiwork,

and ran away forever. In other words, he bowed to a base aspect of our common nature, and did not accept the particular moral duty of our potential nurture:

> I had worked hard for nearly two years, for the sole purpose of infusing life into an inanimate body. For this I had deprived myself of rest and health. I had desired it with an ardor that far exceeded moderation; but now that I had finished, the beauty of the dream vanished, and breathless horror and disgust filled my heart. Unable to endure the aspect of the being I had created, I rushed out of the room . . . A mummy again endued with animation could not be so hideous as that wretch. I had gazed on him while unfinished; he was ugly then; but when those muscles and joints were rendered capable of motion, it became a thing such as even Dante could not have conceived.

31   The very first line of the preface of *Frankenstein* has often been misinterpreted: "The event on which this fiction is founded has been supposed, by Dr. Darwin, and some of the physiological writers of Germany, as not of impossible occurrence." People suppose that "Dr. Darwin" must be Charles of evolutionary fame. But Charles Darwin was born on Lincoln's birthday in 1809, and wasn't even ten years old when Mary Shelley wrote her novel. "Dr. Darwin" is Charles's grandfather Erasmus, one of England's most famous physicians, and an atheist who believed in the material basis of life. (Shelley is referring to his idea that such physical forces as electricity might be harnessed to quicken inanimate matter—for life has no inherently spiritual component, and might therefore emerge from nonliving substances infused with enough energy.)

32   I will, however, close with my favorite moral statement from Charles Darwin, who, like Mary Shelley, also emphasized our duty to foster the favorable specificities that nurture and education can control. Mary Shelley wrote a moral tale, not about hubris or technology, but about responsibility to all creatures of feeling and to the products of one's own hand. The monster's misery arose from the moral failure of other humans, not from his own inherent and unchangeable constitution. Charles Darwin later invoked the same theory of human nature to remind us of duties to all people in universal bonds of brotherhood: "If the misery of our poor be caused not by the laws of nature, but by our institutions, great is our sin."

NOTES AND DISCUSSION

Gould's dual thesis is clearly stated in the opening paragraph: Hollywood films distort the thematic subtlety of their sources beyond all recognition, and Hollywood constantly reiterates the theme that disaster can only result from technology exceeding or subverting the laws of God and nature. Gould then narrows his argument and makes the 1931 screen adaptation of Mary Shelley's *Frankenstein* his primary focus; however, he also confronts the old debate over whether nature or nurture is the more influential determinant operating upon humanity.

For the bulk of the essay, Gould supports his argument by comparing and contrasting selected passages from the 1818 edition of Shelley's novel with corresponding scenes from the Hollywood versions. Notice how he creates an informal tone that invites the reader to join him in laughing at the foibles of Hollywood. It is important to note that if you have not read Shelley's novel or seen the film versions, you must depend entirely upon Gould's selection of passages and description of scenes in attempting to weigh and consider his argument. If you have read the novel or seen either or both Frankenstein films discussed, you then have your own readings and recollections to rely upon as well. Part of Gould's purpose may, in fact, be to interest readers in exploring the different tellings of the Frankenstein story and to consider more deeply the relationship between text and film. If you have read the novel, you will no doubt notice that Gould makes no reference to the subtitle of Shelley's novel, "The Modern Prometheus," or to the religious and mythic themes of the original *Frankenstein*.

STUDY QUESTIONS

For Discussion:

1. Gould's characterization of Hollywood's portrayal of the scientist as evil echoes an image from popular culture. List some other Hollywood portrayals of scientists. Do your findings match Gould's claims?

2. Why, in Gould's opinion, does Hollywood keep telling the same stories? Gould labels Hollywood stories "simplifications." What simplifications take place in Gould's own essay?

For Writing:

1. If you have read Mary Shelley's *Frankenstein*, do you still agree with Gould's central thesis? Alternatively, read a novel that is the basis for a Hollywood film with which you are already familiar. Do you see any of the patterns that Gould identifies emerging?

2. Compare and contrast Heather Pringle's exploration of the "nature vs. nurture" question in "The Way We Woo" with Gould's treatment of the issue. Which essay makes a more convincing argument?

CHARLES DARWIN'S TREE OF LIFE

O. B. Hardison, Jr.

BIOGRAPHICAL NOTE

During a distinguished career, O. B. Hardison, Jr. (1928–90) was director of the Folger Shakespeare Library in Washington, DC, a visiting scholar at many universities, and Professor of English at Georgetown University. He was also a founder of the Quark Club, whose members are scientists and humanists interested in cultural change and exchange. Hardison published two collections of poetry and several books. His last book, *Disappearing Through the Skylight: Culture and Technology in the Twentieth Century* (1989), from which this essay is taken, won the *Los Angeles Times*' Book Prize for 1990.

1   The culmination and—for many Victorians—the vindication of the Baconian tradition in science was Charles Darwin's *The Origin of Species* (1859). Darwin acknowledges his debt to Bacon in his *Autobiography* (1876): "I worked on the true Baconian principles, and without any theory collected facts on a wholesale scale."

2   Wholesale is right. The book brings together twenty years of painstaking, minutely detailed observation ranging over the whole spectrum of organic life. Like Bacon, Darwin made little use of mathematics, although he had attempted (unsuccessfully) to deepen his mathematical knowledge while at Cambridge. Nor was Darwin the sort of scientist whose observations depend on instruments. His four-volume study of barnacles—*Cirripedia* (1851–54)—uses microscopy frequently, but much of his best work could have been written entirely on the basis of direct observation.

3   As soon as it was published, *The Origin of Species* was recognized as one of those books that change history. Its reception was partly a tribute to the overwhelming wealth of detail it offers in support of the theory Darwin finally worked out to hold his enormous bundle of facts together and partly a case of powder waiting for a spark. Darwin was initially criticized for giving insufficient credit to his predecessors, and the third edition of *The Origin of Species* includes a list of important moments in the earlier history of the theory of evolution. It begins with Jean-Baptiste Lamarck, who proposed a generally evolutionary theory of biology in the *Histoire naturelle des animaux* (1815). Charles Lyell's *Principles of Geology* (1832) is not included in the list because it is not specifically evolutionary, but its analysis of the evidence of geological change over time was indispensable to Darwin. Using Lyell, he could be certain that the variations he observed among animals of the same species in the Galápagos Islands had occurred within a relatively short span of geologic time.

4   Another source mentioned in the list and the immediate stimulus to the publication of *The Origin of Species* was an essay by Alfred Russell Wallace entitled "On the Tendency of Varieties to Depart Indefinitely from the Original Type." Wallace sent this essay to Darwin in 1858, and it convinced Darwin that if he did not publish his own work he risked being anticipated. He acknowledges Wallace's paper in his introduction and admits in the *Autobiography* that it "contained exactly the same theory as mine." Again according to the *Autobiography*, it was Darwin's reading of Malthus that suggested, around 1838, that all species are locked in a remorseless struggle for survival.

5   In spite of these and other anticipations, *The Origin of Species* was an immediate sensation. By ignoring religious dogma and wishful thinking, Darwin was able to buckle and bow his mind to the nature of things and to produce the sort of powerful, overarching concept that reveals coherence in a vast area of experience that had previously seemed chaotic.

6   A modern reader can see a kinship between Darwin's passionate interest in all things living, beginning with his undergraduate hobby of collecting beetles, and the outburst of nature poetry that occurred in the Romantic period.

7   Darwin was unaware of this kinship. In the *Autobiography* he says that "up to the age of thirty, or beyond it, poetry of many kinds, such as the works of Milton, Gray, Byron, Wordsworth, Coleridge, and Shelley . . . gave me the greatest pleasure. . . . But now for many years I cannot endure to read a line of poetry." His *Journal of the Voyage of the Beagle* is filled with appreciative comments about tropical landscape and its animals and plants, but he remarks that natural scenery "does not cause me the exquisite delight which it formerly did." He is probably contrasting his own methodical descriptions of landscape with the romanticized landscapes of writers like Byron and painters like Turner. He plays the role of Baconian ascetic collecting "without any theory . . . facts on a wholesale scale." His mind, he says (again in the *Autobiography*), has become "a kind of machine for grinding laws out of large collections of facts."

8   The idea that the mind is a machine that grinds laws out of facts echoes Bacon's injunction to use reason to "deliver and reduce" the imagination. The same asceticism is evident in Darwin's disparaging comments about his literary style. He believed he was writing dry scientific prose for other scientists, and John Ruskin, among others, agreed. Darwin was astounded, gratified, and a little frightened by his popular success.

9   No one can read Darwin today without recognizing that he was wrong about his style. As Stanley Edgar Hyman observes in *The Tangled Bank* (1962), both *The Voyage of the Beagle* and *The Origin of Species* are filled with passages that are beautiful and sensitive, whatever Darwin may have thought of them. The writing is effective precisely because it does not strain for the gingerbread opulence fashionable in mid-Victorian English prose. It has a freedom from pretense, a quality of authority, as moving as the natural descriptions in Wordsworth's *Prelude*. It is effective precisely because it stems from direct observation of the things and relationships that nature comprises. In addition to revealing a mind "buckled and bowed" to nature, it reveals a mind that has surrendered to the kaleidoscope of life around it. Consider the following comment on the life-styles of woodpeckers:

> Can a more striking instance of adaptation be given than that of a woodpecker for climbing trees and seizing insects in chinks in the bark? Yet in North America there are woodpeckers which feed largely on fruit, and others with elongated wings which chase insects on the wing. On the plains of La Plata, where hardly a tree grows, there is a woodpecker . . . which has two toes before and two behind, a long pointed tongue, pointed tail-feathers, sufficiently stiff to support the bird on a post, but not so stiff as in the typical woodpeckers, and a straight strong beak. . . . Hence this [bird] in all essential parts of its structure is a woodpecker. Even in such trifling characters as the colouring, the harsh tone of the voice, and undulatory flight, its close blood-relationship to our common woodpecker is plainly declared; yet . . . in certain large districts it does not climb trees, and it makes its nest in holes in banks! In certain other districts, however . . . this same woodpecker . . . frequents trees, and bores holes in the trunk for its nest.

10   Darwin was familiar with Audubon's *Birds of America*, and remarks that Audubon "is the only observer to witness the frigate-bird, which has all its four toes webbed, alight on the surface of the ocean." In spite of a possible touch of irony in this remark, the affinity between the two naturalists is striking. Darwin fixes things in the middle distance by means of words. The central device in his description of the La Plata woodpecker is detail: elongated wings, insects caught on the wing, two toes before and two behind, stiff tail, elongated beak, harsh voice, a nest in a hole in a bank. The accumulating details express close observation which is also loving observation. They create a thingly poetry, a poetry of the actual.

11   In a similar way, Audubon fixes in images a nature that flaunts itself palpably and colorfully in the middle distance. In the process both Darwin and Audubon create an art of the actual.

12   A year before *The Origin of Species*, Oliver Wendell Holmes published "The Chambered Nautilus." It is a poem that attempts to fix a thing that is out there in the middle distance in verse:

> Year after year behold the silent toil
> That spread his lustrous coil;
> Still as the spiral grew,
> He left the past year's dwelling for the new,
> Stole with soft step its shining archway through, built up its idle door,
> Stretched in his last-found home, and knew the old no more.

13   Here, instead of the scientist becoming poet, the poet becomes a scientist. The problem is that the poem cannot forget it is art. It is more clumsy, finally, than Darwin's description of the La Plata woodpecker. Closer to Darwin are the photographs of Mathew Brady, the histories of Ranke and Burckhardt, and the novels of Balzac, George Eliot, and Turgenev.

14   Feeling is usually implicit in Darwin's prose but repressed. Facts are facts and poetry is poetry. Occasionally, however, Darwin allowed his feelings to bubble to the surface. The closing paragraph of *The Origin of Species* is a case in point. It describes a scene,

> . . . clothed with many plants of many kinds, with birds singing on the bushes, with various insects flitting about, and with worms crawling through the damp earth, and . . . these elaborately constructed forms, so different from each other, and dependent upon each other in so complex a manner, have all been produced by laws acting around us. . . . Thus, from the war of nature, from famine and death, the most exalted object which we are capable of conceiving, namely, the production of the higher animals, directly follows.

15   No passage is more obviously dominated by aesthetic feeling than Darwin's description of the variety of species created by the struggle for existence. The idea of the struggle is central to *The Origin of Species*. It involves a paradox that fascinated Darwin. Out of a silent but deadly struggle comes the infinitely varied and exotically beautiful mosaic of life:

> How have all these exquisite adaptations of one part of the organization to another part, and to the conditions of life, and of one organic being to another being, been perfected? We see these beautiful co-adaptations most plainly in the woodpecker and the mistletoe; and only a little less plainly in the humblest parasite which clings to the hairs of a quadruped or feathers of a bird; in the structure of the beetle which dives through the water; in the plumed seed which is wafted by the gentlest breeze; in short, we see beautiful adaptations everywhere and in every part of the organic world.

16   *Exquisite, perfected, beautiful, humblest, plumed, gentlest.* The world described by these adjectives is not cold, alien, or indifferent. It is a work of art. Nor is Darwin's prose the dispassionate, dry prose of a treatise devoted only to facts. Because it is the work of a naturalist, it pays close attention to detail. The parts are there because they are there in nature in the middle distance: the woodpecker, the mistletoe, the parasite clinging to the quadruped, the feathers of the bird, the water beetle, the plumed seed. They illustrate the harmonious relations created by the struggle for survival—"co-adaptation" is Darwin's word. The prose enacts these harmonies through elegantly controlled rhythms.

17   Darwin's language invites the reader to share experience as well as to understand it. *Exquisite, beautiful,* and *gentle* orient him emotionally at the same time that his attention is focused on the objects that give rise to the emotion—mistletoe, parasite, water beetle, plumed seed.

18   The passage flatly contradicts Darwin's statement in the *Autobiography* that his artistic sensitivity had atrophied by the time he was thirty. That he thought it did shows only that he believed with his contemporaries that science is science and art is art. The problem was in his psyche, not his prose. The tradition that science should be dispassionate and practical, that it is a kind of servitude to nature that demands the banishment of the humanity of the observer, prevented him from understanding that he was, in fact, responding to nature aesthetically and communicating that response in remarkably poetic prose. There is no detectable difference in this passage between a hypothetical figure labeled "scientific observer" and another hypothetical figure named "literary artist."

19   The most striking example of Darwin's artistry occurs in the "summary" of Chapter 3. The passage deals explicitly with the tragic implications of natural selection. It is a sustained meditation on a single image. The image—the Tree of Life—is practical because the branching limbs are a vivid representation of the branching pattern of evolution. However, the image is also mythic, an archetype familiar from Genesis and also from Egyptian, Buddhist, Greek, and other sources. In mythology, the Tree of Life connects the underworld and the heavens. It is the axis on which the spheres turn and the path along which creatures from the invisible world visit and take leave of earth. It is an ever-green symbol of fertility, bearing fruit in winter. It is the wood of the Cross on which God dies and the wood reborn that announces the return of life by sending out new branches in the spring. All of this symbolism is familiar from studies of archetypal and primitive imagery. Behind it is what Rudolf Otto calls, in *The Idea of the Holy*, the terrifying and fascinating mystery of things: *mysterium tremendum et fascinans*.

20   It is surprising to find a scientist, particularly a preeminent Victorian scientist and a self-avowed disciple of Bacon, using an archetypal image. Yet Darwin's elaboration is both sensitive and remarkably full. Central to it is the paradox of life in death, and throughout, one senses the hovering presence of the *mysterium tremendum et fascinans*:

> The affinities of all the beings of the same class have sometimes been represented by a great tree. I believe this simile largely speaks the truth. The green and budding twigs may represent existing species; and those produced during former years may represent the long succession of extinct species. At each period of growth all the growing twigs have tried to branch out on all sides, and to overtop and kill the surrounding twigs and branches, in the same manner as species and groups of species have at all times overmastered other species in the great battle of life. . . . Of the many twigs which flourished when the tree was a mere bush, only two or three, now grown into great branches, yet survive and bear the other branches; so with the species which lived during long-past geological periods, very few have left living . . . descendants.
>
> From the first growth of the tree, many a limb and branch has decayed and dropped off; and all these fallen branches of various sizes may represent those whole orders, families, and genera which have now no living representatives, and which are known to us only in a fossil state. As we here and there see a thin, straggling branch springing from a fork low down in a tree, and which by some chance has been favored and is still alive on its summit, so we occasionally see an animal like the Ornithorhynchus or Lepidosiren, which in some small degree connects by its affinities two large branches of life, and which has apparently been saved from fatal competition by having inhabited a protected station. As buds give rise by growth to fresh buds, and these, if vigorous, branch out and overtop on all sides many a feebler branch, so by generation I believe it has been with the great Tree of Life, which fills with its dead and broken branches the crust of the earth, and covers the surface with its ever-branching and beautiful ramifications.

21   Darwin's music here is stately and somber. The central image is established at the beginning: a great tree green at the top but filled with dead branches beneath the crown. The passage becomes an elegy for all the orders of life that have perished since the tree began. Words suggesting death crowd the sentences: *overtopped, kill, the great battle for life, decayed, dropped off, fallen, no living representative, straggling branch, fatal competition*. As the passage moves toward its conclusion, a change, a kind of reversal, can be felt. Words suggesting life become more frequent: *alive, life, saved, fresh buds, vigorous*. The final sentence restates the central paradox in a contrast between universal desolation—"dead and broken branches [filling] the crust of the earth"—with images of eternal fertility—"ever-branching and beautiful ramifications."

22   In spite of the poetic qualities of *The Origin of Species*, the idea of science as the dispassionate observation of things is central to the Darwinian moment. Observation reveals truth; and once revealed, truth can be generalized.

23   The truths discovered by Darwin were applied almost immediately to sociology and political science. Herbert Spencer had coined the phrase "survival of the fittest" in 1852 in an article on the pressures caused by population growth entitled "A Theory of Population." Buttressed by the prestige of *The Origin of Species*, the concept of the survival of the fittest was used to justify laissez-faire capitalism. Andrew Carnegie remarked in 1900, "A struggle is inevitable [in society] and it is a question of the survival of the fittest." John D. Rockefeller added, "The growth of a large business is merely the survival of the fittest." Capitalism enables the strong to survive while the weak are destroyed. Socialism, conversely, protects the weak and frustrates the strong. Marx turned over the coin: socialism is a later and therefore a higher product of evolution than bourgeois capitalism. Being superior, it will replace capitalism as surely as warm-blooded mammals replaced dinosaurs.

24   Darwin also influenced cultural thought. To say this is to say that he changed not only the way the real was managed but the way it was imagined. The writing of history became evolutionary—so much so that historians often assumed an evolutionary model and tailored their facts to fit. The histories of political systems, national economies, technologies, machinery, literary genres, philosophical systems, and even styles of dress were presented as examples of evolution, usually interpreted to mean examples of progress from simple to complex, with simple considered good, and complex better.

25   And, of course, Darwin's theories were both attacked and supported in the name of religion. Adam Sedgwick, professor of geology at Cambridge, began the long history of attacks on Darwin when he wrote in "Objections to Mr. Darwin's Theory of the Origin of Species" (1860): "I cannot conclude without expressing my detestation of the theory, because of its unflinching materialism." Among the sins for which Darwin was most bitterly attacked was his argument that species are constantly coming into existence and dying, an argument that contradicts the fundamentalist reading of Genesis. He was also attacked for suggesting that struggle, including violent struggle, is ultimately beneficial, and that, by implication, the meek will not inherit the earth. Finally, he was attacked for suggesting that man is an animal sharing a common ancestor with the apes, an idea that is implicit in *The Origin of Species* and stated unequivocally in *The Descent of Man* (1871).

26   Darwin's conclusion to *The Origin of Species* is a summary of his vision. It has a strong emotional coloring even in its initial form. Perhaps because of the attacks, Darwin added the phrase "by the Creator" to the first revised (1860) and later editions of the book: "There is a grandeur in this view of life, with its several powers, having been originally breathed by the Creator into a few forms or into one; and that, whilst this planet has gone cycling on according to the fixed law of gravity, from so simple a beginning endless forms most beautiful and most wonderful have been, and are being evolved."

27   Whether the reference to God represents Darwin's personal view of religion is outside the scope of the present discussion. Probably it does not. At any rate the notion that God is revealed in evolution remains powerfully attractive today both to biologists and, as shown by Teilhard de Chardin's *The Phenomenon of Man* (1955), to those attempting to formulate a scientific theology. More generally, in spite of his literary disclaimers, Darwin initiated a whole genre of writing, typified by the work today of Bertel Bager, Lewis Thomas, and Annie Dillard, which dwells on the intricate beauties of natural design.

28   Many of the applications of Darwin's ideas were, however, patently strained from the beginning. Time revealed the inadequacies of others. Social Darwinism is studied in history classes but is no longer a viable political creed. Evolutionary histories of this and that are still being written, but the approach has been shown to be seriously misleading in many applications. More fundamental, by the middle of the twentieth century Baconian empiricism was no longer adequate to the idea of nature that science had developed. Einstein and Heisenberg made it clear that mind and nature—subject and object—are involved in each other and not separate empires. An objective world that can be "observed" and "understood" if only the imagination can be held in check simply does not exist. Facts are not observations "collected . . . on a wholesale scale." They are knots in a net.

NOTES AND DISCUSSION

Hardison's essay explores the nature of science and scientific writing by focusing on the career and publications of the famous English naturalist, Charles Darwin. Hardison builds his essay upon excerpts from Darwin's writing, seamlessly integrating many quotations into his own writing by using a variety of punctuation. Through his presentation and analysis of Darwin's writing, Hardison defines the nature of Darwin's scientific work, but also reveals much about his own definition and vision of science.

    Consider, for example, the stress he places on the fact that much of Darwin's four volumes of *Cirripedia* "could have been written entirely on the basis of direct observation," without technical support. Furthermore, Darwin's science is said to have been conducted on a "wholesale scale," encompassing the works of previous naturalists, as well as his travels, his collections of natural specimens, and his interest in poetry. Darwin compared his own mind to a machine designed to grind laws out of a large collection of facts. But Hardison rejects this claim, arguing that Darwin's own conception of his science and writing is flawed, and that in fact Darwin combined the roles of scientist and poet. He then provides specific examples—extended passages of Darwin's prose—which he analyzes closely to support his thesis. Hardison next outlines Darwin's influence on social, political, economic, and cultural thought, as well as on literature, again providing specific examples and quotations to support his point. Hardison thus implies that Darwin's holistic approach to science, as well as the artistry of both his science and his scientific writing, were fundamental to his influence. There is no doubt that Hardison also wishes to influence his readers' understanding of the nature of science.

STUDY QUESTIONS

For Discussion:

1. Examine the way Hardison characterizes Darwin's approach to science. What does this characterization imply about the nature and methodology of science in general, and about Hardison's own vision of science, in particular?

2. What does Hardison's final metaphor of "knots in a net" suggest? How does it influence your understanding of the end of the essay?

For Writing:

1. Hardison suggests that Darwin influenced the writing of Annie Dillard, among others. A selection from Dillard is included in this anthology. Write an analysis in which you decide whether the qualities that Hardison perceives in Darwin's writing also appear in Dillard's.

2. Analyze Hardison's own style as he analyzes Darwin's, considering the audience he addresses, and the tone he employs.

WHAT IS AN ELEMENTARY PARTICLE?

Werner Heisenberg

BIOGRAPHICAL NOTE

Werner Heisenberg (1901–1976) was one of the more influential and important theorists of quantum physics of the early twentieth century. He is best known for his writings about quantum uncertainty—that is, the proposition that the position and velocity of subatomic particles cannot be known precisely but can only be calculated in terms of probabilities—and for articulating the "uncertainty principle," the idea that science can neither scrutinize the present nor predict the future with complete exactitude. Heisenberg's universe is, then, very different from Einstein's. He suggests that it is impossible to observe subatomic particles directly: the position of those particles may only be calculated, and even those calculations cannot ever be precise, but are only statistically probable. Einstein greeted Heisenberg's claims with incredulity, declaring that "God does not play dice with the universe."

---

1   The question "What is an elementary particle?" must naturally be answered above all by experiment. So I shall first summarize briefly the most important experimental findings of elementary particle physics during the last fifty years, and will try to show that, if the experiments are viewed without prejudice, the question alluded to has already been largely answered by these findings, and that there is no longer much for the theoretician to add. In the second part I will then go on to enlarge upon the philosophical problems connected with the concept of an elementary particle. For I believe that certain mistaken developments in the

theory of elementary particles—and I fear that there are such—are due to the fact that their authors would claim that they do not wish to trouble about philosophy, but that in reality they unconsciously start out from a bad philosophy, and have therefore fallen through prejudice into unreasonable statements of the problem. One may say, with some exaggeration, perhaps, that good physics has been inadvertently spoiled by bad philosophy. Finally I shall say something of these problematic developments themselves, compare them with erroneous developments in the history of quantum mechanics in which I was myself involved, and consider how such wrong turnings can be avoided. The close of the lecture should therefore be more optimistic again.

2   First, then, to the experimental facts. Not quite fifty years ago, Dirac, in his theory of electrons, predicted that in addition to electrons there would also have to exist the appropriate anti-particles, the positrons; and a few years later the existence of positrons, their origin in pair-creation, and hence the existence of so-called anti-matter, was experimentally demonstrated by Anderson and Blackett. It was a discovery of the first order. For till then it had mostly been supposed that there are two kinds of fundamental particle, electrons and protons, which are distinguished above all others by the fact that they can never be changed, so that their number is always constant as well, and which for that very reason had been called elementary particles. All matter was supposed in the end to be made up of electrons and protons. The experimental proof of pair-creation and positrons showed that this idea was false. Electrons can be created and again disappear; so their number is by no means constant; they are not elementary in the sense previously assumed.

3   The next important step was Fermi's discovery of artificial radioactivity. It was learnt from many experiments that one atomic nucleus can turn into another by emission of particles, if the conservation laws for energy, angular momentum, electric charge, etc., allow this. The transformation of energy into matter, which had already been recognized as possible in Einstein's relativity theory, is thus a very commonly observable phenomenon. There is no talk here of any conservation of the number of particles. But there are indeed physical properties, characterizable by quantum numbers—I am thinking, say, of angular momentum or electric charge—in which the quantum numbers can then take on positive and negative values, and for these a conservation law holds.

4   In the thirties there was yet another important experimental discovery. It was found that in cosmic radiation there are very energetic particles, which, on collision with other particles, say a proton, in the emulsion of a photographic plate, can let loose a shower of many secondary particles. Many physicists believed for a time that such showers can originate only through a sort of cascade formation in atomic nuclei; but it later turned out that, even in a collision between a single pair of energetic particles, the theoretically conjectured multiple production of secondary particles does in fact occur. At the end of the forties, Powell discovered the pions, which play the major part in these showers. This showed that in collisions of high-energy particles, the transformation of energy into matter is quite generally the decisive process, so that it obviously no longer makes sense to speak of a splitting of the original particle. The concept of "division" had come, by experiment, to lose its meaning.

5   In the experiments of the fifties and sixties, this new situation was repeatedly confirmed: many new particles were discovered, with long and short lives, and no unambiguous answer could be given any longer to the question about what these particles consisted of, since this question no longer has a rational meaning. A proton, for example, could be made up of neutron and pion, or Λ-hyperon and kaon, or out of two nucleons and an anti-nucleon; it would

be simplest of all to say that a proton just consists of continuous matter, and all these statements are equally correct or equally false. The difference between elementary and composite particles has thus basically disappeared. And that is no doubt the most important experimental finding of the last fifty years.

6   As a consequence of this development, the experiments have strongly suggested an analogy: the elementary particles are something like the stationary states of an atom or a molecule. There is a whole spectrum of particles, just as there is a spectrum, say, of the iron atom or a molecule, where we may think, in the latter case, of the various stationary states of molecule, or even of the many different possible molecules of chemistry. Among particles, we shall speak of a spectrum of "matter." In fact, during the sixties and seventies, the experiments with the big accelerators have shown that this analogy fits all the findings so far. Like the stationary states of the atom, the particles, too, can be characterized by quantum numbers, that is, by symmetry- or transformation-properties, and the exact or approximately valid conservation principles associated with them decide as to the possibility of the transformations. Just as the transformation properties of an excited hydrogen atom under spatial rotation decide whether it can fall to a lower state by emission of a photon, so too, the question whether a $\varnothing$-boson, say, can degenerate into a ρ-boson by emission of a pion, is decided by such symmetry properties. Just as the various stationary states of an atom have very different lifetimes, so too with particles. The ground state of an atom is stable, and has an infinitely long lifetime, and the same is true of such particles as the electron, proton, deuteron, etc. But these stable particles are in no way more elementary than the unstable ones. The ground state of the hydrogen atom follows from the same Schrödinger equation as the excited states do. Nor are the electron and photon in any way more elementary than, say, a Λ-hyperon.

7   The experimental particle-physics of recent years has thus fulfilled much the same tasks, in the course of its development, as the spectroscopy of the early twenties. Just as, at that time, a large compilation was brought out, the so-called Paschen-Götze tables, in which the stationary states of all atom shells were collected, so now we have the annually supplemented *Reviews of Particle Properties*, in which the stationary states of matter and its transformation-properties are recorded. The work of compiling such a comprehensive tabulation therefore corresponds, say, to the star-cataloging of the astronomers, and every observer hopes, of course, that he will one day find a particularly interesting object in his chosen area.

8   Yet there are also characteristic differences between particle physics and the physics of atomic shells. In the latter we are dealing with such low energies, that the characteristic features of relativity theory can be neglected, and nonrelativistic quantum mechanics used, therefore, for description. This means that the governing symmetry-groups may differ in atomic-shell physics on the one hand, and in particles on the other. The Galileo group of shell physics is replaced, at the particle level, by the Lorentz-group; and in particle physics we also have new groups, such as the isospin group, which is isomorphic to the SU_2 group, and then the SU_3 group, the group of scaling transformations, and still others. It is an important experimental task to define the governing groups of particle physics, and in the past twenty years it has already been largely accomplished.

9   Here we can learn from shell physics, that in those very groups which manifestly designate only approximately valid symmetries, two basically different types may be distinguished. Consider, say, among optical spectra, the O_3 group of spatial rotations, and the $O_3 \times O_3$ group, which governs the multiplet-structure in spectra. The basic equations of quantum

mechanics are strictly invariant with respect to the group of spatial rotations. The states of atoms having greater angular momenta are therefore severely degenerate, that is, there are numerous states of exactly equal energy. Only if the atom is placed in an external electromagnetic field do the states split up, and the familiar fine structure emerge, as in the Zeeman or Stark effect. This degeneracy can also be abolished if the ground state of the system is not rotation-invariant, as in the ground states of a crystal or ferro-magnet. In this case there is also a splitting of levels; the two spin-directions of an electron in a ferro-magnet are no longer associated with exactly the same energy. Furthermore, by a well-known theorem of Goldstone, there are bosons whose energy tends to zero with increasing wavelength, and, in the case of the ferro-magnet, Bloch's spin-waves or magnons.

10   It is different with the group $O_3 \times O_3$, from which result the familiar multiplets of optical spectra. Here we are dealing with an approximate symmetry, which comes about in that the spin-path interactions in a specific region are small, so that the spins and paths of electrons can be skewed counter to each other, without producing much change in the interaction. The $O_3 \times O_3$ symmetry is therefore also a useful approximation only in particular parts of the spectrum. Empirically, the two kinds of broken symmetry are most clearly distinguishable in that, for the fundamental symmetry broken by the ground state, there must, by the Goldstone theorem, be associated bosons of zero rest mass, or long-range forces. If we find them, there is reason to believe that the degeneracy of the ground state plays an important role here.

11   Now if these findings are transferred from atomic-shell physics to particle physics, it is very natural, on the basis of the experiments, to interpret the Lorentz group and the SU_2 group, the isospin group, that is, fundamental symmetries of the underlying law of nature. Electromagnetism and gravitation then appear as the long-range forces associated with symmetry broken by the ground state. The higher groups, SU_3, SU_4, SU_6, or $SU_2 \times SU_2$, $SU_3 \times SU_3$ and so on, would then have to rank as dynamic symmetries, just like $O_3 \times O_3$ in atomic-shell physics. Of the dilatation or scaling group, it may be doubted whether it should be counted among the fundamental symmetries; it is perturbed by the existence of particles with finite mass, and by the gravitation due to masses in the universe. Owing to its close relation to the Lorentz group, it certainly ought to be numbered among the fundamental symmetries. The foregoing assignment of perturbed symmetries to the two basic types is made plausible, as I was already saying, by the experimental findings, but it is not yet possible, perhaps, to speak of a final settlement. The most important thing is that, with regard to the symmetry groups that present themselves in the phenomenology of spectra, the question must be asked, and if possible answered, as to which of the two basic types they belong to.

12   Let me point to yet another feature of shell-physics: among optical spectra there are non-combining, or more accurately, weakly combining term-systems, such as the spectra or para- and ortho-helium. In particle physics we can perhaps compare the division of the fermion spectrum into baryons and leptons with features of this type.

13   The analogy between the stationary states of an atom or molecule, and the particles of elementary particle physics, is therefore almost complete, and with this, so it seems to me, I have also given a complete qualitative answer to the initial question "What is an elementary particle?" But only a qualitative answer! The theorist is now confronted with the further question, whether he can also underpin this qualitative understanding by means of quantitative calculations. For this it is first necessary to answer a prior question: What is it, anyway, to understand a spectrum in quantitative terms?

14   For this we have a string of examples, from both classical physics and quantum mechanics alike. Let us consider, say, the spectrum of the elastic vibrations of a steel plate. If we are not to be content with a qualitative understanding, we shall start from the fact that the plate can be characterized by specific elastic properties, which can be mathematically represented. Having achieved this, we still have to append the boundary conditions, adding, for example, that the plate is circular or rectangular, that it is, or is not, under tension, and from this, at least in principle, the spectrum of elastic or acoustic vibrations can be calculated. Owing to the level of complexity, we shall certainly not, indeed, be able to work out all the vibrations exactly, but may yet, perhaps, calculate the lowest, with the smallest number of nodal lines.

15   Thus two elements are necessary for quantitative understanding: the exactly formulated knowledge, in mathematical terms, of the dynamic behavior of the plate, and the boundary conditions, which can be regarded as "contingent," as determined, that is, by local circumstances; the plate, of course, could also be dissected in other ways. It is like this, too, with the electrodynamic oscillations of a cavity resonator. The Maxwellian equations determine the dynamic behavior, and the shape of the cavity defines the boundary conditions. And so it is, also, with the optical spectrum of the iron atom. The Schrödinger equation for a system with a nucleus and 26 electrons determines the dynamic behavior, and to this we add the boundary conditions, which state in this instance that the wave-function shall vanish at infinity. If the atom were to be enclosed in a small box, a somewhat altered spectrum would result.

16   If we transfer these ideas to particle physics, it becomes a question, therefore, of first ascertaining by experiment the dynamical properties of the matter system, and formulating this in mathematical terms. As the contingent element, we now add the boundary conditions, which here will consist essentially of statements about so-called empty space, i.e., about the cosmos and its symmetry properties. The first step must in any case be the attempt to formulate mathematically a law of nature that lays down the dynamics of matter. For the second step, we have to make statements about the boundary conditions. For without these, the spectrum just cannot be defined. I would guess, for example, that in one of the "black holes" of contemporary astrophysics, the spectrum of elementary particles would look totally different from our own. Unfortunately, we cannot experiment on the point.

17   But now a word more about the decisive first step, namely the formulation of the dynamical law. There are pessimists among particle physicists, who believe that there simply is no such law of nature, defining the dynamic properties of matter. With such a view I confess that I can make no headway at all. For somehow the dynamics of matter has to exist, or else there would be no spectrum; and in that case we should also be able to describe it mathematically. The pessimistic view would mean that the whole of particle physics is directed, eventually, at producing a gigantic tabulation containing the maximum number of stationary states of matter, transition-probabilities, and the like, a "Super-Review of Particle Properties," and thus a compilation in which there is nothing more to understand, and which therefore, no doubt, would no longer be read by anyone. But there is also not the least occasion for such pessimism, and I set particular store by this assertion. For we actually observe a particle spectrum with sharp lines, and so, indirectly, a sharply defined dynamics of matter as well. The experimental findings, briefly sketched above, also contain already very definite indications as to the fundamental invariance properties of this fundamental law of nature, and we know from the dispersion relations a great deal about the level of causality that is formulated in this law. We thus have the essential determinants of the law already to hand, and after so many other spectra in physics have finally been understood to some extent in quantitative terms, it will also be possible here, despite the high degree of complexity involved. At this point—and just because of its complexity—I would sooner not discuss the special proposal that was long ago made by myself, together with Pauli, for a mathematical formulation of the underlying law, and which, even now, I still believe to have the best chances of being the right one. But I would like to point out with all emphasis, that the formulation of such a law is the indispensable precondition for understanding the spectrum of elementary particles. All else is not understanding; it is hardly more than a start to the tabulation project, and as theorists, at least, we should not be content with that.

18   I now come to the philosophy by which the physics of elementary particles is consciously or unconsciously guided. For two and a half millennia, the question has been debated by philosophers and scientists, as to what happens when we try to keep on dividing up matter. What are the smallest constituent parts of matter? Different philosophers have given very different answers to this question, which have all exerted their influence on the history of natural science. The best known is that of the philosopher Democritus. In attempting to go on dividing, we finally light upon indivisible, immutable objects, the atoms, and all materials are composed of atoms. The position and motions of the atoms determine the quality of the materials. In Aristotle and his medieval successors, the concept of minimal particles is not so sharply defined. There are, indeed, minimal particles here for every kind of material—on further division the parts would no longer display the characteristic properties of the material—but these minimal parts are continuously changeable, like the materials themselves. Mathematically speaking, therefore, materials are infinitely divisible; matter is pictured as continuous.

19   The clearest opposing position to that of Democritus was adopted by Plato. In attempting continual division we ultimately arrive, in Plato's opinion, at mathematical forms: the regular solids of stereometry, which are definable by their symmetry properties, and the triangles from which they can be constructed. These forms are not themselves matter, but they shape it. The element earth, for example, is based on the shape of the cube, the element fire on the shape of the tetrahedron. It is common to all these philosophers, that they wish in some way to dispose of the antinomy of the infinitely small, which, as everyone knows, was discussed in detail by Kant.

20   Of course, there are and have been more naïve attempts at rationalizing this antinomy. Biologists, for example, have developed the notion that the seed of an apple contains an invisibly small apple tree, which in turn bears blossom and fruit; that again in the fruit there are seeds, in which once more a still tinier apple tree is hidden, and so *ad infinitum*. In the same way, in the early days of the Bohr–Rutherford theory of the atom as a miniature planetary system, we developed with some glee the thesis that upon the planets of this system, the electrons, there are again very tiny creatures living, who build houses, cultivate fields and do atomic physics, arriving once more at the thesis of their atoms as miniature planetary systems, and so *ad infinitum*. In the background here, as I said already, there is always lurking the Kantian antinomy, that it is very hard, on the one hand, to think of matter as infinitely divisible, but also difficult, on the other, to imagine this division one day coming to an enforced stop. The antinomy, as we know, is ultimately brought about by our erroneous belief that we can also apply our intuition to situations on the very small scale. The strongest influence on the physics and chemistry of recent centuries has undoubtedly been exerted by

the atomism of Democritus. It permits an intuitive description of small-scale chemical processes. The atoms can be compared to the mass-points of Newtonian mechanics, and such a comparison leads to a satisfying statistical theory of heat. The chemist's atoms were not, indeed, mass-points at all, but miniature planetary systems, and the atomic nucleus was composed of protons and neutrons, but electrons, protons, and eventually even neutrons could, it was thought, quite well be regarded as the true atoms, that is, as the ultimate indivisible building-blocks of matter. During the last hundred years, the Democritean idea of the atom had thus become an integrating component of the physicist's view of the material world; it was readily intelligible and to some extent intuitive, and determined physical thinking even among physicists who wanted to have nothing to do with philosophy. At this point I should now like to justify my suggestion, that today in the physics of elementary particles, good physics is unconsciously being spoiled by bad philosophy.

21   We cannot, of course, avoid employing a language that stems from this traditional philosophy. We ask, "What does the proton consist of?" "Can one divide the electron, or is it indivisible?" "Is the light-quantum simple, or is it composite?" But these questions are wrongly put, since the words *divide* or *consist of* have largely lost their meaning. It would thus be our task to adapt our language and thought, and hence also our scientific philosophy, to this new situation engendered by the experiments. But that, unfortunately, is very difficult. The result is that false questions and false ideas repeatedly creep into particle physics, and lead to the erroneous developments of which I am about to speak. But first a further remark about the demand for intuitability.

22   There have been philosophers who have held intuitability to be the precondition for all true understanding. Thus here in Munich, for example, the philosopher Hugo Dingler has championed the view that intuitive Euclidean geometry is the only true geometry, since it is presupposed in the construction of our measuring instruments; and on the latter point, Dingler is quite correct. Hence, he says, the experimental findings which underlie the general theory of relativity should be described in other terms than those of a more general Riemannian geometry, which deviates from the Euclidean; for otherwise we become involved in contradictions. But this demand is obviously extreme. To justify what we do by way of experiment, it is enough that, in the dimensions of our apparatus, the geometry of Euclid holds to a sufficiently good approximation. We must therefore come to agree that the experimental findings on the very small and very large scale no longer provide us with an intuitive picture, and must learn to manage there without intuitions. We then recognize, for example, that the aforementioned antinomy of the infinitely small is resolved, among elementary particles, in a very subtle fashion, in a way that neither Kant nor the ancient philosophers could have thought of, namely inasmuch as the term *divide* loses its meaning.

23   If we wish to compare the findings of contemporary particle physics with any earlier philosophy, it can only be with the philosophy of Plato; for the particles of present-day physics are representations of symmetry groups, so the quantum theory tells us, and to that extent they resemble the symmetrical bodies of the Platonic view.

24   But our purpose here was to occupy ourselves not with philosophy, but with physics, and so I will now go on to discuss that development in theoretical particle physics, which in my view sets out from a false statement of the problem. There is first of all the thesis, that the observed particles, such as protons, pions, hyperons, and many others, are made up of smaller unobserved particles, the quarks, or else from partons, gluons, charmed particles, or whatever these imagined particles may all be called. Here the question has obviously been

asked, "What do protons consist of?" But it has been forgotten in the process, that the term *consist of* only has a halfway clear meaning if we are able to dissect the particle in question, with a small expenditure of energy, into constituents whose rest mass is very much greater than this energy-cost; otherwise, the term *consist of* has lost its meaning. And that is the situation with protons. In order to demonstrate this loss of meaning in a seemingly well-defined term, I cannot forebear from telling a story that Niels Bohr was wont to retail on such occasions. A small boy comes into a shop with twopence in his hand, and tells the shopkeeper that he would like twopence-worth of mixed sweets. The shopkeeper hands him two sweets, and says: "You can mix them for yourself." In the case of the proton, the concept "consist of" has just as much meaning as the concept of "mixing" in the tale of the small boy.

25   Now many will object to this, that the quark hypothesis has been drawn from empirical findings, namely the establishing of the empirical relevance of the SU_3 group; and furthermore, it holds up in the interpretation of many experiments on the application of the SU_3 group as well. This is not to be contested. But I should like to put forward a counter-example from the history of quantum mechanics, in which I myself was involved; a counter-example which clearly displays the weakness of arguments of this type. Prior to the appearance of Bohr's theory, many physicists maintained that an atom must be made up of harmonic oscillators. For the optical spectrum certainly contains sharp lines, and they can only be emitted by harmonic oscillators. The charges on these oscillators would have to correspond to other electromagnetic values than those on the electron, and there would also have to be very many oscillators, since there are very many lines in the spectrum.

26   Regardless of these difficulties, Woldemar Voigt constructed at Göttingen in 1912 a theory of the anomalous Zeeman effect of the D-lines in the optical spectrum of sodium, and did so in the following way: he assumed a pair of coupled oscillators which, in the absence of an external magnetic field, yielded the frequencies of the two D-lines. He was able to arrange a coupling of the oscillators with one another, and with the external field, in such a way that, in weak magnetic fields, the anomalous Zeeman effect came out correct, and that in very strong magnetic fields the Paschen-Back effect was also correctly represented. For the intermediate region of moderate fields, he obtained, for the frequencies and intensities, long and complex quadratic roots; formulae, that is, which were largely incomprehensible, but which obviously reproduced the experiments with great exactness. Fifteen years later, Jordan and I took the trouble to work out the same problem by the methods of the quantum-mechanical theory of perturbation. To our great astonishment, we came out with exactly the old Voigtian formulae, so far as both frequencies and intensities were concerned and this, too, in the complex area of the moderate fields. The reasons for this we were later well able to perceive; it was a purely formal and mathematical one. The quantum-mechanical theory of perturbation leads to a system of coupled linear equations, and the frequencies are determined by the eigen values of the equation-system. A system of coupled harmonic oscillators leads equally, in the classical theory, to such a coupled linear equations-system. Since, in Voigt's theory, the most important parameter had been cancelled out, it was therefore no wonder that the right answer emerged. But the Voigtian theory contributed nothing to the understanding of atomic structure.

27   Why was this attempt of Voigt's so successful on the one hand, and so futile on the other? Because he was only concerned to examine the D-lines, without taking the whole line-spectrum into account. Voigt had made phenomenological use of a certain aspect of the oscillator hypothesis, and had either ignored all the other discrepancies of this model, or

deliberately left them in obscurity. Thus he had simply not taken his hypothesis in real earnest. In the same way, I fear that the quark hypothesis is just not taken seriously by its exponents. The questions about the statistics of quarks, about the forces that hold them together, about the particles corresponding to these forces, about the reasons why quarks never appear as free particles, about the pair-creation of quarks in the interior of the elementary particle—all these questions are more or less left in obscurity. If there was a desire to take the quark hypothesis in real earnest, it would be necessary to make a precise mathematical approach to the dynamics of quarks, and the forces that hold them together, and to show that, qualitatively at least, this approach can reproduce correctly the many different features of particle physics that are known today. There should be no question in particle physics to which this approach could not be applied. Such attempts are not known to me, and I am afraid, also, that every such attempt which is presented in precise mathematical language would be very quickly refutable. I shall therefore formulate my objections in the shape of questions: "Does the quark hypothesis really contribute more to understanding of the particle spectrum, than the Voigtian hypothesis of oscillators contributed, in its day, to understanding of the structure of atomic shells?" "Does there not still lurk behind the quark hypothesis the notion, long ago refuted by experiment, that we are able to distinguish simple and composite particles?"

28   I would now like to take up briefly a few questions of detail. If the SU_3 group plays an important part in the structure of the particle spectrum, and this we must assume on the basis of the experiments, then it is important to decide whether we are dealing with a fundamental symmetry of the underlying natural law, or with a dynamic symmetry, which from the onset can only have approximate validity. If this decision is left unclear, then all further assumptions about the dynamics underlying the spectrum also remain unclear, and then we can no longer understand anything. In the higher symmetrics, such as SU_4, SU_6, SU_{12}, $SU_2 \times SU_2$ and so on, we are very probably dealing with dynamic symmetries, which can be of use in the phenomenology; but their heuristic value could be compared, in my view, with that of the cycles and epicycles in Ptolemaic astronomy. They permit only very indirect back-inferences to the structure of the underlying natural law.

29   Finally, a word more about the most important experimental findings of recent years. Bosons of relatively high mass, in the region of 3–4 GeV, and of long lifetime, have lately been discovered. Such states are basically quite to be expected, as Dürr in particular has emphasized. Whether, owing to the peculiarity of their long lifetime, they can be regarded to some degree as composed of other already known long-lived particles, is, of course, a difficult dynamical question, in which the whole complexity of many-particle physics becomes operative. To me, however, it would appear a quite needless speculation, to attempt the introduction of further new particles *ad hoc*, of which the objects in question are to consist. For this would again be that misstatement of the question, which makes no contribution to the understanding of the spectrum.

30   Again, in the storage-rings at Geneva, and in the Batavia machine, the total action cross-sections for proton–proton collisions at very high energies have been measured. It has turned out that the cross-sections increase as the square of the logarithm of the energy, an effect already long ago surmised, in theory, for the asymptotic region. These results, which have also been found, meanwhile, in the collision of other particles, make it probable, therefore, that in the big accelerators the asymptotic region has already been reached, and hence that there, too, we no longer have any surprises to expect.

31   Quite generally, in new experiments, we should not hope for a *deus ex machina* that will suddenly make the spectrum of particles intelligible. For the experiments of the last fifty years already give a qualitatively quite satisfying, noncontradictory, and closed answer to the question "What is an elementary particle?" Much as in quantum chemistry, the quantitative details can be clarified, not suddenly, but only by much physical and mathematical precision-work over the years.

32   Hence I can conclude with an optimistic look ahead to developments in particle physics which seem to me to give promise of success. New experimental findings are always valuable, of course, even when at first they merely enlarge the tabulated record; but they are especially interesting when they answer critical questions of theory. In theory, we shall have to endeavor, without any semi-philosophical preconceptions, to make precise assumptions concerning the underlying dynamics of matter. This must be taken with complete seriousness, and we should not, therefore, be content with vague hypotheses, in which most things are left obscure. For the particle spectrum can be understood only if we know the underlying dynamics of matter; it is the dynamics that count. All else would be merely a sort of word-painting based on the tabulated record, and in that case the record itself would doubtless be more informative than the word-painting.

NOTES AND DISCUSSION

"What Is an Elementary Particle?" is a model of clear writing; Heisenberg is firmly in control of his material from the start. Notice how the first paragraph embodies the elements of the classic opening paragraph by clearly and succinctly identifying and labelling the aims and various sections of the piece. The first section of the essay deals with "the experimental facts" and is marked by a very careful chronological development, ending with the statements, "The difference between elementary and composite particles has thus basically disappeared. And that is no doubt the most important experimental finding of the last fifty years." The second section, as promised, elaborates some of the complications and implications—for both classical and quantum physics—that arise from that finding. The third section specifically addresses "the philosophy by which the physics of elementary particles is consciously or unconsciously guided."

At a pivotal point in the essay, Heisenberg acknowledges that "we cannot . . . avoid employing a language that stems from . . . traditional philosophy," which permits and even encourages "an intuitive description of small-scale chemical processes." However, traditional language and philosophy only define, and allow for, a way of thinking that is fundamentally wrong-headed when applied to quantum physics. The very questions that they promote "are wrongly put, since the words *divide* or *consist of* have largely lost their meaning." Science, for Heisenberg, is in some significant ways bounded and defined by language and its limits of expression. One of the essay's more arresting claims is that, for true scientific advances to be possible, "bad philosophy," ungrounded biases, and inadequate language must be overcome: an inadequate philosophy will condemn us to inadequate science.

Heisenberg claims, in part, that our language and therefore our ways of thinking have not really caught up to the experimental findings of particle physics. The essay concludes in this way: "For the particle spectrum can be understood only if we know the underlying dynamics of matter; it is the dynamics that count. All else would be merely a sort of word-painting based on the tabulated record, and in that case the record itself would doubtless be more informative than the word-painting." Heisenberg has thus identified a thorny problem: our language and our philosophy dictate the ways we think; the ways we think dictate our science; and our science has shown clearly that our language and philosophy are no longer adequate to describe where science is leading.

STUDY QUESTIONS

For Discussion:

1. Heisenberg claims at the beginning of the essay that he will end on a "positive note," yet he seems to have described a logical circle. Do you see any obvious ways out of the difficulties that Heisenberg suggests we have fallen into?

2. In the course of his discussion, Heisenberg uses some very specific, very technical language and information, from both philosophy and physics. What conclusions can you draw about Heisenberg's assumed audience?

For Writing:

1. One of the implications of Heisenberg's theories is that the borders between philosophy and physics, between the humanities and the sciences, have broken down. In a short essay compare and contrast the notions of science presented in this essay with those presented in this collection by one of the following writers: O. B. Hardison, Jay Ingram, Thomas Kuhn, or Cynthia Ozick.

2. Write a short essay, using definition as the principal rhetorical mode, to discuss Heisenberg's suggestion that "today in the physics of elementary particles, good physics is unconsciously being spoiled by bad philosophy." Be sure to offer definitions of both physics and philosophy.

A PERSON PAPER ON PURITY IN LANGUAGE

William Satire (alias Douglas R. Hofstadter)

BIOGRAPHICAL NOTE

Douglas Hofstadter won the 1979 Pulitzer Prize for his book *Gödel, Escher, Bach: An Eternal Golden Braid*. From January 1981 to June 1983 he wrote the monthly "Metamagical Themas" column for *Scientific American*. Since the mid-1980s he has occupied the Walgreen Chair in the College of Literature, Science, and Arts at the University of Michigan in Ann Arbor, continuing his research in the field of Artificial Intelligence.

1   It's high time someone blew the whistle on all the silly prattle about revamping our language to suit the purposes of certain political fanatics. You know what I'm talking about—those who accuse speakers of English of what they call "racism." This awkward neologism, constructed by analogy with the well-established term "sexism," does not sit well in the ears, if I may mix my metaphors. But let us grant that in our society there may be injustices here and there in the treatment of either race from time to time, and let us even grant these people their terms "racism" and "racist." How valid, however, are the claims of the self-proclaimed "black libbers," or "negrists"—those who would radically change our language in order to "liberate" us poor dupes from its supposed racist bias?

2   Most of the clamor, as you certainly know by now, revolves around the age-old usage of the noun "white" and words built from it, such as *chairwhite, mailwhite, repairwhite, clergywhite, middlewhite, Frenchwhite, forewhite, whitepower, whiteslaughter, oneupswhiteship, straw white, whitehandle,* and so on. The negrists claim that using the word "white," either

on its own or as a component, to talk about *all* members of the human species is somehow degrading to blacks and reinforces racism. Therefore the libbers propose that we substitute "person" everywhere "white" now occurs. Sensitive speakers of our secretary tongue of course find this preposterous. There is great beauty to a phrase such as "All whites are created equal." Our forebosses who framed the Declaration of Independence well understood the poetry of our language. Think how ugly it would be to say "All persons are created equal," or "All whites and blacks are created equal." Besides, as any schoolwhitey can tell you, such phrases are redundant. In most contexts, it is self-evident when "white" is being used in an inclusive sense, in which case it subsumes members of the darker race just as much as fairskins.

3   There is nothing denigrating to black people in being subsumed under the rubric "white"—no more than under the rubric "person." After all, white is a mixture of all the colors of the rainbow, including black. Used inclusively, the word "white" has no connotations whatsoever of race. Yet many people are hung up on this point. A prime example is Abraham Moses, one of the more vocal spokeswhites for making such a shift. For years, Niss Moses, authoroon of the well-known negrist tracts *A Handbook of Nonracist Writing* and *Words and Blacks*, has had nothing better to do than go around the country making speeches advocating the downfall of "racist language" that ble objects to. But when you analyze bler objections, you find they all fall apart at the seams. Niss Moses says that words like "chairwhite" suggest to people—most especially impressionable young whiteys and blackeys—that all chairwhites belong to the white race. How absurd! It is quite obvious, for instance, that the chairwhite of the League of Black Voters is going to be a black, not a white. Nobody need think twice about it. As a matter of fact, the suffix "white" is usually not pronounced with a long "i" as in the noun "white," but like "wit," as in the terms *saleswhite, freshwhite, penwhiteship, first basewhite*, and so on. It's just a simple and useful component in building race-neutral words.

4   But Niss Moses would have you sit up and start hollering "Racism!" In fact, Niss Moses sees evidence of racism under every stone. Ble has written a famous article, in which ble vehemently objects to the immortal and poetic words of the first white on the moon, Captain Nellie Strongarm. If you will recall, whis words were: "One small step for a white, a giant step for whitekind." This noble sentiment is anything but racist; it is simply a celebration of a glorious moment in the history of White.

5   Another of Niss Moses' shrill objections is to the age-old differentiation of whites from blacks by the third-person pronouns "whe" and "ble." Ble promotes an absurd notion: that what we really need in English is a single pronoun covering *both* races. Numerous suggestions have been made, such as "pe," "tey," and others. These are all repugnant to the nature of the English language, as the average white in the street will testify, even if whe has no linguistic training whatsoever. Then there are advocates of usages such as "whe or ble," "whis or bler," and so forth. This makes for monstrosities such as the sentence "When the next President takes office, whe or ble will have to choose whis or bler cabinet with great care, for whe or ble would not want to offend any minorities." Contrast this with the spare elegance of the normal way of putting it, and there is no question which way we ought to speak. There are, of course, some yapping black libbers who advocate writing "bl/whe" everywhere, which, aside from looking terrible, has no reasonable pronunciation. Shall we say "blooey" all the time when we simply mean "whe"? Who wants to sound like a white with a chronic sneeze?

* * *

6   One of the more hilarious suggestions made by the squawkers for this point of view is to abandon the natural distinction along racial lines, and to replace it with a highly unnatural one along sexual lines. One such suggestion—emanating, no doubt, from the mind of a madwhite— would have us say "he" for male whites (and blacks) and "she" for female whites (and blacks). Can you imagine the outrage with which sensible folk of either sex would greet this "modest proposal"?

7   Another suggestion is that the plural pronoun "they" be used in place of the inclusive "whe." This would turn the charming proverb "Whe who laughs last, laughs best" into the bizarre concoction "They who laughs last, laughs best." As if anyone in whis right mind could have thought that the original proverb applied only to the white race! No, we don't need a new pronoun to "liberate" our minds. That's the lazy white's way of solving the pseudoproblem of racism. In any case, it's ungrammatical. The pronoun "they" is a plural pronoun, and it grates on the civilized ear to hear it used to denote only one person. Such a usage, if adopted, would merely promote illiteracy and accelerate the already scandalously rapid nosedive of the average intelligence level in our society.

8   Niss Moses would have us totally revamp the English language to suit bler purposes. If, for instance, we are to substitute "person" for "white," where are we to stop? If we were to follow Niss Moses' ideas to their logical conclusion, we would have to conclude that ble would like to see small blackeys and whiteys playing the game of "Hangperson" and reading the story of "Snow Person and the Seven Dwarfs." And would ble have us rewrite history to say, "Don't shoot until you see the *persons* of their eyes!"? Will pundits and politicians henceforth issue *person* papers? Will we now have egg yolks and egg *persons*? And pledge allegiance to the good old Red, *Person*, and Blue? Will we sing, "I'm dreaming of a *person* Christmas"? Say of a frightened white, "Whe's *person* as a sheet!"? Lament the increase of *person*-collar crime? Thrill to the chirping of bob*persons* in our gardens? Ask a friend to *person* the table while we go visit the *persons'* room? Come off it, Niss Moses—don't personwash our language!

9   What conceivable harm is there is such beloved phrases as "No white is an island," "Dog is white's best friend," or "White's inhumanity to white"? Who would revise such classic book titles as Bronob Jacowski's *The Ascent of White* or Eric Steeple Bell's *Whites of Mathematics*? Did the poet who wrote "The best-laid plans of mice and whites gang aft agley" believe that blacks' plans gang *ne'er* agley? Surely not! Such phrases are simply metaphors; everyone can see beyond that. Whe who interprets them as reinforcing racism must have a perverse desire to feel oppressed.

10   "Personhandling" the language is a habit that not only Niss Moses but quite a few others have taken up recently. For instance, Nrs. Delilah Buford has urged that we drop the useful distinction between "Niss" and "Nrs." (which, as everybody knows, is pronounced "Nissiz," the reason for which nobody knows!). Bler argument is that there is no need for the public to know whether a black is employed or not. *Need* is, of course, not the point. Ble conveniently sidesteps the fact that there is a *tradition* in our society of calling unemployed blacks "Niss" and employed blacks "Nrs." Most blacks—in fact, the vast majority—prefer it that way. They *want* the world to know what their employment status is, and for good reason. Unemployed blacks want prospective employers to know they are available, without

having to ask embarrassing questions. Likewise, employed blacks are proud of having found a job, and wish to let the world know they are employed. This distinction provides a sense of security to all involved, in that everyone knows where ble fits into the scheme of things.

11   But Nrs. Buford refuses to recognize this simple truth. Instead, ble shiftily turns the argument into one about whites, asking why it is that whites are universally addressed as "Master," without any differentiation between employed and unemployed ones. The answer, of course, is that in Anerica and other Northern societies, we set little store by the employment status of whites. Nrs. Buford can do little to change that reality, for it seems to be tied to innate biological differences between whites and blacks. Many white-years of research, in fact, have gone into trying to understand why it is that employment status matters so much to blacks, yet relatively little to whites. It is true that both races have a longer life expectancy if employed, but of course people often do not act so as to maximize their life expectancy. So far, it remains a mystery. In any case, whites and blacks clearly have different constitutional inclinations, and different goals in life. And so I say, *Vive na différence!*

* * *

12   As for Nrs. Buford's suggestion that both "Niss" and "Nrs." be unified into the single form of address "Ns." (supposed to rhyme with "fizz"), all I have to say is, it is arbitrary and clearly a thousand years ahead of its time. Mind you, this "Ns." is an abbreviation concocted out of thin air: it stands for absolutely nothing. Who ever heard of such toying with language? And while we're on this subject, have you yet run across the recently founded *Ns.* magazine, dedicated to the concerns of the "liberated black"? It's sure to attract the attention of a trendy band of black airheads for a little while, but serious blacks surely will see through its thin veneer of slick, glossy Madison Avenue approaches to life.

13   Nrs. Buford also finds it insultingly asymmetric that when a black is employed by a white, ble changes bler firmly name to whis firmly name. But what's so bad about that? Every firm's core consists of a boss (whis job is to make sure long-term policies are well charted out) and a secretary (bler job is to keep corporate affairs running smoothly on a day-to-day basis). They are both equally important and vital to the firm's success. No one disputes this. Beyond them there may of course be other firmly members. Now it's quite obvious that all members of a given firm should bear the same firmly name—otherwise, what are you going to call the firm's products? And since it would be nonsense for the boss to change whis name, it falls to the secretary to change bler name. Logic, not racism, dictates this simple convention.

14   What puzzles me the most is when people cut off their noses to spite their faces. Such is the case with the time-honored colored suffixes "oon" and "roon," found in familiar words such as *ambassadroon*, *stewardoon*, and *sculptroon*. Most blacks find it natural and sensible to add those suffixes onto nouns such as "aviator" or "waiter." A black who flies an airplane may proudly proclaim, "I'm an aviatroon!" But it would sound silly, if not ridiculous, for a black to say of blerself, "I work as a waiter." On the other hand, who could object to my saying that the lively Ticely Cyson is a great actroon, or that the hilarious Quill Bosby is a great comedioon? You guessed it—authoroons such as Niss Mildred Hempsley and Nrs. Charles White, both of whom angrily reject the appellation "authoroon," deep though its roots are in our language. Nrs. White, perhaps one of the finest poetoons of our day, for some reason insists on being know as a "poet." It leads one to wonder, is Nrs.

White *ashamed* of being black, perhaps? I should hope not. White needs Black, and Black needs White, and neither race should feel ashamed.

15   Some extreme negrists object to being treated with politeness and courtesy by whites. For example, they reject the traditional notion of "Negroes first," preferring to open doors for themselves, claiming that having doors opened for them suggests implicitly that society considers them inferior. Well, would they have it the other way? Would these incorrigible grousers prefer to open doors for whites? What do blacks want?

*   *   *

16   Another unlikely word has recently become a subject of controversy: "blackey." This is, of course, the ordinary term for black children (including teen-agers), and by affectionate extension it is often applied to older blacks. Yet, incredible though it seems, many blacks—even teen-age blackeys—now claim to have had their "consciousness raised," and are voguishly skittish about being called "blackeys." Yet it's as old as the hills for blacks employed in the same office to refer to themselves as "the office blackeys." And for their superior to call them "my blackeys" helps make the ambiance more relaxed and comfy for all. It's hardly the mortal insult that libbers claim it to be. Fortunately, most blacks are sensible people and realize that mere words do not demean; they know it's how they are *used* that counts. Most of the time, calling a black—especially an older black—a "blackey" is a thoughtful way of complimenting bler, making bler feel young, fresh, and hirable again. Lord knows, I certainly wouldn't object if someone told me that I looked whiteyish these days!

17   Many young blackeys go through a stage of wishing they had been born white. Perhaps this is due to popular television shows like *Superwhite* and *Batwhite*, but it doesn't really matter. It is perfectly normal and healthy. Many of our most successful blacks were once tomwhiteys and feel no shame about it. Why should they? Frankly, I think tomwhiteys are often the cutest little blackeys—but that's just my opinion. In any case, Niss Moses (once again) raises a ruckus on this score, asking why we don't have a corresponding word for young whiteys who play blackeys' games and generally manifest a desire to be black. Well, Niss Moses, if this were a common phenomenon, we most assuredly *would* have such a word, but it just happens not to be. Who can say why? But given that tomwhiteys are a dime a dozen, it's nice to have a word for them. The lesson is that White must learn to fit language to reality; White cannot manipulate the world by manipulating mere words. An elementary lesson, to be sure, but for some reason Niss Moses and others of bler ilk resist learning it.

18   Shifting from the ridiculous to the sublime, let us consider the Holy Bible. The Good Book is of course the source of some of the most beautiful language and profound imagery to be found anywhere. And who is the central character of the Bible? I am sure I need hardly remind you; it is God. As everyone knows, Whe is male and white, and that is an indisputable fact. But have you heard the latest joke promulgated by tasteless negrists? It is said that one of them died and went to Heaven and then returned. What did ble report? "I have seen God, and guess what? Ble's female!" Can anyone say that this is not blasphemy of the highest order? It just goes to show that some people will stoop to any depths in order to shock. I have shared this "joke" with a number of friends of mine (including several blacks, by the way), and, to a white, they have agreed that it sickens them to the core to see Our Lord so shabbily mocked. Some things are just in bad taste, and there are no two ways about it. It is scum like this who are responsible for some of the great problems in our society today, I am sorry to say.

* * *

19   Well, all of this is just another skirmish in the age-old Battle of the Races, I guess, and we shouldn't take it too seriously. I am reminded of words spoken by the great British philosopher Alfred West Malehead in whis commencement address to my *alma secretaria*, the University of North Virginia: "To enrich the language of whites is, certainly, to enlarge the range of their ideas." I agree with this admirable sentiment wholeheartedly. I would merely point out to the overzealous that there are some extravagant notions about language that should be recognized for what they are: cheap attempts to let dogmatic, narrow minds enforce their views on the speakers lucky enough to have inherited the richest, most beautiful and flexible language on earth, a language whose traditions run back through the centuries to such deathless poets as Milton, Shakespeare, Wordsworth, Keats, Walt Whitwhite, and so many others . . . Our language owes an incalculable debt to these whites for their clarity of vision and expression, and if the shallow minds of bandwagon-jumping negrists succeed in destroying this precious heritage for all whites of good will, that will be, without any doubt, a truly female day in the history of Northern White.

Post Scriptum.

20   Perhaps this piece shocks you. It is meant to. The entire point of it is to use something that we find shocking as leverage to illustrate the fact that something that we usually close our eyes to is also very shocking. The most effective way I know to do so is to develop an extended analogy with something known as shocking and reprehensible. Racism is that thing, in this case. I am happy with this piece, despite—but also because of—its shock value. I think it makes its point better than any factual article could. As a friend of mine said, "It makes you so uncomfortable that you can't ignore it." I admit that rereading it makes even me, the author, uncomfortable!

21   Numerous friends have warned me that in publishing this piece I am taking a serious risk of earning myself a reputation as a terrible racist. I guess I cannot truly believe that anyone would see this piece that way. To misperceive it this way would be like calling someone a vicious racist for telling other people "The word 'nigger' is extremely offensive." If *allusions* to racism, especially for the purpose of satirizing racism and its cousins, are confused with racism itself, then I think it is time to stop writing.

22   Some people have asked me if to write this piece, I simply took a genuine William Safire column (appearing weekly in the *New York Times Magazine* under the title "On Language") and "fiddled" with it. That is far from the truth. For years I have collected examples of sexist language, and in order to produce this piece, I dipped into this collection, selected some of the choicest, and ordered them very carefully. "Translating" them into this alternate world was sometimes extremely difficult, and some words took weeks. The hardest terms of all, surprisingly enough, were "Niss," "Nrs.," and "Ns.," even though "Master" came immediately. The piece itself is not based on any particular article by William Safire, but Safire has without doubt been one of the most vocal opponents of nonsexist language reforms, and therefore merits being safired upon.

23   Interestingly, Master Safire has recently spoken out on sexism in whis column (August 5, 1984). Lamenting the inaccuracy of writing either "Mrs. Ferraro" or "Miss Ferraro" to designate the Democratic vice-presidential candidate whose husband's name is "Zaccaro," whe writes:

> It breaks my heart to suggest this, but the time has come for *Ms.* We are no longer faced with a theory, but a condition. It is unacceptable for journalists to dictate to a candidate that she call herself *Miss* or else use her married name; it is equally unacceptable for a candidate to demand that newspapers print a blatant inaccuracy by applying a married honorific to a maiden name.

24   How disappointing it is when someone finally winds up doing the right thing but for the wrong reasons! In Safire's case, this shift was entirely for journalistic rather than humanistic reasons! It's as if Safire wished that women had never entered the political ring, so that the Grand Old Conventions of English—good enough for our grandfathers—would never have had to be challenged. How heartless of women! How heartbreaking the toll on our beautiful language!

* * *

25   A couple of weeks after I finished this piece, I ran into the book *The Nonsexist Communicator*, by Bobbye Sorrels. In it, there is a satire called "A Tale of Two Sexes," which is very interesting to compare with my "Person Paper." Whereas in mine, I slice the world orthogonally to the way it is actually sliced and then perform a mapping of worlds to establish a disorienting yet powerful new vision of our world, in hers, Ms. Sorrels simply reverses the two halves of our world as it is actually sliced. Her satire is therefore in some ways very much like mine, and in other ways extremely different. It should be read.

26   I do not know too many publications that discuss sexist language in depth. The finest I have come across are the aforementioned *Handbook of Nonsexist Writing*, by Casey Miller and Kate Swift; *Words and Women*, by the same authors; *Sexist Language: A Modern Philosophical Analysis*, edited by Mary Vetterling-Braggin; *The Nonsexist Communicator*, by Bobbye Sorrels; and a very good journal titled *Women and Language News* . . . .

27   My feeling about nonsexist English is that it is like a foreign language that I am learning. I find that even after years of practice, I still have to translate sometimes from my native language, which is sexist English. I know of no human being who speaks Nonsexist as their native tongue. It will be very interesting to see if such people come to exist. If so, it will have taken a lot of work by a lot of people to reach that point.

28   One final footnote: My book *Gödel, Escher, Bach*, whose dialogues were the source of my very first trepidations about my own sexism, is now being translated into various languages, and to my delight, the Tortoise, a green-blooded male if ever there was one in English, is becoming *Madame Tortue* in French, *Signorina Tartaruga* in Italian, and so on. Full circle ahead!

NOTES AND DISCUSSION

In "A Person Paper on Purity in Language," Douglas Hofstadter develops an elaborate analogy to satirize resistance to the emerging practice of writing in a non-sexist or gender-neutral language. By arguing indirectly through an analogy that is calculated to shock, he is able to make the defensiveness and flawed reasoning of his theoretical opponents appear absurd, even dangerous.

Hofstadter creates passages that use "race" in deliberately offensive ways, then pretends to be insensitive to the passages. His purpose is to highlight the offensiveness and insensitivity of his real focus—thoughtless, exclusive use of gender in language.

As well as replacing "man" with "white," Hofstadter replaces standard "gendered" personal pronouns, without explanation or advance warning. In effect, he establishes an internal linguistic convention for his paper to demonstrate that such conventions are open to change, and that certain words are only apparently "necessary." One element that may be lost in Hofstadter's engaging discussion of sexism in language is the very real question of racism in language. Hofstadter seems to assume that his audience is not racist. You might want to compare this essay with Goodman's in this anthology. Goodman argues that, while race is a myth, racism is very real.

STUDY QUESTIONS

For Discussion:

1. Imagine the audience's reaction if Hofstadter had titled his essay "A Feminist Paper on Gendering in Language," and had argued the issue head on. What are the advantages and disadvantages of his more indirect title and approach?

2. Does Hofstadter's essay focus your attention more on racism or on sexism?

For Writing:

1. Find, either elsewhere in this collection or in a journal or textbook in your field of studies, an article or a passage that does not try to eliminate sexist terminology or gender-specific language, and rewrite it in a more neutral style. To get a sense of the range and types of substitutions Hofstadter uses, and the mental adjustments you yourself have been making in reading his essay, you might want to set up an equivalency chart, matching Hofstadter's words with the ones we would ordinarily use or expect: for example, chairwhite/chairman; Niss/Miss; authoroon/author.

2. Hofstadter's essay exposes one of the ways we try to "blame the victims" of discriminatory practices, rather than the practices themselves, in order to preserve comfortable but potentially damaging attitudes, conventions, or precedents. Think of another field where this happens, and try to devise a short satirical analogy in the spirit of Hofstadter's piece.

WOMEN IN CHEMISTRY BEFORE 1900

Sherida Houlihan and John H. Wotiz

BIOGRAPHICAL NOTE

Sherida Houlihan and John H. Wotiz presented the original version of this essay in 1973 to the 166th American Chemical Society National Meeting in Chicago, while they were colleagues at Southern Illinois University in Carbondale, IL. A revised version of the essay appeared in the *Journal of Chemical Education* in June 1975.

---

1   Historians have accorded women a very small part in chemistry throughout the ages. However, the earliest recorded "chemists" were women. They were the Perfumeresses Tapputi-Belatekallim and ( )ninu. These names were found on cuneiform tablets of ancient Mesopotamia dating to about 2,000 BC. The second name is not completely known because of blanks on the tablet. The name Belatekallim means that Tapputi was a mistress of a household[1] and in charge of the manufacture of perfume. ( )ninu is the author of an ancient text on perfumery.[2]

2   A typical list of tools for perfumery included a metal pot (*diaqaru*) and a lid, a measuring cup (*kasu*), a sieve (*girbal*), a ladle (*migrafa*), a large wooden bowl (*qas'a*), and an oven (*tannur*). All of these things could be found in an ancient kitchen. Instructions for carrying out the operations in perfumery were very similar to cooking instructions.[3]

3   Some origins of chemistry came from the mystic art of alchemy. One of the most prolific writers of the alchemical period was Zosimos of Panopolis, who lived ~300 AD. Some alchemist writings mentioned four women, Theosebia his sister, Mary the Jewess, Cleopatra, and Paphnutia the Virgin.

Reprinted with permission from the *Journal of Chemical Education*, vol. 52, no. 6, June 1975, pp. 362–64; copyright © 1975, Division of Chemical Education, Inc.

4   A great deal of controversy occurred between historians over the actual existence of Cleopatra and Mary the Jewess. Some writers maintain that the Cleopatra prominent in alchemy is not the Egyptian queen, but others state there is no proof that she was not. Cleopatra is credited with the invention of the alembic or still, which was an important laboratory equipment of the early alchemists.[4]

5   Two of the early alchemical writings "Dialogue of Cleopatra and the Philosophers" and "The Gold-Making of Cleopatra" are also ascribed to Cleopatra. The latter is particularly important because it is one of the earliest known examples of the use of symbols for gold, silver, mercury, possibly lead–copper alloy, and arsenic in chemical writings. Drawings are also included that illustrate her theme of the unity of all things, death, and revivification through a "water." A drawing of a distillation apparatus is also shown.[5] Some accounts mention Cleopatra's study of the solvent action of vinegar on pearls.

6   Mary the Jewess was identified by several names: "The Jewess," "Maria Prophetissa," Miriam the sister to Moses and Aaron, and Maria the Jewess. Some historians question the fact that she actually existed.[6] Mary is credited with some alchemical writings and the invention of the *kerotakis* and the *Balneum Mariae* (the prototype of an autoclave), and a water bath, which the French still call the *bainmarie*. The *kerotakis* was used for sublimation and as a still.[7] She also discovered a material, Mary's Black, which had the required black hue needed in the alchemical production of "gold." It was purified by fusing a lead–copper alloy with sulfur.

7   In the following thousand years women had very little direct influence on the evolution of chemistry. In 1666 Marie Meurdrac wrote *La Chymie charitable et facile en faveur des dames* which is probably the first chemistry book written by a woman.[8] She considered chemistry to deal with objects that are a mixture of the three "basic principles" (salt, sulfur, and mercury), which can be separated by two general operations, "solution and congelation." The book is divided into six parts that deal with Laboratory operations and weights, Separations, Animals, Metals, Preparation of medicinals, and Preserving and increasing the beauty of "Ladies." In her foreword Marie Meurdrac expressed the opinion that she was the first woman that wrote a chemistry treatise.

8   In 1758 Marie Anne Pierrette Paulze was born in France, the daughter of Jacques Paulze, a member of the *Ferme-Génerale*. The *Ferme* was a tax collecting enterprise where private citizens collected taxes on a profit-sharing basis with the King. One of Jacques Paulze's colleagues in the *Ferme* was Antoine Lavoisier. In 1771 Jacques arranged a marriage between the pair even though Marie was only 14 and Lavoisier was twice her age. The large age difference seemed to make no difference and the couple was quite happy.

9   Madame Lavoisier gave her husband a great deal of assistance in his scientific work. She translated the work of many contemporary British chemists into French, e.g., Kirwan's "Essay on Phlogiston" and "Strength of Acids and the Proportion of Ingredients in Neutral Salts."[9] This translation also showed that Marie had enough knowledge of chemical theory and practice to comment intelligently and constructively on the work through footnotes of the translator.

10   Some of Marie's best known accomplishments were the thirteen illustrations for her husband's book, *Traité de Chimie*, Paris, 1789. The original sketches and plates still exist and show her painstaking work. There are at least four different versions of each plate which vary in details of her corrections. She also published Antoine Lavoisier's *Mémoires de Chimie* after her husband was executed by the French revolutionists in 1794. He left behind the whole sec-

ond, a large part of the first, and fragments of the fourth volume of a projected collection of eight volumes. He was correcting the proofs while he was in prison. Marie asked his former collaborator Seguin to assist her and write a preface. Since they quarreled, she wrote her own introduction and published the memoirs in 1805. The *Mémoires* were never put on sale but Madame Lavoisier gave copies to the most distinguished scientist of the day.[10]

11   After Antoine's death, she had many suitors. In 1801 or 1802 she met Count Rumford, founder of the Royal Institution. Rumford was forty-eight and she was forty-three. They seemed well suited for each other. They were both interested in science and liked to travel.[11] The wedding took place in Paris in 1805. Marie insisted on retaining her first husband's name and was known as Madame Lavoisier de Rumford. Unfortunately their marital bliss soon turned to despair. The problem occurred because Rumford expected the marriage to give him financial security and that Marie would follow his every wish. However, Marie was used to living her own life and had no intention of giving up her independence.

12   During the late eighteenth and the first half of the nineteenth century, Jane Marcet became one of the most important women in the history of early chemistry. Her *Conversations on Chemistry* was used as a textbook in Great Britain and the United States for 30 years. She was born Jane Haldiman in London in 1769 to Swiss parents. In 1799 Jane married Alexander Marcet, a distinguished Swiss physician and chemist who worked on several ideas with Berzelius. Upon Jane's father's death she inherited a large fortune. Dr. Marcet resigned his post at Guy's Hospital in London, gave up medicine entirely, and devoted all his time to experimental chemistry. He encouraged his wife's interest in science and made a great deal of information available to her through his numerous acquaintances and his broad knowledge of chemistry. This appears to be the only schooling Jane received in the scientific field.[12]

13   *Conversations on Chemistry* was first published anonymously in 1805. The public would not have reacted favorably to a book on science written by a woman. The format of the book was an informal dialogue between Mrs. Bryan, the teacher, and Emily and Caroline, the pupils. Mrs. Bryan described the discoveries of Galvani, Volta, Franklin, Count Rumford, Priestley, Oersted, Berzelius, Berthollet, Cavendish, Lavoisier, Davy, and other important men in the field. In the preface to this book she stated, "In venturing to offer the public . . . an introduction to chemistry, the author . . . a woman, conceives that some explanation may be required; and she feels it the more necessary to apologize for the present undertaking as her knowledge of the subject is but recent, and as she can have no real claims to the title of chemist."[13] The readers believed a man had to be the author of the work even after reading the preface. The book was illustrated with woodcuts of laboratory apparatus.

14   Mrs. Marcet's book was left at the bookbindery where Michael Faraday was an apprentice. Faraday credited Mrs. Marcet with being a primary reason for beginning his study of chemistry. Later, Faraday always sent Mrs. Marcet copies of his publications.[14]

15   One of Jane Marcet's most important contributions was her method of teaching chemistry to beginners through experimental demonstrations, a practice that was not yet accepted as a teaching method. Mrs. Marcet revised and corrected the later editions of her work as new discoveries and applications were made, e.g., gaslight, the miner's lamp, electro-magnetism, and the doctrine of Definite Proportions.[15] When Jane Marcet died in London in 1858 at the age of 89, all of the world of science, and especially the field of chemistry, owed her a huge debt of gratitude. *Conversations of Chemistry* went through sixteen editions.

16   Jacob Berzelius appreciated the potential contribution of women to chemistry. He was very impressed with Madame Lavoisier when he visited her Paris salon in 1819. The Marcets

and Berzelius were good friends and Berzelius was their constant visitor in London in 1812. Dr. Marcet helped Berzelius achieve recognition in the French–English scientific circles.

17   In 1819 while he was abroad, Berzelius was elected secretary of the Swedish Academy of Science and was given an apartment and laboratory in the house of the Academy. Berzelius then needed to establish his household, and to deal with that problem he wrote to one of his friends[16]:

> I have thought a great deal about how to organize my household, particularly with respect to service and I have decided to employ a maid rather than a man servant, who would be more expensive and of little use. Anna, who is now employed at the Callins, has waited on me for almost ten years. She is the best maid I know of; she is careful, honest, prompt, and ugly, all qualities which a bachelor's maid should have, and I know that she has often been on the verge of leaving the Callin family. Talk to her on my behalf and ask her if she would like to continue to take care of my person and my reagents, and if she accepts the offer, then grant her whatever she wants in wages and board. Should she be difficult try to persuade her, for being an untidy person, I need someone I can rely on; furthermore she is already familiar with all my pieces of equipment and their names that I almost believe she could be started off right away distilling hydrochloric acid.

18   Anna Christina Persdotter Sundstrom moved his apparatus and laboratory equipment from his old residence before Berzelius returned from his travels. She was born in 1795 and died in 1871 and dedicated sixteen years of her life to the care of Berzelius' household and the cleaning of his laboratory. Anna played an important role in Berzelius' laboratory and made a strong impression on his coworkers. Friends of Berzelius often remembered Anna in their letter with "kind regards and greetings." She was a very independent individual as seen in a letter from Berzelius to Wöhler, "Anna sends many regards and says that Moses (Mosander) is a pig, and that of all the gentlemen who have been in the laboratory, none is as neat as Dr. Wöhler and none as amiable as Henrik Rose." Wöhler seems to have known Anna very well for he replies, "That '*die gute und gestrenge Anna*' prefers to wash chemical glassware instead of plates and drinking glasses and would rather prepare hydrogen sulfide than food, is evidence of her scientific turn of mind. Please convey warmest greetings to her from one of her former pupils."[17]

19   For a long time Berzelius held the view that chlorine was oxidized muriatic acid. This belief prompted a quotation which has become famous. In 1823, Anna remarked that the retort she was cleaning gave off a bad odor of 'oxymuriatic acid.' Berzelius replied, "Listen, Anna, you should not say 'oxymuriatic acid' any more, you should say 'chlorine' instead. It is better."[18]

20   In 1835 Berzelius married and his wife pressured him to dismiss Anna. Quite probably his bride was jealous of the respect and mutual admiration Anna and Berzelius had for each other, and felt their relationship threatened her importance. To keep the peace, Berzelius reluctantly let Anna go to find a new position.

21   There are reports of two other women chemists at the turn of the eighteenth century. However there is very little known about Elizabeth Fulhame except that she was the wife of a doctor and an early convert to Lavoisier's theory on combustion.[19] In London in 1794 she published "Essay on Combustion." This publication generated a great deal of interest. Priestley mentioned her book and experiments. Mrs. Fulhame performed some of the experiments for him in London. She also carried out experiments on the reduction of gold salts by light which were repeated by Count Rumford. Mrs. Fulhame says: "I shall en-

deavour to show that the hydrogen of water is the only substance that restores oxygenated bodies to their combustible state, and that water is the only source of the oxygen, which oxygenates combustible bodies." She was elected an honorary member of the Philadelphia Chemical Society after the book was reprinted there is 1810.[20]

22   Mary Sommervile (1780-1872) was interested in Faraday's work and they corresponded during 1833-34.[21] She was the author of *Connexion of the Physical Sciences* which was printed in at least three editions. She revised her third edition to announce that "Dr. Faraday has proved, by recent experiments, . . . that chemical affinity is merely a result of the electrical state of the particles of the matter."

23   In the United States Benjamin Rush set up a chemistry course for girls. In 1787 he was one of the organizers of the Young Ladies Academy in Philadelphia. His idea of education for girls was very straightforward; in a pioneer country, girls should learn useful, rather than entertaining subjects.[22] Since chemistry and physics were constantly applied in the management of the home, they should be taught. The Rush-taught course contained seven lectures which brought forth basic chemical doctrines and showed the applications of chemistry to homemaking. He also performed a few experiments to illustrate his lectures. It is not known if the course was taught more than once.

24   It should be obvious that the contributions of Maria Sklodowska Curie (1867-1934) made her the most important woman scientist before 1900. Since her life and work is well known and recorded it is not reviewed here.

25   The first known chemists were two women perfumeresses of ancient Mesopotamia. It seems logical that women would go into a science which is similar to cooking. Jane Marcet is not important today but during the middle of the nineteenth century her book influenced thousands of young chemistry students. Women like Jane Marcet and Marie Lavoisier were encouraged and aided by their husbands in their work, but at the turn of the twentieth century, Pierre Curie was aiding his wife Maria. Since that time women are finding their rightful place in science and society. Thus the prophecy of T. P. Smith in 1798 was realized:[23]* "I shall now present you with the last and most pleasing revolution that has occurred in chemistry. Hitherto we have beheld this science entirely in the hands of *men*; we are now about to behold *women* assert their just, though too long neglected claims, of being participators in the pleasures arising from a knowledge of chemistry."

LITERATURE CITED

1. Edward Farber, *Great Chemists* (New York: Interscience Publishers, 1961), p. 3.

2. Martin Levey, *Chemistry and Chemical Technology in Ancient Mesopotamia* (New York: Elsevier, 1959), p. 142.

3. *Ibid.*, p. 134.

4. John Read, *Prelude to Chemistry* (New York: Macmillan, New York, 1937), p. 15.

5. Frank S. Taylor, *The Alchemists* (New York: H. Schuman, 1949), p. 58.

---

*   Reference 23 contains on p. 41 another interesting quote from *Letters for Literary Ladies* of unknown date: "Chemistry is a science particularly suited to women, suited to their talents and their situation; chemistry is not a science of parade, it affords occupation and infinite variety; . . ."

6. Levey, *op. cit.*, p. 142

7. Taylor, *op. cit.,* p. 39.

8. Lloyd O. Bishop, and Will S. DeLoach, *J. CHEM. EDUC.*, 47, 448 (1970).

9. Dennis I. Duveen, *Chymia* 4, 14 (1953).

10. *Ibid.*

11. *Ibid.*

12. Eva V. Armstrong, *J. CHEM. EDUC.*, 15, 53 (1938).

13. *Ibid.*

14. *Ibid.*

15. *Ibid.*

16. Johan E. Jorpes, *Jac. Berzelius, His Life and Work* (Stockholm: Almquist & Wiksell, 1966), p. 84.

17. *Ibid.*, p. 86.

18. *Ibid.*, p. 105.

19. James R. Partington, *A History of Chemistry* (London: Macmillan, 1971), p. 708.

20. *Ibid.*

21. Trevor H. Levere, *Affinity and Matter* (London: Clarendon Press,1971), p. 111.

22. Farber, *op. cit.*, p. 310.

23. Edgar F. Smith, *Chemistry in America. Chapters from the History of Science in the United States* (New York: D. Appleton and Company, 1914), p. 35.

NOTES AND DISCUSSION

Houlihan and Wotiz's essay surveys of the history women in chemistry before 1900, providing an introduction or overview as a starting point for those who are interested in performing more in-depth research. It is structured chronologically, starting with the earliest known women chemists (2000 BC) and advancing rapidly to 1900. The brevity of the essay suggests (rightly or wrongly) that the history of women in chemistry is slight, though Houlihan and Wotiz don't address the reasons for this lack of female contribution directly. The authors apply the same template to each woman chemist, presenting all the available information for each, thus essentially creating a terse and perfunctory list. It is worth considering whether this result is due to the collaborative writing process. In any case, for each of the women, Houlihan and Wotiz provide information about her historical context, family circumstances, education, contributions to chemical theory, knowledge, or apparatus, and associations with male chemists. Comparisons and contrasts between the women chemists are only implied.

Much of this essay focuses on the domestic side of science, attributing women's supposedly innate cooking and cleaning skills to their role in chemistry, and examining their scientific partnerships or "marriages." Notice the way these women chemists are named, and compare these naming conventions to those for male scientists. Then consider what effect Houlihan and Wotiz achieve, and whether they diminish or elevate these women's right to recognition.

As a research paper, the essay pulls together information from a variety of sources to create something new: a paper that focuses specifically on the role of women in chemistry. Note how Houlihan and Wotiz draw upon a variety of sources—both primary (chemistry texts by women) and secondary (other authors' accounts of women chemists)—to compile their information, and how they report controversy among earlier sources.

STUDY QUESTIONS

For Discussion:

1. Notice how few of the female chemists mentioned in this paper are "famous." One purpose of this essay is to commemorate some of these significant, but forgotten, women scientists. Why is it important to remember them?

2. What do the eighteenth- and nineteenth-century female chemists have in common in terms of education and their role in the development of chemistry?

For Writing:

1. Research and prepare an account of the career of Jane Marcet, Mary Sommervile, or Elizabeth Fulhame.

2. Read Hilary Rose's essay on Curie and Marić. Describe how Rose's observations apply to the women whose careers are sketched out in Houlihan and Wotiz's essay.

MYTH AND

MALEVOLENCE

Michael Ignatieff

BIOGRAPHICAL NOTE

Michael Ignatieff has been a history professor at the University of British Columbia, and a research fellow of King's College, Cambridge. He is now a writer and broadcaster in London, England. His works include *The Russian Album* (1987), a family memoir that won the Governor General's Award for non-fiction, and *Blood and Belonging: Journeys into the New Nationalism* (1993).

1   In the summer of 1992, when Serbian militias were viciously "cleansing" the Muslim villages of southeastern Bosnia, journalists asked the Serbs of Foca and Goradze why people they had lived with for centuries deserved such treatment. The Serbs seemed surprised by the question. Didn't everybody know that Muslims killed Serbian children and floated their crucified bodies down the river Drina? Several old women, doing their washing by the riverbank, swore they had seen them with their own eyes.

2   No one could persuade these old women otherwise. They were in the grip of one of the oldest atrocity myths in Western culture. The Romans accused the early Christians of just this sort of child sacrifice. When the Christians got a state church of their own, they turned the same myth against the Jews. The earliest recorded accusation occurred in the English town of Norwich in 1144, when the Jewish community was accused of killing a Christian child and draining his blood for use in satanic rituals. In all its apparitions, the tortured or crucified child surfaces, like an image in a nightmare, whenever an ethnic or religious majority has to read into its subconscious to justify the persecution of a minority. As the millennium ends,

Muslim Europeans find themselves the target of a myth that, when the millennium began, was a blood libel against the Jews.

3   Myths endure because they offer repertoires of moral justification. Myths turn crime into fate and murder into necessity; they both justify atrocity and perpetuate it. The Balkan wars have been among the most inhuman in an inhuman century. Intrastate wars, the war of village against village, neighbor against neighbor, will usually engender more atrocities than the impersonal wars between states. Small wonder that the three urban communities most thoroughly destroyed by the Balkan conflict—Vukovar, Mostar, and Sarajevo—had the highest rates of ethnic intermarriage.

4   It is as if the very intermingling of the combatants forced these communities into displays of terror and destruction to demarcate the territories and values they were defending. What Serbs once shared with their neighbors had to be defiled, so that sharing would never be possible again. Atrocities draw the innocent bystander into collusion with the guilty perpetrator and engrave the myth of inhuman otherness in the subconscious of both sides.

5   This myth of inhuman otherness does such violence to the facts that it can gain a foothold only if ordinary people on every side can be made to forget that in reality their differences are small. It is nonsense to call the Balkan communities ethnic groups at all. Intermarriage down the centuries has blurred ethnic differences to the vanishing point; religious differences have collapsed in the general secularization of Balkan culture; modernization has converged material aspirations toward the same Mercedes cars and Swiss-style chalets. Nationalism in the Balkans is what Freud called the narcissism of minor difference. Lies, demagoguery, and propaganda have turned permeable identities into bunkered mentalities. Serbs and Croats who once shared the same language are being told that Serbian and Croatian are as distinct as the Cyrillic and Latin scripts in which they are written. Nationalistic narcissism is a hothouse for atrocity myths that blossom forth in order to portray each community as the blameless victim of the motiveless malevolence of the other.

6   In the Balkans these myths collapse time. The past can never safely become the past. It remains immobilized in a neurotic, hysterical present. The very name each group gives the other locks both sides into a past that is a nightmare. Serbs call all Croatian fighters Ustase, the fascist minority of World War II Croatia. Croatians call the Serbs Chetniks, the fascist minority on the other side. The naming process is intended to visit the sins of the fathers upon the sons forever.

7   Renaming enemies rewrites the past so that their very identity can be expunged from history. The Bosnian Serbs assert that the Muslims don't really exist, since they are renegade Serbs who converted to Islam in order to gain land and privileges from their Ottoman overlords. Thorvald Stoltenberg, the former U.N. mediator, has been heard to repeat this preposterous fable. In other ways too the outside world ignorantly colludes in Balkan mythmaking. The Western fantasy that all Muslims are fanatics and all Islam is fundamentalist underwrites the Serbs' myth that they, like the Christian host turning back the Turks at the gates of Vienna in 1683, are holding the Islamic tide from Europe's southern flank.

8   There is no easy awakening from the nightmare of their history. But outsiders can do something to break the demonic hold of myth. War-crimes tribunals and human-rights commissions are not the irrelevance they seem. Their function is to plunge the burning coals of myth into the icy bath of evidence; to hold the remaining ember of truth aloft for all to see; to show that history never justifies crime; and to teach people that they need truth as much as they need peace, and can't hope to get one without the other.

NOTES AND DISCUSSION

Michael Ignatieff illustrates in grotesque detail the effects of the abuse of language that Orwell writes of and warns against in "Politics and the English Language." He opens with an example of euphemism: the word "cleansing," which substitutes for "genocide." Later, he discusses the purposes and effects of name-calling in human affairs. Interestingly, he himself seems to use the word "myth" euphemistically, sometimes to mean "fantasy," sometimes to mean "legend," and frequently to mean "lies and propaganda."

Ignatieff's primary focus is a recent example of one particular atrocity myth that has been a propaganda tool throughout Western history. He uses the cause-and-effect and process analysis methods to explain how myths become "necessary" and are employed to "justify" atrocity, particularly in the "narcissistic" realm of modern nationalism. As language, such myths are a form of violence in themselves, and can lead to violence of a bloodier kind.

Note as well the intense figurative language Ignatieff uses in his conclusion. Orwell writes of the dangers of outmoded metaphors, and advises that figures of speech be kept fresh. In a piece that looks at how some language never gets a chance to become stale, Ignatieff's metaphors might seem flamboyant and sensational; but then, maybe a plea such as his for truth and sanity in such extreme circumstances needs to be made in extreme language.

STUDY QUESTIONS

For Discussion:

1. Ignatieff calls on outsiders to intervene to settle bloody local feuds, since they are uncontaminated by local myths. Are outsiders necessarily less contaminated? Might not imported myths become just as dangerous in such emotionally charged conflicts? For example, what role might the religion of a "peace-keeping" force play?

2. Look up Freud's analysis of the Narcissus myth, as well as the classical account of the myth (from Ovid's *Metamorphoses*). Note in particular Freud's use of "narcissism of minor differences." Think about the ways Freud has adapted the classical myth of Narcissus, which is itself a cautionary tale. How has Ignatieff further adapted the myth through his appropriation of Freud?

For Writing:

1. One of the practices Ignatieff alludes to is the use of euphemism—replacing an ugly word with a prettier one to hide or to glorify reality. He draws attention to the word "cleansing" when used to refer to genocide. Euphemism is part of the job of "renaming" that precedes and accompanies atrocities, or, in a less violent situation, an unpopular or risky political decision. Discuss this practice in relation to those that Orwell describes in "Politics and the English Language," and look for some examples of these practices in the "political" vocabulary of your own local or national government.

2. Are you aware of other myths that are used to excuse the persecution of unwanted members of a population, or to define another group of people as less than human or as unworthy of humane treatment? Relate one or two such myths, and explain how they make the unpleasant and irresponsible seem "natural." Be specific, both about the myth itself and about its ramifications.

   (This analysis need not refer to "society" in general, but could refer to a myth or story circulating within a group you are part of, or excluded from. For example, numerous "urban myths" of random violence caution us against various criminal elements. These are myths because they are not borne out by crime statistics, but serve to keep people on edge and on the defensive.)

THE ATOM'S IMAGE PROBLEM

Jay Ingram

BIOGRAPHICAL NOTE

Jay Ingram is a science writer and broadcaster. He may be best known to Canadians as the former host of CBC Radio's science program "Quirks and Quarks." He is the author of several books on science and everyday life and the co-host of @discovery.ca, a daily science news magazine on television's Discovery Channel. He also writes a column for Equinox magazine, from which this essay is taken.

1   What do you envision when you hear the word *atom*? I bet if you see anything at all it is a miniature solar system, with the nucleus of the atom as the sun, and tiny electrons whirling planetlike around it. And why not? A stylized version of this has long been synonymous with atomic power. It's probably the atom you saw in public school and is, indeed, a model rooted in science. The science is, however, a little out of date—by at least 70 years. If you try to redraw the atom as scientists imagine it today, it is transformed. What was solid becomes wispy and foggy, what was compact becomes vast, and, most important of all, what was predictable is not.

2   This revolution in the concept of the atom was largely accomplished in a few years of incredible scientific progress during the 1920s. So why are we nonscientists so out of date in our mental image of the atom? Is it because atomic science is so incompatible with everyday experience that we simply can't form and hold an image of it?

3   In his 1928 book *The Nature of the Physical World*, the great English astrophysicist Sir Arthur Eddington cast his eye back to the nineteenth century and said, "It was the boast of the Victorian physicist that he would not claim to understand a thing until he could make a

First published in Equinox, no. 87, June 1996. Reprinted by permission of the author.

model of it; and by a model he meant something constructed of levers, geared wheels, squirts, or other appliances familiar to an engineer." I suspect that most of us, if we are physicists at all, are Victorian. And I wonder if the Victorian physicists Eddington described weren't revealing something about human psychology that holds for most of us today.

4   By the time Eddington published his book, the solar-system model of the atom had already been out of favour for two years, replaced by the infinitely more challenging imagery of quantum mechanics. In fact, the solar-system atom, for all its hold on the popular imagination, held sway among scientists for little more than a decade. In that sense, it takes its place beside the cowboy: the Wild West has had much greater staying power in popular culture than it did in reality.

5   However brief the scientific reign of the solar-system atom, its beginnings were honest. In 1911 Ernest Rutherford made public the experiment that set the stage for its appearance. When he aimed highly energized subatomic particles at thin sheets of gold foil, he was shocked to see that in some cases the particles bounced right back. Rutherford said, "It was almost as incredible as if you had fired a 15-inch shell at a piece of tissue paper and it came back and hit you." Rutherford concluded that the atoms of gold in the sheet couldn't be likened (as had been suggested) to miniature raisin buns—blobs of positive electrical charge stuffed with tiny negative charges. Instead, the positive charge had to be intensely concentrated at a point inside the atom. Only such a compact object could deflect the particles Rutherford had aimed at it. He didn't go so far as to limit the outer negative charges (the electrons) to precise orbits, and in that sense he was more in tune with the modern vision of the atom.

6   However, in 1912, shortly after this experiment, the Danish physicist Niels Bohr came to work with Rutherford, and by 1913 he put the electrons firmly in orbits about the nucleus. In doing so, Bohr solved what had been a major problem in previous theories: classical physics had predicted that as electrons circled in orbits, they would steadily radiate away their energy; as this happened, their orbits would decay and they would eventually spiral into the nucleus like satellites reentering the earth's atmosphere. In one scientist's words, "matter would incandesce and collapse." Bohr argued that continuous processes such as radiating energy and decaying orbits were out-of-date concepts, failing to capture the inner workings of the atom. He suggested that electrons were restricted to certain stable orbits, in which they could move without loss of energy, and could only jump from one to another by emitting or absorbing a packet, or quantum, of energy.

7   So by the beginning of World War I, the solar-system atom was in place, but by the mid-1920s, it was gone. It couldn't withstand the brilliant onslaught of experimentation and thought that swept through physics in Europe during that decade. A who's who of science repainted our portrait of the atom, even if we haven't noticed. Perhaps the most radical change was that, as seen from the quantum-theory point of view, such particles as electrons could behave as waves. So Erwin Schrödinger, an Austrian-born Irish physicist, was able to dispense with the precise orbits of the electrons, filling the same space with waves radiating outward from the nucleus, the peaks of which corresponded to the now-defunct orbits. Max Born, a theoretical physicist, altered that idea slightly by claiming that the waves' peaks didn't really show where electrons were but, rather, where they might be.

8   In 1927 German physicist Werner Heisenberg elevated that sense of uncertainty into a principle, called (guess what?) Heisenberg's Uncertainty Principle. He established that it was not just difficult but literally impossible to pinpoint both the position and the momen-

tum (or velocity) of an electron at the same time—the very act of measurement would inevitably disturb the object being measured. In physics, the relationship has mathematical precision: you can know where the electron is, but then you don't know where it's going; if you endeavour to detect where it's going, you lose track of where it is. Is it any wonder that the solar-system model of the atom was trashed? It was replaced by a dissonant sort of picture—in tune with physicists' thinking but out of tune with the rest of us.

9   In today's atom, the electrons are still there outside the nucleus (although they often venture perilously close to it), but they are represented not by miniplanets but by probabilities, clouds of likelihood that suggest, "this is where you might find it." Sometimes there are gaps in those clouds—places forbidden to electrons, yet these seem to present no barrier to the electrons' ability to materialize, first on one side of the gap, then on the other.

10   There's also the nucleus, the image of which has evolved from a tightly bound cluster of protons and neutrons to something that might be like a drop of liquid, spinning, pulsating, and quivering with the movements of the particles inside. Or it might be more like a series of Russian doll-like shells, nestled one inside the other. And as important as the nucleus is, it occupies only a minuscule fraction of the total size of the atom.

11   It has always struck me that physicists and chemists are, for the most part, perfectly happy to think of and talk about the atom as the sum of a set of equations. I'm sure they all believe these equations represent something in the real world, but it is probably not possible any more to say exactly what. The indeterminate and unknowable have replaced precision and prediction.

12   That's fine if you're a physicist—it's necessary—but it doesn't work very well for the rest of us. We don't have the language and skills to understand the atom as math; we need a model that squares with intuition. Clouds of probability don't; balls moving in orbits do.

13   Much is made these days of the idea that we are coping with the twentieth century equipped with only a Stone Age hunter—gatherer brain. It follows, then, that the brain should be particularly skilled at doing things useful for hunter—gatherers. Imagination is certainly one of those skills, but imagination of what? Of solid, substantial objects moving around each other in regular fashion? Or of pointlike particles that can't be localized and that behave like waves and move in strange and unpredictable ways?

14   And why should you care what the atom is like? If you are at all interested in the natural world, you have to care. The atom isn't just another feature of nature—it *is* nature. Unfortunately, the solar-system atom was likely about as much as we could handle in concrete conceptual terms. When scientists left the concept behind forever in the 1920s, it seems they left the rest of us behind too. They have their mathematical atom to contemplate. We have only our mental pictures.

NOTES AND DISCUSSION

Ingram's subject in this essay is in some ways the same as Heisenberg's in "What Is an Elementary Particle?", but Ingram's approach is very different. He spends the length of the essay trying to destroy an analogy and create an alternative—the essay hinges on a series of analogies, metaphors, images, and similes—in order to make concrete and imaginable some of the abstract concepts of modern particle science. Even he admits that these concepts may, finally, be too complex to articulate in the terms that he is using.

Ingram gives several metaphors and similes to try to capture the essence of electrons and the nucleus of an atom: the electrons are "clouds of likelihood"; the nucleus is "like a drop of liquid" or "like a series of Russian doll-like shells." He tries hard to find an analogy, a metaphor, a simile, or an image that will capture what he wants to say, but nothing can do justice to the conceptual complexities. Analogies are powerful tools, but they also can also lead to serious misconceptions. Note that Ingram begins his essay with an example of a wildly inaccurate image that, he claims, has stubbornly stayed fixed in popular conceptions of the atom; in fact, it is the image that is used to denote atomic power. However, Ingram's difficulty may be the result of an inaccurate assumption: he seems to claim that having an image of something is the same as having an understanding of that thing. He writes, towards the end of the essay, that "we need a model that squares with intuition." In comparison, see Heisenberg's essay about elementary particles, and note that Heisenberg makes no effort to construct mental pictures for his readers. Ingram may, in fact, be trying to do something that is just not possible.

STUDY QUESTIONS

For Discussion:

1. Consider your beliefs about and understanding of atoms. Is your understanding of the atom contingent on a mental "image"? Notice Ingram's final two sentences: "They have their mathematical atom to contemplate. We have only our mental pictures." Discuss Ingram's assumption that part of understanding something is having "mental pictures" of it.

2. Examine Ingram's apparent belief that the relationship of "scientists" (especially physicists) to "the rest of us" is an "us vs. them" relationship. Compare and contrast the image of the scientist presented here with the one in Stephen Jay Gould's "The Monster's Human Nature."

For Writing:

1. In an essay, compare and contrast Ingram's essay with Heisenberg's "What Is an Elementary Particle?" Describe what, specifically, are the strengths and weaknesses of each approach.

2. Ingram works largely from analogies, metaphors, and similes in this piece. Write an analogy of your own that tries to capture in an appropriate image something that is very complex.

CLONE MAMMALS . . . CLONE MAN?

Axel Kahn

BIOGRAPHICAL NOTE

Axel Kahn is director of the INSERM (Institut National de la Santé et de la Recherche de Molecule) laboratory of Research on Genetics and Molecular Pathology at the Cochin Institute of Molecular Genetics in Paris, France.

1   The experiments of I. Wilmut et al. (*Nature* 385, 810; 1997) demonstrate that sheep embryonic eggs (oocytes) can reprogramme the nuclei of differentiated cells, enabling the cells to develop into any type. The precise conditions under which this process can occur remain to be elucidated; the factors determining the success of the technique, and the long-term prospects for animals generated in this way, still need to be established. But, of course, the main point is that Wilmut et al. show that it is now possible to envisage cloning of adult mammals in a completely asexual fashion.

2   The oocyte's only involvement is the role of its cytoplasm in reprogramming the introduced nucleus and in contributing intracellular organelles—mainly mitochondria—to the future organism. This work will undoubtedly open up new perspectives in research in biology and development, for example, in understanding the functional plasticity of the genome and chromatin during development, and the mechanisms underlying the stability of differentiated states. Another immediate question is to ask whether a species barrier exists. Could an embryo be produced, for example, by implanting the nucleus of a lamb in an enucleated mouse oocyte? Any lambs born in this way would possess a mouse mitochondrial genome.

3   The implications for humans are staggering. One example is that the technique suggests that a woman suffering from a serious mitochondrial disease might in future be able to produce children free of the disease by having the nucleus of her embryo implanted in a donor oocyte (note that this process is not the same as "cloning").

Would Cloning Humans Be Justified?

4   But the main question raised by the paper by Wilmut et al. is that of the possibility of human cloning. There is no *a priori* reason why humans should behave very differently from other mammals where cloning is possible, so the cloning of an adult human could become feasible using the techniques reported.

5   What medical and scientific "justification" might there be for cloning? Previous debates have identified the preparation of immuno-compatible differentiated cell lines for transplantation, as one potential indication. We could imagine everyone having their own reserve of therapeutic cells that would increase their chance of being cured of various diseases, such as cancer, degenerative disorders, and viral or inflammatory diseases.

6   But the debate has in the past perhaps paid insufficient attention to the current strong social trend towards a fanatical desire for individuals not simply to have children but to ensure that these children also carry their genes. Achieving such biological descendance was impossible for sterile men until the development of ICSI (intracytoplasmic sperm injection), which allows a single sperm to be injected directly into the oocyte.

7   But human descendance is not only biological, as it is in all other species, but is also emotional and cultural. The latter is of such importance that methods of inheritance where both parents' genes are not transmitted—such as adoption and insemination with donor sperm—are widely accepted without any major ethical questions being raised.

8   But today's society is characterized by an increasing demand for biological inheritance, as if this were the only desirable form of inheritance. Regrettably, a person's personality is increasingly perceived as being largely determined by his or her genes. Moreover, in a world where culture is increasingly internationalized and homogenized, people may ask themselves whether they have anything else to transmit to their children apart from their genes. This pressure probably accounts for the wide social acceptance of ICSI, a technique which was widely made available to people at a time when experimental evidence as to its safety was still flimsy. ICSI means that men with abnormal sperm can now procreate.

9   Going further upstream, researchers have now succeeded in fertilizing a mouse oocyte using a diploid nucleus of a spermatogonium: apparently normal embryonic development occurs, at least in the early stages. But there are also severe forms of sterility—such as dysplasia or severe testicular atrophy—or indeed lesbian couples, where no male germ line exists. Will such couples also demand the right to a biological descendance?

10   Applying the technique used by Wilmut et al. in sheep directly to humans would yield a clone "of the father" and not a shared descendant of both the father and mother. Nevertheless, for a woman the act of carrying a fetus can be as important as being its biological mother. The extraordinary power of such "maternal reappropriation" of the embryo can be seen from the strong demand for pregnancies in post-menopausal women, and for embryo and oocyte donations to circumvent female sterility. Moreover, if cloning techniques were ever to be used, the mother would be contributing something—her mitochondrial genome. We cannot exclude the possibility that the current direction of public opinion will tend to legitimize the resort to cloning techniques in cases where, for example, the male partner in a couple is unable to produce gametes.

11   The creation of human clones solely for spare cell lines would, from a philosophical point of view, be in obvious contradiction to an ethical principle expressed by Immanuel Kant: that of human dignity. This principle demands that an individual—and I would extend this to read human life—should never be thought of only as a means, but always also as an end. Creating human life for the sole purpose of preparing therapeutic material would clearly not be for the dignity of the life created.

12   Analysing the use of cloning as a means of combating sterility is much more difficult, as the explicit goal is to create a life with the right to dignity. Moreover, individuals are not determined entirely by their genome, as of course the family, cultural, and social environment have a powerful "humanizing" influence on the construction of a personality. Two human clones born decades apart would be much more different psychologically than identical twins raised in the same family.

Threat of Human "Creators"

13   Nonetheless, part of the individuality and dignity of a person probably lies in the uniqueness and unpredictability of his or her development. As a result, the uncertainty of the great lottery of heredity constitutes the principal protection against biological predetermination imposed by third parties, including parents. One blessing of the relationship between parents and children is their inevitable difference, which results in parents loving their children for what they are, rather than trying to make them what they want. Allowing cloning to circumvent sterility would lead to it being tolerated in cases where it was imposed, for example, by authorities. What would the world be like if we accepted that human "creators" could assume the right to generate creatures in their own likeness, beings whose very biological characteristics would be subjugated to an outside will?

14   The results of Wilmut et al. undoubtedly have much merit. One effect of them is to oblige us to face up to our responsibilities. It is not a technical barrier that will protect us from the perspectives I have mentioned, but a moral one, originating from a reflection of the basis of our dignity. That barrier is certainly the most dignified aspect of human genius.

This article is a slightly edited version of a commentary first published on *Nature's* Web site on February 27, 1997.

NOTES AND DISCUSSION

This essay responds to the publication of the paper "Viable Offspring Derived from Fetal and Adult Mammalian Cells" by Ian Wilmut et al., which appeared in *Nature* on February 27, 1997, and which is included in this anthology. You may wish to read the Wilmut essay in conjunction with Kahn's response. The appearance of "Viable Offspring" in *Nature* prompted significant media coverage. Dolly, the cloned sheep, became a minor celebrity; President Clinton asked the White House Bioethics Commission to investigate the implications of this "stunning" research.

Kahn's essay is in three distinct parts. He begins by summarizing and reiterating the central results of Wilmut's study in more common language and terminology. He also briefly suggests that Wilmut's work may have implications and applications in fields other than that of human cloning. However, in the second section of the essay, it becomes clear that *human cloning* is Kahn's focus. Consider what tone and meaning he implies by punctuating the word "justification." This essay is a personal response to a complicated ethical issue. Notice how Kahn uses generalized statements and claims, standard transitional words and phrases, and rhetorical questions to advance his opinion rapidly and forcefully.

The essay compares and contrasts different visions of humanity and its need to procreate and nurture its young. Clearly, in discussing cloning, Kahn enters into the on-going debate over "nature vs. nurture": he reflects on what creates identity and family, thus making cloning not simply a remote issue grounded in ethical and scientific debates, but an area of more immediate interest to a general readership. The essay's title contains the word "man," although its subtitle and content use the more neutral and collective "humankind" or "humanity." Consider why "man" might have been chosen for the title.

Toward the essay's conclusion, Kahn uses the first person "I," further personalizing his argument. He concludes that the decisions involved in cloning are not just technical and scientific, but are a collective moral responsibility.

STUDY QUESTIONS

For Discussion:

1. Identify and then compare and contrast the different visions of humanity, and the need to procreate and nurture its young, that Kahn's essay presents.

2. Identify the transitional words and phrases Kahn uses to structure his argument. Then examine and describe the organizational and rhetorical impact these words and phrases have on the essay's overall structure and the success of its argument.

For Writing:

1. Read the essay by Wilmut et al. that inspired this essay. Analyze what Kahn has interpreted and extrapolated from Wilmut's report and decide which of his conclusions seem valid and which do not. Be sure to fully explain the reasons behind your decisions.

2. Research some of the ethical debates surrounding cloning. Explain in detail, through references to specific articles and authors, whether Kahn is justified in suggesting that "the debate has in the past perhaps paid insufficient attention to the current strong social trend towards a fanatical desire for individuals not simply to have children but to ensure that these children also carry their genes."

WHY JOHNNY CAN'T THINK

Walter Karp

BIOGRAPHICAL NOTE

Walter Karp (1934–89) produced eight books and over two hundred articles during his passionate writing career. His twin obsessions were American politics and history.

---

1   Until very recently, remarkably little was known about what actually goes on in America's public schools. There were no reliable answers to even the most obvious questions. How many children are taught to read in overcrowded classrooms? How prevalent is rote learning and how common are classroom discussions? Do most schools set off gongs to mark the change of "periods"? Is it a common practice to bark commands over public address systems in the manner of army camps, prisons, and banana republics? Public schooling provides the only intense experience of a public realm that most Americans will ever know. Are school buildings designed with the dignity appropriate to a great republican institution, or are most of them as crummy-looking as one's own?

2   The darkness enveloping America's public schools is truly extraordinary considering that 38.9 million students attend them, that we spend nearly $134 billion a year on them, and that foundations ladle out generous sums for the study of everything about schooling—except what really occurs in the schools. John I. Goodlad's eight-year investigation of a mere thirty-eight of America's 80,000 public schools—the result of which, *A Place Called School* (McGraw-Hill, 1984), was published last year—is the most comprehensive study ever undertaken. Hailed as a "landmark in American educational research," it was financed with great difficulty. The darkness, it seems, has its guardians.

3 Happily, the example of Goodlad, a former dean of UCLA's Graduate School of Education, has proven contagious. A flurry of new books shed considerable light on the practice of public education in America. In *The Good High School* (Basic Books, 1985), Sara Lawrence Lightfoot offers vivid "portraits" of six distinctive American secondary schools. In *Horace's Compromise* (Houghton Mifflin, 1985), Theodore R. Sizer, a former dean of Harvard's Graduate School of Education, reports on his two-year odyssey through public high schools around the country. Even *High School* (Harper & Row, 1985), a white paper issued by Ernest L. Boyer and the Carnegie Foundation for the Advancement of Teaching, is supported by a close investigation of the institutional life of a number of schools. Of the books under review, only *A Nation at Risk* (U.S. Government Printing Office, 1984), the report of the Reagan Administration's National Commission on Excellence in Education, adheres to the established practice of crass special pleading in the dark.

4 Thanks to Goodlad et al., it is now clear what the great educational darkness has so long concealed: the depth and pervasiveness of political hypocrisy in the common schools of the country. The great ambition professed by public school managers is, of course, education for citizenship and self-government, which harks back to Jefferson's historic call for "general education to enable every man to judge for himself what will secure or endanger his freedom." What the public schools practice with remorseless proficiency, however, is the prevention of citizenship and the stifling of self-government. When 58 percent of the thirteen-year-olds tested by the National Assessment for Educational Progress think it is against the law to start a third party in America, we are dealing not with a sad educational failure but with a remarkably subtle success.

5 Consider how effectively America's future citizens are trained not to judge for themselves about anything. From the first grade to the twelfth, from one coast to the other, instruction in America's classrooms is almost entirely dogmatic. Answers are "right" and answers are "wrong," but mostly answers are short. "At all levels, [teacher-made] tests called almost exclusively for short answers and recall of information," reports Goodlad. In more than a thousand classrooms visited by his researchers, "only *rarely*" was there "evidence to suggest instruction likely to go much beyond mere possession of information to a level of understanding its implications." Goodlad goes on to note that "the intellectual terrain is laid out by the teacher. The paths for walking through it are largely predetermined by the teacher." The give-and-take of genuine discussion is conspicuously absent. "Not even 1%" of institutional time, he found, was devoted to discussions that "required some kind of open response involving reasoning or perhaps an opinion from students. . . . The extraordinary degree of student passivity stands out."

6 Sizer's research substantiates Goodlad's. "No more important finding has emerged from the inquiries of our study than that the American high school student, *as student*, is all too often docile, compliant, and without initiative." There is good reason for this. On the one hand, notes Sizer, "there are too few rewards for being inquisitive." On the other, the heavy emphasis on "the right answer . . . smothers the student's efforts to become an effective intuitive thinker."

7 Yet smothered minds are looked on with the utmost complacency by the educational establishment—by the Reagan Department of Education, state boards of regents, university education departments, local administrators, and even many so-called educational reformers. Teachers are neither urged to combat the tyranny of the short right answer nor trained to do so. "Most teachers simply do not know how to teach for higher levels of thinking," says Goodlad. Indeed, they are actively discouraged from trying to do so.

8   The discouragement can be quite subtle. In their orientation talks to new, inexperienced teachers, for example, school administrators often indicate that they do not much care what happens in class so long as no noise can be heard in the hallway. This thinly veiled threat virtually ensures the prevalence of short-answer drills, workbook exercises, and the copying of long extracts from the blackboard. These may smother young minds, but they keep the classroom quiet.

9   Discouragement even calls itself reform. Consider the current cry for greater use of standardized student tests to judge the "merit" of teachers and raise "academic standards." If this fake reform is foisted on the schools, dogma and docility will become even more prevalent. This point is well made by Linda Darling-Hammond of the Rand Corporation in an essay in *The Great School Debate* (Simon & Schuster, 1985). Where "important decisions are based on test scores," she notes, "teachers are more likely to teach to the tests" and less likely to bother with "nontested activities, such as writing, speaking, problem-solving, or real reading of books." The most influential promoter of standardized tests is the "excellence" brigade in the Department of Education; so clearly one important meaning of "educational excellence" is greater proficiency in smothering students' efforts to think for themselves.

10   Probably the greatest single discouragement to better instruction is the overcrowded classroom. The Carnegie report points out that English teachers cannot teach their students how to write when they must read and criticize the papers of as many as 175 students. As Sizer observes, genuine discussion is possible only in small seminars. In crowded classrooms, teachers have difficulty imparting even the most basic intellectual skills, since they have no time to give students personal attention. The overcrowded classroom inevitably debases instruction, yet it is the rule in America's public schools. In the first three grades of elementary school, Goodlad notes, the average class has twenty-seven students. High school classes range from twenty-five to forty students, according to the Carnegie report.

11   What makes these conditions appalling is that they are quite unnecessary. The public schools are top-heavy with administrators and rife with sinecures. Large numbers of teachers scarcely ever set foot in a classroom, being occupied instead as grade advisers, career counselors, "coordinators," and supervisors. "Schools, if simply organized," Sizer writes, "can have well-paid faculty and fewer than eighty students per teacher [sixteen students per class] without increasing current per-pupil expenditure." Yet no serious effort is being made to reduce class size. As Sizer notes, "Reducing teacher load is, when all the negotiating is over, a low agenda item for the unions and school boards." Overcrowded classrooms virtually guarantee smothered minds, yet the subject is not even mentioned in *A Nation at Risk*, for all its well-publicized braying about a "rising tide of mediocrity."

12   Do the nation's educators really want to teach almost 40 million students how to "think critically," in the Carnegie report's phrase, and "how to judge for themselves," in Jefferson's? The answer is, if you can believe that you will believe anything. The educational establishment is not even content to produce passive minds. It seeks passive spirits as well. One effective agency for producing these is the overly populous school. The larger schools are, the more prison-like they tend to be. In such schools, guards man the stairwells and exits. ID cards and "passes" are examined at checkpoints. Bells set off spasms of anarchy and bells quell the student mob. PA systems interrupt regularly with trivial fiats and frivolous announcements. This "malevolent intruder," in Sizer's apt phrase, is truly ill willed, for the PA system is actually an educational tool. It teaches the huge student mass to respect the authority of disembodied voices and the rule of remote and invisible agencies. Sixty-three percent of all high school students in America attend schools with enrollments of five thousand or more. The common excuse for these mobbed schools is economy, but in fact they cannot be shown to save taxpayers a penny. Large schools "tend to create passive and compliant students," notes Robert B. Hawkins, Jr., in an essay in *The Challenge to American Schools* (Oxford University Press, 1987). That is their chief reason for being.

13   "How can the relatively passive and docile roles of students prepare them to participate as informed, active, and questioning citizens?" asks the Carnegie report, in discussing the "hidden curriculum" of passivity in the schools. The answer is, they were not meant to. Public schools introduce future citizens to the public world, but no introduction could be more disheartening. Architecturally, public school buildings range from drab to repellent. They are often disfigured by demoralizing neglect—"cracked sidewalks, a shabby lawn, and peeling paint on every window sash," to quote the Carnegie report. Many big-city elementary schools have numbers instead of names, making them as coldly dispiriting as possible.

14   Public schools stamp out republican sentiment by habituating their students to unfairness, inequality, and special privilege. These arise inevitably from the educational establishment's long-standing policy (well described by Diane Ravitch in *The Troubled Crusade* [Basic Books, 1985]) of maintaining "the correlation between social class and educational achievement." In order to preserve that factitious "correlation," public schooling is rigged to favor middle-class students and to ensure that working-class students do poorly enough to convince them that they fully merit the lowly station that will one day be theirs. "Our goal is to get these kids to be like their parents," one teacher, more candid than most, remarked to a Carnegie researcher.

15   For more than three decades, elementary schools across the country practiced a "progressive" non-phonetic method of teaching reading that had nothing much to recommend it save its inherent social bias. According to Ravitch, this method favored "children who were already motivated and prepared to begin reading" before entering school, while making learning to read more difficult for precisely those children whose parents were ill-read or ignorant. The advantages enjoyed by the well-bred were thus artificially multiplied tenfold, and 23 million adult Americans are today "functional illiterates." America's educators, notes Ravitch, have "never actually accepted full responsibility for making all children literate."

16   That describes a malicious intent a trifle too mildly. Reading is the key to everything else in school. Children who struggle with it in the first grade will be "grouped" with the slow readers in the second grade and will fall hopelessly behind in all subjects by the sixth. The schools hasten this process of falling behind, report Goodlad and others, by giving the best students the best teachers and struggling students the worst ones. "It is ironic," observes the Carnegie report, "that those who need the most help get the least." Such students are commonly diagnosed as "culturally deprived" and so are blamed for the failures inflicted on them. Thus they are taught to despise themselves even as they are inured to their inferior station.

17   The whole system of unfairness, inequality, and privilege comes to fruition in high school. There, some 15.7 million youngsters are formally divided into the favored few and the ill-favored many by the practice of "tracking." About 35 percent of America's public secondary-school students are enrolled in academic programs (often sub-divided into "gifted" and "non-gifted" tracks); the rest are relegated to some variety of non-academic schooling. Thus the tracking system, as intended, reproduces the divisions of the class system. "The honors programs," notes Sizer, "serve the wealthier youngsters, and the general tracks (whatever their titles) serve the working class. Vocational programs are often a cruel social dumping

ground." The bottom-dogs are trained for jobs as auto mechanics, cosmeticians, and institutional cooks, but they rarely get the jobs they are trained for. Pumping gasoline, according to the Carnegie report, is as close as an auto-mechanics major is likely to get to repairing a car. "Vocational education in the schools is virtually irrelevant to job fate," asserts Goodlad. It is merely the final hoax that the school bureaucracy plays on the neediest, one that the federal government has been promoting for seventy years.

18   The tracking system makes privilege and inequality blatantly visible to everyone. It creates under one roof "two worlds of schooling," to quote Goodlad. Students in academic programs read Shakespeare's plays. The commonality, notes the Carnegie report, are allowed virtually no contact with serious literature. In their English classes they practice filling out job applications. "Gifted" students alone are encouraged to think for themselves. The rest are subjected to sanctimonious wind, chiefly about "work habits" and "career opportunities."

19   "If you are a child of low-income parents," reports Sizer, "the chances are good that you will receive limited and often careless attention from adults in your high school. If you are the child of upper-middle-income parents, the chances are good that you will receive substantial and careful attention." In Brookline High School in Massachusetts, one of Lightfoot's "good" schools, a few fortunate students enjoy special treatment in their Advanced Placement classes. Meanwhile, students tracked into "career education" learn about "institutional cooking and clean-up" in a four-term Food Service course that requires them to mop up after their betters in the school cafeteria.

20   This wretched arrangement expresses the true spirit of public education in America and discloses the real aim of its hidden curriculum. A favored few, pampered and smiled upon, are taught to cherish privilege and despise the disfavored. The favorless many, who have majored in failure for years, are taught to think ill of themselves. Youthful spirits are broken to the world and every impulse of citizenship is effectively stifled. John Goodlad's judgment is severe but just: "There is in the gap between our highly idealistic goals for schooling in our society and the differentiated opportunities condoned and supported in schools a monstrous hypocrisy."

21   The public schools of America have not been corrupted for trivial reasons. Much would be different in a republic composed of citizens who could judge for themselves what secured or endangered their freedom. Every wielder of illicit or undemocratic power, every possessor of undue influence, every beneficiary of corrupt special privilege would find his position and tenure at hazard. Republican education is a menace to powerful, privileged, and influential people, and they in turn are a menace to republican education. That is why the generation that founded the public schools took care to place them under the suffrage of local communities, and that is why the corrupters of public education have virtually destroyed that suffrage. In 1932 there were 127,531 school districts in America. Today there are approximately 15,840 and they are virtually impotent, their proper role having been usurped by state and federal authorities. Curriculum and textbooks, methods of instruction, the procedures of the classroom, the organization of the school day, the cant, the pettifogging, and the corruption are almost uniform from coast to coast. To put down the menace of republican education its shield of local self-government had to be smashed, and smashed it was.

22   The public schools we have today are what the powerful and the considerable have made of them. They will not be redeemed by trifling reforms. Merit pay, a longer school year, more homework, special schools for "the gifted," and more standardized tests will not even begin to turn our public schools into nurseries of "informed, active, and questioning citizens."

They are not meant to. When the authors of *A Nation at Risk* call upon the schools to create an "educated work force," they are merely sanctioning the prevailing corruption, which consists precisely in the reduction of citizens to credulous workers. The education of a free people will not come from federal bureaucrats crying up "excellence" for "economic growth," any more than it came from their predecessors who cried up schooling as a means to "get a better job."

23   Only ordinary citizens can rescue the schools from their stifling corruption, for nobody else wants ordinary children to become questioning citizens at all. If we wait for the mighty to teach America's youth what secures or endangers their freedom, we will wait until the crack of doom.

NOTES AND DISCUSSION

Walter Karp's standard method of writing was to do what he called "investigative reading," that is, to read everything that he could find on a given topic, begin each essay with a brief summary of the facts, and analyze the topic by paying close attention to pertinent details that had been ignored in previous discussions of the problem.

This essay is an example of a well-developed argument. It has a strong, provocative thesis that is clearly stated, and it uses evidence from a variety of sources to support its position. The argument that there is something wrong with North American school systems is familiar, but Karp's thesis is a surprising reversal of that position: he goes beyond the idea that the education system is doing a bad job, to suggest that it is doing exactly the job it was designed to do.

STUDY QUESTIONS

For Discussion:

1. What is Karp's thesis? How is that thesis defended in this essay?
2. Do you think it is true, as Karp claims, that "reading is the key to everything else in school"? Can you suggest any other possible keys? During your discussion, consider the essay's audience, especially in the context of Karp's closing "call to arms."

For Writing:

1. Does Karp's description of schools agree with your own experience? Write a paragraph discussing whether you and your classmates come from the "gifted elite" of which Karp speaks.
2. Karp spends a good deal of time comparing various models of education. What is his preferred model? Would he draw any distinctions between the kinds of education science students usually receive and the kind humanities students do? In a short analytical essay, discuss the two different models of education.

INDIA

Perri Klass

BIOGRAPHICAL NOTE

Perri Klass is a pediatrician who attended Harvard Medical School. In addition to writing novels and collections of short stories, she has contributed essays to magazines and newspapers such as *Mademoiselle* and *The New York Times*. This essay is taken from a book about her years as a medical student, *A Not Entirely Benign Procedure* (1987).

---

1   *The people look different.* The examining room is crowded with children and their parents, gathered hopefully around the doctor's desk, jockeying for position. Everyone seems to believe, if the doctor gets close to *my* child everything will be okay. Several Indian medical students are also present, leaning forward to hear their professor's explanations as they watch one particular child walk across the far end of the room. I stand on my toes, straining to see over the intervening heads so I, too, can watch this patient walk. I can see her face, intent, bright dark eyes, lips pinched in concentration. She's about ten years old. I can see her sleek black head, the two long black braids pinned up in circles over her ears in the style we used to call doughnuts. All she's wearing is a long loose shirt, so her legs can be seen, as with great difficulty she wobbles across the floor. At the professor's direction, she sits down on the floor and then tries to get up again; she needs to use her arms to push her body up.

2   I'm confused. This patient looks like a child with absolutely classic muscular dystrophy, but muscular dystrophy is a genetic disease carried on the Y chromosome, like hemophilia. It therefore almost never occurs in girls. Can this be one of those one-in-a-trillion cases? Or is it a more unusual form of muscle disease, one that isn't sex-linked in inheritance?

3	Finally the child succeeds in getting up on her feet, and her parents come forward to help her dress. They pull her over near to where I'm standing, and as they're helping with the clothing, the long shirt slides up over the child's hips. No, this isn't one of those one-in-a-trillion cases. I've been watching a ten-year-old boy with muscular dystrophy; he comes from a Sikh family, and Sikh males don't cut their hair. Adults wear turbans, but young boys often have their hair braided and pinned up in those two knots.

4	Recently I spent some time in India, working in the pediatric department of an important New Delhi hospital. I wanted to learn about medicine outside the United States, to work in a pediatric clinic in the Third World, and I suppose I also wanted to test my own medical education, to find out whether my newly acquired skills are in fact transferable to any place where there are human beings, with human bodies, subject to their range of ills and evils.

5	But it wasn't just a question of my medical knowledge. In India, I found that my cultural limitations often prevented me from thinking clearly about patients. Everyone looked different, and I was unable to pick up any clues from their appearance, their manner of speech, their clothing. This is a family of Afghan refugees. This family is from the south of India. This child is from a very poor family. This child has a Nepalese name. All the clues I use at home to help me evaluate patients, clues ranging from what neighborhood they live in to what ethnic origin their names suggest, were hidden from me in India.

6	The people don't just look different on the outside, of course. It might be more accurate to say *the population is different*. The gene pool, for example: there are some genetic diseases that are much more common here than there, cystic fibrosis, say, which you have to keep in mind when evaluating patients in Boston, but which would be show-offy and highly unlikely diagnosis-out-of-a-book for a medical student to suggest in New Delhi (I know—in my innocence I suggested it).

7	And all of this, in the end, really reflects human diversity, though admittedly it's reflected in the strange warped mirror of the medical profession; it's hard to exult in the variety of human genetic defects, or even in the variety of human culture, when you're looking at it as a tool for examining a sick child. Still, I can accept the various implications of a world full of different people, different populations.

8	*The diseases are different.* The patient is a seven-year-old boy whose father says that over the past week and a half he has become more tired, less active, and lately he doesn't seem to understand everything going on around him. Courteously, the senior doctor turns to me, asks what my assessment is. He asks this in a tone that suggests that the diagnosis is obvious, and as a guest I'm invited to pronounce it. The diagnosis, whatever it is, is certainly not obvious to me. I can think of a couple of infections that might look like this, but no single answer. The senior doctor sees my difficulty and offers a maxim, one that I've heard many times back in Boston. Gently, slightly reprovingly, he tells me, "Common things occur commonly. There are many possibilities, of course, but I think it is safe to say that this is almost certainly tuberculous meningitis."

9	Tuberculous meningitis? Common things occur commonly? Somewhere in my brain (and somewhere in my lecture notes) "the complications of tuberculosis" are filed away, and yes, I suppose it can affect the central nervous system, just as I can vaguely remember that it can affect the stomach and the skeletal system. . . . To tell the truth, I've never even seen a case of straightforward tuberculosis of the lung in a small child, let alone what I would have thought of as a rare complication.

10　　And hell, it's worse than that. I've done a fair amount of pediatrics back in Boston, but there are an awful lot of things I've never seen. When I was invited in New Delhi to give an opinion on a child's rash, I came up with quite a creative list of tropical diseases, because guess what? I had never seen a child with measles before. In the United States, children are vaccinated against measles, mumps, and rubella at the age of one year. There are occasional outbreaks of measles among college students, but the disease is now very rare in small children. ("Love this Harvard medical student. Can't recognize tuberculous meningitis. Can't recognize measles or mumps. What the hell do they teach them over there in pediatrics?")

11　　And this, of course, is one of the main medical student reasons for going to study abroad, the chance to see diseases you wouldn't see at home. The pathology, we call it, as in "I got to see some amazing pathology while I was in India." It's embarrassing to find yourself suddenly ignorant, but it's interesting to learn all about a new range of diagnoses, symptoms, treatments, all things you might have learned from a textbook and then immediately forgotten as totally outside your own experience.

12　　The difficult thing is that these differences don't in any way, however tortured, reflect the glory of human variation. They reflect instead the sad partitioning of the species, because they're almost all preventable diseases, and their prevalence is a product of poverty, of lack of vaccinations, of malnutrition and poor sanitation. And therefore, though it's all very educational for the medical student (and I'm by now more or less used to parasitizing my education off of human suffering), this isn't a difference to be accepted without outrage.

13　　*The expectations are different.* The child is a seven-month-old girl with diarrhea. She has been losing weight for a couple of weeks, she won't eat or drink, she just lies there in her grandmother's arms. The grandmother explains: one of her other grandchildren has just died from very severe diarrhea, and this little girl's older brother died last year, not of diarrhea but of a chest infection. . . . I look at the grandmother's face, at the faces of the baby's mother and father, who are standing on either side of the chair where the grandmother is sitting with the baby. All these people believe in the possibility of death, the chance that the child will not live to grow up. They've all seen many children die. These parents lost a boy last year, and they know that they may lose their daughter.

14　　The four have traveled for almost sixteen hours to come to this hospital, because after the son died last year, they no longer have faith in the village doctor. They're hopeful, they offer their sick baby to this famous hospital. They're prepared to stay in Delhi while she's hospitalized, the mother will sleep in the child's crib with her, the father and grandmother may well sleep on the hospital grounds. They've brought food, cooking pots, warm shawls because it's January and it gets cold at night. They're tough, and they're hopeful, but they believe in the possibility of death.

15　　Back home, in Boston, I've heard bewildered, grieving parents say, essentially, "Who would have believed that in the 1980s a child could just die like that?" Even parents with terminally ill children, children who spend months or years getting sicker and sicker, sometimes have great difficulty accepting that all the art and machinery of modern medicine are completely helpless. They expect every child to live to grow up.

16　　In India, it isn't that parents are necessarily resigned, and certainly not that they love their children less. They may not want to accept the dangers, but poor people, people living in poor villages or in urban slums, know the possibility is there. If anything, they may be even more terrified than American parents, just because perhaps they're picturing the death of some other loved child, imagining this living child going the way of that dead one.

17   I don't know. This is a gap I can't cross. I can laugh at my own inability to interpret the signals of a different culture, and I can read and ask questions and slowly begin to learn a little about the people I'm trying to help care for. I can blush at my ignorance of diseases uncommon in my home territory, study up in textbooks, and deplore inequalities that allow preventable diseases to ravage some unfortunate populations while others are protected. But I can't draw my lesson from this grandmother, these parents, this sick little girl. I can't imagine their awareness, their accommodations of what they know. I can't understand how they live with it. I can't accept their acceptance. My medical training has taken place in a world where all children are supposed to grow up, and the exceptions to this rule are rare horrible diseases, disastrous accidents. That is the attitude, the expectation I demand from patients. I'm left most disturbed not by the fact of children dying, not by the different diseases from which they die, or the differences in the medical care they receive, but by the way their parents look at me, at my profession. Perhaps it is only in this that I allow myself to take it all personally.

NOTES AND DISCUSSION

"India" is a comparison-and-contrast essay with a strong narrative component. It is a personal essay about the difficulties of experiencing "difference" first-hand. Note its striking stylistic features: the use of a vulnerable first person narrator, of italics as a structural device, and of frequent parenthetical asides and commentaries to the reader after some action has taken place.

Klass's essay is organized around a list of three "differences": "The people look different"; "The diseases are different"; "The expectations are different." Notice that these are all partial comparisons. Klass leaves the reader to fill in the blank that she has deliberately left: different from what? This absence is the real crux of the essay: people are dying every day in India from diseases that are, as Klass writes in paragraph 12, "almost all preventable diseases, and their prevalence is a product of poverty, of lack of vaccinations, of malnutrition and poor sanitation." Klass writes from a firm position in the first world, where excellent medical care is taken for granted. This first-world reality is very different from the third-world reality that she experiences in India. The essay thus becomes in part a plea for the expansion of medical borders, for a closing of gaps—between rich and poor, between first and third worlds—that need not exist.

STUDY QUESTIONS

For Discussion:

1. The differences that Klass feels so acutely no doubt affect her ability to perform as a pediatrician. It is apparent in this essay that she likely will not remain in India for an extended period. What impact will the experience have on her medical practice?
2. Notice the essay's strong focus on children. While this focus exists in part because Klass is a pediatrician, it lends the essay an impact that it might otherwise not have. Compare the emotional impact of this essay with that of Selzer's essay on the epidemic of AIDS in Haiti, especially among the island's prostitutes. How much of the difference between the two

essays is due to the choice of subjects, and how those subjects are constructed, not only in the essays themselves, but in society?

For Writing:

1. Describe—as a narrative, or as a comparison and contrast essay—a situation in which you felt acutely displaced, perhaps because your knowledge was not adequate for what was expected of you.

2. Write a short analysis of this essay's informal, almost chatty tone. To what extent is this tone a feature of the essay's subject—children—as opposed to its style? While the subject of the essay is children, the issue is their needless death and disease. How well suited are Klass's tone and style to the content of the essay? Why do you think Klass has made the technical choices that she has?

THE ROUTE TO NORMAL SCIENCE

Thomas S. Kuhn

BIOGRAPHICAL NOTE

Thomas Kuhn has taught at Harvard, Berkeley, Princeton, and MIT, and is well known for his writings on the history of science. "The Route to Normal Science" is excerpted from his 1962 book *The Structure of Scientific Revolutions*. Kuhn's ideas on paradigm shifts have also been appreciated and cited in many non-scientific fields. His other books include *The Copernican Revolution* (1957), *The Essential Tension* (1977), and *Black-Body Theory and the Quantum Discontinuity* (1987).

1   In this essay, "normal science" means research firmly based upon one or more past scientific achievements, achievements that some particular scientific community acknowledges for a time as supplying the foundation for its further practice. Today such achievements are recounted, though seldom in their original form, by science textbooks, elementary and advanced. These textbooks expound the body of accepted theory, illustrate many or all of its successful applications, and compare these applications with exemplary observations and experiments. Before such books became popular early in the nineteenth century (and until even more recently in the newly matured sciences), many of the famous classics of science fulfilled a similar function. Aristotle's *Physica*, Ptolemy's *Almagest*, Newton's *Principia* and *Opticks*, Franklin's *Electricity*, Lavoisier's *Chemistry*, and Lyell's *Geology*—these and many other works served for a time implicitly to define the legitimate problems and methods of a research field for succeeding generations of practitioners. They were able to do so because

they shared two essential characteristics. Their achievement was sufficiently unprecedented to attract an enduring group of adherents away from competing modes of scientific activity. Simultaneously, it was sufficiently open-ended to leave all sorts of problems for the redefined group of practitioners to resolve.

2   Achievements that share these two characteristics I shall henceforth refer to as "paradigms," a term that relates closely to "normal science." By choosing it, I mean to suggest that some accepted examples of actual scientific practice—examples which include law, theory, application, and instrumentation together—provide models from which spring particular coherent traditions of scientific research. These are the traditions which the historian describes under such rubrics as "Ptolemaic astronomy" (or "Copernican"), "Aristotelian dynamics" (or "Newtonian"), "corpuscular optics" (or "wave optics"), and so on. The study of paradigms, including many that are far more specialized than those named illustratively above, is what mainly prepares the student for membership in the particular scientific community with which he will later practice. Because he there joins men who learned the bases of their field from the same concrete models, his subsequent practice will seldom evoke overt disagreement over fundamentals. Men whose research is based on shared paradigms are committed to the same rules and standards for scientific practice. That commitment and the apparent consensus it produces are prerequisites for normal science, i.e., for the genesis and continuation of a particular research tradition.

3   Because in this essay the concept of a paradigm will often substitute for a variety of familiar notions, more will need to be said about the reasons for its introduction. Why is the concrete scientific achievement, as a locus of professional commitment, prior to the various concepts, laws, theories, and points of view that may be abstracted from it? In what sense is the shared paradigm a fundamental unit for the student of scientific development, a unit that cannot be fully reduced to logically atomic components which might function in its stead? . . . Answers to these questions and to others like them will prove basic to an understanding both of normal science and of the associated concept of paradigms. That more abstract discussion will depend, however, upon a previous exposure to examples of normal science or of paradigms in operation. In particular, both these related concepts will be clarified by noting that there can be a sort of scientific research without paradigms, or at least without any so unequivocal and so binding as the ones named above. Acquisition of a paradigm and of the more esoteric type of research it permits is a sign of maturity in the development of any given scientific field.

4   If the historian traces the scientific knowledge of any selected group of related phenomena backward in time, he is likely to encounter some minor variant of a pattern here illustrated from the history of physical optics. Today's physics textbooks tell the student that light is photons, i.e., quantum-mechanical entities that exhibit some characteristics of waves and some of particles. Research proceeds accordingly, or rather according to the more elaborate and mathematical characterization from which this usual verbalization is derived. That characterization of light is, however, scarcely half a century old. Before it was developed by Planck, Einstein, and others early in this century, physics texts taught that light was transverse wave motion, a conception rooted in a paradigm that derived ultimately from the optical writings of Young and Fresnel in the early nineteenth century. Nor was the wave theory the first to be embraced by almost all practitioners of optical science. During the eighteenth century the paradigm for this field was provided by Newton's *Opticks*, which taught that light

was material corpuscles. At that time physicists sought evidence, as the early wave theorists had not, of the pressure exerted by light particles impinging on solid bodies.[1]

5   These transformations of the paradigms of physical optics are scientific revolutions, and the successive transition from one paradigm to another via revolution is the usual developmental pattern of mature science. It is not, however, the pattern characteristic of the period before Newton's work, and that is the contrast that concerns us here. No period between remote antiquity and the end of the seventeenth century exhibited a single generally accepted view about the nature of light. Instead there were a number of competing schools and subschools, most of them espousing one variant or another of Epicurean, Aristotelian, or Platonic theory. One group took light to be particles emanating from material bodies; for another it was a modification of the medium that intervened between the body and the eye; still another explained light in terms of an interaction of the medium with an emanation from the eye; and there were other combinations and modifications besides. Each of the corresponding schools derived strength from its relation to some particular metaphysic, and each emphasized, as paradigmatic observations, the particular cluster of optical phenomena that its own theory could do most to explain. Other observations were dealt with by *ad hoc* elaborations, or they remained as outstanding problems for further research.[2]

6   At various times all these schools made significant contributions to the body of concepts, phenomena, and techniques from which Newton drew the first nearly uniformly accepted paradigm for physical optics. Any definition of the scientist that excludes at least the more creative members of these various schools will exclude their modern successors as well. Those men were scientists. Yet anyone examining a survey of physical optics before Newton may well conclude that, though the field's practitioners were scientists, the net result of their activity was something less than science. Being able to take no common body of belief for granted, each writer on physical optics felt forced to build his field anew from its foundations. In doing so, his choice of supporting observation and experiment was relatively free, for there was no standard set of methods or of phenomena that every optical writer felt forced to employ and explain. Under these circumstances, the dialogue of the resulting books was often directed as much to the members of other schools as it was to nature. That pattern is not unfamiliar in a number of creative fields today, nor is it incompatible with significant discovery and invention. It is not, however, the pattern of development that physical optics acquired after Newton and that other natural sciences make familiar today.

7   The history of electrical research in the first half of the eighteenth century provides a more concrete and better known example of the way a science develops before it acquires its first universally received paradigm. During that period there were almost as many views about the nature of electricity as there were important electrical experimenters, men like Hauksbee, Gray, Desaguliers, Du Fay, Nollett, Watson, Franklin, and others. All their numerous concepts of electricity had something in common—they were partially derived from one or another version of the mechanico-corpuscular philosophy that guided all scientific research of the day. In addition, all were components of real scientific theories, of theories that had been drawn in part from experiment and observation and that partially determined the choice and interpretation of additional problems undertaken in research. Yet though all the experiments were electrical and though most of the experimenters read each other's works, their theories had no more than a family resemblance.[3]

8   One early group of theories, following seventeenth-century practice, regarded attraction and frictional generation as the fundamental electrical phenomena. This group tended

to treat repulsion as a secondary effect due to some sort of mechanical rebounding and also to postpone for as long as possible both discussion and systematic research on Gray's newly discovered effect, electrical conduction. Other "electricians" (the term is their own) took attraction and repulsion to be equally elementary manifestations of electricity and modified their theories and research accordingly. (Actually, this group is remarkably small—even Franklin's theory never quite accounted for the mutual repulsion of two negatively charged bodies.) But they had as much difficulty as the first group in accounting simultaneously for any but the simplest conduction effects. Those effects, however, provided the starting point for still a third group, one which tended to speak of electricity as a "fluid" that could run through conductors rather than as an "effluvium" that emanated from non-conductors. This group, in its turn, had difficulty reconciling its theory with a number of attractive and repulsive effects. Only through the work of Franklin and his immediate successors did a theory arise that could account with something like equal facility for very nearly all these effects and that therefore could and did provide a subsequent generation of "electricians" with a common paradigm for its research.

9   Excluding those fields, like mathematics and astronomy, in which the first firm paradigms date from prehistory and also those, like biochemistry, that arose by division and recombination of specialties already matured, the situations outlined above are historically typical. Though it involves my continuing to employ the unfortunate simplification that tags an extended historical episode with a single and somewhat arbitrarily chosen name (e.g., Newton or Franklin), I suggest that similar fundamental disagreements characterized, for example, the study of motion before Aristotle and of statics before Archimedes, the study of heat before Black, of chemistry before Boyle and Boerhaave, and of historical geology before Hutton. In parts of biology—the study of heredity, for example—the first universally received paradigms are still more recent; and it remains an open question what parts of social science have yet acquired such paradigms at all. History suggests that the road to a firm research consensus is extraordinarily arduous.

10   History also suggests, however, some reasons for the difficulties encountered on that road. In the absence of a paradigm or some candidate for a paradigm, all of the facts that could possibly pertain to the development of a given science are likely to seem equally relevant. As a result, early fact-gathering is a far more nearly random activity than the one that subsequent scientific development makes familiar. Furthermore, in the absence of a reason for seeking some particular form of more recondite information, early fact-gathering is usually restricted to the wealth of data that lie ready to hand. The resulting pool of facts contains those accessible to casual observation and experiment together with some of the more esoteric data retrievable from established crafts like medicine, calendar making, and metallurgy. Because the crafts are one readily accessible source of facts that could not have been casually discovered, technology has often played a vital role in the emergence of new sciences.

11   But though this sort of fact-collecting has been essential to the origin of many significant sciences, anyone who examines, for example, Pliny's encyclopedic writings or the Baconian natural histories of the seventeenth century will discover that it produces a morass. One somehow hesitates to call the literature that results scientific. The Baconian "histories" of heat, color, wind, mining, and so on, are filled with information, some of it recondite. But they juxtapose facts that will later prove revealing (e.g., heating by mixture) with others (e.g., the warmth of dung heaps) that will for some time remain too complex to be integrated with the-

ory at all.[4] In addition, since any description must be partial, the typical natural history often omits from its immensely circumstantial accounts just those details that later scientists will find sources of important illumination. Almost none of the early "histories" of electricity, for example, mention that chaff, attracted to a rubbed glass rod, bounces off again. That effect seemed mechanical, not electrical.[5] Moreover, since the casual fact-gatherer seldom possesses the time or the tools to be critical, the natural histories often juxtapose descriptions like the above with others, say, heating by antiperistasis (or by cooling), that we are now quite unable to confirm.[6] Only very occasionally, as in the cases of ancient statics, dynamics, and geometrical optics, do facts collected with so little guidance from pre-established theory speak with sufficient clarity to permit the emergence of a first paradigm.

12   This is the situation that creates the schools characteristic of the early stages of a science's development. No natural history can be interpreted in the absence of at least some implicit body of intertwined theoretical and methodological belief that permits selection, evaluation, and criticism. If that body of belief is not already implicit in the collection of facts—in which case more than "mere facts" are at hand—it must be externally supplied, perhaps by a current metaphysic, by another science, or by personal and historical accident. No wonder, then, that in the early stages of the development of any science different men confronting the same range of phenomena, but not usually all the same particular phenomena, describe and interpret them in different ways. What is surprising, and perhaps also unique in its degree to the fields we call science, is that such initial divergences should ever largely disappear.

13   For they do disappear to a very considerable extent and then apparently once and for all. Furthermore, their disappearance is usually caused by the triumph of one of the pre-paradigm schools, which, because of its own characteristic beliefs and preconceptions, emphasized only some special part of the too sizable and inchoate pool of information. Those electricians who thought electricity a fluid and therefore gave particular emphasis to conduction provide an excellent case in point. Led by this belief, which could scarcely cope with the known multiplicity of attractive and repulsive effects, several of them conceived the idea of bottling the electrical fluid. The immediate fruit of their efforts was the Leyden jar, a device which might never have been discovered by a man exploring nature casually or at random, but which was in fact independently developed by at least two investigators in the early 1740s.[7] Almost from the start of his electrical researches, Franklin was particularly concerned to explain that strange and, in the event, particularly revealing piece of special apparatus. His success in doing so provided the most effective of the arguments that made his theory a paradigm, though one that was still unable to account for quite all the known cases of electrical repulsion.[8] To be accepted as a paradigm, a theory must seem better than its competitors, but it need not, and in fact never does, explain all the facts with which it can be confronted.

14   What the fluid theory of electricity did for the subgroup that held it, the Franklinian paradigm later did for the entire group of electricians. It suggested which experiments would be worth performing and which, because directed to secondary or to overly complex manifestations of electricity, would not. Only the paradigm did the job far more effectively, partly because the end of inter-school debate ended the constant reiteration of fundamentals and partly because the confidence that they were on the right track encouraged scientists to undertake more precise, esoteric, and consuming sorts of work.[9] Freed from the concern with any and all electrical phenomena, the united group of electricians could pursue selected phenomena in far more detail, designing much special equipment for the task and

employing it more stubbornly and systematically than electricians had ever done before. Both fact collection and theory articulation became highly directed activities. The effectiveness and efficiency of electrical research increased accordingly, providing evidence for a societal version of Francis Bacon's acute methodological dictum: "Truth emerges more readily from error than from confusion."[10]

15   We shall be examining the nature of this highly directed or paradigm-based research in the next section, but must first note briefly how the emergence of a paradigm affects the structure of the group that practices the field. When, in the development of a natural science, an individual or group first produces a synthesis able to attract most of the next generation's practitioners, the older schools gradually disappear. In part their disappearance is caused by their members' conversion to the new paradigm. But there are always some men who cling to one or another of the older views, and they are simply read out of the profession, which thereafter ignores their work. The new paradigm implies a new and more rigid definition of the field. Those unwilling or unable to accommodate their work to it must proceed in isolation or attach themselves to some other group.[11] Historically, they have often simply stayed in the departments of philosophy from which so many of the special sciences have been spawned. As these indications hint, it is sometimes just its reception of a paradigm that transforms a group previously interested merely in the study of nature into a profession or, at least, a discipline. In the sciences (though not in fields like medicine, technology, and law, of which the principal *raison d'être* is an external social need), the formation of specialized journals, the foundation of specialists' societies, and the claim for a special place in the curriculum have usually been associated with a group's first reception of a single paradigm. At least this was the case between the time, a century and a half ago, when the institutional pattern of scientific specialization first developed and the very recent time when the paraphernalia of specialization acquired a prestige of their own.

16   The more rigid definition of the scientific group has other consequences. When the individual scientist can take a paradigm for granted, he need no longer, in his major works, attempt to build his field anew, starting from first principles and justifying the use of each concept introduced. That can be left to the writer of textbooks. Given a textbook, however, the creative scientist can begin his research where it leaves off and thus concentrate exclusively upon the subtlest and most esoteric aspects of the natural phenomena that concern his group. And as he does this, his research communiqués will begin to change in ways whose evolution has been too little studied but whose modern end products are obvious to all and oppressive to many. No longer will his researches usually be embodied in books addressed, like Franklin's *Experiments . . . on Electricity* or Darwin's *The Origin of Species*, to anyone who might be interested in the subject matter of the field. Instead they will usually appear as brief articles addressed only to professional colleagues, the men whose knowledge of a shared paradigm can be assumed and who prove to be the only ones able to read the papers addressed to them.

17   Today in the sciences, books are usually either texts or retrospective reflections upon one aspect or another of the scientific life. The scientist who writes one is more likely to find his professional reputation impaired than enhanced. Only in the earlier, pre-paradigm, stages of the development of the various sciences did the book ordinarily possess the same relation to professional achievement that it still retains in other creative fields. And only in those fields that still retain the book, with or without the article, as a vehicle for research communication are the lines of professionalization still so loosely drawn that the layman may hope to follow progress by reading the practitioners' original reports. Both in mathematics and astronomy, research reports had ceased already in antiquity to be intelligible to a generally educated audience. In dynamics, research became similarly esoteric in the later Middle Ages, and it recaptured general intelligibility only briefly during the early seventeenth century when a new paradigm replaced the one that had guided medieval research. Electrical research began to require translation for the layman before the end of the eighteenth century, and most other fields of physical science ceased to be generally accessible in the nineteenth. During the same two centuries similar transitions can be isolated in the various parts of the biological sciences. In parts of the social sciences they may well be occurring today. Although it has become customary, and is surely proper, to deplore the widening gulf that separates the professional scientist from his colleagues in other fields, too little attention is paid to the essential relationship between that gulf and the mechanisms intrinsic to scientific advance.

18   Ever since prehistoric antiquity one field of study after another has crossed the divide between what the historian might call its prehistory as a science and its history proper. These transitions to maturity have seldom been so sudden or so unequivocal as my necessarily schematic discussion may have implied. But neither have they been historically gradual, coextensive, that is to say, with the entire development of the fields within which they occurred. Writers on electricity during the first four decades of the eighteenth century possessed far more information about electrical phenomena than had their sixteenth-century predecessors. During the half-century after 1740, few new sorts of electrical phenomena were added to their lists. Nevertheless, in important respects, the electrical writings of Cavendish, Coulomb, and Volta in the last third of the eighteenth century seem further removed from those of Gray, Du Fay, and even Franklin than are the writings of these early eighteenth-century electrical discoverers from those of the sixteenth century.[12] Sometime between 1740 and 1780, electricians were for the first time enabled to take the foundations of their field for granted. From that point they pushed on to more concrete and recondite problems, and increasingly they then reported their results in articles addressed to other electricians rather than in books addressed to the learned world at large. As a group they achieved what had been gained by astronomers in antiquity and by students of motion in the Middle Ages, of physical optics in the late seventeenth century, and of historical geology in the early nineteenth. They had, that is, achieved a paradigm that proved able to guide the whole group's research. Except with the advantage of hindsight, it is hard to find another criterion that so clearly proclaims a field a science.

END NOTES

1. Joseph Priestley, *The History and Present State of Discoveries Relating to Vision, Light, and Colours* (London, 1772), pp. 385-90.

2. Vasco Ronchi, *Histoire de la lumière*, trans. Jean Taton (Paris, 1956), chaps. i-iv.

3. Duane Roller and Duane H. D. Roller, *The Development of the Concept of Electric Charge: Electricity from the Greeks to Coulomb* ("Harvard Case Histories in Experimental Science," Case 8; Cambridge, Mass., 1954); and I. B. Cohen, *Franklin and Newton: An Inquiry into Speculative Newtonian Experimental Science and Franklin's Work in Electricity as an Example Thereof* (Philadelphia, 1956), chaps. vii-xii. For some of the analytic detail in the paragraph that follows in the text, I am indebted to a still unpublished

paper by my student John L. Heilbron. Pending its publication, a somewhat more extended and more precise account of the emergence of Franklin's paradigm is included in T. S. Kuhn, "The Function of Dogma in Scientific Research," in A. C. Crombie (ed.), "Symposium on the History of Science, University of Oxford, July 9-15, 1961," to be published by Heinemann Educational Books, Ltd.

4. Compare the sketch for a natural history of heat in Bacon's *Novum Organum*, Vol. VIII of *The Works of Francis Bacon*, ed. J. Spedding, R. L. Ellis, and D. D. Heath (New York, 1869), pp. 179-203.

5. Roller and Roller, *op. cit.*, pp. 14, 22, 28, 43. Only after the work recorded in the last of these citations do repulsive effects gain general recognition as unequivocally electrical.

6. Bacon, *op. cit.*, pp. 235, 337, says, "Water slightly warm is more easily frozen than quite cold." For a partial account of the earlier history of this strange observation, see Marshall Clagett, *Giovanni Marliani and Late Medieval Physics* (New York, 1941), chap. iv.

7. Roller and Roller, *op. cit.*, pp. 51-54.

8. The troublesome case was the mutual repulsion of negatively charged bodies, for which see Cohen, *op. cit.*, pp. 491-94, 531-43.

9. It should be noted that the acceptance of Franklin's theory did not end quite all debate. In 1759 Robert Symmer proposed a two-fluid version of that theory, and for many years thereafter electricians were divided about whether electricity was a single fluid or two. But the debates on this subject only confirm what has been said above about the manner in which a universally recognized achievement unites the profession. Electricians, though they continued divided on this point, rapidly concluded that no experimental tests could distinguish the two versions of the theory and that they were therefore equivalent. After that, both schools could and did exploit all the benefits that the Franklinian theory provided (*ibid.*, pp. 543-46, 548-54).

10. Bacon, *op. cit.*, p. 210.

11. The history of electricity provides an excellent example which could be duplicated from the careers of Priestley, Kelvin, and others. Franklin reports that Nollet, who at mid-century was the most influential of the Continental electricians, "lived to see himself the last of his Sect, except Mr. B.—his Eleve and immediate Disciple" (Max Farrand [ed.], *Benjamin Franklin's Memoirs* [Berkeley, Calif., 1949], pp. 384-86). More interesting, however, is the endurance of whole schools in increasing isolation from professional science. Consider, for example, the case of astrology, which was once an integral part of astronomy. Or consider the continuation in the late eighteenth and early nineteenth centuries of a previously respected tradition of "romantic" chemistry. This is the tradition discussed by Charles C. Gillispie in "The *Encyclopédie* and the Jacobin Philosophy of Science: A Study in Ideas and Consequences," *Critical Problems in the History of Science*, ed. Marshall Clagett (Madison, Wis., 1959), pp. 255-89; and "The Formation of Lamarck's Evolutionary Theory," *Archives internationales d'histoire des sciences*, XXXVII (1956), 323-38.

12. The post-Franklinian developments include an immense increase in the sensitivity of charge detectors, the first reliable and generally diffused techniques for measuring charge, the evolution of the concept of capacity and its relation to a newly refined notion

of electric tension, and the quantification of electrostatic force. On all of these see Roller and Roller, *op. cit.*, pp. 66-81; W. C. Walker, "The Detection and Estimation of Electric Charges in the Eighteenth Century," *Annals of Science*, I (1936), 66-100; and Edmund Hoppe, *Geschichte der Elektrizität* (Leipzig, 1884), Part I, chaps. iii-iv.

NOTES AND DISCUSSION

In this essay, note the heavy reliance on definitions, and on the repetition of the root word "paradigm," especially early on. Remember that Kuhn is trying to introduce a new concept and tie it to existing principles or expectations. Particularly important are his opening definition of "normal science" and his extended definition of "paradigm." Kuhn also provides some historical examples of the patterns of scientific development and progress in order to illustrate the contributions of shared paradigms, and to resurrect some largely forgotten or under-appreciated figures in the history of science.

Kuhn is also concerned with what shared paradigms allow or make possible, and with what they prevent or make difficult. He is particularly concerned with the problem of communicating science. While a shared paradigm helps to create a community that shares a set of assumptions and understands what constitutes good or productive research, that community will have to communicate in the specialized language of the paradigm, producing articles that can be understood only by the privileged few who have the particular knowledge.

Of course, paradigms guide research and complicate communication not only in science, but in the humanities as well. See, for example, Cynthia Ozick's essay, "Crocodiled Moats in the Kingdom of Letters," for a discussion of the influence of paradigms in another discipline.

Definitions are extremely important to Kuhn, but consider also his reliance on aphorisms, his own as well as those of others. For example, he claims "Acquisition of a paradigm and of the more esoteric type of research it permits is a sign of maturity in the development of any given scientific field." Later he quotes Bacon: "Truth emerges more readily from error than from confusion." What Kuhn means by "maturity" and Bacon means by "truth" might be open to interpretation.

Finally, note that Kuhn, by Douglas Hofstadter's standards at least (see "A Person Paper on Purity in Language"), has an unacknowledged paradigm of his own, namely, that science is a male field: "Men whose research is based on shared paradigms are committed to the same rules and standards for scientific practice." This gender-specific language may be more a reflection of the linguistic standards at the time of writing than of any inherent prejudice, but presents an interesting example of unconscious exclusion through vocabulary.

STUDY QUESTIONS

For Discussion:

1. In a lecture, textbook, or elsewhere, find a passage that uses too much jargon or inside knowledge for you to understand it. What was your reaction as a reader?

2. Discuss the degree to which the problem of unintelligibility, of privileged language, in science, is linked with the public suspicion of science. In your answer, consider the portrayal of a scientist in a current newspaper or news magazine, or Stephen Jay Gould's discussion of scientists in "The Monster's Human Nature."

For Writing:

1. Assess Kuhn's use of the techniques of definition, explaining how they work individually and collectively.

2. Kuhn writes, "History suggests that the road to a firm research consensus is extraordinarily arduous." As a research topic, find and assess the role of a paradigm or a major paradigm shift in the development of your major field of study, or consider whether such a shift is in progress right now.

SENSE AND SENSIBILITY

Lewis H. Lapham

BIOGRAPHICAL NOTE

Lewis H. Lapham is the editor of *Harper's Magazine* and the author of many articles and books concerned with contemporary American life. "Sense and Sensibility" is from the column he writes for *Harper's* entitled "Notebook." The column usually takes as its topic some facet of modern American society; the pieces often have a political or cultural dimension, as does this one.

---

1   *The ocean is closed.*
             —Sign posted at 5:00 P.M. by the management of a Miami Beach hotel

2   On a Tuesday afternoon in late July, in a taxi stalled for an hour in traffic on the Brooklyn Bridge, I listened to a New York literary agent praise his daughter's gift for refined political sentiment. Twenty years ago a proud father might have praised a daughter's talent for music or gymnastics, but the times have changed, and it is the exquisiteness of the moral aesthetic that prompts the cue for applause. The girl was fifteen, a student at one of the city's better private schools, already word perfect in her catechism of correct opinions. Her father was a successful dealer in high-priced pulp, and his daughter kept up with the latest cultural trends as they made their way around the beaches and lawns of East Hampton.

3   At the beginning of the spring term her biology class had taken up the study of primitive organisms, and the girls were asked to look through microscopes at a gang of bacteria toiling in a drop of water. The agent's daughter refused. No, she said, she would not look. She would not invade the privacy of the bacteria. They might be weak and small and without

important friends in Congress, but they were entitled to their rights, and she, for one, would grant them a measure of respect. After what apparently was a moment of stunned silence in the classroom, the teacher congratulated the girl for her principled dissent. Of course she didn't have to look at the bacteria. She had taught the class a lesson that couldn't be learned from a microscope.

4   The story seemed to me proof of the inanity of much of what goes by the name of higher education, but the agent was so pleased with it, so suffused with the light of virtue, that I smiled politely and said something genial and optimistic about his daughter's chances of going to Harvard. By that time the taxi had crossed the bridge, and I was glad to escape into the less rarefied atmosphere of Second Avenue before the agent began to explain his theory of global harmony. I once had listened to him give a speech on the subject to a conference of publishers, and I knew that he was capable of long recitations in what he believed to be the language of the Oglala Sioux.

5   Two days later I was still thinking about the innocent and disenfranchised bacteria when I came across a news item on an inside page of the *New York Times* that matched the literary agent's story with its appropriate corollary. The narrative was very brief, no more than a few paragraphs, and sketchy in its details, but the moral lesson was as solemn as an auto-da-fé. Well after sunset on the evening of July 16, an eight-year-old boy in Tampa, Florida, looked through the window of a building near his home and saw a man and a woman (both unmarried and both in their middle thirties) making love in a hot tub. The hot tub was in the bathroom of a condominium that the man had rented three weeks earlier, and the blinds on the window had been drawn closed. The boy reported the event to his father, who called the sheriff's office. While awaiting the arrival of the men in uniform, a small crowd gathered outside the bathroom window, and another neighbor took it upon himself to record the scene in the hot tub on videotape. He was, he said, assembling evidence.

6   "They knew we were out there," he said. "They were exhibitionists. I shot right through the blinds."

7   Both the man and the woman were arrested on charges of committing a lewd and lascivious act. They spent the rest of the night in jail, and the next morning they each had to post $15,000 bail before being let loose in the streets.

8   The vigilant schoolboy in Florida reminded me of the sensitive schoolgirl in New York, and I wondered why it was that both prodigies seemed to partake of the same spirit. At first glance they seemed so unlike each other, and it was easy enough to contrast the differences of age, sex, education, and regional prejudice. Their acts of piety expressed contradictory notions of the public good, and I could imagine each of their fathers thinking that the other father had stumbled into the snares of the Antichrist. The boy quite clearly had been born under the star of the political right. Given world enough and time, he stood a good chance of growing up to vote Republican, enforce the drug laws, and distribute Bibles or the collected works of Allan Bloom. The girl had been raised under the sign of the political left, and once she completes the formality of the curriculum at Harvard, I expect that she will write funding guidelines for the federal government or scripts for Kevin Costner.

9   The ideological differences matter less than the common temperament or habit of mind. Both the boy and the girl apparently were the kind of people who sift the grains of human feeling and experience through the cloth of milk-white abstraction, and I didn't doubt but that they never would have much use for historical circumstance or the exception that proves the rule.

10   I wish I didn't think that such people now speak for the American majority, or that the will toward conformity crowds so close to the surface of so many nominally political disputes. The spirit of the age favors the moralist and the busybody, and the instinct to censor and suppress shows itself not only in the protests for and against abortion or multiculturalism but also in the prohibitions against tobacco and pet birds. It seems that everybody is forever looking out for everybody else's spiritual or physical salvation. Doomsday is at hand, and the community of the blessed (whether defined as the New York Yacht Club or the English department at Duke) can be all too easily corrupted by the wrong diet, the wrong combination of chemicals, the wrong word. The preferred modes of address number only three—the sermon, the euphemism, and the threat—and whether I look to the political left or the political right I'm constantly being told to think the right thoughts and confess the right sins.

11   Passing through Portsmouth, Rhode Island, I see a sign on a public bus that says Do Drugs and Kiss Your Federal Benefits Goodbye. I leaf through *The Dictionary of Cautionary Words and Phrases*, compiled by a tribunal of purified journalists (the 1989 Multicultural Management Program Fellows), and I learn that I must be very, very careful when using the words "man," "woman," "watermelon," "barracuda," "community," "banana," and "impotent." Given a careless inflection or an ambiguous context, the words can be construed as deadly insults.

12   The prompters of the public alarm sound their dismal horns from so many points on the political compass that I suspect that what they wish to say isn't political. The would-be saviors in our midst worry about the moral incoherence of a society distracted by its fears— fear of apples, fear of Mexicans, fear of bankruptcy, fear of the rain—and they seek to construct the citadel of the New Jerusalem with whatever materials come most easily or obviously to hand. Every few days the newspapers bear further witness to the jury-rigged orthodoxies meant to redeem the American moral enterprise and reclaim the American soul.

13 •   The village of Chester, New York, passes a law to the effect that all the signs on all the stores of a new shopping mall must be painted blue. A merchant neglects to read the fine print on the lease and plans to put up the red sign under which he has been doing business for thirteen years. No good. Unacceptable. Either he paints the sign blue or he goes elsewhere. The village clerk, Elizabeth Kreher, overrules his objections with an air of sublime self-righteousness. "He shouldn't be complaining; he should be thankful to have such a nice place to move his store into. Plus it's a beautiful color—I just love blue."

14 •   The chairman of General Public Utilities Corporation, a married man named Hoch, admits to a love affair with a woman employed by the company as vice president of communications. The news of their liaison arrived by anonymous letter. Hoch resigns, but the woman keeps her office and title. Various spokespersons explain that a public utility depends for its rate increases on the grace and favor of the federal government and therefore must align its manners with the prevailing political trends. The feminist lobby in Washington is as loud as it is judgmental. Goodbye, Hoch.

15 •   A waiter and a waitress working in a restaurant south of Seattle refuse to serve a pregnant woman a rum daiquiri in order to lead her out of the paths of temptation. When the woman persists in her folly, the waiter and waitress (both in their early twenties and very devout in their beliefs about health and hygiene) lecture her on the evils of alcohol and read her the surgeon general's warning about drinking and birth defects.

16 •   A woman in California kisses her boyfriend goodnight on the steps of her own house, and a committee of disapproving neighbors reprimands her for lowering the tone and

character of the block. For precisely the same reason, a committee of neighbors in Illinois censures a man for parking a vulgar pickup truck in his own driveway.

17 •   Joseph Epstein, the editor of *The American Scholar* and a writer well-known both for his wit and neo-classical political views, publishes an essay in a literary journal in which he refers to "the snarling humorlessness" of various feminist critics and professors. He makes the mistake of repeating the joke about the couple in Manhattan who cannot decide whether to get a revolver or a pit bull in order to protect themselves against burglars. They compromise by hiring a feminist. The joke incites so much rage within some of the nation's more advanced universities that Epstein feels constrained to write a letter of explanation to the *New York Times* conceding that "one attempts humor at one's peril."

18   Like Queen Victoria and the National Endowment for the Arts, the Puritan spirit is not easily amused. Over the last seven or eight years I've noticed that my own experiments with irony or satire in mixed or unknown company require some introductory remark (comparable to a warning from the surgeon general) announcing the arrival of a joke that might prove harmful to somebody's self-esteem.

19   A society in which everybody distrusts everybody else classifies humor as a dangerous substance and entertains itself with cautionary tales. The news media magnify the fear of death by constantly reciting the alphabet of doom (abortion, AIDS, alcohol, asbestos, cancer, cigarettes, cocaine, etc.), and the public-service advertising extols the virtues of chastity and abstinence. The more urgent the causes of alarm, the more plausible the justifications for stricter controls. Stricter controls necessarily entail the devaluation of any and all systems of thought (most of them humanist) that make invidious distinctions between man and beast, man and moth, man and blood specimen, and I've noticed that the puritanical enthusiasms of the last several years complement and sustain the attitude of mind that assigns to human beings a steadily lower and more disreputable place in the hierarchy of multicellular life forms.

20   The rules and exhortations run to so many cross-purposes (more freedom and more rights, but also more laws and more police; no to fornication, yes to free contraceptives in the schools; yes to the possession of automatic weapons, no to the possession of cocaine) that it's hard to know what sort of perfect society our saviors have in mind. Presumably it will be clean and orderly and safe, but who will be deemed worthy of inhabiting the spheres of blameless abstraction? Maybe only the bacteria. Human beings make too much of a mess with their emotions and their wars. They poison the rivers and litter the fields with Styrofoam cups, and very few of them can be trusted with kitchen matches or the works of Aristotle.

21   I see so many citizens armed with the bright shields of intolerance that I wonder how they would agree on anything other than a need to do something repressive and authoritarian. I have no way of guessing how they will cleanse the world of its impurities, but if I were in the business of advising newly minted college graduates, I would encourage them to think along the lines of a career in law enforcement. Not simply the familiar and sometimes unpleasant forms of law enforcement—not merely the club, the handcuffs, and the noose—but law enforcement broadly and grandly conceived, law enforcement as a philosophy and way of life, as the presiding spirit that defines not only the duty of the prison guard and police spy but also the work of the food inspector, the newspaper columnist, the federal regulator, and the museum director. The job opportunities seem to me as numberless as the microbes still at large (and presumably up to no good) in the depths of the cold and unruly sea.

NOTES AND DISCUSSION

"Sense and Sensibility" is an interesting example of a comparison–contrast essay that does not side with either of the conflicting camps under discussion. Note the way Lapham uses evidence from each "side" to undermine its own argument, while making it clear throughout that his own views belong to neither camp (both of which he deems ridiculous), but are based, apparently, on reason and "common sense." Notice also his discussion of humour and satire, particularly the series of "cautionary tales" for the education and amusement of his audience. Consider who might be his targets of satire or irony.

The essay's title is clearly a reference to Jane Austen's novel *Sense and Sensibility*, with the girl of the opening paragraphs cast as a twentieth-century Marianne Dashwood. We are to remember that Austen's Marianne is romantic, eager, impetuous, and generally imprudent in her passions. The girl's counterpart, the boy in the second anecdote, is aligned with the seducer in Andrew Marvell's poem "To His Coy Mistress" through the line, "given world enough and time."

STUDY QUESTIONS

For Discussion:

1. Lapham uses literary allusions extensively in this essay. Discuss the purposes of such references, and comment on their effectiveness. Closely connected to the technique of allusion is his use of startling comparisons and contrasts. For example, Lapham writes that the girl is likely to grow up to "write funding guidelines for the federal government or scripts for Kevin Costner." What effect do such comparisons have on the reader?

2. Consider Lapham's strategies in this essay. What purpose does the epigraph serve? Is the strategy of using such a multitude of examples effective? Should Lapham have documented his cases more fully (and why do you think he has chosen not to do so)? Why does he set off the series of "cautionary tales," using bullets and spacing, in the middle of the essay?

For Writing:

1. Write a paragraph discussing the extent to which this essay is satirical. Consider in your answer how you think Lapham would respond to Hofstadter's "A Person Paper."

2. In paragraph 18, Lapham notes that "Over the last seven or eight years I've noticed that my own experiments with irony or satire in mixed or unknown company require some introductory remark . . . announcing the arrival of a joke that might prove harmful to somebody's self-esteem." Analyze Lapham's implicit claim in this paragraph that nobody's "self-esteem" should be harmed by humour, that humour is, or should be, fundamentally harmless.

A, B, AND C: THE HUMAN ELEMENT IN MATHEMATICS

Stephen Leacock

BIOGRAPHICAL NOTE

Stephen Leacock (1869–1944) trained as an economist, and was for many years a prominent member of the Department of Economics and Political Science at McGill University. He published in a variety of fields, including political science, literary criticism, and history. However, he is best known for his nearly thirty books of humour, of which *Sunshine Sketches of a Little Town* (1912) is the most famous and widely studied. The piece reprinted here is from his first book of humour, *Literary Lapses* (1910). The Stephen Leacock Award for Humour is presented annually in his honour in his hometown of Orillia, Ontario.

1   The student of arithmetic who has mastered the first four rules of his art, and successfully striven with money sums and fractions, finds himself confronted by an unbroken expanse of questions known as problems. These are short stories of adventure and industry with the end omitted, and though betraying a strong family resemblance, are not without a certain element of romance.

2   The characters in the plot of a problem are three people called A, B, and C. The form of the question is generally of this sort:

3   "A, B, and C do a certain piece of work. A can do as much work in one hour as B in two, or C in four. Find how long they work at it."

4   Or thus:

5   "A, B, and C are employed to dig a ditch. A can dig as much in one hour as B can dig in two, and B can dig twice as fast as C. Find how long, etc. etc."

6   Or after this wise:

7   "A lays a wager that he can walk faster than B or C. A can walk half as fast again as B, and C is only an indifferent walker. Find how far, and so forth."

8   The occupations of A, B, and C are many and varied. In the older arithmetics they contented themselves with doing "a certain piece of work." This statement of the case, however, was found too sly and mysterious, or possibly lacking in romantic charm. It became the fashion to define the job more clearly and to set them at walking matches, ditch-digging, regattas, and piling cord wood. At times, they became commercial and entered into partnership, having with their old mystery a "certain" capital. Above all they revel in motion. When they tire of walking-matches—A rides on horseback, or borrows a bicycle and competes with his weaker-minded associates on foot. Now they race on locomotives; now they row; or again they become historical and engage stage-coaches; or at times they are aquatic and swim. If their occupation is actual work they prefer to pump water into cisterns, two of which leak through holes in the bottom and one of which is watertight. A, of course, has the good one; he also takes the bicycle, and the best locomotive, and the right of swimming with the current. Whatever they do they put money on it, being all three sports. A always wins.

9   In the early chapters of the arithmetic, their identity is concealed under the names John, William, and Henry, and they wrangle over the division of marbles. In algebra they are often called X, Y, Z. But these are only their Christian names, and they are really the same people.

10   Now to one who has followed the history of these men through countless pages of problems, watched them in their leisure hours dallying with cord wood, and seen their panting sides heave in the full frenzy of filling a cistern with a leak in it, they become something more than mere symbols. They appear as creatures of flesh and blood, living men with their own passions, ambitions, and aspirations like the rest of us. Let us view them in turn. A is a full-blooded blustering fellow, of energetic temperament, hot-headed and strong-willed. It is he who proposes everything, challenges B to work, makes the bets, and bends the others to his will. He is a man of great physical strength and phenomenal endurance. He has been known to walk forty-eight hours at a stretch, and to pump ninety-six. His life is arduous and full of peril. A mistake in the working of a sum may keep him digging a fortnight without sleep. A repeating decimal in the answer might kill him.

11   B is a quiet, easy-going fellow, afraid of A and bullied by him, but very gentle and brotherly to little C, the weakling. He is quite in A's power, having lost all his money in bets.

12   Poor C is an undersized, frail man, with a plaintive face. Constant walking, digging, and pumping has broken his health and ruined his nervous system. His joyless life has driven him to drink and smoke more than is good for him, and his hand often shakes as he digs ditches. He has not the strength to work as the others can; in fact, as Hamlin Smith has said, "A can do more work in one hour than C in four."

13   The first time that I ever saw these men was one evening after a regatta. They had all been rowing in it, and it had transpired that A could row as much in one hour as B in two, or C in four. B and C had come in dead fagged and C was coughing badly. "Never mind, old fellow," I heard B say, "I'll fix you up on the sofa and get you some hot tea." Just then A came blustering in and shouted, "I say, you fellows, Hamlin Smith has shown me three cisterns in his garden and he says we can pump them until to-morrow night. I bet I can beat you both. Come on. You can pump in your rowing things, you know. Your cistern leaks a little, I think, C." I heard B growl that it was a dirty shame and that C was used up now, but they went, and presently I could tell from the sound of the water that A was pumping four times as fast as C.

14   For years after that I used to see them constantly about town and always busy. I never heard of any of them eating or sleeping. Then owing to a long absence from home, I lost sight

of them. On my return I was surprised to no longer find A, B, and C at their accustomed tasks; on inquiry I heard that work in this line was now done by N, M, and O, and that some people were employing for algebraical jobs, four foreigners called Alpha, Beta, Gamma, and Delta.

15   Now it chanced one day that I stumbled upon old D, in the little garden in front of his cottage, hoeing in the sun. D is an aged labouring man who used occasionally to be called in to help A, B, and C. "Did I know 'em, sir?" he answered, "why, I knowed 'em ever since they was little fellows in brackets. Master A, he were a fine lad, sir, though I always said, give me Master B for kind-heartedness-like. Many's the job as we've been on together, sir, though I never did no racing nor aught of that, but just the plain labour, as you might say. I'm getting a bit too old and stiff for it nowadays, sir—just scratch about in the garden here and grow a bit of a logarithm, or raise a common denominator or two. But Mr. Euclid he use me still for them propositions, he do."

16   From the garrulous old man I learned the melancholy end of my former acquaintances. Soon after I left town, he told me, C had been taken ill. It seems that A and B had been rowing on the river for a wager, and C had been running on the bank and then sat in a draught. Of course the bank had refused the draught and C was taken ill. A and B came home and found C lying helpless in bed. A shook him roughly and said, "Get up, C, we're going to pile wood." C looked so worn and pitiful that B said, "Look here, A, I won't stand this, he isn't fit to pile wood to-night." C smiled feebly and said, "Perhaps I might pile a little if I sat up in bed." Then B, thoroughly alarmed, said, "See here, A, I'm going to fetch a doctor; he's dying." A flared up and answered, "You've no money to fetch a doctor." "I'll reduce him to his lowest terms," B said firmly, "that'll fetch him." C's life might even then have been saved but they made a mistake about the medicine. It stood at the head of the bed on a bracket, and the nurse accidentally removed it from the bracket without changing the sign. After the fatal blunder C seems to have sunk rapidly. On the evening of the next day, as the shadows deepened in the little room, it was clear to all that the end was near. I think that even A was affected at the last as he stood with bowed head, aimlessly offering to bet with the doctor on C's laboured breathing. "A," whispered C, "I think I'm going fast." "How fast do you think you'll go, old man?" murmured A. "I don't know," said C, "but I'm going at any rate."—The end came soon after that. C rallied for a moment and asked for a certain piece of work that he had left downstairs. A put it in his arms and he expired. As his soul sped heavenward A watched its flight with melancholy admiration. B burst into a passionate flood of tears and sobbed, "Put away his little cistern and the rowing clothes he used to wear, I feel as if I could hardly ever dig again."—The funeral was plain and unostentatious. It differed in nothing from the ordinary, except that out of deference to sporting men and mathematicians, A engaged two hearses. Both vehicles started at the same time, B driving the one which bore the sable parallelopiped containing the last remains of his ill-fated friend. A on the box of the empty hearse generously consented to a handicap of a hundred yards, but arrived first at the cemetery by driving four times as fast as B. (Find the distance to the cemetery.) As the sarcophagus was lowered, the grave was surrounded by the broken figures of the first book of Euclid.—It was noticed that after the death of C, A became a changed man. He lost interest in racing with B, and dug but languidly. He finally gave up his work and settled down to live on the interest of his bets.—B never recovered from the shock of C's death; his grief preyed upon his intellect and it became deranged. He grew moody and spoke only in monosyllables. His disease became rapidly aggravated, and he presently spoke only in words whose spelling was regular and which presented no difficulty to the beginner.

Realizing his precarious condition he voluntarily submitted to be incarcerated in an asylum, where he abjured mathematics and devoted himself to writing the History of the Swiss Family Robinson in words of one syllable.

NOTES AND DISCUSSION

Leacock, or his persona, takes his examples from the arithmetic texts and primers of "another era," which, we assume, is a period earlier than Leacock's own. He achieves the humour in this piece through the deceptively simple practice of writing about something abstract as though it were concrete. In moving from one level of discourse or frame of reference to another, the narrator displays what George Meredith identifies as a key element of humour: the failure to act with common sense. The narrator even casts himself as a character in the lives of the symbols, as when he interviews D.

Equally humorous are A, B, and C themselves (and their various aliases, disguises, and successors). In their predictable behaviours and fixed relationships, they illustrate another theory: Bergson's belief that humour results from the grafting of the mechanical or automatic onto the human.

There are other witty elements here as well, including puns, such as those surrounding C's fatal illness. Moreover, the essay seems at times a parody of literary analysis and criticism: the speaker calls the problems "short stories," and children's elementary spelling and reading lessons are often called their "A-B-Cs."

STUDY QUESTIONS

For Discussion:

1. Leacock's technique of shifting from the world of mathematics to the world of the "short story" would be much more difficult with more advanced texts and their array of more complex symbols. Do you think there is a limit to how simple or complex the "problem" can be? Discuss whether models of symbolic "behaviour" are all the same beneath the surface, regardless of their complexity.

2. What does Leacock's essay have to say about our human tendency to find or create narrative? Hayden White, the historiographer, suggests that historians define the beginnings and ends of "historical events" by the transition or failure of transition into new moral levels. In what ways is this moral shaping of events at work, in the "lives" of A, B, and C?

For Writing:

1. Attempt a humorous effect similar to Leacock's by transferring the terms or symbols from a course you are currently taking into a brief narrative relating their misadventures; or displace some literary figures into "roles" as symbols in a formula or calculation. Remember that mathematical symbols have "grammatical" functions: the variables are nouns, while the function symbols, such as the equal sign, are verbs.

2. Analyze the essay's final paragraph for tone and humorous technique. What is the effect of the funeral story, and of what happens to B? That is, how does the paragraph extend and complete the work of the rest of the essay?

FINGER-POINTING

Robert W. Lucky

BIOGRAPHICAL NOTE

Robert W. Lucky, a long-time columnist for *IEEE Spectrum*, has written three books: *Principles of Data Communication* (1968), *Computer Communications* (1975), and *Silicon Dreams: Information, Man, and Machine* (1989). The latter book was written while he was Executive Director of Research for AT&T Bell Labs and deals with the representation of information in appropriate formats for both people and computers. In 1987 he received the Marconi International Fellowship.

1   Have you ever been associated with a failed project? Probably you haven't; no one else I know has either. All the biographies I read speak of successes. Failure does not occur. Yet somehow I remember various schedules that weren't met, programs that didn't function, research that fizzled, and products that didn't sell. It's funny—all the people are successful; it is only the projects that fail.

2   There are some basic laws of life involved here. We all know that things will go wrong, as is well documented in the classic paper by Murphy. With electrical engineering projects as complicated as they are these days, there is no question that things will inevitably become a muddle. The only question is—who will be blamed?

3   It seems that we all have an innate ability to escape guilt. Either that, or finger-pointing is the immediate subject of on-the-job training, because little of our educational experiences seem relevant. When you fail a test in college, your name is at the top of the paper, next to the "F"; pointing your finger at other people is not effective. In the complexities of the real

world there is no "F" at the top of the paper, but—more important—there is no name there either.

4   Why is there no name to be blamed at the top of a real-life test? Most companies talk tough about rewards for success and penalties for failure. It just seems that in the latter case no one can be found to assume responsibility. (In the case of success, there does not seem to be a problem finding a plethora of responsible parties.)

5   In the event of failure, there are often organizational reasons why no guilty person can be found. In the turmoil of modern life in the high-tech world, reorganizations are so frequent that it is not clear in retrospect who was in charge at the time the failure occurred, since this instant cannot be properly isolated. It would be a simplification to say this is exactly like a game of musical chairs where someone is left standing at the moment the music stops. Picture instead the music fading away gradually and the cast of players constantly changing in confusion, while a maintenance crew is mysteriously removing chairs in the midst of the competition.

6   Have you ever noticed that some executives seem to leave behind a wake of disastrous projects, always being promoted out of a job before it sours? They can always insist the project would have been a success had they remained in charge. Timing is everything, but even extraordinarily bad timing can be overcome if the management level is high enough. For example, I have even heard a theory of promotional advancement that depends upon being at the helm of a debacle when it crashes. Naturally one's career undergoes a momentary lull, but in later years people forget the history of the unfortunate project and remember only the name of the manager. "Oh, of course I remember Stan," they say. "We'd be lucky to have someone as well known as he to accept this modest promotion."

7   At the bottom of the organizational structure, the tactics for guilt avoidance are necessarily different. Cunning and craftiness are often needed to supplement questionable engineering. There is a strategy usually referred to only by its acronym, CYA, that many believe to be effective. For example, before a final design is submitted, you issue a memorandum pointing out possible weaknesses in the data and components supplied by other company divisions. Of course, it will be necessary to defend your own design against their allegations, but always leave yourself an out. Your design utilizes the finest technology and the latest principles, but you are depending on the integrated widget being available on schedule and meeting certain specifications. You would not recommend your backup design. (Don't worry about the integrated-widget people becoming the villains should things go awry—they are depending on the device department, which in turn has been promised certain materials from a subcontractor.)

8   I wonder how George Washington would handle all this if he were an electrical engineer? Chopping down cherry trees isn't in vogue the way it used to be. If George were a designer, he would be anxious to admit to any error that he had committed. "I cannot tell a lie," he would tell his associates. "It was my design of the bus interface board which caused our product to fail."

9   His friends would give him wise counsel, both because George looks like an up-and-coming engineer and because guilt in an organization can bring lightning from the corporate sky. "George, you're not being modern," they would say. "How could you have known that the systems department had underspecified the drive capability your board would need? The marketing people added features at the last moment. It has nothing to do with us, George."

10   I don't think George would have been dissuaded. Believing in the domino theory of "for want of a nail, etc.," George would go to his department head and confess "I cannot tell a lie," he would repeat. "It was my design that caused our company's quarterly return to be below expectations."

11   At the next board meeting the president would be fuming about the dismal performance in the market. "Heads will roll for this," he would threaten. His underlings would jump to the defenses. "We have already conducted an investigation, and we have identified the person responsible. His name is George Washington. He works in the widget design department." I can imagine the president becoming very irritated at this disclosure. "I never heard of George Washington," he might shout. "I want to fire someone important! What is the name of Washington's department head?"

12   In the contemporary engineering world guilt is a very abstract concept. When I think of my George Washington fantasy, I realize how difficult it would be even to claim guilt. So why do I see all the finger-pointing and people covering themselves against contingencies?

13   Perhaps it is all a game we see played out elsewhere in the business world. Somehow, I'd like to think engineers are just a little above all that. Maybe tomorrow George Washington will come into my office with his confession, and I'll see how well I fare with my own convictions.

NOTES AND DISCUSSION

In "Finger-Pointing" Robert Lucky establishes an informal, personal tone in the opening paragraph by asking the reader a direct question. He also asks questions at transitional points in paragraphs 2, 4, 6, and 8, as he moves into new topics, and, in paragraph 12, as he shifts into his conclusion. Each developmental section answers the question that begins it. The tone is also gently humorous, though he asks his readers to consider a serious problem.

For coherency, Lucky repeats key words, especially in the introduction. For clarity, he provides examples and illustrations and, in paragraph 5, develops an analogy using the familiar game of musical chairs.

Finally, note that, even though this is a "factual" essay, Lucky creates an imaginary scenario that builds another analogy out of a U.S. cultural hero. Through this analogy he personalizes a situation that, he argues, is often left impersonal and anonymous for reasons that the dialogue makes clear. You might want to compare Lucky's fictional support with John Ruskin's fictitious dialogue in "The English Villa," or with David Suzuki's analogy of the car-crash in "The Road from Rio," or with Rachel Carson's story in "A Fable for Tomorrow."

Study Questions

For Discussion:

1. Lucky does not name as failures any specific people or real companies. In what ways does this lack of documentary evidence help or hinder his argument? What does he rely on instead of evidence?

2. Contrast Lucky's discussion of failure with Henry Petroski's in "Lessons from Play; Lessons from Life." If failure is just a necessary part of the creative process (as Petroski claims), why are so many people trying to deny or avoid association with it (as Lucky claims)?

For Writing:

1. As a research project, find and report examples of engineers or other professionals who blew the whistle on what they considered faulty projects or practices.

2. Write a memo regarding the perceived problems with a *hypothetical* project or situation defined by the class.

BEGINNING TO UNDERSTAND THE BEGINNING

Rick McConnell

BIOGRAPHICAL NOTE

Rick McConnell writes a regular column in the "Life" section of the *Edmonton Journal*. Following his graduation from the Journalism program at the Southern Alberta Institute of Technology (SAIT), he worked for smaller newspapers in North Battleford and Moose Jaw, Saskatchewan, covering a range of fields, from farm news to city council. He started at the *Journal* in 1989 as a general reporter. Because his assigned subject is now "life," he says, "I like to think I'm doing research all the time."

1   All beginnings are hard.

2   Novelist Chaim Potok was right when he wrote that. Beginnings are hard. All of them.

3   Whether you are starting a lifetime of education with your first day of kindergarten, or beginning a friendship, a marriage, or a new job, it's important to get started on the right foot.

4   Those of us in the writing game know this as well as anyone. Every column, every news story, every short story, even an epic novel, has to get off to a good start. That crucial first sentence is, well . . . just that, crucial. If we don't get you interested right from the start, you might get bored and wander over to the comics page or close the book and flip on the TV.

5   In the newspaper business we call these first sentences "leads." We agonize over them, sweat over them, talk about them, put them off as long as possible. Sometimes we'll walk around the room and bother other people; if you can't think of a good lead, at least you can keep someone else from getting started on what they're doing while you're not doing what you should be doing.

First published in the *Edmonton Journal*, May 9, 1996. Reprinted with permission of the *Edmonton Journal*.

6   The best newspaper lead I ever saw was written by James (Scotty) Reston of the *New York Times*. On November 22, 1963, Reston was at the *Times* Washington bureau when word came in that President John F. Kennedy had been assassinated. While the main news stories about the shooting, the arrest of a suspect, and the swearing in of the new president fell to reporters in the field, Reston was asked to sum up the feelings of a nation for the next day's front page. So he sat down at his old manual typewriter and opened a vein, as sportswriter Red Smith liked to put it. This two-sentence lead was the result:

7   "America wept tonight, not alone for its dead young president, but for itself. The grief was general, for somehow the worst in the nation had prevailed over the best."

8   I didn't have to look that up to get it right. I know those two lines better than any I have ever written myself. What Reston wrote that day was simply the best beginning to a newspaper story ever. The rest of us can spend the rest of eternity trying to write the second best.

9   Because I love beginnings so much, I use them as a way to judge all writing. I even shop for books by opening to the first page and reading the opening sentence. If I like it, I'll flip inside and read the beginnings of a couple of other chapters. Then I'll read the blurb on the jacket.

10   Then I'll take it home and, often as not, find out I bought the same book two years ago and have already read it twice.

11   Poking through my shelves the other day I found two copies of Normal Mailer's *The Naked and the Dead*. If I lose one, I'll still be able to turn to the opening page and read his first sentence. "Nobody could sleep." That's all it says. I've read that line dozens of times and the whole book three times. It never puts me to sleep.

12   "In our family, there was no clear line between religion and fly fishing." Maybe not, but Norman Maclean knew there was a line between good writing and boring writing when he used that sentence to open his novella *A River Runs Through It*. I've been hooked on his writing for years.

13   Here are some other opening lines I love:

14   "My father said he saw him years later playing in a tenth-rate commercial league in a textile town in Carolina, wearing shoes and an assumed name." (*Shoeless Joe* by W. P. Kinsella.)

15   "Above the town, on the hill brow, the stone angel used to stand." (*The Stone Angel* by Margaret Laurence.)

16   Beginnings can be wacky:

17   "We were somewhere around Barstow on the edge of the desert when the drugs began to take hold." (*Fear and Loathing in Las Vegas* by Hunter S. Thompson.)

18   Or dramatic:

19   "She only stopped screaming when she died." (*Kane and Abel* by Jeffery Archer.)

20   Or they can just set a nice scene:

21   "When Augustus came out on the porch the blue pigs were eating a rattlesnake—not a very big one." (*Lonesome Dove* by Larry McMurtry.)

22   "A few miles south of Soledad, the Salinas River drops in close to the hillside bank and runs deep and green." (*Of Mice and Men* by John Steinbeck.)

23   But the fact remains, all beginnings are hard and good ones are even harder.

24   That's why I stole the beginning of this column from Chaim Potok. It's actually the first line of his novel *In the Beginning*.

25   Potok knew what he was talking about. Then again, maybe Clive Barker put it better. He started his 1987 novel *Weaveworld* with this sentence:

26   "Nothing ever begins."

27   Hmmm. I'll have to think about that.

NOTES AND DISCUSSION

Ask any writer which sentence is the most difficult to write in any piece, and the answer is most commonly "the first." Even (or especially) professionals sweat to find or craft this crucial sentence, as Rick McConnell attests. Often the problem with beginnings arises because the writer has not yet decided what to say, or has not done enough pre-writing. For student writers, the problem often stems from trying to be perfect too early in the writing process. Sometimes they solve the problem by writing a general opening statement, which, if it names or is directly related to the topic, can help focus the reader's attention. However, an opening statement about the history of the world or a general concept of life, science, or literature is of little benefit.

McConnell knows that a good lead speaks for itself and draws readers into the world of the piece. He offers little advice but many examples; plenty of writing texts list techniques for writing effective openings and point out the flaws of bad ones. McConnell does not explain much; he lets the words work on his reader the way they have worked on him. In effect, he provides models, rather than theories, and writing and rhetoric teachers since the ancient Greeks have advised their students to seek good models to emulate.

STUDY QUESTIONS

For Discussion:

1. Examine the opening sentences of several essays in this collection. Which seem most effective, and why? Consider such matters as length, vocabulary, rhythm, structure, and figures of speech (similes, metaphors, etc.). How do the effective openings get the reader interested or set the mood for what follows?

2. Some of McConnell's examples are from non-fiction; others, from fiction. Draw up your own list of examples from a variety of sources, and see if the techniques of fiction are significantly different from those of nonfiction. Consider these, for example:

   A screaming comes across the sky. (Thomas Pynchon, *Gravity's Rainbow*)

   It was in Burma, a sodden morning of the rains. (George Orwell, "A Hanging")

   Under the pale outrage of a breaking sky, the plane thuds. (Aritha van Herk, *The Tent Peg*)

   A strange place it was, that place where the world began. (Margaret Laurence, "Where the World Began")

   With a clamour of bells that set the swallows soaring, the Festival of Summer came to the city of Omelas, bright-towered by the sea. (Ursula LeGuin, "The Ones Who Walk Away from Omelas")

FOR WRITING:

1. Explain how the titles and opening sentences of several essays work together to complement each other and to focus the reader's attention and engage his or her interest.

2. Concluding sentences are often as hard to write as openings, because the essay should end gracefully, but not terminate interest in the topic. When you find effective openings, compare their content and form to the concluding sentences of the essays. Do the conclusions return to key words or concepts? Echo the tone? How do they announce "the end" without ending with a rhetorical thud?

WHY THE DEFICIT IS A GODSEND

AND FIVE OTHER ECONOMIC HERESIES

Walter Russell Mead

BIOGRAPHICAL NOTE

Walter Russell Mead is a writer and contributing editor to *Harper's Magazine*. This essay was first published in *Harper's*.

---

1   "A rise in the corporate tax rate is not likely to raise additional revenue," Bruce Bartlett announced to the nation, via the opinion page of *The Wall Street Journal*, less than twelve hours after President Clinton had finished his February 17 address to a joint session of Congress. In seven paragraphs he summoned no fewer than nine "statistics" from, as he put it, "the data"; and the piece was accompanied by a tidy graph. Bartlett, who was a senior economist at the Treasury Department during the Reagan and Bush administrations, is now comfortably ensconced at the libertarian Cato Institute, one of numerous Washington "think tanks" that serve as the Delphic temples for our rather colorless oracles, the economists.

2   The ancient Romans used to send for the augurs. In Washington you send for the economists. The Romans were probably better served. Augury, the practice of reading the future from such portents as the flight of birds and the entrails of sacrificial cattle, was about as scientific as economics, but the Roman priests were often men of wide practical experience whose predictions and warnings may have represented the best available advice. American economists, by contrast, are mostly visiting scholars or tenured academics—that is, people who do not really know how anything works and have little incentive to learn.

3   That this circumstance has not kept economists from divining and forewarning, soothsaying and prophesying, has never been more obvious than in recent months. With Clinton's

announcement of his plan to raise the income tax of the wealthy, establish a broad-based energy tax, trim the funding of dozens of government programs, and spend $16 billion more on an assortment of others—all in the name of stimulating the economy in the short term, trimming the federal deficit by 1996, and creating more and better jobs by century's end—the nation's capital has been besieged by economists. One glimpses them whispering in the ears of Lloyd Bentsen and Dan Rostenkowski, waving computer-generated rows of figures before White House correspondents, uttering sibylline predictions of weal or woe into the clip-on microphones provided by Ted Koppel and Jim Lehrer.

4   Where else but in the nation's capital could economists count on such prestige, such reverence? Because who more than elected politicians have a need to dress up the favors asked by their most influential constituents and campaign backers with crunched statistics, policy jargon, and elegant theories? It should surprise no one that the numbers and notions that form the canon of the true economic faith in Washington today are those that promise to keep the nation's elite well provided for in this world, if not in the next.

5   Allow me to borrow an image from Voltaire: Until the last host of a Sunday-morning public-affairs program is strangled in the entrails of the last economist, those whose standard of living is not the concern of the Brookings Institution, the American Enterprise Institute, et al.—that is, most of us—would do well to practice an attitude of militant heresy. Turn a deaf ear to the false prophets. Take no action based on their superstitious mutterings. Scoff at their warnings and trample upon their edicts. Study, for the sake of demystification, the following articles of faith, proclaimed by the defenders of orthodoxy. And pray that none of their superstitions, however widely believed, comes to influence public policy.

I. THE NATIONAL DEBT AND THE ANNUAL FEDERAL BUDGET DEFICIT ARE WICKED AND CORRUPTING.

6   This particular belief has won many recent converts, no doubt due to its being fervidly embraced by H. Ross Perot, a man who also remains convinced the North Vietnamese sent hit squads to get him. Perot, of course, got religion from the economists (who somehow—and this may be the only miracle economists are capable of—manage to gain influence with rich men only *after* they've made their fortunes).

7   Try to find a Washington economist who is not sure that the national debt is a harbinger of doom. Watch Federal Reserve Chairman Alan Greenspan or Brookings Institution cleric Henry J. Aaron do impressions of the prophet Jeremiah. We have been spending too much and saving too little—alackaday and alas! We are eating the seed corn, consuming the resources that ought to have ensured the prosperity of our children. *O tempora! O mores!*

8   The superstitious and the ill-informed—a group by no means confined to the social sciences—have railed against government deficits and debts ever since the inspired Whig merchants of London created the Bank of England to fund British foreign policy and stabilize domestic affairs after the Glorious Revolution. About a hundred years later, Alexander Hamilton established the foundations for a strong federal republic here on the proper reasoning that the national debt is also a national asset. Hamilton rightly saw the national debt as a political blessing: bondholders are the last people to want the government to collapse. He predicted that the debt would unite those in each of the thirteen states who purchased the new government's bonds; after all, if the government fell, so would the price of their interest-bearing certificates. He was totally, brilliantly right.

9   The principle still holds. The governments of Germany and Japan are much more willing to support the economic policies of the United States than we have any right to expect. The reason? U.S. government obligations held by their citizens, their corporations, and
their central banks create a mighty bond of interest between them and us. If we go down,
they come too.

10   Fear of the national debt, it should be said, is not a recent superstition. Thomas Jefferson
thought the national debt would ruin the country when it stood at $75 million. It had grown
to more than thirty times that size by the end of the Civil War, when President Andrew
Johnson warned that this level of debt made the American people "slaves" to tax gatherers
and bondholders. During the next two generations those same "enslaved" Americans built
the transcontinental railroads, among other things, and the country became the greatest industrial power in the world.

11   The cries of doom became louder when World War I sent the debt to $24 billion; what
actually resulted was the Roaring Twenties, a decade of economic expansion and growing
federal debt not unlike the Reagan Eighties. One might well argue that the money the US government spent in the 1980s (on the defense buildup, for example) was money spent un-
wisely, or that the taxes the government chose not to collect (on the well-to-do, for example)
were tax revenues that justice demanded be collected. But these are *political* matters, not economic ones. What the black-cowled economists claim is that debt—debt *by definition* and
in and of itself—tends to inflate the currency, drive up interest rates, and crowd out private
borrowing. The 1980s simply failed to prove this theorem.

12   During the Reagan and Bush administrations, as the annual budget deficit rose to nearly
$300 billion, the annual rate of inflation fell from 13.5 percent (in 1980) to 2.9 percent (in
1992). Turning to interest rates, throughout the 1980s both nominal and real interest rates generally fell, even as the "ruinous" deficit rose. Interest rates on federal overnight funds—
loans commercial banks make to one another—were at 16.4 percent in 1981, when the deficit
began to widen; they were down to 3.5 percent when Clinton took office. And interest rates
on long-term government bonds fell from a peak of 14 percent in 1982 to about 7 percent last
fall, at the very time Ross Perot was turning the deficit into a major campaign issue.

13   As to the alleged Washington-driven credit crunch: Did the increased borrowing of the
national government drive private borrowers from the capital markets? Well, no. The 1980s
were years of great speculative bubbles, leveraged buyouts, and other corporate profligacy,
all of which drove corporations deeper into debt than ever before. Such shenanigans on the
part of our corporate barons *were* disgraceful, true. But all this had nothing to do with any
inability of CEOs to borrow money. The decade saw a frenzy of debt, an orgy of debt. A
stock-market crash like that of October 1987 does not bring down countless "margin buy-
ers" unless loans are easy to come by. The 1980s were not starved for capital; they were a
decade awash with capital, and investors seeking a quick fortune rather than long-term productive investments shoveled their borrowed dollars into the hands of any scoundrel with a
plausible story to tell.

14   Historically, much more damage has come from efforts to pay down the national debt than
from running it up. Herbert Hoover, warning of "the tears and anguish of universal bankruptcy," dutifully worked to reduce the national debt right up to the advent of the Great
Depression, which his policies helped usher in. And Franklin Roosevelt actually gave the
Depression a second wind when he tried to balance the budget in his second term.

15   Give the deficit some respect: let it grow within reason—and the current $300 billion deficit, which is only 5 percent of the gross domestic product, is not pushing the envelope. Be nice to the deficit, and it will be nice to you.

II. RAISE THE TAXES OF THE RICH, AND BAD TIMES WILL SOON BE AT HAND.

16   Next to the evils of the deficit, the subject that calls forth the most heartrending lamentations from economists is the crushing burden of taxation on those who make the most. "Envy and demagoguery," Harvard economist Lawrence Lindsey has insisted, are solely responsible for high taxes on the well-to-do. Commenting on Clinton's plan to increase from 31 percent to 36 percent the rate of taxation on those whose joint income is more than $140,000, Alan Reynolds, director of economic research at the Hudson Institute, declared that "the proposed steep tax penalties on success demoralize the ambitious, reducing the incentive for young people to do the difficult things required to earn high incomes in the future." Progressive income taxes and capital-gains taxes, the orthodox economists would have us believe, destroy the incentives of the rich to make money, to save, and to invest. The result is slow growth and poorer prospects for everyone else.

17   The evidence points precisely the other way. Prosperous economic periods are linked not only to times of high government deficits but to times when the rich are heavily taxed. Take the Twenties. Those who earned more than $1 million in 1921 paid 73 percent tax on their additional income; the economy grew 15.8 percent. This was the best year of the Roaring Twenties. By 1929 the marginal tax on the rich had fallen to 24 percent. Amazingly enough, the economy responded by falling into depression.

18   Taxes rose again, quite dramatically, during World War II, and the top nominal marginal tax rates never dropped below 70 percent between 1940 and 1970. In 1981 Ronald Reagan came to power, determined to cut the fetters that had so tragically thwarted the incentive of a generation of American entrepreneurs. Although tax reforms moderated the impact, nominal tax rates sank rapidly; the top rate fell from 63 percent in 1980 to 33 percent in 1986. Fortunately, Reagan was careful to nurture a healthy national debt. Thanks to the burgeoning deficits of the 1980s, low tax rates on the rich did not bring about a depression—they only slowed down our growth, which averaged 2.9 percent in the Reagan--Bush years.

19   How to explain the relationship between high taxes on the rich and prosperity? High welfare payments are opposed on the grounds that they take away the incentive of poor people to work. Conceivably, rich people may think the same way. Once you've got the yacht, why keep working? If you can live well by just parking your money in the bank or in bonds, why back an entrepreneur? Increasing their taxes drives the rich to invest more cleverly and to work harder in the same way that cutting social benefits forces working people to look harder for work and to take jobs they might otherwise turn down.

20   More important is that the high-growth postwar decades were periods not simply of high taxes but of fixed exchange rates, controls on the movement of capital across national frontiers, and increased government involvement in industry and labor markets. A government that taxes highly also tends to be a government that understands an active role in the economy extends beyond firing unionized air-traffic controllers. High-taxing administrations have historically been those that encourage powerful unions, which, in turn, can demand the good wages the spending of which fuels growth. Try to find an economist in Washington

these days arguing the place of strong unions in easing joblessness and creating economic growth! Such blasphemies are seldom uttered.

III. INFLATION IS THE ROOT OF ALL EVIL.

21   Inflation is a disease, not a sin—but don't expect to be invited to any Washington economic conference if you say so.

22   Actually, inflation is best thought of as a family of diseases, like cancer. The rather terrible bout of inflation that swept the Western world in the 1970s was a rare strain. It was caused by the collapse of the Bretton Woods currency system. The price of gold moved from $35 an ounce in 1971 to $400 an ounce by late 1979. This was, in effect, a massive devaluation of paper money against gold, and it set off a chain reaction as producers of raw materials—especially Middle Eastern producers of oil—sought to protect their incomes, as measured in gold, from the devaluation of the dollar. Inflation jumped in every country—in the United States it peaked at 13.5 percent in 1980—before easing in the mid-1980s.

23   To summon up the Carter years as an excuse not to fund government programs is a politician's tactic and an economist's trick. Most bouts of inflation are simply a manifestation of the business cycle of a healthy economy. As an economic expansion matures, the productive capacity of the economy nears its limits. Factories are busy, and raw materials and labor are in short supply. The demand allows producers and workers to raise their prices, and these rising prices ricochet throughout the economy. Ultimately, this kind of inflation causes the economy to overheat and go into recession; but, however annoying, it does not bring about economic collapse.

24   There is no threat of inflation just now. If there is a danger today, it is *de*-flation. The collapse of the commercial real-estate market and the decline of housing prices throughout the English-speaking world in the late 1980s triggered a wider recession that is now afflicting Europe and Japan. Meanwhile there are continuing signs in the world's major industries—automobiles, aerospace, steel, and even computers—of an enormous excess capacity, usually a sure sign of deflation. Real wages continue to fall in the United States; unemployment in Europe is climbing. These are not signs of inflation.

25   History teaches that deflation has a tendency to increase international tensions. Western Europe, the United States, and Japan are bickering with one another when they should be working together to nurture global growth. Trade tension between the developing industries of the south and the glutted markets of the north is turning into real political tension—especially between China, as well as other, smaller East Asian nations, and the United States. Western Europe is refusing to open its markets to the world-be producers of the East, increasing the likelihood of anarchy in the formerly Communist world.

26   One thing to keep in mind that economists often forget: inflation makes people unhappy; deflation causes wars.

IV. INTERNATIONAL FREE TRADE CAN BE ACHIEVED FOR THE GOOD OF ALL.

27   In economic theory, free trade refers to a condition under which no legal or social barriers impede trade among any number of economic entities. Investors, workers, farmers, and factory owners in countries A, B, and C can buy and sell labor, capital, farm goods, or any other commodity in any of the three countries. This is absolute free trade, and it is as impossible to achieve as absolute zero—although you would not think it if you sat through a Senate hearing on the General Agreement on Tariffs and Trade (GATT) or the North American Free Trade Agreement (NAFTA), the two trade agreements now on the national agenda.

28   Free trade is a theoretical horizon, not a practical goal. New York today does not have absolute free trade with Connecticut; lawyers, doctors, stockbrokers, and cabdrivers licensed in one state cannot operate freely in the other. Although absolute free trade never has existed anywhere in the world, it is an important concept for economic theory because it represents one of the conditions under which economies theoretically approach their optimum performance. It is an appealing idea to toss before voters because freedom itself is appealing. Why should governments limit the right of consumers to buy and the right of producers to sell?

29   Unfortunately, economists tend not to think very clearly about the relation of absolute free trade to concrete trade policy proposals. Yes, absolute free trade might well be the best of all imaginable trading regimens. Yes, in general the reduction of barriers to trade between nations is a good thing. But economists, many of whom have never held in their hands, much less ever read, the proposed text of either GATT or NAFTA, stumble uncritically into the absurd position of defending these agreements because they are "free trade" agreements. This is flat-out wrong. Both GATT and NAFTA are *managed* trade agreements, and they are bad ones at that. They lower some barriers to trade, keep others high, and contain vast and lucrative loopholes that benefit interest groups who were successful at lobbying powerful elected officials.

30   The Uruguay Round of GATT talks aims at a peculiar kind of trade regimen. Capital will be as free as possible to migrate around the world in search of better investment opportunities. Goods will be freer than ever before to travel around the world in search of better markets and higher prices. Only labor will wear chains: workers from Bangladesh have no chance to better their wages by moving to Brussels. The ability of companies to use low-wage countries to produce goods for high-wage markets is the centerpiece of GATT's economic strategy.

31   This is not a new system in world history. Great Britain had a similar system in the late eighteenth century. Goods and capital were free to circulate in the British economy, but the movement of labor was restricted by poor laws dating back to the reign of Elizabeth I. These laws made it virtually impossible for working people to move from the parish where they were born—where wages might be low and opportunities limited—to a parish where conditions were better. Adam Smith denounced the tendency of these laws to produce illegal "aliens" and irrational, costly wage differentials, and his followers attacked and denounced the poor laws until they were repealed in 1834.

32   This system that Smith attacked is the system that GATT wants to set up worldwide—and that NAFTA wants to establish in North America. Nations are to become the new parishes; immigration police assume the role of parish wardens, deporting illegals and enforcing an irrational, discriminatory, and costly system of market regulation—one likely to slow down world growth and technological progress.

33   New investment in management, training, and technology is the engine of productivity growth. When labor is expensive, managers have an incentive to reduce their use of labor by investing in new technologies and methods. When labor is cheap, this incentive is reduced. Japan, with its aging population and its reluctance to allow immigration, has led the way in

raising industrial productivity through capital-intensive investments. GATT and NAFTA will improve access to low-wage labor and therefore will reduce the economic advantage of technological investment; it is not unreasonable to expect a slowdown in the rate of development and introduction of new technologies. One can even note that both U.S. productivity growth and real wages have declined substantially since the Tokyo Round of GATT talks, concluded in 1979, increased the ability of multi-national companies to use labor in low-wage countries.

V. WHAT THE WORLD'S POOR NEED IS LAISSEZ-FAIRE CAPITALISM.

34   Economists are never as confident or as dogmatic as when they are giving advice to developing countries. From the World Bank and the International Monetary Fund, to say nothing of Washington's think tanks, pour forth the encyclicals and injunctions: Open your markets to foreign capital and goods. Respect intellectual-property rights. Pay your debts. Deregulate your domestic markets. Dismantle your state planning agencies and trust in the benevolence of the invisible hand.

35   This advice has only one disadvantage: it doesn't work and never has. No country that has successfully developed has ever followed this path. Countries that eschew the laws of laissez-faire perform demonstrably better than countries that embrace it. This has been true from the start of the Industrial Revolution, and it is true today.

36   Even nineteenth-century Britain and America, portrayed in economic lore as the most virtuously laissez-faire of rising economies, were never free traders. Britain developed its infant industries behind the walls of high tariffs and a tight technical embargo. It was illegal to export blueprints of textile machinery. Britain did not begin to embrace the god of the invisible hand until its own industries had achieved technological supremacy.

37   George Washington, Alexander Hamilton, and Thomas Jefferson were all protectionists. So were Abraham Lincoln and Teddy Roosevelt. The United States developed behind high tariff barriers. Intellectual-property rights were scoffed at; for most of its first century of independence the United States refused to recognize foreign copyrights of any kind. American states repudiated their foreign debts—Mississippi is still in default from the time of Andrew Jackson. The guiding hand of government was visible in tariff policy, and it consciously selected which industries to foster and which to expose to international competition. From the Northwest Ordinance to the Homestead Act and the subsidized development of the transcontinental railroad, the American government acted vigorously and decisively to impose a basic plan on the nation's development and to support key industries. Even today, the most successful American export industry—aerospace—is the one most heavily guided, subsidized, and promoted by the American government.

38   France, Germany, Japan, Italy, Sweden: any list of industrial nations that are rich today—that have successfully passed through a process of development—is a list of countries that diligently and consciously practiced protection and national planning. All of them have sheltered infant industries, ruthlessly trodden on the intellectual rights of foreigners, and developed on the basis of state planning. In fact, only in the economic backwaters of Latin America and Eastern Europe do government officials still listen patiently to the platitudinous tautologies of Cambridge and the intricate dogmas of Chicago. And even in Poland, the former Czechoslovakia, and Russia they are beginning to have their doubts. Mayor Anatoly

Sobchak, for one, recently attributed St. Petersburg's relative economic success to the city's having fewer Harvard-trained economists around than any other Russian city.

VI. ECONOMICS IS A SCIENCE.

39   Here we get to the central pillar of the faith: the notion that economics is a science, an organized body of knowledge built on objective experiments. The difference between scientific and theological propositions, as we all were taught, is that the former can be tested and disproved, and the latter cannot. Ultimately, the truth of a scientific hypothesis is established when a predicted result comes to pass time and again.

40   By this test, economics is clearly a faith and not a science. To say that economists have an abysmal record of predicting the future is putting it mildly. To choose but one example: In mid-1990, on the eve of the country's most recent recession, thirty-five out of forty leading economists predicted another twelve months of economic growth. If physicists or chemists were getting results like this, would we call physics or chemistry a science?

41   Economists cannot predict tomorrow's economy; they cannot agree on the state of the economy today; they cannot even arrive at a consensus on why the economy behaved as it did in the past. There is too much economists cannot gauge. The essence of experiment has to do with control—with the ability to rule out extraneous factors and to repeat the experiment at a later date. It is not possible to design an experiment that could definitively test, for example, whether high taxes on the rich help or hinder prosperity. There is no way to measure all the variables, or even to decide who and what are causes and effects.

42   This is unsettling. Prosperity is the key to political and national success. It is the key to avoiding world war. We can't stand the thought that things this important may not be fully subject to rational understanding or control. And so we raise up a priesthood, cloak its members in our illusions, and listen respectfully as they tell us how to propitiate the angry gods.

43   This may be comforting, but it is neither noble nor smart. If we are going to have religions, then let us have real ones: religions based on things like love and human dignity, not on increasing the GDP. And if we are going to try to shape our economic future for the better, let us begin with an honest admission of how little we know about the economy. We may not ever be able to build a positive science of economics based on empirical knowledge, but that is no reason to wrap the little we know in a pseudoscientific fog of superstition.

NOTES AND DISCUSSION

Walter Russell Mead takes a provocative stance in this analytical essay regarding deficit reduction. He argues that, far from being the embodiment of evil, as many claim, the deficit is healthy, natural, and positive for most people and most economies. He organizes his analysis into six main subsections, each of which is set off with a number and heading. Those headings summarize the essay's topics very succinctly: the national debt, consideration of the taxation of the rich, inflation, international free trade, and the relationship between the poor and laissez-faire capitalism. The essay ends with what has been lurking as one of Mead's main points all along: that economics is not a science, though economists claim to be scientists. Mead's proposal, analysis, and conclusion—that a deficit is actually good for national economies—fly in the face of the current popular economic wisdom. Mead explicitly discredits—indeed, mocks— economic theories, which drive some political parties and governments almost exclusively.

STUDY QUESTIONS

For Discussion:

1. Mead structures his essay around six fundamental tenets advanced by economists, whom he likens to peculiar religious practitioners. This comparison is not fair, and it is unlikely that Mead means to be fair. What is the effect of this unfairness on your attitudes as a reader?

2. How would you characterize Mead's tone? How does he treat "the common person"? Is that common person Mead's audience? What do you think of his treatment of people in power, and his tendency to create humour by making them look foolish?

For Writing:

1. Mead analyzes economic trends, using various figures and statistics to support his claims. In what other ways can you analyze the figures that Mead presents?

2. While Mead's essay is an analysis, it relies heavily on a striking analogy. He compares economists to a religious order: "we raise up a priesthood, cloak its members in our illusions, and listen respectfully as they tell us how to propitiate the angry gods." Write a short analysis of Mead's analogy, taking particular notice of how he portrays both economics and religion. As a pre-writing exercise, you might want to construct precise models of Mead's view of religion and economics. Those models may also take into account some of Mead's assumptions about scholars and academics mentioned at the beginning of this piece.

BEHIND THE FORMALDEHYDE CURTAIN

Jessica Mitford

BIOGRAPHICAL NOTE

Jessica Mitford was born in England in 1917 and moved to the United States when she was still a young woman. She began her prolific career as a writer in the 1950s. Her work often displays the investigative journalism she shows in this essay, which has been taken from her book *The American Way of Death* (1963). Her other works include a companion volume, *The American Way of Birth* (1993); *Kind and Usual Punishment: The Prison Business* (1973); an investigation of journalism itself entitled *Poison Penmanship: The Gentle Art of Mudraking* (1979); and various biographies, including *Faces of Philip: A Memoir of Philip Toynbee* (1984).

1   The drama begins to unfold with the arrival of the corpse at the mortuary.

2   Alas, poor Yorick! How surprised he would be to see how his counterpart of today is whisked off to a funeral parlor and is in short order sprayed, sliced, pierced, pickled, trussed, trimmed, creamed, waxed, painted, rouged, and neatly dressed—transformed from a common corpse into a Beautiful Memory Picture. This process is known in the trade as embalming and restorative art, and is so universally employed in the United States and Canada that the funeral director does it routinely, without consulting corpse or kin. He regards as eccentric those few who are hardy enough to suggest that it might be dispensed with. Yet no law requires embalming, no religious doctrine commends it, nor is it dictated by considerations of health, sanitation, or even of personal daintiness. In no part of the world but in Northern America is it widely used. The purpose of embalming is to make the corpse presentable for viewing in a suitably costly container; and here too the funeral director routinely, without first consulting the family, prepares the body for public display.

3   Is all this legal? The processes to which a dead body may be subjected are after all to some
extent circumscribed by law. In most states, for instance, the signature of next of kin must
be obtained before an autopsy may be performed, before the deceased may be cremated,
before the body may be turned over to a medical school for research purposes; or such pro-
vision must be made in the decedent's will. In the case of embalming, no such permission
is required nor is it ever sought. A textbook, *The Principles and Practices of Embalming*, comments on this: "There is some question regarding the legality of much that is done within the
preparation room." The author points out that it would be most unusual for a responsible member of a bereaved family to instruct the mortician, in so many words, to "*embalm*" the body
of a deceased relative. The very term "embalming" is so seldom used that the mortician
must rely upon custom in the matter. The author concludes that unless the family specifies
otherwise, the act of entrusting the body to the care of a funeral establishment carries with
it an implied permission to go ahead and embalm.

4   Embalming is indeed a most extraordinary procedure, and one must wonder at the
docility of Americans who each year pay hundreds of millions of dollars for its perpetuation,
blissfully ignorant of what it is all about, what is done, how it is done. Not one in ten thousand has any idea of what actually takes place. Books on the subject are extremely hard to
come by. They are not to be found in most libraries or bookshops.

5   In an era when huge television audiences watch surgical operations in the comfort of their
living rooms, when, thanks to the animated cartoon, the geography of the digestive system
has become familiar territory even to the nursery school set, in a land where the satisfaction
of curiosity about almost all matters is a national pastime, the secrecy surrounding embalming
can, surely, hardly be attributed to the inherent gruesomeness of the subject. Custom in this
regard has within this century suffered a complete reversal. In the early days of American
embalming, when it was performed in the home of the deceased, it was almost mandatory
for some relative to stay by the embalmer's side and witness the procedure. Today, family
members who might wish to be in attendance would certainly be dissuaded by the funeral
director. All others, except apprentices, are excluded by law from the preparation room.

6   A close look at what does actually take place may explain in large measure the undertaker's intractable reticence concerning a procedure that has become his major *raison d'être*.
Is it possible he fears that public information about embalming might lead patrons to wonder if they really want this service? If the funeral men are loath to discuss the subject outside the trade, the reader may, understandably, be equally loath to go on reading at this
point. For those who have the stomach for it, let us part the formaldehyde curtain. . . .

7   The body is first laid out in the undertaker's morgue—or rather, Mr. Jones is reposing
in the preparation room—to be readied to bid the world farewell.

8   The preparation room in any of the better funeral establishments has the tiled and sterile
look of a surgery, and indeed the embalmer–restorative artist who does his chores there is
beginning to adopt the term "dermasurgeon" (appropriately corrupted by some mortician–
writers as "demi-surgeon") to describe his calling. His equipment, consisting of scalpels, scissors, augers, forceps, clamps, needles, pumps, tubes, bowls, and basins, is crudely imitative
of the surgeon's, as is his technique, acquired in a nine- or twelve-month post-high school
course in an embalming school. He is supplied by an advanced chemical industry with a
bewildering array of fluids, sprays, pastes, oils, powders, creams, to fix or soften tissue,
shrink or distend it as needed, dry it here, restore the moisture there. There are cosmetics,
waxes, and paints to fill and cover features, even plaster of Paris to replace entire limbs.

There are ingenious aids to prop and stabilize the cadaver: a Vari-Pose Head Rest, the Edwards Arm and Hand Positioner, the Repose Block (to support the shoulders during the embalming), and the Throop Foot Positioner, which resembles an old-fashioned stocks.

9   Mr. John H. Eckels, president of the Eckels College of Mortuary Science, thus describes the first part of the embalming procedure: "In the hands of a skilled practitioner, this work may be done in a comparatively short time and without mutilating the body other than by slight incision—so slight that it scarcely would cause serious inconvenience if made upon a living person. It is necessary to remove the blood, and doing this not only helps in the disinfecting, but removes the principal cause of disfigurements due to discoloration."

10   Another textbook discusses the all-important time element: "The earlier this is done, the better, for every hour that elapses between death and embalming will add to the problems and complications encountered. . . ." Just how soon should one get going on the embalming? The author tells us, "On the basis of such scanty information made available to this profession through its rudimentary and haphazard system of technical research, we must conclude that the best results are to be obtained if the subject is embalmed before life is completely extinct—that is, before cellular death has occurred. In the average case, this would mean within an hour after somatic death." For those who feel that there is something a little rudimentary, not to say haphazard, about this advice, a comforting thought is offered by another writer. Speaking of fears entertained in early days of premature burial, he points out, "One of the effects of embalming by chemical injection, however, has been to dispel fears of live burial." How true; once the blood is removed, chances of live burial are indeed remote.

11   To return to Mr. Jones, the blood is drained out through the veins and replaced by embalming fluid pumped in through the arteries. As noted in *The Principles and Practices of Embalming*, "every operator has a favorite injection and drainage point—a fact which becomes a handicap only if he fails or refuses to forsake his favorites when conditions demand it." Typical favorites are the carotid artery, femoral artery, jugular vein, subclavian vein. There are various choices of embalming fluid. If Flextone is used, it will produce a "mild, flexible rigidity. The skin retains a velvety softness, the tissues are rubbery and pliable. Ideal for women and children." It may be blended with B. and G. Products Company's Lyf-Lyk tint, which is guaranteed to reproduce "nature's own skin texture . . . the velvety appearance of living tissue." Suntone comes in three separate tints: Suntan; Special Cosmetic Tint, a pink shade "especially indicated for young female subjects"; and Regular Cosmetic Tint, moderately pink.

12   About three to six gallons of a dyed and perfumed solution of formaldehyde, glycerin, borax, phenol, alcohol, and water is soon circulating through Mr. Jones, whose mouth has been sewn together with a "needle directed upward between the upper lip and gum and brought out through the left nostril," with the corners raised slightly "for a more pleasant expression." If he should be buck-toothed, his teeth are cleaned with Bon Ami and coated with colorless nail polish. His eyes, meanwhile, are closed with flesh-tinted eye caps and eye cement.

13   The next step is to have at Mr. Jones with a thing called a trocar. This is a long, hollow needle attached to a tube. It is jabbed into the abdomen, poked around the entrails and chest cavity, the contents of which are pumped out and replaced with "cavity fluid." This done, and the hole in the abdomen sewn up, Mr. Jones's face is heavily creamed (to protect the skin from burns which may be caused by leakage of the chemicals), and he is covered with a sheet and

left unmolested for a while. But not for long—there is more, much more, in store for him. He has been embalmed, but not yet restored, and the best time to start the restorative work is eight to ten hours after embalming, when the tissues have become firm and dry.

14   The object of all this attention to the corpse, it must be remembered, is to make it presentable for viewing in an attitude of healthy repose. "Our customs require the presentation of our dead in the semblance of normality . . . unmarred by the ravages of illness, disease, or mutilation," says Mr. J. Sheridan Mayer in his *Restorative Art*. This is rather a large order since few people die in the full bloom of health, unravaged by illness and unmarked by some disfigurement. The funeral industry is equal to the challenge: "In some cases the gruesome appearance of a mutilated or disease-ridden subject may be quite discouraging. The task of restoration may seem impossible and shake the confidence of the embalmer. This is the time for intestinal fortitude and determination. Once the formative work is begun and affected tissues are cleaned or removed, all doubts of success vanish. It is surprising and gratifying to discover the results which may be obtained."

15   The embalmer, having allowed an appropriate interval to elapse, returns to the attack, but now he brings into play the skill and equipment of sculptor and cosmetician. Is a hand missing? Casting one in plaster of Paris is a simple matter. "For replacement purposes, only a cast of the back of the hand is necessary; this is within the ability of the average operator and is quite adequate." If a lip or two, a nose, or an ear should be missing, the embalmer has at hand a variety of restorative waxes with which to model replacements. Pores and skin texture are simulated by stippling with a little brush, and over this cosmetics are laid on. Head off? Decapitation cases are rather routinely handled. Ragged edges are trimmed, and head joined to torso with a series of splints, wires, and sutures. It is a good idea to have a little something at the neck—a scarf or a high collar—when time for viewing comes. Swollen mouth? Cut out tissue as needed from inside the lips. If too much is removed, the surface contour can easily be restored by padding with cotton. Swollen necks and cheeks are reduced by removing tissue through the vertical incisions made down each side of the neck. "When the deceased is casketed, the pillow will hide the suture incisions . . . as an extra precaution against leakage, the suture may be painted with liquid sealer."

16   The opposite condition is more likely to present itself—that of emaciation. His hypodermic syringe now loaded with massage cream, the embalmer seeks out and fills the hollowed and sunken areas by injection. In this procedure the backs of the hands and fingers and the under-chin area should not be neglected.

17   Positioning the lips is a problem that recurrently challenges the ingenuity of the embalmer. Closed too tightly, they tend to give a stern, even disapproving expression. Ideally, embalmers feel, the lips should give the impression of being ever so slightly parted, the upper lip protruding slightly for a more youthful appearance. This takes some engineering, however, as the lips tend to drift apart. Lip drift can sometimes be remedied by pushing one or two straight pins through the inner margin of the lower lip and then inserting them between the two front upper teeth. If Mr. Jones happens to have no teeth, the pins can just as easily be anchored in his Armstrong Face Former and Denture Replacer. Another method to maintain lip closure is to dislocate the lower jaw, which is then held in its new position by a wire run through holes which have been drilled through the upper and lower jaws at the midline. As the French are fond of saying, *il faut souffrir pour être belle*.

18   If Mr. Jones has died of jaundice, the embalming fluid will very likely turn him green. Does this deter the embalmer? Not if he has intestinal fortitude. Masking pastes and cosmetics are heavily laid on, burial garments and casket interiors are color-correlated with particular

care, and Jones is displayed beneath rose-colored lights. Friends will say "How *well* he looks." Death by carbon monoxide, on the other hand, can be rather a good thing from the embalmer's viewpoint: "One advantage is the fact that this type of discoloration is an exaggerated form of a natural pink coloration." This is nice because the healthy glow is already present and needs but little attention.

19 The patching and filling completed, Mr. Jones is now shaved, washed, and dressed. Cream-based cosmetic, available in pink, flesh, suntan, brunette, and blond, is applied to his hands and face, his hair is shampooed and combed (and, in the case of Mrs. Jones, set), his hands manicured. For the horny-handed son of toil special care must be taken; cream should be applied to remove ingrained grime, and the nails cleaned. "If he were not in the habit of having them manicured in life, trimming and shaping is advised for better appearance—never questioned by kin."

20 Jones is now ready for casketing (this is the present participle of the verb "to casket"). In this operation his right shoulder should be depressed slightly "to turn the body a bit to the right and soften the appearance of lying flat on the back." Positioning the hands is a matter of importance, and special rubber positioning blocks may be used. The hands should be cupped slightly for a more lifelike, relaxed appearance. Proper placement of the body requires a delicate sense of balance. It should lie as high as possible in the casket, yet not so high that the lid, when lowered, will hit the nose. On the other hand, we are cautioned, placing the body too low "creates the impression that the body is in a box."

21 Jones is next wheeled into the appointed slumber room where a few last touches may be added—his favorite pipe placed in his hand or, if he was a great reader, a book propped into position. (In the case of little Master Jones a Teddy bear may be clutched.) Here he will hold open house for a few days, visiting hours 10 A.M. to 9 P.M.

22 All now being in readiness, the funeral director calls a staff conference to make sure that each assistant knows his precise duties. Mr. Wilber Kriege writes: "This makes your staff feel that they are a part of the team, with a definite assignment that must be properly carried out if the whole plan is to succeed. You never heard of a football coach who failed to talk to his entire team before they go on the field. They have drilled on the plays they are to execute for hours and days, and yet the successful coach knows the importance of making even the bench-warming third-string substitute feel that he is important if the game is to be won." The winning of *this* game is predicted upon glass-smooth handling of the logistics. The funeral director has notified the pallbearers whose names were furnished by the family, has arranged for the presence of clergyman, organist, and soloist, has provided transportation for everybody, has organized and listed the flowers sent by friends. In *Psychology of Funeral Service* Mr. Edward A. Martin points out: "He may not always do as much as the family thinks he is doing, but it is his helpful guidance that they appreciate in knowing they are proceeding as they should. . . . The important thing is how well his services can be used to make the family believe they are giving unlimited expression to their own sentiment."

23 The religious service may be held in a church or in the chapel of the funeral home; the funeral director vastly prefers the latter arrangement, for not only is it more convenient for him but it affords him the opportunity to show off his beautiful facilities to the gathered mourners. After the clergyman has had his say, the mourners queue up to file past the casket for a last look at the deceased. The family is *never* asked whether they want an open-casket ceremony; in the absence of their instruction to the contrary, this is taken for granted. Consequently well over 90 per cent of all American funerals feature the open casket—a

custom unknown in other parts of the world. Foreigners are astonished by it. An English woman living in San Francisco described her reaction in a letter to the writer:

> I myself have attended only one funeral here—that of an elderly fellow worker of mine. After the service I could not understand why everyone was walking towards the coffin (sorry, I mean casket), but thought I had better follow the crowd. It shook me rigid to get there and find the casket open and poor old Oscar lying there in his brown tweed suit, wearing a suntan makeup and just the wrong shade of lipstick. If I had not been extremely fond of the old boy, I have a horrible feeling that I might have giggled. Then and there I decided that I could never face another American funeral—even dead.

24   The casket (which has been resting throughout the service on a Classic Beauty Ultra Metal Casket Bier) is now transferred by a hydraulically operated device called Porto-Lift to a balloon-tired, Glide Easy casket carriage which will wheel it to yet another conveyance, the Cadillac Funeral Coach. This may be lavender, cream, light green—anything but black. Interiors, of course, are color-correlated, "for the man who cannot stop short of perfection."

25   At graveside, the casket is lowered into the earth. This office, once the prerogative of friends of the deceased, is now performed by a patented mechanical lowering device. A "Lifetime Green" artificial grass mat is at the ready to conceal the sere earth, and overhead, to conceal the sky, is a portable Steril Chapel Tent ("resists the intense heat and humidity of summer and the terrific storms of winter . . . available in Silver Grey, Rose, or Evergreen"). Now is the time for the ritual scattering of earth over the coffin, as the solemn words "earth to earth, ashes to ashes, dust to dust" are pronounced by the officiating cleric. This can today be accomplished "with a mere flick of the wrist with the Gordon Leak-Proof Earth Dispenser. No grasping of a handful of dirt, no soiled fingers. Simple, dignified, beautiful, reverent! The modern way!" The Gordon Earth Dispenser (at $5) is of nickel-plated brass construction. It is not only "attractive to the eye and long wearing"; it is also "one of the 'tools' for building better public relations" if presented as "an appropriate non-commercial gift" to the clergyman. It is shaped something like a saltshaker.

26   Untouched by human hand, the coffin and the earth are now united.

27   It is in the function of directing the participants through this maze of gadgetry that the funeral director has assigned to himself his relatively new role of "grief therapist." He has relieved the family of every detail, he has revamped the corpse to look like a living doll, he has arranged for it to nap for a few days in a slumber room, he has put on a well-oiled performance in which the concept of *death* has played no part whatsoever—unless it was inconsiderately mentioned by the clergyman who conducted the religious service. He has done everything in his power to make the funeral a real pleasure for everybody concerned. He and his team have given their all to score an upset victory over death.

NOTES AND DISCUSSION

This essay is an outstanding and skillful example of a process analysis. Jessica Mitford is very methodical, detailed, and precise as she describes the practice of embalming. Embalming, she says, is at present surrounded by secrecy. This essay aims to "lift the curtain" on that secrecy.

Mitford describes in (sometimes uncomfortable) detail the process of embalming. She states that embalming is a curious practice unique to North America; her essay is designed to critique this practice and suggest that the funeral industry is performing a service that is wholly unnecessary, and probably highly destructive to the survivors.

Mitford begins with "the arrival of the corpse at the mortuary," and describes the process of what happens there until, "untouched by human hand, the coffin and the earth are now united." She concludes her essay with the stunning observation that *death* plays no part in death whatsoever. Mitford's point is, in part, that the mourning process has become commercialized and dehumanized; an entire industry has been constructed to make sure that death is, in Mitford's words, "simple, dignified, beautiful, reverent!" The mortician becomes part chemist, part surgeon, part choreographer, part artist and sculptor. The funeral itself has become a play: note the word "drama" in the first paragraph, and the description of the funeral director in the last paragraph as someone who plays a "role" and delivers a "performance." The reader is left to ask, "What for?"

STUDY QUESTIONS

For Discussion:

1. What is Mitford's attitude toward the process she is analyzing? How do you know? How would you characterize the essay's tone? Note Mitford's careful use of euphemisms: at times she exposes them; at others, she deliberately uses them.

2. Mitford's essay is distinctive not only because of the abundance of detail, but also because of its grim humour. There are many examples of that humour, but notice, in particular, the list of verbs in the second paragraph. What is your response to the essay's humour, given its subject matter?

For Writing:

1. Write a description of a process with which you are familiar, making sure to include as many pertinent details as possible.

2. The image of lifting a curtain implies not only disclosure, but also a theatrical performance. Shakespeare is invoked through the reference in the second paragraph to Yorick from *Hamlet*. Do you agree with Mitford that funerals, and by implication, other modern public rituals are needlessly commercialized? Consider a public ritual in which you have been involved recently—a baptism, a wedding, a graduation, or some other celebration—and write a response to Mitford. The commercialization of those public rituals is not limited to the people who supply the services. Discuss the degree to which the participants are implicated as well.

THE REVIVAL OF HANDICRAFT

William Morris

BIOGRAPHICAL NOTE

William Morris (1834–1896) was a painter, businessman, poet, designer, furniture maker, printer, weaver, novelist, and political agitator and essayist. His boundless energy and his wide range of interests and abilities made him the inspiration for the Arts and Crafts movements in both England and North America. Like John Ruskin, a friend whom he counted as one of his literary masters, Morris became progressively dissatisfied with the drabness and false ornamentation of the modern industrial world. In later years he became convinced that a political revolution was needed to restore to humanity a society in which work could once more be enjoyed, without the exploitation that seemed to him so prevalent in Victorian England.

Morris was an important supporter of the Pre-Raphaelites—an idealistic and somewhat naturalistic school of art and poetry that fashioned as a model for themselves, in part from reading Malory's *Morte D'Arthur*, a medieval world that had never really existed. The Pre-Raphaelite Brotherhood was formed initially by three idealistic young painters—William Holman Hunt, Dante Gabriel Rossetti, and John Everett Millais—as a reaction to what they perceived to be the false and artificial aesthetic values of other Victorian painters and writers.

1   For some time past there has been a good deal of interest shown in what is called in our modern slang Art Workmanship, and quite recently there has been a growing feeling that this art workmanship to be of any value must have some of the workman's individuality imparted to it beside whatever of art it may have got from the design of the artist who has planned, but not executed the work. This feeling has gone so far that there is growing up a fashion for demanding handmade goods even when they are not ornamented in any way, as, for instance, woollen and linen cloth spun by hand and woven without power, hand-knitted hosiery, and the like. Nay, it is not uncommon to hear regrets for the hand labour in the

fields, now fast disappearing from even backward districts of civilised countries. The scythe, the sickle, and even the flail are lamented over, and many are looking forward with drooping spirits to the time when the hand-plough will be as completely extinct as the quern, and the rattle of the steam-engine will take the place of the whistle of the curly-headed plough-boy through all the length and breadth of the land. People interested, or who suppose that they are interested, in the details of the arts of life feel a desire to revert to methods of handicraft for production in general; and it may therefore be worth considering how far this is a mere reactionary sentiment incapable of realisation, and how far it may foreshadow a real coming change in our habits of life as irresistible as the former change which has produced the system of machine production, the system against which revolt is now attempted.

2   In this paper I propose to confine the aforesaid consideration as much as I can to the effect of machinery versus handicraft upon the arts; using that latter word as widely as possible, so as to include all products of labour which have any claims to be considered beautiful. I say as far as possible; for as all roads lead to Rome, so the life, habits, and aspirations of all groups and classes of the community are founded on the economical conditions under which the mass of the people live, and it is impossible to exclude socio-political questions from the consideration of aesthetics. Also, although I must avow myself a sharer in the above-mentioned reactionary regrets, I must at the outset disclaim the mere aesthetic point of view which looks upon the ploughman and his bullocks and his plough, the reaper, his work, his wife, and his dinner, as so many elements which compose a pretty tapestry hanging, fit to adorn the study of a contemplative person of cultivation, but which it is not worth while differentiating from each other except in so far as they are related to the beauty and interest of the picture. On the contrary, what I wish for is that the reaper and his wife should have themselves a due share in all the fullness of life; and I can, without any great effort, perceive the justice of their forcing me to bear part of the burden of its deficiencies, so that we may together be forced to attempt to remedy them, and have no very heavy burden to carry between us.

3   To return to our aesthetics: though a certain part of the cultivated classes of to-day regret the disappearance of handicraft from production, they are quite vague as to how and why it is disappearing, and as to how and why it should or may reappear. For to begin with the general public is grossly ignorant of all the methods and processes of manufacture. This is of course one result of the machine-system we are considering. Almost all goods are made apart from the life of those who use them; we are not responsible for them, our will has had no part in their production, except so far as we form a part of the market on which they can be forced for the profit of the capitalist whose money is employed in producing them. The market assumes that certain wares are wanted; it produces such wares, indeed, but their kind and quality are only adapted to the needs of the public in a very rough fashion, because the public needs are subordinated to the interest of the capitalist masters of the market, and they can force the public to put up with the less desirable article if they choose, as they generally do. The result is that in this direction our boasted individuality is a sham; and persons who wish for anything that deviates ever so little from the beaten path have either to wear away their lives in a wearisome and mostly futile contest with a stupendous organisation which disregards their wishes, or to allow those wishes to be crushed out for the sake of a quiet life.

4   Let us take a few trivial but undeniable examples. You want a hat, say, like that you wore last year; you go to the hatter's, and find you cannot get it there, and you have no re-

source but in submission. Money by itself won't buy you the hat you want; it will cost you three months' hard labour and twenty pounds to have an inch added to the brim of your wideawake; for you will have to get hold of a small capitalist (of whom but few are left), and by a series of intrigues and resolute actions which would make material for a three-volume novel, get him to allow you to turn one of his hands into a handicraftsman for the occasion; and a very poor handicraftsman he will be, when all is said. Again, I carry a walking-stick, and like all sensible persons like it to have a good heavy end that will swing out well before me. A year or two ago it became the fashion to pare away all walking-sticks to the shape of attenuated carrots, and I really believe I shortened my life in my attempts at getting a rea-sonable staff of the kind I was used to, so difficult it was. Again, you want a piece of furniture which the trade (mark the word, Trade, not Craft!) turns out, blotched over with idiotic sham ornament; you wish to dispense with this degradation, and propose it to your uphol-sterer, who grudgingly assents to it; and you find that you have to pay the price of two pieces of furniture for the privilege of indulging your whim of leaving out the trade finish (I decline to call it ornament) on the one you have got made for you. And this is because it has been made by handicraft instead of machinery. For most people, therefore, there is a prohibitive price put upon the acquirement of the knowledge of methods and processes. We do not know how a piece of goods is made, what the difficulties are that beset its man-ufacture, what it ought to look like, feel like, smell like, or what it ought to cost apart from the profit of the middleman. We have lost the art of marketing, and with it the due sympa-thy with the life of the workshop, which would, if it existed, be such a wholesome check on the humbug of party politics.

5   It is a natural consequence of this ignorance of the methods of making wares, that even those who are in revolt against the tyranny of the excess of division of labour in the occu-pations of life, and who wish to recur more or less to handicraft, should also be ignorant of what that life of handicraft was when all wares were made by handicraft. If their revolt is to carry any hope with it, it is necessary that they should know something of this. I must assume that many or perhaps most of my readers are not acquainted with Socialist literature, and that few of them have read the admirable account of the different epochs of production given in Karl Marx's great work entitled *Capital*. I must ask to be excused, therefore, for stating very briefly what, chiefly owing to Marx, has become a commonplace of Socialism, but is not generally known outside it. There have been three great epochs of production since the beginning of the Middle Ages. During the first or medieval period all production was indi-vidualistic in method; for though the workmen were combined into great associations for pro-tection and the organisation of labour, they were so associated as citizens not as mere workmen. There was little or no division of labour, and what machinery was used was sim-ply of the nature of a multiplied tool, a help to the workman's hand labour and not a supplanter of it. The workman worked for himself and not for any capitalistic employer, and he was ac-cordingly master of his work and his time: this was the period of pure handicraft. When in the latter half of the sixteenth century the capitalist employer and the so-called free workman began to appear, the workmen were collected into workshops, the old tool-machines were improved, and at last a new invention, the division of labour, found its way into the work-shops. The division of labour went on growing throughout the seventeenth century, and was perfected in the eighteenth, when the unit of labour became a group and not a single man; or in other words the workman became a mere part of a machine composed sometimes wholly of human beings, and sometimes of human beings plus labour-saving machines,

which towards the end of this period were being copiously invented; the fly-shuttle may be taken for an example of these. The latter half of the eighteenth century saw the beginning of the last epoch of production that the world has known, that of the automatic machine which supersedes hand labour, and turns the workman who was once a handicraftsman helped by tools, and next a part of a machine, into a tender of machines. And as far as we can see, the revolution in this direction as to kind is complete, though as to degree, as pointed out by Mr. David A. Wells last year (1887), the tendency is towards the displacement of ever more and more "muscular" labour, as Mr. Wells calls it.

6   This is very briefly the history of the evolution of industry during the last five hundred years; and the question now comes: Are we justified in wishing that handicraft may in its turn supplant machinery? Or it would perhaps be better to put the question in another way; will the period of machinery evolve itself into a fresh period of machinery more independent of human labour than anything we can conceive of now, or will it develop its contradictory in the shape of a new and improved period of production by handicraft? The second form of the question is the preferable one, because it helps us to give a reasonable answer to what people who have any interest in external beauty will certainly ask: Is the change from handicraft to machinery good or bad? And the answer to that question is to my mind that, as my friend Belfort Bax has put it, statically it is bad, dynamically it is good. As a condition of life, production by machinery is altogether an evil; as an instrument for forcing on us better conditions of life it has been, and for some time yet will be, indispensable.

7   Having thus tried to clear myself of mere reactionary pessimism let me attempt to show why statically handicraft is to my mind desirable, and its destruction a degradation of life. Well, first I shall not shrink from saying bluntly that production by machinery necessarily results in utilitarian ugliness in everything which the labour of man deals with, and that this is a serious evil and a degradation of human life. So clearly is this the fact that though few people will venture to deny the latter part of the proposition, yet in their hearts the greater part of cultivated civilised persons do not regard it as an evil, because their degradation has already gone so far that they cannot, in what concerns the sense of seeing, discriminate between beauty and ugliness: their languid assent to the desirableness of beauty is with them only a convention, a superstitious survival from the times when beauty was a necessity to all men. The first part of the proposition (that machine industry produces ugliness) I cannot argue with these persons, because they neither know, nor care for, the difference between beauty and ugliness; and with those who do understand what beauty means I need not argue it, as they are but too familiar with the fact that the produce of all modern industrialism is ugly, and that whenever anything which is old disappears, its place is taken by something inferior to it in beauty; and that even out in the very fields and open country. The art of making beautifully all kinds of ordinary things, carts, gates, fences, boats, bowls, and so forth, let alone houses and public buildings, unconsciously and without effort has gone; when anything has to be renewed among these simple things the only question asked is how little it can be done for, so as to tide us over our responsibility and shift its mending on to the next generation.

8   It may be said, and indeed I have heard it said, that since there is some beauty still left in the world and some people who admire it, there is a certain gain in the acknowledged eclecticism of the present day, since the ugliness which is so common affords a contrast whereby the beauty, which is so rare, may be appreciated. This I suspect to be only another form of the maxim which is the sheet anchor of the laziest and most cowardly group of our

cultivated classes, that it is good for the many to suffer for the few; but if any one puts forward in good faith the fear that we may be too happy in the possession of pleasant surroundings, so that we shall not be able to enjoy them, I must answer that this seems to me a very remote terror. Even when the tide at last turns in the direction of sweeping away modern squalor and vulgarity, we shall have, I doubt, many generations of effort in perfecting the transformation, and when it is at last complete, there will be first the triumph of our success to exalt us, and next the history of the long wade through the putrid sea of ugliness which we shall have at last escaped from. But furthermore, the proper answer to this objection lies deeper than this. It is to my mind that very consciousness of the production of beauty for beauty's sake which we want to avoid; it is just what is apt to produce affectation and effeminacy amongst the artists and their following. In the great times of art conscious effort was used to produce great works for the glory of the City, the triumph of the Church, the exaltation of the citizens, the quickening of the devotion of the faithful; even in the higher art, the record of history, the instruction of men alive and to live hereafter, was the aim rather than beauty; and the lesser art was unconscious and spontaneous, and did not in any way interfere with the rougher business of life, while it enabled men in general to understand and sympathise with the nobler forms of art. But unconscious as these producers of ordinary beauty may be, they will not and cannot fail to receive pleasure from the exercise of their work under these conditions, and this above all things is that which influences me most in my hope for the recovery of handicraft. I have said it often enough, but I must say it once again, since it is so much a part of my case for handicraft, that so long as man allows his daily work to be mere unrelieved drudgery he will seek happiness in vain. I say further that the worst tyrants of the days of violence were but feeble tormentors compared with those Captains of Industry who have taken the pleasure of work away from the workmen. Furthermore, I feel absolutely certain that handicraft joined to certain other conditions, of which more presently, would produce the beauty and the pleasure in work above mentioned; and if that be so, and this double pleasure of lovely surroundings and happy work could take the place of the double torment of squalid surroundings and wretched drudgery, have we not good reason for wishing, if it might be, that handicraft should once more step into the place of machine production?

9   I am not blind to the tremendous change which this revolution would mean. The maxim of modern civilisation to a well-to-do man is, Avoid taking trouble! Get as many of the functions of your life as you can performed by others for you! Vicarious life is the watchword of our civilisation, and we well-to-do and cultivated people live smoothly enough while it lasts. But, in the first place, how about the vicars, who do more for us than the singing of mass for our behoof for a scanty stipend? Will they go on with it for ever? For indeed the shuffling off of responsibilities from one to the other has to stop at last, and somebody has to bear the burden in the end. But let that pass, since I am not writing politics, and let us consider another aspect of the matter. What wretched lop-sided creatures we are being made by the excess of the division of labour in the occupations of life! What on earth are we going to do with our time when we have brought the art of vicarious life to perfection, having first complicated the question by the ceaseless creation of artificial wants which we refuse to supply for ourselves? Are all of us (we of the great middle class I mean) going to turn philosophers, poets, essayists, men of genius, in a word, when we have come to look down on the ordinary functions of life with the same kind of contempt wherewith persons of good breeding look down upon a good dinner, eating it sedulously however? I shudder

when I think of how we shall bore each other when we have reached that perfection. Nay, I think we have already got in all branches of culture rather more geniuses than we can comfortably bear, and that we lack, so to say, audiences rather than preachers. I must ask pardon of my readers; but our case is at once so grievous and so absurd that one can scarcely help laughing out of bitterness of soul. In the very midst of our pessimism we are boastful of our wisdom, yet we are helpless in the face of the necessities we have created, and which, in spite of our anxiety about art, are at present driving us into luxury unredeemed by beauty on the one hand, and squalor unrelieved by incident or romance on the other, and will one day drive us into mere ruin.

10   Yes, we do sorely need a system of production which will give us beautiful surroundings and pleasant occupation, and which will tend to make us good human animals, able to do something for ourselves, so that we may be generally intelligent instead of dividing ourselves into dull drudges or duller pleasure-seekers according to our class, on the one hand, or hapless pessimistic intellectual personages, and pretenders to that dignity, on the other. We do most certainly need happiness in our daily work, content in our daily rest; and all this cannot be if we hand over the whole responsibility of the details of our daily life to machines and their drivers. We are right to long for intelligent handicraft to come back to the world which it once made tolerable amidst war and turmoil and uncertainty of life, and which it should, one would think, make happy now we have grown so peaceful, so considerate of each other's temporal welfare.

11   Then comes the question, How can the change be made? And here at once we are met by the difficulty that the sickness and death of handicrafts is, it seems, a natural expression of the tendency of the age. We willed the end, and therefore the means also. Since the last days of the Middle Ages the creation of an intellectual aristocracy has been, so to say, the spiritual purpose of civilisation side by side with its material purpose of supplanting the aristocracy of status by the aristocracy of wealth. Part of the price it has had to pay for its success in that purpose (and some would say it is comparatively an insignificant part) is that this new aristocracy of intellect has been compelled to forgo the lively interest in the beauty and romance of life, which was once the portion of every artificer at least, if not of every workman, and to live surrounded by an ugly vulgarity which the world amidst all its changes has not known till modern times. It is not strange that until recently it has not been conscious of this degradation; but it may seem strange to many that it has now grown partially conscious of it. It is common now to hear people say of such and such a piece of country or suburb: "Ah! it was so beautiful a year or so ago, but it has been quite spoilt by the building." Forty years back the building would have been looked on as a vast improvement; now we have grown conscious of the hideousness we are creating, and we go on creating it. We see the price we have paid for our aristocracy of intellect, and even that aristocracy itself is more than half regretful of the bargain, and would be glad if it could keep the gain and not pay the full price for it. Hence not only the empty grumbling about the continuous march of machinery over dying handicraft, but also various elegant little schemes for trying to withdraw ourselves, some of us, from the consequences (in this direction) of our being superior persons; none of which can have more than a temporary and very limited success. The great wave of commercial necessity will sweep away all these well-meant attempts to stem it, and think little of what it has done, or whither it is going.

12   Yet after all even these feeble manifestations of discontent with the tyranny of commerce are tokens of a revolutionary epoch, and to me it is inconceivable that machine pro-

duction will develop into mere infinity of machinery, or life wholly lapse into a disregard of life as it passes. It is true indeed that powerful as the cultivated middle class is, it has not the power of re-creating the beauty and romance of life; but that will be the work of the new society which the blind progress of commercialism will create, nay, is creating. The cultivated middle class is a class of slave-holders, and its power of living according to its choice is limited by the necessity of finding constant livelihood and employment for the slaves who keep it alive. It is only a society of equals which can choose the life it will live, which can choose to forgo gross luxury and base utilitarianism in return for the unwearying pleasure of tasting the fullness of life. It is my firm belief that we shall in the end realise this society of equals, and also that when it is realised it will not endure a vicarious life by means of machinery; that it will in short be the master of its machinery and not the servant, as our age is.

13   Meantime, since we shall have to go through a long series of social and political events before we shall be free to choose how we shall live, we should welcome even the feeble protest which is now being made against the vulgarisation of all life: first because it is one token amongst others of the sickness of modern civilisation; and next, because it may help to keep alive memories of the past which are necessary elements of the life of the future, and methods of work which no society could afford to lose. In short, it may be said that though the movement towards the revival of handicraft is contemptible on the surface in face of the gigantic fabric of commercialism; yet, taken in conjunction with the general movement towards freedom of life for all, on which we are now surely embarked, as a protest against intellectual tyranny, and a token of the change which is transforming civilisation into socialism, it is both noteworthy and encouraging.

NOTES AND DISCUSSION

Morris begins his essay by stating the general problem he will address: true handicraft, and the kind of artistry that goes with it, has been replaced by machinery; true aesthetics have been replaced by a narrow, uninspired utilitarianism and empty ornamentation. He then provides a series of specific examples, bemoaning the loss of the true "handicraftsman." Next, Morris briefly sketches Marx's history of production, which has led to industrialization, and its de-humanization of the worker. Morris proposes two possible futures for humanity: in one "the period of machinery evolve[s] itself into a fresh period of machinery more independent of human labour than anything we can conceive of now"; alternatively, the future may take "the shape of a new and improved period of production by handicraft." The essay then ends with a call for a revolution, to establish that second future: "to me it is inconceivable that machine production will develop into mere infinity of machinery, or life wholly lapse into a disregard of life as it passes." Morris sees his essay, finally, as a plea for humanity itself.

The urgency of Morris's message gives this essay an almost biblical, oratorical tone. Notice in particular his selective and effective use of archaisms like "nay." Notice, too, his skillful weaving of fabric/textile/weaving metaphors into the essay, reflecting his own love of that craft.

STUDY QUESTIONS

For Discussion:

1. If Morris was dismayed by the mechanization of industry in the late nineteenth century, how do you think he would respond to living conditions in the late twentieth century? Does either of the possible futures Morris predicts in paragraph 6 appear to be coming true, or do you see a third possibility, one unforeseen by Morris?

2. One crux of Morris's argument is that, "as a condition of life, production by machinery is altogether an evil; as an instrument for forcing on us better conditions of life it has been, and for some time yet will be, indispensable." Do you agree? Whether or not you agree discuss some of the implications of this statement.

For Writing:

1. Compare and contrast Morris's stance against the mechanization of modern life with Wendell Berry's. Which argument is more convincing?

2. The utopian future, free of machinery, that Morris envisions in this essay is articulated more fully in his novel *News from Nowhere*. Using that novel as a research base, analyze Morris's version of the history of production. To what extent does Morris's image of future perfection depend upon an idealized image of the past?

"STATE-OF-THE-ART CAR": THE FERRARI TESTAROSSA

Joyce Carol Oates

BIOGRAPHICAL NOTE

Joyce Carol Oates has been called America's "most prolific major writer." She has written over two dozen novels and collections of short stories, as well as plays and many volumes of poetry. She is also an accomplished essayist who writes on an amazingly diversity of subjects. A feminist, she frequently examines the symbols and rituals of male-dominated aspects of North American society.

1   Speak of the Ferrari Testarossa to men who know cars and observe their immediate visceral response: the virtual dilation of their eyes in sudden focused *interest*. The Testarossa!—that domestic rocket of a sports car, sleek, low-slung, aggressively wide; startlingly beautiful even in the eyes of non-car aficionados; so spectacular a presence on the road that—as I can personally testify —heads turn, faces break into childlike smiles in its wake. As one observer has noted, the Testarossa drives "civilians" crazy.

2   Like a very few special cars, the Ferrari Testarossa is in fact a meta-car, a poetic metaphor or trope: an *object* raised to the level of a near-spiritual *value*. Of course it has a use—as a Steinway concert grand or a Thoroughbred racing horse has a use—but its significance hovers above and around mere use. What can one say about a street car (as opposed to a racing car) capable of traveling 177 effortless miles per hour?—accelerating, as it does, again without effort, from 0 mph to 60 mph in 5 seconds, 107 mph in 13.3 seconds? A car that sells for approximately $104,000—if you can get one? (The current waiting period is twelve months and will probably get longer.) There are said to be no more than 450 Testarossas in

private ownership in the United States; only about three hundred models are made by Ferrari yearly. So popular has the model become, due in part to its much-publicized presence in the television series *Miami Vice* (in which, indeed, fast cars provide a sort of subtextual commentary on the men who drive them), that a line of child-sized motorized "Testarossas" is now being marketed—which extravagant toys range in price from $3,500 to $13,000. (Toys bought by parents who don't want to feel guilty, as one Ferrari dealer remarked.)

3   For all its high-tech styling, its racing-car image, the Ferrari Testarossa is a remarkably easy car to drive: its accelerative powers are first unnerving, then dangerously seductive. You think you are traveling at about 60 miles per hour when in fact you are moving toward 100 miles per hour (with your radar detector—"standard issue for this model"—in operation). In the luxury-leather seats, low, of course, and accommodatingly wide, you have the vertiginous impression of being somehow below the surface of the very pavement, skimming, flying, *rocketing* past vehicles moving at ordinary speeds; as if in a dream, or an "action" film. (Indeed, viewed through the discreetly tinted windshield of a Testarossa, the world, so swiftly passing, looks subtly altered: less assertive in its dimensions, rather more like "background.") Such speeds are heady, intoxicating, clearly addictive: if you are moving at 120 mph so smoothly, why not 130 mph? why not 160 mph? why not the limit—if, indeed, there *is* a limit? "Gusty/Emotions on wet roads on autumn nights" acquire a new significance in a car of such unabashed romance. What godly maniacal power: you have only to depress the accelerator of the Ferrari Testarossa and you're at the horizon. Or beyond.

4   The mystique of high-performance cars has always intrigued me with its very opacity. Is it lodged sheerly in speed?—mechanical ingenuity?—the "art" of a finely tuned beautifully styled vehicle (as the mere physical fact of a Steinway piano constitutes "art")?—the adrenal thrill of courting death? Has it primarily to do with display (that of male game fowl, for instance)? Or with masculine prowess of a fairly obvious sort? (Power being, as the cultural critic Henry Kissinger once observed, the ultimate aphrodisiac.)

5   Or is it bound up with the phenomenon of what the American economist Thorstein Veblen so wittily analyzed as "conspicuous consumption" in his classic *Theory of the Leisure Class* (1899)—Veblen's theory being that the consumption of material goods is determined not by the inherent value of goods but by the social standing derived from their consumption. (Veblen noted how in our capitalistic-democratic society there is an endless "dynamics" of style as the wealthiest class ceaselessly strives to distinguish itself from the rest of society and its habits of consumption trickle down to lower levels.)

6   Men who work with high-performance cars, however, are likely to value them as ends in themselves: they have no time for theory, being so caught up, so mesmerized, in practice. To say that certain cars at certain times determine the "state-of-the-art" is to say that such machinery, on its most refined levels, constitutes a serious and speculative and ever-changing (improving?) art. The Ferrari Testarossa is not a *car* in the generic sense in which, say, a Honda Accord—which my husband and I own—is a *car*. (For one thing, the Accord has about 90 horsepower; the Testarossa 380.) Each Ferrari is more or less unique, possessed of its own mysterious personality; its peculiar ghost-in-the-machine. "It's a good car," I am told, with typical understatement, by a Testarossa owner named Bill Kontes, "—a *good* car." He pauses, and adds, "But not an antique. This is a car you can actually drive."

7   (Though it's so precious—the lipstick-red model in particular such an attention-getter—that you dare not park it in any marginally public place. Meta-cars arouse emotions at all points of the spectrum.)

8   Bill Kontes, in partnership with John Melniczuk, owns and operates Checkered Flag Cars in Vineland, New Jersey—a dealership of such choice content (high-performance exotic cars, "vintage" classics, others) as to make it a veritable Phillips Collection amid its larger rivals in the prestige car market. It was by way of their hospitality that I was invited to test-drive the Ferrari Testarossa for *Quality*, though my only qualifications would seem to have been that I knew how to drive a car. (Not known to Mr. Kontes and Mr. Melniczuk was the ambiguous fact that I did once own, in racier days, a sports car of a fairly modest species—a Fiat Spider also in audacious lipstick-red. I recall that it was always stalling. That it gave up, so to speak, along a melancholy stretch of interstate highway in the approximate vicinity of Gary, Indiana, emitting actual flames from its exhaust. That the garage owner to whose garage it was ignominiously towed stared at it and said contemptuously, "A pile of junk!" That we sold it soon afterward and never bought another "sports" car again.)

9   It was along a semideserted stretch of South Jersey road that Mr. Kontes turned the Ferrari Testarossa over to me, gallantly, and surely bravely: and conscious of the enormity of the undertaking—a sense, very nearly, that the honor of "woman writerhood" might be here at stake, a colossal blunder or actual catastrophe reflecting not only upon the luckless perpetrator but upon an entire generation and gender—I courageously drove the car, and, encouraged by Mr. Kontes, and by the mysterious powers of the radar detector to detect the presence of uniformed and sanctioned enforcers of the law (which law, I fully understand, *is* for our own good and in the best and necessary interests of the commonwealth), I did in fact accelerate through all five gears to a speed rather beyond one I'd anticipated: though not to 120 mph, which was Mr. Kontes's fairly casual speed a few minutes previously. (This particular Testarossa, new to Vineland, had been driven at 160 mph by Mr. Melniczuk the other day, along a predawn stretch of highway presumably sanctioned by the radar detector. To drive behind the Testarossa, as I also did, and watch it—suddenly—ease away toward the horizon is an eerie sight: if you don't look closely you're likely to be startled into asking, Where did it go?)

10   But the surprise of the Testarossa, *pace Miami Vice* and the hyped-up media image, is that it is an easy, even comfortable car to drive: user-friendly, as the newly coined cliché would have it. It reminded me not at all of the tricky little Spider I'd quite come to hate by the time of our parting but, oddly, of the unnerving but fiercely exhilarating experience of being behind the controls—so to speak—of a two-seater open-cockpit plane. (My father flew sporty airplanes years ago, and my childhood is punctured with images of flight: the wind-ravaged open-cockpit belonged to a former navy bomber recycled for suburban airfield use.) As the Testarossa was accelerated I felt that visceral sense of an irresistibly gathering and somehow condensing power—"speed" being in fact a mere distillation or side effect of power—and, within it, contained by it, an oddly humble sense of human smallness, frailty. One of the perhaps unexamined impulses behind high-speed racing must be not the mere "courting" of death but, on a more primary level, its actual pre-experience; its taste.

11   But what have such thoughts to do with driving a splendid red Ferrari Testarossa in the environs of Vineland, New Jersey, one near-perfect autumn day, an afternoon shading romantically into dusk? Quite beyond, or apart from, the phenomenal machinery in which Bill Kontes and I were privileged to ride I was acutely conscious of the spectacle we and it presented to others' eyes. Never have I seen so many heads turn!—so much staring!—*smiling*! While the black Testarossa may very well resemble, as one commentator has noted, Darth Vader's personal warship, the lipstick-red model evokes smiles of pleasure, envy, awe—most pointedly in young men, of course, but also in older, even elderly women. Like royalty, the Testarossa seems to bestow a gratuitous benison upon its spectators. Merely to watch it pass is to feel singled out, if, perhaps, rather suddenly drab and anonymous. My thoughts drifted onto the pomp of kings and queens and maharajahs, the legendary excesses of the Gilded Age of Morgan, Carnegie, Rockefeller, Mellon, Armour, McCormick, et al.— Edith Rockefeller McCormick, just to give one small example, served her dinner guests on china consisting of over a thousand pieces containing 11,000 ounces of gold—the Hope Diamond, and Liz Taylor's diamonds, and the vision of Mark Twain, in impeccable dazzling white, strolling on Fifth Avenue while inwardly chafing at his increasing lack of privacy. If one is on public display one is of course obliged not to be conscious of it; driving a $104,000 car means being equal to the car in dignity and style. Otherwise the public aspect of the performance is contaminated: we are left with merely conspicuous consumption, an embarrassment in such times of economic trepidation and worldwide hunger.

12   Still, it's the one incontrovertible truth about the Ferrari Testarossa: no matter who is behind the wheel people stare, and they stare in admiration. Which might not otherwise be the case.

NOTES AND DISCUSSION

An interesting irony underlies this essay: the writer looks at a car, its effects on men, and its metaphoric place in a male-centred value system; but the writing "I," the person appreciating the car, its features, and its effects on observers, is a woman. She seems as interested in the car as a test of gender characteristics and perspectives as she is in it as a machine.

Parts of the essay read like standard automotive journalism or product performance reports. However, Oates consistently takes the report past the standard and ordinary into the exceptional and extraordinary. A segment that begins by characterizing the Testarossa as "a remarkably easy car to drive" continues by describing its "unnerving" and "dangerously seductive" acceleration. She refers to the Testarossa as a "meta-car"—a car that is "about" cars, or about the essence of "car."

The different sections of the essay comment on the car's different aspects: its technical data and physical features; its role as a consumer item and an item of display; its connection with popular culture; its effect on the writer/driver; its effect on those who watch it go by (or pull away).

Overall, Oates wants to explore the journalistic *why* as much as, or more than, the *what*. Why do people admire this car and its drivers? Why does it have such an appeal and mystique, such "value" beyond its price?

STUDY QUESTIONS

For Discussion:

1. Apply Veblen's theory of "conspicuous consumption," as introduced and defined here, to other products on the market. What are the dominant means of displaying ownership and a capacity for consumption in some social group you are familiar with or a member of? And what, if any, are the gender implications behind that ownership, display, and consumption?

2. Are you aware of other products whose "worth" is derived from appearances in television, movies, or other popular cultural activities? Are you aware that manufacturers pay to have their cars, clothes, labels, etc., appear in such venues? Discuss some of the possible implications of these hidden advertisements on artistic freedom.

FOR WRITING:

1. Describe a consumer item in both its physical and its social contexts, exploring not only what it is, but what it "means." Attempt to link the two frames of reference to show how the product's "meaning" is built into its physical design.

2. As a research project, find E.B. White's essay "Farewell, My Lovely" and read it. There are interesting similarities, and telling differences, between the car described by White and the one in this essay—not only in the cars themselves, but also in the ways each author writes about them. Compare and contrast several features such as the names and physical details of the vehicles, the use of figures of speech, the tone, etc. Ask yourself questions like these: just what does "Testarossa" mean, anyway? what does it *sound* like it means? what does it appear to refer to?

POLITICS AND THE ENGLISH LANGUAGE

George Orwell

BIOGRAPHICAL NOTE

George Orwell (1903–1950) is the pseudonym of Eric Blair. Orwell was an English novelist, essayist, and social commentator. He was a life-long opponent of totalitarianism in its various forms. He is perhaps best known for two novels, *Animal Farm* (1946) and *Nineteen Eighty-Four* (1947). This essay, which is from a collection entitled *Shooting an Elephant and Other Stories*, has been frequently anthologized.

---

1   Most people who bother with the matter at all would admit that the English language is in a bad way, but it is generally assumed that we cannot by conscious action do anything about it. Our civilization is decadent and our language—so the argument runs—must inevitably share in the general collapse. It follows that any struggle against the abuse of language is a sentimental archaism, like preferring candles to electric light or hansom cabs to aeroplanes. Underneath this lies the half-conscious belief that language is a natural growth and not an instrument which we shape for our own purpose.

2   Now, it is clear that the decline of a language must ultimately have political and economic causes: it is not due simply to the bad influence of this or that individual writer. But an effect can become a cause, reinforcing the original cause and producing the same effect in an intensified form, and so on indefinitely. A man may take to drink because he feels himself to be a failure, and then fail all the more completely because he drinks. It is rather the same thing that is happening to the English language. It becomes ugly and inaccurate because our thoughts are foolish, but the slovenliness of our language makes it easier for us to have

foolish thoughts. The point is that the process is reversible. Modern English, especially written English, is full of bad habits which spread by imitation and which can be avoided if one is willing to take the necessary trouble. If one gets rid of these habits one can think more clearly, and to think clearly is a necessary first step towards political regeneration: so that the fight against bad English is not frivolous and is not the exclusive concern of professional writers. I will come back to this presently, and I hope that by that time the meaning of what I have said here will have become clearer. Meanwhile, here are five specimens of the English language as it is now habitually written.

3   These five passages have not been picked out because they are especially bad—I could have quoted far worse if I had chosen—but because they illustrate various of the mental vices from which we now suffer. They are a little below the average, but are fairly representative samples. I number them so that I can refer back to them when necessary:

(1) I am not, indeed, sure whether it is not true to say that the Milton who once seemed not un-like a seventeenth-century Shelley had not become, out of an experience ever more bitter in each year, more alien [*sic*] to the founder of that Jesuit sect which nothing could induce him to tolerate.

PROFESSOR HAROLD LASKI (ESSAY IN *FREEDOM OF EXPRESSION*)

(2) Above all, we cannot play ducks and drakes with a native battery of idioms which prescribes such egregious collocations of vocables as the Basic *put up with* for *tolerate* or *put at a loss* for *bewilder*.

PROFESSOR LANCELOT HOGBEN (*INTERGLOSSA*)

(3) On the one side we have the free personality: by definition it is not neurotic, for it has neither conflict nor dream. Its desires, such as they are, are transparent, for they are just what institutional approval keeps in the forefront of consciousness; another institutional pattern would alter their number and intensity; there is little in them that is natural, irreducible, or culturally dangerous. But *on the other side*, the social bond itself is nothing but the mutual reflection of these self-secure integrities. Recall the definition of love. Is not this the very picture of a small academic? Where is there a place in this hall of mirrors for either personality or fraternity?

ESSAY ON PSYCHOLOGY IN *POLITICS* (NEW YORK)

(4) All the "best people" from the gentlemen's clubs, and all the frantic fascist captains, united in common hatred of Socialism and bestial horror of the rising tide of the mass revolutionary movement, have turned to acts of provocation, to foul incendiarism, to medieval legends of poisoned wells, to legalize their own destruction of proletarian organizations, and rouse the agitated petty-bourgeoisie to chauvinistic fervour on behalf of the fight against the revolutionary way out of the crisis.

COMMUNIST PAMPHLET

(5) If a new spirit *is* to be infused into this old country, there is one thorny and contentious reform which must be tackled, and that is the humanization and galvanization of the BBC. Timidity here will bespeak cancer and atrophy of the soul. The heart of Britain may be sound

and of strong beat, for instance, but the British lion's roar at present is like that of Bottom in Shakespeare's *Midsummer Night's Dream*—as gentle as any sucking dove. A virile new Britain cannot continue indefinitely to be traduced in the eyes or rather ears of the world by the effete languors of Langham Place, brazenly masquerading as "standard English." When the Voice of Britain is heard at nine o'clock, better far and infinitely less ludicrous to hear aitches honestly dropped than the present priggish, inflated, inhibited, school-ma'amish arch braying of blameless bashful mewing maidens!

L<small>ETTER IN</small> *T<small>RIBUNE</small>*

4   Each of these passages has faults of its own, but, quite apart from avoidable ugliness, two qualities are common to all of them. The first is staleness of imagery; the other is lack of precision. The writer either has a meaning and cannot express it, or he inadvertently says something else, or he is almost indifferent as to whether his words mean anything or not. This mixture of vagueness and sheer incompetence is the most marked characteristic of modern English prose, and especially of any kind of political writing. As soon as certain topics are raised, the concrete melts into the abstract and no one seems able to think of turns of speech that are not hackneyed: prose consists less and less of *words* chosen for the sake of their meaning, and more and more of *phrases* tacked together like the sections of a prefabricated henhouse. I list below, with notes and examples, various of the tricks by means of which the work of prose-construction is habitually dodged:

DYING METAPHORS

5   A newly invented metaphor assists thought by evoking a visual image, while on the other hand a metaphor which is technically "dead" (e.g., *iron resolution*) has in effect reverted to being an ordinary word and can generally be used without loss of vividness. But in between these two classes there is a huge dump of worn-out metaphors which have lost all evocative power and are merely used because they save people the trouble of inventing phrases for themselves. Examples are: *Ring the change on, take up the cudgels for, toe the line, ride roughshod over, stand shoulder to shoulder with, play into the hands of, no axe to grind, grist to the mill, fishing in troubled waters, on the order of the day, Achilles' heel, swan song, hotbed.* Many of these are used without knowledge of their meaning (what is a "rift," for instance?), and incompatible metaphors are frequently mixed, a sure sign that the writer is not interested in what he is saying. Some metaphors now current have been twisted out of their original meaning without those who use them even being aware of the fact. For example, *toe the line* is sometimes written *tow the line*. Another example is *the hammer and the anvil*, now always used with the implication that the anvil gets the worst of it. In real life it is always the anvil that breaks the hammer, never the other way about: a writer who stopped to think what he was saying would be aware of this, and would avoid perverting the original phrase.

OPERATORS OR VERBAL FALSE LIMBS

6   These save the trouble of picking out appropriate verbs and nouns, and at the same time pad each sentence with extra syllables which give it an appearance of symmetry. Characteristic phrases are: *render inoperative, militate against, make contact with, be subjected to, give rise to, give grounds for, have the effect of, play a leading part* (role) *in, make itself felt, take ef-*

fect, exhibit a tendency to, serve the purpose of, etc., etc. The keynote is the elimination of simple verbs. Instead of being a single word, such as *break, stop, spoil, mend, kill,* a verb becomes a *phrase,* made up of a noun or adjective tacked on to some general-purposes verb such as *prove, serve, form, play, render.* In addition, the passive voice is wherever possible used in preference to the active, and noun constructions are used instead of gerunds (*by examination of* instead of *by examining*). The range of verbs is further cut down by means of the *-ize* and *de-* formation, and the banal statements are given an appearance of profundity by means of the *not un-* formation. Simple conjunctions and prepositions are replaced by such phrases as *with respect to, having regard to, the fact that, by dint of, in view of, in the interests of, on the hypothesis that*; and the ends of sentences are saved from anticlimax by such resounding commonplaces as *greatly to be desired, cannot be left out of account, a development to be expected in the near future, deserving of serious consideration, brought to a satisfactory conclusion*, and so on and so forth.

PRETENTIOUS DICTION

7   Words like *phenomenon, element, individual* (as noun), *objective, categorical, effective, virtual, basic, primary, promote, constitute, exhibit, exploit, utilize, eliminate, liquidate,* are used to dress up simple statements and give an air of scientific impartiality to biased judgments. Adjectives like *epoch-making, epic, historic, unforgettable, triumphant, age-old, inevitable, inexorable, veritable,* are used to dignify the sordid processes of international politics, while writing that aims at glorifying war usually takes on an archaic colour, its characteristic words being: *realm, throne, chariot, mailed fist, trident, sword, shield, buckler, banner, jackboot, clarion.* Foreign words and expressions such as *cul de sac, ancien régime, deus ex machina, mutatis mutandis, status quo, gleichschaltung, weltanschauung,* are used to give an air of culture and elegance. Except for the useful abbreviations *i.e., e.g.,* and *etc.*, there is no real need for any of the hundreds of foreign phrases now current in English. Bad writers, and especially scientific, political, and sociological writers, are nearly always haunted by the notion that Latin and Greek words are grander than Saxon ones, and unnecessary words like *expedite, ameliorate, predict, extraneous, deracinated, clandestine, subaqueous,* and hundreds of others constantly gain ground from their Anglo-Saxon opposite numbers.[1] The jargon peculiar to Marxist writing (*hyena, hangman, cannibal, petty bourgeois, these gentry, lacquey, flunkey, mad dog, White Guard,* etc.) consists largely of words and phrases translated from Russian, German, or French; but the normal way of coining a new word is to use a Latin or Greek root with the appropriate affix and, where necessary, the *-ize* formation. It is often easier to make up words of this kind (*deregionalize, impermissible, extramarital, nonfragmentatory,* and so forth) than to think up the English words that will cover one's meaning. The result, in general, is an increase in slovenliness and vagueness.

MEANINGLESS WORDS

8   In certain kinds of writing, particularly in art criticism and literary criticism, it is normal to come across long passages which are almost completely lacking in meaning.[2] Words like *romantic, plastic, values, human, dead, sentimental, natural, vitality,* as used in art criticism, are strictly meaningless in the sense that they not only do not point to any discoverable

object, but are hardly ever expected to do so by the reader. When one critic writes, "The outstanding feature of Mr. X's work is its living quality," while another writes, "The immediately striking thing about Mr. X's work is its peculiar deadness," the reader accepts this as a simple difference of opinion. If words like *black* and *white* were involved, instead of the jargon words *dead* and *living*, he would see at once that language was being used in an improper way. Many political words are similarly abused. The word *Fascism* has now no meaning except in so far as it signifies "something not desirable." The words *democracy, socialism, freedom, patriotic, realistic, justice*, have each of them several different meanings which cannot be reconciled with one another. In the case of a word like *democracy*, not only is there no agreed definition, but the attempt to make one is resisted from all sides. It is almost universally felt that when we call a country democratic we are praising it: consequently the defenders of every kind of régime claim that it is a democracy, and fear that they might have to stop using the word if it were tied down to any one meaning. Words of this kind are often used in a consciously dishonest way. That is, the person who uses them has his own private definition, but allows his hearer to think he means something quite different. Statements like *Marshal Pétain was a true patriot, The Soviet Press is the freest in the world, The Catholic Church is opposed to persecution*, are almost always made with intent to deceive. Other words used in variable meanings, in most cases more or less dishonestly, are: *class, totalitarian, science, progressive, reactionary, bourgeois, equality*.

9   Now that I have made this catalogue of swindles and perversions, let me give another example of the kind of writing that they lead to. This time it must of its nature be an imaginary one. I am going to translate a passage of good English into modern English of the worst sort. Here is a well-known verse from *Ecclesiastes*:

10   "I returned and saw under the sun, that the race is not to the swift, nor the battle to the strong, neither yet bread to the wise, nor yet riches to men of understanding, nor yet favour to men of skill; but time and chance happeneth to them all."

11   Here it is in modern English:

12   "Objective consideration of contemporary phenomena compels the conclusion that success or failure in competitive activities exhibits no tendency to be commensurate with innate capacity, but that a considerable element of the unpredictable must invariably be taken into account."

13   This is a parody, but not a very gross one. Exhibit (3), above, for instance, contains several patches of the same kind of English. It will be seen that I have not made a full translation. The beginning and ending of the sentence follow the original meaning fairly closely, but in the middle the concrete illustrations—race, battle, bread—dissolve into the vague phrase "success or failure in competitive activities." This had to be so, because no modern writer of the kind I am discussing—no one capable of using phrases like "objective consideration of contemporary phenomena"—would ever tabulate his thoughts in that precise and detailed way. The whole tendency of modern prose is away from concreteness. Now analyse these two sentences a little more closely. The first contains forty-nine words but only sixty syllables, and all its words are those of everyday life. The second contains thirty-eight words of ninety syllables: eighteen of its words are from Latin roots, and one from Greek. The first sentence contains six vivid images, and only one phrase ("time and chance") that could be called vague. The second contains not a single fresh, arresting phrase, and in spite of its ninety syllables it gives only a shortened version of the meaning contained in the first. Yet without a doubt it is the second kind of sentence that is gaining ground in modern

English. I do not want to exaggerate. This kind of writing is not yet universal, and outcrops of simplicity will occur here and there in the worst-written page. Still, if you or I were told to write a few lines on the uncertainty of human fortunes, we should probably come much nearer to my imaginary sentence than to the one from *Ecclesiastes*.

14   As I have tried to show, modern writing at its worst does not consist in picking out words for the sake of their meaning and inventing images in order to make the meaning clearer. It consists in gumming together long strips of words which have already been set in order by someone else, and making the results presentable by sheer humbug. The attraction of this way of writing is that it is easy. It is easier—even quicker, once you have the habit—to say *In my opinion it is a not unjustifiable assumption that* than to say *I think*. If you use ready-made phrases, you not only don't have to hunt about for words; you also don't have to bother with the rhythms of your sentences, since these phrases are generally so arranged as to be more or less euphonious. When you are composing in a hurry—when you are dictating to a stenographer, for instance, or making a public speech—it is natural to fall into a pretentious, Latinized style. Tags like *a consideration which we should do well to bear in mind* or *a conclusion to which all of us would readily assent* will save many a sentence from coming down with a bump. By using stale metaphors, similes, and idioms, you save much mental effort, at the cost of leaving your meaning vague, not only for your reader but for yourself. This is the significance of mixed metaphors. The sole aim of a metaphor is to call up a visual image. When these images clash—as in *The Fascist octopus has sung its swan song, the jackboot is thrown into the melting pot*—it can be taken as certain that the writer is not seeing a mental image of the objects he is naming; in other words he is not really thinking. Look again at the examples I gave at the beginning of this essay. Professor Laski (1) uses five negatives in fifty-three words. One of these is superfluous, making nonsense of the whole passage, and in addition there is the slip *alien* for akin, making further nonsense, and several avoidable pieces of clumsiness which increase the general vagueness. Professor Hogben (2) plays ducks and drakes with a battery which is able to write prescriptions, and, while disapproving of the everyday phrase *put up with*, is unwilling to look *egregious* up in the dictionary and see what it means. (3), if one takes an uncharitable attitude towards it, is simply meaningless: probably one could work out its intended meaning by reading the whole of the article in which it occurs. In (4), the writer knows more or less what he wants to say, but an accumulation of stale phrases chokes him like tea leaves blocking a sink. In (5), words and meaning have almost parted company. People who write in this manner usually have a general emotional meaning—they dislike one thing and want to express solidarity with another—but they are not interested in the detail of what they are saying. A scrupulous writer, in every sentence that he writes, will ask himself at least four questions, thus: What am I trying to say? What words will express it? What image or idiom will make it clearer? Is this image fresh enough to have an effect? And he will probably ask himself two more: Could I put it more shortly? Have I said anything that is avoidably ugly? But you are not obliged to go to all this trouble. You can shirk it by simply throwing your mind open and letting the ready-made phrases come crowding in. They will construct your sentences for you—even think your thoughts for you, to a certain extent—and at need they will perform the important service of partially concealing your meaning even from yourself. It is at this point that the special connection between politics and the debasement of language becomes clear.

15   In our time it is broadly true that political writing is bad writing. Where it is not true, it will generally be found that the writer is some kind of rebel, expressing his private opinions and not a "party line." Orthodoxy, of whatever colour, seems to demand a lifeless, imitative style. The political dialects to be found in pamphlets, leading articles, manifestos, White Papers, and the speeches of under-secretaries do, of course, vary from party to party, but they are all alike in that one almost never finds in them a fresh, vivid, home-made turn of speech. When one watches some tired hack on the platform mechanically repeating the familiar phrases—*bestial atrocities, iron heel, bloodstained tyranny, free peoples of the world, stand shoulder to shoulder*—one often has a curious feeling that one is not watching a live human being but some kind of dummy: a feeling which suddenly becomes stronger at moments when the light catches the speaker's spectacles and turns them into blank discs which seem to have no eyes behind them. And this is not altogether fanciful. A speaker who uses that kind of phraseology has gone some distance towards turning himself into a machine. The appropriate noises are coming out of his larynx, but his brain is not involved as it would be if he were choosing his words for himself. If the speech he is making is one that he is accustomed to make over and over again, he may be almost unconscious of what he is saying, as one is when one utters the responses in church. And this reduced state of consciousness, if not indispensable, is at any rate favourable to political conformity.

16   In our time, political speech and writing are largely the defence of the indefensible. Things like the continuance of British rule in India, the Russian purges and deportations, the dropping of the atom bombs on Japan, can indeed be defended, but only by arguments which are too brutal for most people to face, and which do not square with the professed aims of political parties. Thus political language has to consist largely of euphemism, question-begging, and sheer cloudy vagueness. Defenceless villages are bombarded from the air, the inhabitants driven out into the countryside, the cattle machine-gunned, the huts set on fire with incendiary bullets: this is called *pacification*. Millions of peasants are robbed of their farms and sent trudging along the roads with no more than they can carry: this is called *transfer of population* or *rectification of frontiers*. People are imprisoned for years without trial, or shot in the back of the neck, or sent to die of scurvy in Arctic lumber camps: this is called *elimination of unreliable elements*. Such phraseology is needed if one wants to name things without calling up mental pictures of them. Consider for instance some comfortable English professor defending Russian totalitarianism. He cannot say outright, "I believe in killing off your opponents when you can get good results by doing so." Probably, therefore, he will say something like this:

17   "While freely conceding that the Soviet régime exhibits certain features which the humanitarian may be inclined to deplore, we must, I think, agree that a certain curtailment of the right to political opposition is an unavoidable concomitant of transitional periods, and that the rigours which the Russian people have been called upon to undergo have been amply justified in the sphere of concrete achievement."

18   The inflated style is itself a kind of euphemism. A mass of Latin words falls upon the facts like soft snow, blurring the outlines and covering up all the details. The great enemy of clear language is insincerity. When there is a gap between one's real and one's declared aims, one turns as it were instinctively to long words and exhausted idioms, like a cuttlefish squirting out ink. In our age there is no such thing as "keeping out of politics." All issues are political issues, and politics itself is a mass of lies, evasions, folly, hatred, and schizophrenia. When the general atmosphere is bad, language must suffer. I should expect to find—this is a guess which I have not sufficient knowledge to verify—that the German, Russian, and Italian languages have all deteriorated in the last ten or fifteen years, as a result of dictatorship.

19   But if thought corrupts language, language can also corrupt thought. A bad usage can spread by tradition and imitation, even among people who should and do know better. The debased language that I have been discussing is in some ways very convenient. Phrases like *a not unjustifiable assumption, leaves much to be desired, would serve no good purpose, a consideration which we should do well to bear in mind*, are a continuous temptation, a packet of aspirins always at one's elbow. Look back through this essay, and for certain you will find that I have again and again committed the very faults I am protesting against. By this morning's post I have received a pamphlet dealing with conditions in Germany. The author tells me that he "felt impelled" to write it. I open it at random, and here is almost the first sentence that I see: "[The Allies] have an opportunity not only of achieving a radical transformation of Germany's social and political structure in such a way as to avoid a nationalistic reaction in Germany itself, but at the same time of laying the foundations of a co-operative and unified Europe." You see, he "feels impelled" to write—feels, presumably, that he has something new to say—and yet his words, like cavalry horses answering the bugle, group themselves automatically into the familiar dreary pattern. This invasion of one's mind by ready-made phrases (*lay the foundations, achieve a radical transformation*) can only be prevented if one is constantly on guard against them, and every such phrase anaesthetizes a portion of one's brain.

20   I said earlier that the decadence of our language is probably curable. Those who deny this would argue, if they produced an argument at all, that language merely reflects existing social conditions, and that we cannot influence its development by any direct tinkering with words and constructions. So far as the general tone or spirit of a language goes, this may be true, but it is not true in detail. Silly words and expressions have often disappeared, not through any evolutionary process but owing to the conscious action of a minority. Two recent examples were *explore every avenue* and *leave no stone unturned*, which were killed by the jeers of a few journalists. There is a long list of flyblown metaphors which could similarly be got rid of if enough people would interest themselves in the job; and it should also be possible to laugh the *not un-* formation out of existence,[3] to reduce the amount of Latin and Greek in the average sentence, to drive out foreign phrases and strayed scientific words, and, in general, to make pretentiousness unfashionable. But all these are minor points. The defence of the English language implies more than this, and perhaps it is best to start by saying what it does *not* imply.

21   To begin with it has nothing to do with archaism, with the salvaging of obsolete words and turns of speech, or with the setting up of a "standard English" which must never be departed from. On the contrary, it is especially concerned with the scrapping of every word or idiom which has outworn its usefulness. It has nothing to do with correct grammar and syntax, which are of no importance so long as one makes one's meaning clear, or with the avoidance of Americanisms, or with having what is called a "good prose style." On the other hand it is not concerned with fake simplicity and the attempt to make written English colloquial. Nor does it even imply in every case preferring the Saxon word to the Latin one, though it does imply using the fewest and shortest words that will cover one's meaning. What is above all needed is to let the meaning choose the word, and not the other way about. In prose, the worst thing one can do with words is to surrender to them. When you think of a concrete object, you think wordlessly, and then, if you want to describe the thing you

have been visualizing you probably hunt about till you find the exact words that seem to fit. When you think of something abstract you are more inclined to use words from the start, and unless you make a conscious effort to prevent it, the existing dialect will come rushing in and do the job for you, at the expense of blurring or even changing your meaning. Probably it is better to put off using words as long as possible and get one's meaning as clear as one can through pictures or sensations. Afterwards one can choose—not simply *accept*—the phrases that will best cover the meaning, and then switch round and decide what impression one's words are likely to make on another person. This last effort of the mind cuts out all stale or mixed images, all prefabricated phrases, needless repetitions, and humbug and vagueness generally. But one can often be in doubt about the effect of a word or a phrase, and one needs rules that one can rely on when instinct fails. I think the following rules will cover most cases:

(i)   Never use a metaphor, simile, or other figure of speech which you are used to seeing in print.

(ii) Never use a long word where a short one will do.

(iii) If it is possible to cut a word out, always cut it out.

(iv) Never use the passive where you can use the active.

(v)   Never use a foreign phrase, a scientific word, or a jargon word if you can think of an everyday English equivalent.

(vi) Break any of these rules sooner than say anything outright barbarous.

These rules sound elementary, and so they are, but they demand a deep change of attitude in anyone who has grown used to writing in the style now fashionable. One could keep all of them and still write bad English, but one could not write the kind of stuff that I quoted in those five specimens at the beginning of this article.

22   I have not here been considering the literary use of language, but merely language as an instrument for expressing and not for concealing or preventing thought. Stuart Chase and others have come near to claiming that all abstract words are meaningless, and have used this as a pretext for advocating a kind of political quietism. Since you don't know what Fascism is, how can you struggle against Fascism? One need not swallow such absurdities as this, but one ought to recognize that the present political chaos is connected with the decay of language, and that one can probably bring about some improvement by starting at the verbal end. If you simplify your English, you are freed from the worst follies of orthodoxy. You cannot speak any of the necessary dialects, and when you make a stupid remark its stupidity will be obvious, even to yourself. Political language—and with variations this is true of all political parties, from Conservatives to Anarchists—is designed to make lies sound truthful and murder respectable, and to give an appearance of solidity to pure wind. One cannot change this all in a moment, but one can at least change one's own habits, and from time to time one can even, if one jeers loudly enough, send some worn-out and useless phrase—some *jackboot, Achilles' heel, hotbed, melting pot, acid test, veritable inferno*, or other lump of verbal refuse—into the dustbin where it belongs.

ENDNOTES

1. An interesting illustration of this is the way in which the English flower names which were in use till very recently are being ousted by Greek ones, *snapdragon* becoming *antirrhinum*, *forget-me-not* becoming *myosotis*, etc. It is hard to see any practical reason for this change of fashion: it is probably due to an instinctive turning-away from the more homely word and a vague feeling that the Greek word is scientific.

2. Example: "Comfort's catholicity of perception and image, strangely Whitmanesque in range, almost the exact opposite in aesthetic compulsion, continues to evoke that trembling atmospheric accumulative hinting at a cruel, an inexorably serene timelessness . . . Wrey Gardiner scores by aiming at simple bull's-eyes with precision. Only they are not so simple, and through this contented sadness runs more than the surface bittersweet of resignation" (*Poetry Quarterly*).

3. One can cure oneself of the *not un-* formation by memorizing this sentence: *A not unblack dog was chasing a not unsmall rabbit across a not ungreen field.*

NOTES AND DISCUSSION

"Politics and the English Language" has been widely admired and studied since its first publication in 1946. It has often been used as a model for what English prose should be and too often is not. Orwell argues forcibly against the use of "dying metaphors," "operators or verbal false limbs," "pretentious diction," and "meaningless words," and for clarity, above all.

However, this essay is more than a humourless, didactic manual on plain style and a list of linguistic offences. Orwell provides several clues as to how we should read his essay. For instance, in the opening paragraph, he calls language "an instrument which we shape for our own purposes," yet in the first sentence of that paragraph, he uses that instrument rather carelessly: the referent of the pronoun "it" is unclear. Indeed, later in the essay, Orwell himself announces, "Look back through this essay, and for certain you will find that I have again and again committed the very faults I am protesting against." Many of those faults not only do appear throughout the essay, but make their first appearance in the opening paragraph. Thus Orwell criticizes, on one hand, the careless use of language, and, on the other, the didactic policing of language that, if followed rigorously, would make written expression virtually impossible.

Orwell's most valuable lesson to us in this essay is to be diligent, both in reading and in writing, to always think clearly about what we are saying, and about what is being said to us.

STUDY QUESTIONS

For Discussion:

1. How would you characterize Orwell's persona in this essay? How seriously do you think that persona should be taken? Notice the narrator's tendency to make sweeping generalizations like "it is clear that the decline of a language must ultimately have political and economic causes," and to use metaphors and similes like "a mass of Latin words falls upon the facts like soft snow." Which is easier to find, examples of Orwell following his own

instructions, or of him breaking his own rules? Armed with your findings, discuss Orwell's observation in the last sentence of the first paragraph that many people have a "half-conscious belief that language is a natural growth and not an instrument which we shape for our own purposes."

2. This essay contains several lists: Orwell's five examples of bad writing; the list that can be constructed from the subheadings that name particular faults; the four questions that "a scrupulous writer . . . will ask himself," and the "two more" that he should add; and the list of rules in the penultimate paragraph. Discuss the effect of those lists and subheadings on the reader.

For Writing:

1. What is Orwell's thesis? Write an analysis of his thesis and his method of arguing for it.
2. Find an example in a newspaper of what Orwell calls "political language," and analyze it according to his criteria. Ask yourself what exactly Orwell means by "politics" in his title. Does your analysis support his claim that political language is largely the "defence of the indefensible"?

CROCODILED MOATS IN THE KINGDOM OF LETTERS

Cynthia Ozick

BIOGRAPHICAL NOTE

Cynthia Ozick was born and raised in New York City. She has written widely about the various tensions between scientists and humanists, one of the topics of this essay. Her essays, novels, and short stories have earned her wide praise and many awards, including a Guggenheim Fellowship. In her most recent collection of essays, entitled *Fame & Folly*, Ozick examines the often vexed relationship between life and literature by referring to subjects as wide-ranging as Salman Rushdie and Anthony Trollope.

For constantly I felt I was moving among two groups—comparable in intelligence, identical in race, not grossly different in social origin, earning about the same incomes, who had almost ceased to communicate at all, who in intellectual, moral, and psychological climate had so little in common that . . . one might have crossed an ocean.
—C. P. Snow, *"The Two Cultures and the Scientific Revolution"*

1   Disraeli in his novel *Sybil* spoke of "two nations," the rich and the poor. After the progress of more than a century, the phrase (and the reality) remains regrettably apt. But in the less than three decades since C. P. Snow proposed his "two cultures" thesis—the gap of incomprehension between the scientific and literary elites—the conditions of what we still like to call culture have altered so drastically that Snow's arguments are mostly dissolved into pointlessness. His compatriot and foremost needler, the Cambridge critic F. R. Leavis, had in any case set out to flog Snow's hypothesis from the start. Snow, he said, "rides on an advancing swell of cliché," "doesn't know what literature is," and hasn't "had the advantage

of an intellectual discipline of any kind." And besides—here Leavis emitted his final boom—"there is only one culture."

2   In the long run both were destined to be mistaken—Leavis perhaps more than Snow. In 1959, when Snow published "The Two Cultures," we had already had well over a hundred years to get used to the idea of science as a multidivergent venture—dozens and dozens of disciplines, each one nearly a separate nation with its own governance, psychology, entelechy. It might have been possible to posit, say, a unitary medical culture in the days when barbers were surgeons; but in recent generations we don't expect our dentist to repair a broken kneecap, or our orthopedist to practice cardiology. And nowadays we are learning that an ophthalmologist with an understanding of the cornea is likely to be a bit shaky on the subject of the retina. Engineers are light-years from astrophysicists. Topology is distinct from topography, paleobotany from paleogeology, particle physics from atomic. In reiterating that scientific culture is specialist culture—who doesn't know this?—one risks riding an advancing swell of cliché. Yet science, multiplying, fragmented, in hot pursuit of split ends, is in a way a species of polytheism, or, rather, animism: every grain of matter, every path of conceptualization, has its own ruling spirit, its differentiated lawgiver and traffic director. Investigative diversity and particularizing empiricism have been characteristic of science since—well, since alchemy turned into physical chemistry (and lately into superconductivity); since the teakettle inspired the locomotive; since Icarus took off his wax wings to become Pan Am; since Archimedes stepped out of his tub into Einstein's sea.

3   Snow was in command of all this, of course—he was pleased to identify himself as an exceptional scientist who wrote novels—and still he chose to make a monolith out of splinters. Why did he do it? In order to have one unanimity confront another. While it may have been a polemical contrivance to present a diversiform scientific culture as unitary, it was patently not wrong, thirty years ago, to speak of literary culture as a single force or presence. That was what was meant by the peaceable word "humanities." And it was what Leavis meant, too, when he growled back at Snow that one culture was all there was worth having. "Don't mistake me," Leavis pressed, "I am not preaching that we should defy, or try to reverse, the accelerating movement of external civilization (the phrase sufficiently explains itself, I hope) that is determined by advancing technology. . . . What I *am* saying is that such a concern is not enough—disastrously not enough." Not enough, he argued, for "a human future . . . in full intelligent possession of its full humanity." For Leavis, technology was the mere outer rind of culture, and the job of literature (the hot core at the heart of culture) was not to oppose science but to humanize it. Only in Snow's wretchedly deprived mind did literature stand apart from science; Snow hardly understood what literature was *for*. And no wonder; Snow's ideas about literary intellectuals came, Leavis sneered, from "the reviewing in the Sunday papers."

4   It has never been easy to fashion a uniform image of science—which is why we tend to say "the sciences." But until not very long ago one could take it for granted (despite the headlong decline of serious high art) that there was, on the humanities side, a concordant language of sensibility, an embracing impulse toward integration, above all the conviction of human connectedness—even if that conviction occasionally partook of a certain crepuscular nostalgia we might better have done without. Snow pictured literature and science as two angry armies. Leavis announced that there was only one army, with literature as its commander in chief. Yet it was plain that both Leavis and Snow, for all their antagonisms, saw the kingdom of letters as an intact and enduring power.

5   This feeling for literary culture as a glowing wholeness—it *was* a feeling, a stirring, a flush of idealism—is now altogether dissipated. The fragrant term that encapsulated it—belles-lettres—is nearly archaic and surely effete: it smacks of leather tooling for the moneyed, of posturing. But it was once useful enough. Belles-lettres stood for a binding thread of observation and civilizing emotion. It signified not so much that letters are beautiful as that the house of letters is encompassingly humane and undivisive, no matter how severally its windows are shaped, or who looks out or in. Poets, scholars, journalists, librarians, novelists, playwrights, art critics, philosophers, historians, political theorists, and all the rest may have inhabited different rooms, differently furnished, but it was indisputably one house with a single roof and plenty of connecting doors and passageways. And sometimes—so elastic and compressive was the humanist principle—poet, scholar, essayist, philosopher, etc., all lived side by side in the same head. Seamlessness (even if only an illusion) never implied locked and separate cells.

6   And now? Look around. Now "letters" suggest a thousand enemy camps, "genres" like fortresses, professions isolated by crocodiled moats. The living tissue of intuition and inference that nurtured the commonalty of the humanities is ruptured by an abrupt invasion of specialists. In emulation of the sciences? But we don't often hear of astronomers despising molecular biologists; in science, it may be natural for knowledge to run, like quicksilver, into crannies.

7   In the ex-community of letters, factions are in fashion, and the business of factions is to despise. Matthew Arnold's mild and venerable dictum, an open-ended, open-armed, definition of literature that clearly intends a nobility of inclusiveness—"the best that is known and thought in the world"—earns latter-day assaults and jeers. What can all that mean now but "canon," and what can a received canon mean but reactionary, racist, sexist, elitist closure? Politics presses against disinterestedness; all categories are suspect, no category is allowed to display its wares without the charge of enslavement by foregone conclusion and vested interest. What Arnold called the play of mind is asked to show its credentials and prove its legitimacy. "Our organs of criticism," Arnold complained in 1864 (a period as uninnocent as our own), "are organs of men and parties having practical ends to serve, and with them those practical ends are the first thing and the play of mind the second."

8   And so it is with us. The culture of the humanities has split and split and split again, always for reasons of partisan ascendancy and scorn. Once it was not unusual for writers— Dreiser, Stephen Crane, Cather, Hemingway!—to turn to journalism for a taste of the workings of the world. Today novelists and journalists are alien breeds reared apart, as if imagination properly belonged only to the one and never to the other; as if society and instinct were designed for estrangement. The two crafts are contradictory even in method; journalists are urged to tell secrets in the top line; novelists insinuate suspensefully, and wait for the last line to spill the real beans. Dickens, saturated in journalism, excelled at shorthand; was a court reporter; edited topical magazines.

9   In the literary academy, Jacques Derrida has the authority that Duns Scotus had for medieval scholastics—and it is authority, not literature, that mainly engages faculties. In the guise of maverick or rebel, professors kowtow to dogma. English departments have set off after theory, and use culture as an instrument to illustrate doctrinal principles, whether Marxist or "French Freud." The play of mind gives way to signing up and lining up. College teachers were never so cut off from the heat of poets dead or alive as they are now; only think of the icy distances separating syllables by, say, Marianne Moore, A. R. Ammons, May Swenson, or Amy Clampitt from the papers read at last winter's Modern Language Association meeting—*viz.*, "Written Discourse as Dialogic Interaction," "Abduction, Transference, and the Reading Stage," "The Politics of Feminism and the Discourse of Feminist Literary Criticism."

10   And more: poets trivialize novelists, novelists trivialize poets. Both trivialize critics. Critics trivialize reviewers. Reviewers report that they *are* critics. Short-story writers assert transfigurations unavailable to novelists. Novelists declare the incomparable glories of the long pull. Novelizing estheticians, admitting to literature no claims of moral intent, ban novelizing moralists. The moralists condemn the estheticians as precious, barren, solipsist. Few essayists essay fiction. Few novelists hazard essays. Dense-language writers vilify minimalists. Writers of plain prose ridicule complex sentences. Professors look down on commercial publishers. Fiction writers dread university presses. The so-called provinces envy and despise the provinciality of New York. New York sees sour grapes in California and everywhere else. The so-called mainstream judges which writers are acceptably universal and which are to be exiled as "parochial." The so-called parochial, stung or cowardly or both, fear all particularity and attempt impersonation of the acceptable. "Star" writers—recall the International PEN Congress in New York last year—treat lesser-knowns as invisible, negligible. The lesser-knowns, crushed, disparage the stars.

11   And even the public library, once the unchallenged repository of the best that is known and thought, begins to split itself off, abandons its mandate and rents out Polaroid cameras and videotapes, like some semiphilanthropic Crazy Eddie. My own local library, appearing to jettison the basic arguments of the age, flaunts, shelf after shelf prominently marked Decorating, Consumer Power, How-To, Cookery, Hooray for Hollywood, Accent on You, What Makes Us Laugh, and many more such chitchat categories. But there are no placards for Literature, History, Biography; and Snow and Leavis, whom I needed to moon over in order to get started on this essay, were neither one to be had. (I found them finally in the next town, in a much smaller if more traditionally bookish library.)

12   Though it goes against the grain of respected current belief to say so, literature is really *about* something. It is about us. That may be why we are drawn to think of the kingdom of letters as a unity, at least in potential. Science, teeming and multiform, is about how the earth and the heavens and the microbes and the insects and our mammalian bodies are constructed, but literature is about the meaning of the finished construction. Or, to set afloat a more transcendent vocabulary: science is about God's work; literature is about our work. If our work lies untended (and what is our work but aspiration?), if literary culture falls into a heap of adversial splinters—into competing contemptuous clamorers for turf and mental dominance—then what will be left to tell us that we are one human presence?

13   To forward that strenuous telling, Matthew Arnold (himself now among the jettisoned) advised every reader and critic to "try and possess one great literature, at least, besides his own; and the more unlike his own, the better." Not to split off from but to add on to the kingdom of letters: so as to uncover its human face.

14   An idea which—in a time of ten thousand self-segregating literary technologies—may be unwanted, if not obsolete.

NOTES AND DISCUSSION

A physicist and a novelist, C. P. Snow saw himself as unusually—perhaps uniquely—qualified to discuss the differences between what he calls "The Two Cultures." His essay of that title was first published in 1956, and revised and expanded in 1959. It provoked an immediate and heated response from F. R. Leavis, who was probably the most respected and influential literary critic of his day. His position, as Ozick notes, was that "the job of literature . . . was not to oppose science but to humanize it."

Ozick's essay was first published in 1987. While it begins as a response to Snow and Leavis and their divisive debate, by the end, Ozick admits to using Snow and Leavis merely "to moon over in order to get started on this essay." Her essay, it turns out, is not really a response at all, but an addendum to the discussion, and a nostalgic obituary about the passing of a single, unified discipline called "the humanities."

In addition to the references to Snow and Leavis, Ozick refers throughout the essay to Matthew Arnold, among others. Note her use of Arnold's definition of literature in the seventh paragraph: "the best that is known and thought in the world."

Note also her use of figurative language to advance her own position. This is from paragraph two: "Investigative diversity and particularizing empiricism have been characteristic of science since—well, since alchemy turned into physical chemistry (and lately into superconductivity); since the teakettle inspired the locomotive; since Icarus took off his wax wings to become Pan Am; since Archimedes stepped out of his tub into Einstein's sea."

STUDY QUESTIONS

For Discussion:

1. Although Ozick is quite clear about her disapproval of the tone of the debate between Snow and Leavis, is she equally clear about her own notions of the differences between science and literature? In your response, consider Ozick's paraphrase of Leavis's claim that "technology [is] the mere outer rind of culture." What are the implications of that metaphor?

2. Ozick discusses the "Kingdom of Letters" extensively in this essay. One part of that kingdom is "Literature." By her own definition, is Ozick's essay literature? To what extent is Ozick's essay an example of a "paradigm shift" in the humanities, like those that Thomas Kuhn claims govern scientific investigation?

For Writing:

1. Write an analytical paragraph about Ozick's definitions of science and of literature. Do you agree with her definitions? What would you add to them? In the course of your answer, consider where you think writing about science falls, in each of the three traditions—Snow's, Leavis's, and Ozick's—presented here.

2. Ozick uses the "split" that divided Leavis and Snow to start her discussion, but she is much more concerned with other, more current splits in the "Kingdom of Letters." In a short research essay, investigate some of the figures and positions that Ozick names. Do you agree that the splits she is concerned about are more profound and disturbing than the one between Leavis and Snow? Is Ozick's original split—between the sciences and the humanities—still an important one?

LESSONS FROM PLAY; LESSONS FROM LIFE

Henry Petroski

BIOGRAPHICAL NOTE

Henry Petroski is a professor of civil engineering at Duke University and a regular columnist for *American Scientist* magazine. He has written several books, all of which are concerned with problems and questions in engineering and design. His books include *The Pencil: A History of Design and Circumstance* (1990) and *The Evolution of Useful Things* (1992).

1   When I want to introduce the engineering concept of fatigue to students, I bring a box of paper clips to class. In front of the class I open one of the paper clips flat and then bend it back and forth until it breaks in two. That, I tell the class, is failure by fatigue, and I point out that the number of back and forth cycles it takes to break the paper clip depends not only on how strong the clip is but also on how severely I bend it. When paper clips are used normally, to clip a few sheets of paper together, they can withstand perhaps thousands or millions of the slight openings and closings it takes to put them on and take them off the papers, and thus we seldom experience their breaking. But when paper clips are bent open so wide that they look as if we want them to hold all the pages of a book together, it might take only ten or twenty flexings to bring them to the point of separation.

2   Having said this, I pass out a half dozen or so clips to each of the students and ask them to bend their clips to breaking by flexing them as far open and as far closed as I did. As the students begin this low-budget experiment, I prepare at the blackboard to record how many back and forth bendings it takes to break each paper clip. As the students call out the numbers, I plot them on a bar graph called a histogram. Invariably the results fall clearly under a bell-shaped normal curve that indicates the statistical distribution of the results, and I

elicit from the students the explanations as to why not all the paper clips broke with the same number of bendings. Everyone usually agrees on two main reasons: not all paper clips are equally strong, and not every student bends his clips in exactly the same way. Thus the students recognize at once the phenomenon of fatigue and the fact that failure by fatigue is not a precisely predictable event.

3   Many of the small annoyances of daily life are due to predictable—but not precisely so—fractures from repeated use. Shoelaces and light bulbs, as well as many other familiar objects, seem to fail us suddenly and when it is least convenient. They break and burn out under conditions that seem no more severe than those they had been subjected to hundreds or thousands of times before. A bulb that has burned continuously for decades may appear in a book of world records, but to an engineer versed in the phenomenon of fatigue, the performance is not remarkable. Only if the bulb had been turned on and off daily all those years would its endurance be extraordinary, for it is the cyclic and not the continuous heating of the filament that is its undoing. Thus, because of the fatiguing effect of being constantly changed, it is the rare scoreboard that does not have at least one bulb blown.

4   Children's toys are especially prone to fatigue failure, not only because children subject them to seemingly endless hours of use but also because the toys are generally not overdesigned. Building a toy too rugged could make it too heavy for the child to manipulate, not to mention more expensive than its imitators. Thus, the seams of rubber balls crack open after so many bounces, the joints of metal tricycles break after so many trips around the block, and the heads of plastic dolls separate after so many nods of agreement.

5   Even one of the most innovative electronic toys of recent years has been the victim of mechanical fatigue long before children (and their parents) tire of playing with it. Texas Instruments' Speak & Spell effectively employs one of the first microelectronic voice synthesizers. The bright red plastic toy asks the child in a now-familiar voice to spell a vocabulary of words from the toy's memory. The child pecks out letters on the keyboard, and they appear on a calculator-like display. When the child finishes spelling a word, the ENTER key is pressed and the computer toy says whether the spelling is correct and prompts the child to try again when a word is misspelled. Speak & Spell is so sophisticated that it will turn itself off if the child does not press a button for five minutes or so, thus conserving its four C-cells.

6   My son's early model Speak & Spell had given him what seemed to be hundreds of hours of enjoyment when one day the ENTER key broke off at its plastic hinge. But since Stephen could still fit his small finger into the buttonhole to activate the switch, he continued to enjoy the smart, if disfigured, toy. Soon thereafter, however, the E key snapped off, and soon the T and O keys followed suit. Although he continued to use the toy, its keyboard soon became a maze of missing letters and, for those that were saved from the vacuum cleaner, taped-on buttons.

7   What made these failures so interesting to me was the very strong correlation between the most frequently occurring letters in the English language and the fatigued keys on Stephen's Speak & Spell. It is not surprising that the ENTER key broke first, since it was employed for inputting each word and thus got more use than any one letter. Of the seven most common letters—in decreasing occurrence, E, T, A, O, I, N, S, R—five (E, T, O, S, and R) were among the first keys to break. All other letter keys, save for the two seemingly anomalous failures of P and Y, were intact when I first reported this serendipitous experiment on the fatigue phenomenon in the pages of *Technology Review*.

8   If one assumes that all Speak & Spell letter keys were made as equally well as manufacturing processes allowed, perhaps about as uniformly as or even more so than paper
clips, then those plastic keys that failed must generally have been the ones pressed most
frequently. The correlation between letter occurrence in common English words and the
failure of the keys substantiates that this did indeed happen, for the anomalous failures seem
also to be explainable in terms of abnormally high use. Because my son is right-handed,
he might be expected to favor letters on the right-hand side of the keyboard when guessing
spellings or just playing at pressing letters. Since none of the initial failed letters occurs in
the four left-most columns of Speak & Spell, this proclivity could also explain why the
common-letter keys A and N were still intact. The anomalous survival of the I key may be
attributed to its statistically abnormal strength or to its underuse by a gregarious child. And
the failure of the infrequently occurring P and Y might have been a manifestation of the
statistical weakness of the keys or of their overuse by my son. His frequent spelling of his
name and the name of his cat, Pollux, endeared the letter *P* to him, and he had learned early
that *Y* is sometimes a vowel. Furthermore, each time the Y key was pressed, Speak & Spell
would ask the child's favorite question, "Why?"

9   Why the fatigue of its plastic buttons should have been the weak link that destroyed the
integrity of my son's most modern electronic toy could represent the central question for understanding engineering design. Why did the designers of the toy apparently not anticipate
this problem? Why did they not use buttons that would outlast the toy's electronics? Why did
they not obviate the problem of fatigue, the problem that has defined the lifetimes of mechanical and structural designs for ages? Such questions are not unlike those that are asked
after the collapse of a bridge or the crash of an airplane. But the collapse of a bridge or the
crash of an airplane can endanger hundreds of lives, and thus the possibility of the fatigue
of any part can be a lesson from which its victims learn nothing. Yet the failure of a child's
toy, though it may cause tears, is but a lesson for a child's future of burnt-out light bulbs and
broken shoelaces. And years later, when his shoelaces break as he is rushing to dress for an
important appointment, he will be no less likely to ask, "Why?"

10   After I wrote about the found experiment, my son retrieved his Speak & Spell from my
desk and resumed playing with the toy—and so continued the experiment. Soon another
key failed, the vowel key U in the lower left position near where Stephen held his thumb. Next
the A key broke, another vowel and the third most frequently occurring letter of the alphabet. The experiment ended with that failure, however, for Stephen acquired a new model of
Speak & Spell with the new keyboard design that my daughter, Karen, had pointed out to me
at an electronics store. Instead of having individually hinged plastic buttons, the new model
has its keyboard printed on a single piece of rubbery plastic stretched over the switches.
The new model Stephen has is called an E. T. Speak & Spell, after the little alien creature
in the movie, and I am watching the plastic sheet in the vicinity of those two most frequently occurring letters to see if the fatigue gremlin will strike again.

11   Not long after I had first written about my son's Speak & Spell I found out from readers that their children too had had to live with disfigured keyboards. It is a tribute to the in-
geniousness of the toy—and the attachment that children had developed for it—that they
endured the broken keys and adapted in makeshift ways, as they would have to throughout a life of breakdowns and failures in our less than perfect world. Some parents reported
that their children apparently discovered that the eraser end of a pencil fit nicely into the holes
of the old Speak & Spell and thus could be used to enter the most frequently used letters with-

out the children having to use their fingertips. I have wondered if indeed this trick was actually discovered by the parents who loved to play with the toy, for almost any child's finger should easily fit into the hole left by the broken button, but Mommy and Daddy's certainly would not.

12   Nevertheless, this resourcefulness suggests that the toy would have been a commercial success even with its faults, but the company still improved the keyboard design to solve the problem of key fatigue. The new buttonless keyboard is easily cleaned and pressed by even the clumsiest of adult fingers. The evolution of the Speak & Spell keyboard is not an atypical example of the way mass-produced items, though not necessarily planned that way, are debugged through use. Although there may have been some disappointment among parents who had paid a considerable amount of money for what was then among the most advanced applications of microelectronics wizardry, their children, who were closer to the world of learning to walk and talk and who were still humbled by their skinned knees and twisted tongues, took the failure of the keys in stride. Perhaps the manufacturer of the toy, in the excitement of putting the first talking computer on the market, overlooked some of the more mundane aspects of its design, but when the problem of the fractured keys came to its attention, it acted quickly to improve the toy's mechanical shortcomings.

13   I remember being rather angry when my son's Speak & Spell lost its first key. For all my understanding of the limitations of engineering and for all my attempted explanations to my neighbors of how failures like the Hyatt Regency walkways and the DC-10 could happen without clear culpability, I did not extend my charity to the designers of the toy. But there is a difference in the design and development of things that are produced by the millions and those that are unique, and it is generally the case that the mass-produced mechanical or electronic object undergoes some of its debugging and evolution after it is offered to the consumer. Such actions as producing a new version of a toy or carrying out an automobile recall campaign are not possible for the large civil engineering structure, however, which must be got right from the first stages of construction. So my charity should have extended to the designers of the Speak & Spell, for honest mistakes can be made by mechanical and electrical as well as by civil engineers. Perhaps someone had underestimated the number of *E*s it would take a child to become bored with the new toy. After all, most toys are put away long before they break. If this toy, which is more sophisticated than any I ever had in my own childhood, could tell me when I misspelled words I never could keep straight, then I would demand from it other superhuman qualities such as indestructibility. Yet we do not expect that of everything.

14   Although we might all be annoyed when a light bulb or a shoelace breaks, especially if it does so at a very inconvenient time, few if any of us would dream of taking it back to the store claiming it had malfunctioned. We all know the story of Thomas Edison searching for a suitable filament for the light bulb, and we are aware of and grateful for the technological achievement. We know, almost intuitively it seems, that to make a shoelace that would not break would involve compromises that we are not prepared to accept. Such a lace might be undesirably heavy or expensive for the style of shoe we wear, and we are much more willing to have the option of living with the risk of having the lace break at an inopportune time or of having the small mental burden of anticipating when the lace will break so that we might replace it in time. Unless we are uncommonly fastidious, we live dangerously and pay little attention to preventive maintenance of our fraying shoelaces or our aging

light bulbs. Though we may still ask "Why?" when they break, we already know and accept the answer.

15   As the consequences of failure become more severe, however, the forethought we must give to them becomes more a matter of life and death. Automobiles are manufactured by the millions, but it would not do to have them failing with a snap on the highways the way light bulbs and shoelaces do at home. The way an automobile could fail must be anticipated so that, as much as possible, a malfunction does not lead to an otherwise avoidable deadly accident. Since tires are prone to flats, we want our vehicles to be able to be steered safely to the side of the road when one occurs. Such a failure is accepted in the way light bulb and shoelace failures are, and we carry a spare tire to deal with it. Other kinds of malfunctions are less acceptable. We do not want the brakes on all four wheels and the emergency braking system to fail us suddenly and simultaneously. We do not want the steering wheel to come off in our hands as we are negotiating a snaking mountain road. Certain parts of the automobile are given special attention, and in the rare instances when they do fail, leading to disaster, massive lawsuits can result. When they become aware of a potential hazard, automobile manufacturers are compelled to eliminate what might be the causes of even the most remote possibilities of design-related accidents by the massive recall campaigns familiar to us all.

16   As much as it is human to make mistakes, it is also human to want to avoid them. Murphy's Law, holding that anything that can go wrong will, is not a law of nature but a joke. All the light bulbs that last until we tire of the lamp, all the shoelaces that outlast their shoes, all the automobiles that give trouble-free service until they are traded in have the last laugh on Murphy. Just as he will not outlive his law, so nothing manufactured can be or is expected to last forever. Once we recognize this elementary fact, the possibility of a machine or a building being as near to perfect for its designed lifetime as its creators may strive to be for theirs is not only a realistic goal for engineers but also a reasonable expectation for consumers. It is only when we set ourselves such an unrealistic goal as buying a shoelace that will never break, inventing a perpetual motion machine, or building a vehicle that will never break down that we appear to be fools and not rational beings.

17   Oliver Wendell Holmes is remembered more widely for his humor and verse than for the study entitled "The Contagiousness of Puerperal Fever" that he carried out as Parkman Professor of Anatomy and Philosophy at Harvard Medical School. Yet it may have been his understanding of the seemingly independent working of the various parts of the human body that helped him to translate his physiological experiences into a lesson for structural and mechanical engineers. Although some of us go first in the knees and others in the back, none of us falls apart all at once in all our joints. So Holmes imagined the foolishness of expecting to design a horse-drawn carriage that did not have a weak link.

18   Although intended as an attack on Calvinism, in which Holmes uses the metaphor of the "one-hoss shay" to show that a system of logic, no matter how perfect it seems, must collapse if its premises are false, the poem also holds up as a good lesson for engineers. Indeed, Micro-Measurements, a Raleigh, North Carolina-based supplier of devices to measure the stresses and strains in engineering machines and structures, thinks "The Deacon's Masterpiece" so apt to its business that it offers copies of the poem suitable for framing. The firm's advertising copy recognizes that although ". . . Holmes knew nothing of . . . modern-day technology when he wrote about a vehicle with no weak link among its components," he did realize the absurdity of attempting to achieve "the perfect engineering feat."

19   In Holmes's poem, which starts on p. 223, the Deacon decides that he will build an indestructible shay, with every part as strong as the rest, so that it will not break down. However, what the Deacon fails to take into account is that everything has a lifetime, and if indeed a shay could be built with "every part as strong as the rest," then every part would "wear out" at the same time and whoever inherited the shay from the Deacon, who himself would pass away before his creation, would be taken by surprise one day. While "The Deacon's Masterpiece" is interesting in recognizing that breaking down is the wearing out of one part, the weakest link, it is not technologically realistic in suggesting that all parts could have exactly the same lifetime. That premise is contrary to the reality that we can only know that this or that part will last for *approximately* this or that many years, just as we can only state the probability that any one paper clip will break after so many bendings. The exact lifetime of a part, a machine, or a structure is known only after it has broken.

20   Just as we are expected to know our own limitations, so should we know those of the inanimate world. Even the pyramids in the land of the Sphinx, whose riddle reminds us that we all must crawl before we walk and that we will not walk forever, have been eroded by the sand and the wind. Nothing on this earth is inviolate on the scale of geological time, and nothing we create will last at full strength forever. Steel corrodes and diamonds can be split. Even nuclear waste has a half-life.

21   Engineering deals with lifetimes, both human and otherwise. If not fatigue or fracture, then corrosion or erosion; if not war or vandalism, then taste or fashion claim not only the body but the very souls of once-new machines. Some lifetimes are set by the intended use of an engineering structure. As such an offshore oil platform may be designed to last for only the twenty or thirty years that it will take to extract the oil from the rock beneath the sea. It is less easy to say when the job of a bridge will be completed, yet engineers will have to have some clear idea of a bridge's lifetime if only to specify when some major parts will have to be inspected, serviced, or replaced. Buildings have uses that are subject to the whims of business fashion, and thus today's modern skyscraper may be unrentable in fifty years. Monumental architecture such as museums and government buildings, on the other hand, should suggest a permanence that makes engineers think in terms of centuries. A cathedral, a millennium.

22   The lifetime of a structure is no mere anthropomorphic metaphor, for how long a piece of engineering must last can be one of the most important considerations in its design. We have seen how the constant on and off action of a child's toy or a light bulb can cause irreparable damage, and so it is with large engineering structures. The ceaseless action of the sea on an offshore oil platform subjects its welded joints to the very same back and forth forces that cause a paper clip or a piece of plastic to crack after so many flexures. The bounce of a bridge under traffic and the sway of a skyscraper in the wind can also cause the growth of cracks in or the exhaustion of strength of steel cables and concrete beams, and one of the most important calculations of the modern engineer is the one that predicts how long it will take before cracks or the simple degradation of its materials threaten the structure's life. Sometimes we learn more from experience than calculations, however.

23   Years after my son had outgrown Speak & Spell, and within months of his disaffection with the video games he once wanted so much, he began to ask for toys that required no batteries. First he wanted a BB gun, which his mother and I were reluctant to give him, and then he wanted a slingshot. This almost biblical weapon seemed somehow a less violent toy and evoked visions of a Norman Rockwell painting, in which a boy-being-a-boy conceals his

homemade slingshot from the neighbor looking out a broken window. It is almost as inno-cent a piece of Americana as the baseball hit too far, and no one would want to ban sling-shots or boys.

24   I was a bit surprised, however, to learn that my son wanted to *buy* a slingshot ready-made, and I was even more surprised to learn that his source would not be the Sears Catalog, which might have fit in with the Norman Rockwell image, but one of the catalogs of several discount stores that seem to have captured the imagination of boys in this age of high-tech toys. What my son had in mind for a slingshot was a mass-produced, metal-framed object that was as far from my idea of a slingshot as an artificial Christmas tree is from a fir.

25   Stephen was incredulous as I took him into the woods behind our house looking for the proper fork with which to make what I promised him would be a *real* slingshot. We collected a few pieces of trees that had fallen in a recent wind storm, and we took them up to our deck to assemble what I had promised. Unfortunately, I had forgotten how easily pine and dry cottonwood break, and my first attempts to wrap a rubber band around the sloping arms of the benign weapon I was making met with structural failure. We finally were able to find pieces strong enough to withstand the manipulation required for their transformation into slingshots, but their range was severely limited by the fact that they would break if pulled back too far.

26   My son was clearly disappointed in my inability to make him a slingshot, and I feared that he had run away disillusioned with me when he disappeared for an hour or so after dinner that evening. But he returned with the wyes of tree branches stronger and more sup-ple than any I found behind our house. We were able to wrap our fattest rubber bands around these pieces of wood without breaking them, and they withstood as much pull as we were able or willing to supply. Unfortunately, they still did not do as slingshots, for the rubber bands kept slipping down the inclines of the Y and the bands were difficult to hold without the stones we were using for ammunition slipping through them or going awry.

27   After almost a week of frustration trying to find the right branch-and-rubber band com-bination that would produce a satisfactory slingshot that would not break down, I all but promised I would buy one if we could not make a top-notch shooter out of the scraps of wood scattered about our basement. Stephen was patient if incredulous as I sorted through odd pieces of plywood and selected one for him to stand upon while I sawed out of it the shape of the body of a slingshot. He was less patient when I drilled holes to receive a rubber band, and I acceded to his impatience in not sanding the plywood or rounding the edges before giv-ing the device the test of shooting. I surprised him by producing some large red rubber bands my wife uses for her manuscripts, and he began to think he might have a real sling-shot when I threaded the ends of a rubber band through the holes in the plywood Y. With the assembly completed I demonstrated how far a little pebble could be shot, but I had to admit, at least to myself, that it was very difficult to keep the pebble balanced on the slender rub-ber band. My son was politely appreciative of what I had made for him, but he was properly not ecstatic. The pebbles he tried to shoot dropped in weak arcs before his target, and he knew that his slingshot would be no match for the one his friend had bought through the catalog.

28   In my mind I admitted that the homemade slingshot was not well designed, and in a desperate attempt to save face with my son I decided to add a second rubber band and large pocket to improve not only the range but also the accuracy of the toy. These proved to be tremendous improvements, and with them the slingshot seemed almost unlimited in range and very comfortable to use. Now we had a slingshot of enormous potential, and my son was

ready to give it the acid test. We spent an entire weekend practicing our aim at a beer bottle a good thirty yards away. The first hit was an historic event that pinged off the glass and the second a show of power that drilled a hole clear through the green glass and left the bottle standing on only a prayer. As we got better at controlling the pebbles issuing from our homemade slingshot we changed from bottles to cans for our targets and hit them more and more.

29   With all our shooting, the rubber bands began to break from fatigue. This did not bother my son, and he seemed to accept it as something to be expected in a slingshot, for it was just another toy and not a deacon's masterpiece. As rubber bands broke, we replaced them. What proved to be more annoying was the slipping of the rubber band over the top of the slingshot's arm, for we had provided no means of securing the band from doing so. In time, however, we came to wrap the broken rubber bands around the tops of the arms to keep the functioning ones in place. This worked wonderfully, and the satisfaction of using broken parts to produce an improved slingshot was especially appealing to my son. He came to believe that his slingshot could outperform any offered in the catalogs, and the joy of producing it ourselves from scrap wood and rubber bands gave him a special pleasure. And all the breaking pieces of wood, slipping rubber bands, and less-than-perfect functioning gave him a lesson in structural engineering more lasting than any textbook's—or any fanciful poem's. He learned to make things that work by steadily improving upon things that did not work. He learned to learn from mistakes. My son, at eleven, had absorbed one of the principal lessons of engineering, and he had learned also the frustrations and the joys of being an engineer.

APPENDIX

The Deacon's Masterpiece
Or, the Wonderful "One-Hoss Shay"
A Logical Story

By Oliver Wendell Holmes

Have you heard of the wonderful one-hoss shay,
That was built in such a logical way
It ran a hundred years to a day,
And then, of a sudden, it—ah, but stay,
I'll tell you what happened without delay,
Scaring the parson into fits,
Frightening people out of their wits—
Have you ever heard of that, I say?

Seventeen hundred and fifty-five.
Georgius Secundus *was then alive,—*
Snuffy old drone from the German hive.
That was the year when Lisbon-town
Saw the earth open and gulp her down,
And Braddock's army was done so brown,
Left without a scalp to its crown.
It was on the terrible Earthquake-day
That the Deacon finished the one-hoss shay.
A general flavor of mild decay,
But nothing local, as one may say.
There couldn't be,—for the Deacon's art
Had made it so like in every part
That there wasn't a chance for one to start.
For the wheels were just as strong as the thills,
And the floor was just as strong as the sills,
And the panels just as strong as the floor,
And the whipple-tree neither less nor more,
And the back crossbar as strong as the fore,
And spring and axle and hub encore.
And yet, as a whole, it is past a doubt
In another hour it will be worn out!

First of November, 'Fifty-five!
This morning the parson takes a drive.
Now, small boys, get out of the way!
Here comes the wonderful one-hoss shay,
Drawn by a rat-tailed, ewe-necked bay.
"Huddup!" said the parson.—Off went they.

The parson was working his Sunday's text,—
Had got to fifthly, *and stopped perplexed*
At what the—Moses—was coming next.
All at once the horse stood still,
'Close by the meet'n'-house on the hill.
First a shiver, and then a thrill,
Then something decidedly like a spill,—
And the parson was sitting upon a rock,
At half past nine by the meet'n'-house clock,—
Just the hour of the Earthquake shock!
What do you think the parson found,
When he got up and stared around?
The poor old chaise in a heap or mound,
As if it had been to the mill and ground!
You see, of course, if you're not a dunce,
How it went to pieces all at once,—
All at once, and nothing first,—
Just as bubbles do when they burst.

End of the wonderful one-hoss shay.
Logic is logic. That's all I say.

NOTES AND DISCUSSION

This essay is a chapter from Henry Petroski's book *To Engineer is Human: The Role of Failure in Successful Design* (1985). In that book, Petroski argues that failures in general, but mechanical and structural failures (which are both failures of design) in particular, are responsible for many more significant advances in knowledge than any number of successes could be. This essay discusses "fatigue failure" and the steady development of a successful design for a slingshot for Petroski's son Stephen. Notice Petroski's strategy of beginning his discussion with an anecdote and continuing to include bits of narrative, such as the stories about the Speak & Spell electronic games and the evolution of the perfect slingshot. Note, too, the importance of play in this essay: Petroski draws parallels between play and more "serious" scientific investigation. Finally, notice that the essay implicitly compares engineering to the human condition through its title, conclusion, and techniques such as nostalgia, allusion, and anecdote.

STUDY QUESTIONS

For Discussion:

1. Implicit in this essay is the notion that play is an important part of learning—for children, for students, and for engineering professors. What are the connotations of this notion?
2. This essay suggests that engineering principles such as fatigue are essential parts of everyday life, and that curious people are all, to some degree, engineers at heart. Do you agree with that proposal? Why, or why not? How would you define an engineer?

For Writing:

1. Write a brief report on mechanical fatigue discussing what it is, how it comes about, and why it is important. Compare your report with Petroski's essay. How and why are they different?

2. Write a narrative about a time in your life when simple technology failed you. What did you learn from that experience?

THE WAY WE WOO

Heather Pringle

BIOGRAPHICAL NOTE

Heather Pringle, a science journalist based in Vancouver, has written on various aspects of archaeology for magazines such as *New Scientist, Omni, Canadian Geographic,* and *Saturday Night.* She has received both the National Magazine Award and the Canadian Archaeological Association's Public Writing Award. She recently published *In Search of Ancient North America* (1996), and is currently working on a book about the Maya.

---

1   Helen Fisher slips into a ringside seat, amusement stirring in her dark eyes. It's just after eight on a steamy Friday night at the Mad Hatter Restaurant and Pub, one of dozens of softly lit singles bars on Manhattan's prosperous Upper East Side. A bevy of young businessmen, ties loosened and beer glasses in hand, lean against the railings, sizing up each female who walks in the door. On the street outside, barhoppers stream by the plate-glass windows like tropical fish. "There's constant motion here," says Fisher. "It looks like a real good pickup bar."

2   Elegantly dressed in a black skirt and sweater set, Fisher looks more like a society columnist than someone about to settle down for an evening in a singles bar. But the 48-year-old anthropologist has spent the past decade deciphering the mysteries of human mating behaviour, and she still relishes the odd evening in the field. "Men and women have no idea the amount of sexual signals they are sending out to each other," she says, angling her chair for a better view. "They'd be amazed."

First published in *Equinox*, November/December 1993. Reprinted with permission of the author and *Equinox* magazine. The photographs that originally accompanied the article have been dropped.

3   Fisher, a research associate in the department of anthropology at the American Museum of Natural History in New York, is one of a new scientific breed seeking out the biological and genetic roots of our love lives. Unwilling to accept traditional views, she and her colleagues have begun taking a fresh look at human romance—from the first twinges of physical attraction to the heady flush of courtship and the bitter acrimony of divorce. Taking clues from the animal kingdom and anthropology, they are turning up answers to some of the most enduring mysteries of romance: why men fall for pretty faces and women pine for men of means; why males roam from bed to bed, while females dream of Mr. Right; and why love is so intoxicating and divorce so commonplace.

4   As she glances across the room, Fisher begins pointing out some of the subtleties of human courtship, patterns of behaviour that seem to stem from a distant past. Those men by the railing, for example? Fisher grins. Singles bars, she explains, work much like the mating grounds of sage grouse and other birds. After staking out individual territories in the most prominent area in the bar, the men are now attempting to attract females with simple courtship displays: stretching, exaggerating simple movements, and laughing heartily. "One of them is even swinging from side to side, which is a real gesture of approachability," she says.

5   Fisher points out a miniskirted woman deep in conversation with a man at the bar. "See how she's gesturing and swaying and preening?" Fisher asks. "She keeps on touching her eyes, her nose, and her mouth." Stroking her face as if stroking that of her companion, she is flashing a series of intention cues—messages that she wants to touch him. But he remains strangely impassive, refusing to turn even his shoulders toward her. The conversation may be flowing, says Fisher, but the courtship ritual is rapidly stalling. As we watch, shameless voyeurs, the animated discussion slowly sputters and dies. "The pickup runs on messages," concludes Fisher, shaking her head, "and every one of them has to be returned." Turning to the bartender, the woman asks for her bill, then hurries out into the night.

6   What is ultimately going on here? Beyond the rejected advances and the private humiliations, Fisher sees the workings of an age-old ritual. After years of study and debate, she and other evolutionary anthropologists now suggest that human romance has been shaped by biology and the forces of natural selection. According to this controversial line of thought, humans conduct their love lives in much the same manner around the world. From the singles bars of North America to the marriage brokers of Asia, we attract, court, and discard mates in ways that subtly but surely promote the survival of our species.

7   It's a theory that challenges decades of entrenched thinking. Historians have long insisted that love itself was a cultural invention, an emotion first conceived by the courtly poets of Europe some eight hundred years ago and subsequently passed on to Europe's idle rich. In time, went this thinking, the idea of romantic love percolated to the lower classes, who in turn carried it to colonies far and wide. Such views dovetailed nicely with modern anthropological thought. Since the 1920s, when American scientist Margaret Mead returned from fieldwork on the South Seas islands of Samoa, most anthropologists believed that human behaviour was shaped largely by culture. Children, they noted, were as impressionable as clay. "It's a view that there is basically no human nature," says David Buss, a professor of psychology at the University of Michigan in Ann Arbor, "that humans are simply a product of their environment."

8   Over the past two decades, however, serious cracks have appeared in those theoretical walls. Influenced by Charles Darwin, a small but vocal group of social scientists now suggest that natural selection, not culture, has shaped certain key human behaviours. Over

hundreds of thousands of years, they theorize, evolution has moulded not only anatomy but the human psyche itself, favouring certain social behaviours, certain states of mind, that promote survival and reproductive success. In other words, biology lies just beneath the surface of much human psychology. Could our romances, they ask, be guided by certain evolved mechanisms? Could the human heart be unconsciously governed by the ancient encodings of our genes?

9   Psychologists Martin Daly and Margo Wilson think the answers are in little doubt. After fifteen years of research, the husband-and-wife team at McMaster University in Hamilton, Ontario, conclude that love runs a remarkably similar course around the world. Wilson smiles as she observes that men tend to be attracted to the same qualities in women every-where—even in traditional Islamic cultures, where females are veiled from head to shoulder. "The fact that you have these flirtatious eyes looking out from a whole black garb must just stimulate the imagination far beyond what is beneath the veil," she laughs. "Mystery is sexually exciting."

10   Wilson's interest in human romance first arose in the mid-1970s, when she and Daly came across the writings of those investigating the evolutionary basis of social behaviour in animals. After examining the life histories of animals as diverse as the dung fly, the Jamaican lizard, and the elephant seal, researchers had noted that males and females often approached the mating game very differently as a result of basic reproductive biology. Among most mammal species, for instance, females slave away much of their adult lives caring for their young—nurturing embryos, nursing infants, and often protecting litters alone. Absorbed by maternal duties, they are physically incapable of producing as many young as their male counterparts are. With a greater investment in their young, females tend to pick mates carefully, selecting those best able to help their brood survive. Most males, on the other hand, are spared such intensive parental labour. Serving largely as sperm donors, they take a different tactic, favouring quantity over quality in mating and inseminating as many fertile females as possible.

11   Intrigued, Daly and Wilson wondered how the behaviour of *Homo sapiens* fit into this pattern. Like other mammalian females, women invest long months in pregnancy, breast-feeding, and early childcare, keeping their families small. Men, however, are less burdened. (One eighteenth-century Moroccan emperor reputedly fathered seven hundred sons and more than three hundred daughters before celebrating his fiftieth birthday.) Could such radical biological differences shape human romance? Would men the world over, for example, be more promiscuous than women?

12   While comprehensive statistics were scarce, the team soon began piecing together an astonishing case. In an American study of middle-aged couples published in 1970, one social scientist reported that twice as many males as females had committed adultery. In a German study of young working-class singles, 46 percent of the males, compared with only 6 percent of the females, were interested in casual sex with an attractive stranger. All around the world, from the Amazonian rainforest to the Kalahari Desert, field accounts of anthropologists lined up on this point: men of all ages craved far more sexual variety than women. Quips Wilson, "Male sexual psychology seems to be that you're willing to do it with, you know, chickens or anything."

13   Daly and Wilson found one other sweeping pattern in the anthropological literature: in every society, men and women entered into marriages—formal, long-standing unions that

Passion Play: A Step-by-Step Script

After spending long, smoky evenings observing couples in North American singles bars, researchers have discerned several steps in human courtship:

Approach: As a rule, it is the female who begins the mating ritual, walking up to a male or taking a seat beside him. If he reciprocates her interest by turning and looking, a conversation ensues.

Talk: As the two chat, accents and manner of speech are highly revealing. "Talking is an enormous escalation point," notes Helen Fisher. "How many people have opened their mouth and had a horrible accent, and you just realized, no way? A lot of pickups end there." But if a man and a woman successfully negotiate that hurdle, they slowly turn to face each other, moving first their heads, then their shoulders and, finally, their entire bodies.

Touch: Generally, the woman will touch first, brushing her hand briefly along a man's arm or shoulder. If the man responds in kind, touching becomes more frequent.

Gaze: As the conversation becomes more intense and pleasurable, the couple begin glancing into each other's eyes, until they are finally unable to look away. Researchers call this the "copulatory gaze."

Body Synchrony: Mesmerized by talk and touch, the couple begin moving in harmony. If the female lifts her glass for a sip, the male does too. If he slouches in his chair to the right, she mirrors his movement. "I would like to speculate," writes Timothy Perper in his book *Sex Signals: The Biology of Love*, "that by the time they are fully synchronized, each person is physiologically prepared for intercourse."

gave legitimacy to the resulting children. Had basic biology also shaped wedlock? If the biologists were right, women would marry men most capable of contributing to their children's well-being, while men would marry the most fertile females they could find.

14   In fact, the psychologists discovered, men generally wed younger women—a finding that squared well with evolution-minded predictions. As Wilson points out, women in their early twenties are much more fertile than those in their thirties; older men are far more likely to have acquired the kind of wealth and social status that could shelter their children from harm. And, notes Wilson, research shows that the attractiveness of a male in most cultures is judged more by his maturity, skills, and status than by a square-cut jaw and fine features. "Like Henry Kissinger," says Wilson of the former US Secretary of State. "People used to say he was really handsome. He was in a high-status position, a very powerful position."

15   To study human tastes in mates in more detail, David Buss drew up a list of thirty-one attributes and arranged for men and women in Africa, Asia, Europe, and South America to grade them by importance. "The results amazed me in that they basically confirmed the evolutionary predictions that others had speculated about," he notes. In the thirty-seven cultures polled, responses were strongly consistent, suggesting a universal, biological truth

honed over millennia of evolution. While both sexes graded traits such as intelligence and kindness highly, they diverged sharply in two areas. "Women place a premium on status, older age and maturity, and resources," says Buss. "Men place a premium on youth and physical attractiveness."

16   Buss suggests that the male predilection for beauty is informed by sound biological logic. How else could a man judge the potential fertility of his mate? "The capacity of a woman to bear children is not stamped on her forehead," he writes in a recent paper. "It is not part of her social reputation, so no one is in a position to know. Even the woman herself lacks direct knowledge of her fertility and reproductive value." But certain visual cues, he explains, could serve as rough measures. Shapely legs, shiny hair, lustrous eyes, and a clear, unblemished complexion in a female all signal health and youth. And some researchers have suggested that symmetrical facial features—particularly eyes of well-matched colour and alignment—could indicate mutation-free genes. Ancestral males drawn to such qualities, notes Buss, would have likely fathered more children than men attracted to other physical traits.

17   The differing biological goals of the sexes also have profound effects on human relations and courtship behaviour. While women need time to size up a man's finances and social status, men can measure beauty and youth with a mere flicker of an eye. Consider the recently published results of a study at the Florida State University at Tallahassee. Psychologists Russell Clark and Elaine Hatfield dispatched young men to different corners of the campus, instructing each to pitch one of three questions to female strangers: "Would you go out with me tonight?" "Would you come over to my apartment tonight?" or "Would you go to bed with me tonight?" While 56 percent of the females consented to a date, only 6 percent agreed to visit the male's apartment—and not one consented to sex. But when a female approached male strangers with the same questions, 50 percent of the men agreed to a date, 69 percent consented to an apartment visit—and 75 percent offered to go to bed with her that night.

18   As Buss and other psychologists slowly piece together the evolution of physical attraction, other researchers examine the biological and genetic origins of the emotion of love itself. At the University of Nevada, Las Vegas, just a short stroll away from the rotund cupids and neon hearts adorning the city's all-night wedding chapels, anthropologist William Jankowiak is sweeping aside earlier cultural theories. Passionate attachments, he suggests, "must have evolved for some sense of adaptation. [They] must have helped *Homo sapiens* survive in the battle against the cockroach."

19   A soft-spoken but intense scholar, Jankowiak became interested in the evolution of love some six years ago while conducting fieldwork in Inner Mongolia. During casual reading of ancient Chinese folktales, he was amazed to discover descriptions of passionate love that could have been penned today. "I said, 'My God, I wonder if this has been universal in Chinese history,' and it was. And then I started wondering if this was universal all over."

20   Turning to the scientific literature, Jankowiak unearthed two studies published in the 1960s by American psychologist Paul Rosenblatt. Interested in the emergence of love as a basis for marriage, Rosenblatt had pored over anthropological reports for dozens of human cultures, concluding that less than two-thirds had any concept of the emotion of love. As Jankowiak read the studies, however, he could see that Rosenblatt had missed a key source of information—the folklore of tribal peoples. Troubled by the omission, Jankowiak decided to start from scratch, eager to see whether love was an emotion present in all cultures.

Harlequin's Lock on Our Hearts

Every month, Harlequin Enterprises Limited ships its purple prose around the globe—from Abu Dhabi to Zimbabwe and from Iceland to Tonga. Selling more than two hundred million books a year, the Canadian firm claims to have made "the language of love universal, crossing social, cultural, and geographical borders with an ease unrivalled by any other publisher." What is its secret of success?

As it turns out, Harlequin editors understand human desire pretty well. According to company guidelines for the Harlequin Regency line of novels, for example, heroines must be attractive and quick-witted and range in age between eighteen and twenty-eight years old. The objects of their affections, on the other hand, must be virile and prosperous, possess high societal positions—"we prefer peers," say the editors—and range in age from twenty-four to thirty-five years old.

Such matches are made in heaven, according to mate-preference studies conducted by Douglas Kenrick and an associate at Arizona State University in Tempe. As Kenrick notes, females are strongly drawn to men who possess leadership skills and occupy the top rungs of a hierarchy. Moreover, they crave mates up to eight or nine years older than themselves. Men, on the other hand, are not particularly charmed by leadership. Instead, they hanker after beautiful females in their twenties—something that Harlequin editors seem to have known all along.

21   With graduate student Edward Fischer, Jankowiak settled into the work, searching for love songs, tales of elopement, and other signs of romantic entanglements. In cultures where no trace of passion could be found in the literature, Jankowiak called up the anthropologists themselves to enquire whether any relevant evidence had been left out. In the end, the two researchers recorded romantic love in a resounding 88.5 percent of the 166 cultures they studied. For Jankowiak, the results strongly suggested that love is a common part of the human condition, an experience owing more to biology than to culture.

22   Still, some scholars puzzled over the small number of societies where no sign of romantic love had been uncovered. If love was a universal condition, how had inhabitants of these cultures mustered such resistance? At the University of California, Santa Barbara, doctoral candidate Helen Harris decided to take a closer look at one such society—the Mangaians of the South Pacific. According to anthropological reports, the inhabitants of Mangaia had developed a highly sexual culture. At the age of thirteen or so, boys on the island were trained by older women to bring female partners to orgasm several times before reaching climaxes of their own. The craft perfected, the young men began courting the favours of island women—averaging three orgasms a night, seven nights a week. But according to an anthropologist who lived among the Mangaians in the 1950s, neither sex ever experienced the emotion of love. "He said that when he talked about it, the Mangaians didn't understand," notes Harris.

23   Perplexed, Harris began her own fieldwork, interviewing males and females who had been adolescents during the 1950s. As her research proceeded, she could see that the sensational tales of sexual prowess had obscured the rich emotional life of Mangaia. Now middle-aged, the men and women recounted tales of deep passion, even love at first sight. "One of the women said she was in one of the stores on the island, she turned around, and she saw this man," recalls Harris. "She did not know him, but feelings just came over her that she had never felt before. . . . She analyzed it and said, 'I think it was just God's way of getting two people together. It's natural for people to feel this way.' And she and this man finally married after some years."

24   While it seems likely that romantic love arose in all human cultures, from the lean reindeer herders of Lapland to the now silent scholars of the Sung Dynasty, it is less clear just when and why this emotional state evolved. Researchers have yet to discern any convincing evidence of such strong emotions in the animal kingdom, for instance. And surveys have shown that intimate, long-lasting associations between a male and a female are strikingly rare even among our close primate relatives. "Yet the hallmark of the human animal is that we form these pair bonds," says Helen Fisher, sitting down with a glass of iced tea in her small Manhattan apartment. "So how come?"

25   In search of clues, Fisher turned to the zoological literature, studying several species that form such intimate bonds. In foxes, she found a clear biological imperative. Bearing some five helpless kits at a time, female red foxes become virtual prisoners of their broods. Equipped with only thin, low-fat milk, mothers must nurse each of their young every two to three hours. Without a male to help feed her, a female would soon starve to death. "But when the kits begin to wander off," says Fisher, "the pair bond breaks up. It lasts only long enough to raise those kits through infancy."

26   As Fisher sees it, hominid females may have become similarly vulnerable some four million years ago. With climatic change, our simian ancestors were forced from the receding forests of Africa onto vast grassy plains, where stealthy predators stalked. "What I think," says Fisher, who has just published her theories in a new book, *Anatomy of Love: The Natural History of Monogamy, Adultery, and Divorce*, "is that we came down from the trees and we were forced onto two legs instead of four. Females suddenly needed to carry their babies in their arms instead of on their backs. What a huge reproductive burden," she says with a wince. "They also had to start carrying sticks and stones for tools and weapons in this dangerous place. So women needed a mate to help rear their young."

27   As they roamed farther onto the grasslands, early human males also found compelling reasons to pair off with females. Along the vast savannas, food sources such as cashew trees, berry patches, and the occasional meaty carcass were widely scattered. Constantly roaming, males were unable to feed or defend large harems. "Polygyny was almost impossible for men," says Fisher, "and pair bonding was critical for women." So males who fell in love and formed pairs with females were more successful in passing on their genes, thus perpetuating the penchant for intimacy.

28   Setting down her iced tea, Fisher points out that science has yet to prove her theories conclusively. No one, for instance, has located specific genes capable of turning love on or off in the human psyche. Even so, some medical research supports her contention. At the New York State Psychiatric Institute in New York City, researcher Michael Liebowitz suggests that the powerful emotion of love is created by a tidal wave of certain naturally produced

The Universal Seven-Year Itch

While North Americans vow at the altar to forsake all others, less than 50 percent make good on their promise. But Canadians and Americans are not alone in their adulteries; infidelity is the rule rather than the exception around the world.

The Kuikuru of the Amazonian rainforest, for example, often seek out lovers just a few months after marriage. Kuikuru men and women have been known to juggle as many as twelve extra partners at a time, and their affairs are discussed with great openness and delight in the Amazonian society.

Among traditional Hindu communities in India, adultery is strongly discouraged. But infidelity clearly flourishes anyway. Notes one Sanskrit proverb: "Only when fire will cool, the moon burn, or the ocean fill with tasty water will a woman be pure."

In Japan, specially designated love hotels cater to adulterous couples. Furnished with such exotica as wall-to-wall mirrors, video recorders, whips and handcuffs, rooms are rented by the hour and enjoy a brisk trade during the day and early evening.

chemicals in the brain. And others have suggested that the taps for these chemicals might be directly controlled by our genes.

29   A psychiatrist who specializes in the treatment of anxiety and depression, Liebowitz first began to suspect the chemical basis of love in the early 1980s after noticing the profound effects of particular antidepressants on patients who were addicted to the thrill of new relationships. After researching the matter carefully, he now suggests that the sheer intoxication of love—the warm, reckless euphoria that sweeps over us and drives away all other thoughts—may be caused by certain chemical excitants flooding into brain structures thought to control love and emotional arousal.

30   One of the most likely chemical candidates, he says, is phenylethylamine, a natural amphetaminelike substance that has been found by other researchers to have some powerful effects on the behaviour of certain laboratory animals. Mice injected with the substance squeal exuberantly and leap into the air like popcorn, and rhesus monkeys given a closely related compound make kissing sounds. And there is evidence that humans are highly susceptible too. When Liebowitz and colleague Donald Klein treated romance junkies with antidepressants that raise the levels of phenylethylamine in the brain, the patients gradually gave up their hungry search for new mates. "They could settle down and accept life with more stable and appropriate partners," explains Liebowitz.

31   Impressed by such evidence, he suggests that neural chemicals play a key part in sparking the giddy excitement of attraction. But the effects of such chemicals are temporary. As time passes, Liebowitz theorizes, nerve endings in the brain may cease to respond to phenylethylamine and a second chemical system kicks into place. Based on such natural narcotics as endorphins, it can endow lovers with the warm, comfortable feelings of a secure attachment. "Unfortunately, that leads people to take dependable partners too much for

granted," says Liebowitz. "They think, oh well, somebody else is very attractive, and my long-term relationship is not as exciting as that." Thirsting for the amphetamine high again, many will eventually abandon their partners for someone new.

32   Even here, in betrayal and divorce, evolutionary theorists such as Fisher see a form of natural logic. Research has shown, she notes, that the powerful attraction phase of love generally lasts from two to three years. And statistics suggest that divorce rates peak in and around the fourth year of marriage. In Fisher's view, the timing is significant. As it happens, women in traditional hunting and gathering societies—which resemble those in which humans first evolved—frequently nurse infants for as long as four years. During that period, they depend on their mates to supply some food and protection. But once a child is weaned and can be cared for by others, the mother may consider switching mates.

33   "I think four million years ago, there would have been advantages to primitive divorce," says Fisher. "If a male and a female raised a child through infancy and then broke up and formed new pair bonds, what they would actually be doing is creating genetic variety. And that's really critical to evolution."

34   But, as Fisher concedes, such biologically based codes of conduct may have served us far better in the grasslands of Africa than they do today in a world of divorce lawyers, property settlements, and child-custody battles. As she sets her empty glass on the table, the anthropologist shakes her head at the irony of it all. "Look at the incredible problem we're in. A drive to make a commitment, to love, to remain together. A drive to break up and pair again. And a drive to be adulterous on the side. No wonder we all struggle in every culture in the world." She pauses and smiles. "We are built to struggle."

NOTES AND DISCUSSION

Pringle opens her essay with a hook: an attractive woman sits in the Mad Hatter Restaurant and Pub, declaring that the place looks like "a real good pickup bar." This scenario recalls the openings of countless books, movies, and television shows. The reader expects a narrative, a story, a romance. However, in the next paragraph, Pringle undermines that expectation: the woman is not "on the make"; she is an anthropologist who studies human mating behaviour.

Pringle's essay researches and reports on recent studies by anthropologists who, influenced by Darwin's theories of natural selection, believe that human mating behaviour is genetically programmed, rather than culturally determined. Think about whether Pringle herself implicitly argues in favour of one of these hypotheses and about how successfully she maintains the position of an objective reporter who introduces experts and summarizes their findings.

Pringle recounts the anthropologists' studies using a variety of rhetorical strategies: she conducts a step-by-step process analysis of the body language of courting couples; compares and contrasts human behaviour with animal and human behaviour across different cultures; presents statistics from anthropological studies to support interpretations of human mating behaviour; and draws analogies between the mating and courtship behaviours of early hominids and those of twentieth-century humans.

STUDY QUESTIONS

For Discussion:

1. What elements identified and discussed in this essay agree or disagree with your own observations of mating behaviour? For instance, does our society equate symmetry with beauty? Does the fact that we are not hominids living in "the grasslands of Africa," but *Homo sapiens* living in the late twentieth century weaken the essay's arguments?

2. Conduct some field research of your own in a public place on campus. Do you observe the mating behaviours described in Pringle's essay?

For Writing:

1. Outline the major ideas discussed in this essay and examine how Pringle moves from point to point.

2. Decide whether Pringle believes nature or nurture to be the determining factor in human mating behaviour. To answer this question, consider which points in the essay are most convincing and why. Are certain points made more or less convincing by the way Pringle presents them?

MARIE CURIE
AND MILEVA
EINSTEIN MARÍC

Hilary Rose

BIOGRAPHICAL NOTE

Hilary Rose is the author of *Science and Society* (1969) and *Love, Power, and Knowledge: Towards a Feminist Transformation of the Sciences* (1994), from which this essay is excerpted.

---

1   Perhaps it was partly that the Nobel Prize was so new—not yet gelled in its prestige status—that made it possible in 1903 not only to invite Henri Becquerel and Pierre Curie to share the Physics Prize, but also to include Marie Curie at the astonishingly youthful age of 36.[1] (The terms of the Nobel award mean that it may be shared a maximum of three ways.) The introductory address on behalf of the committee spoke not only of the discoveries opening "a new epoch in the history of physics" and of the close relationships of their producers, but of how:

> Les découvertes et les travaux de M. Becquerel et de M. et Mme. Curie sont en relations intimes les uns avec les autres: et les deux derniers ont travaillé en commun. Aussi L'Académie Royale des Sciences n'a-t-elle pas cru devoir séparer ces éminents savants, quand il s'est agi de récompenser par un prix Nobel la découverte de la radio-activité spontanée.[2]*

Equal producers the Curies may have been, but it was Pierre alone who was to give the Nobel address at Stockholm. There was perhaps some justification for this as he was eight

---

*The discoveries and work of [Monsieur] Becquerel and of [Monsieur] and [Madame] Curie are closely related to one another: and the latter two worked together. Also the Royal Academy of the Sciences does not believe that it should separate these eminent scholars, when it is deciding to award a Nobel Prize for the discovery of spontaneous radioactivity. (Author's translation)

From *Love, Power, and Knowledge* by Hilary Rose. Reprinted with permission of Indiana University Press.

years older than Marie, and had not been educated in a Warsaw lycée or transferred countries and languages before studying at the Faculty of Science in Paris. Nor did his father have the relatively modest occupation of a teacher in a Warsaw lycée, but was a French medical doctor. Marie and Pierre had met and researched together at the Ecole Physique and were married in 1895; in the same year he was appointed to a chair. (At the time of receiving the prize Marie had not yet defended her doctorate thesis.) Within two years of the marriage their first daughter, Irène, was born. Personal life and work thread Marie's notebooks; she describes her daughter's first steps, then speaks of the element she and Pierre have found which they propose to call radium; her next entry reports the consolidation of Irène's walking. They shared a common commitment to socialism and to feminism, the last a matter of no small significance for the history of science.[3]

2   Because for the rest of the century this astonishing woman has been held up to all, and especially to all women scientists, as the example of what women are capable of achieving,[4] Elizabeth Crawford's[5] study of the early years of the Nobel Institution makes salutary reading. She reveals that the recognition of Marie's contribution to her and Pierre's achievement was not uncontentious; we suddenly find that we are back in an old story, recognizable all too often from our own lives. At the first hurdle, that of nominations, the French Academy had only put forward the names of Henri Becquerel and Pierre Curie. Marie, as a woman, was not seen as capable of producing scientific knowledge, and therefore was outside the committee's consideration either as a potential member or as a nominee.[6]

3   Within the politics of Swedish science things were a little better but still complicated. Ironically it was the monarchist "right-wing" mathematician Gösta Mittag Leffler, a highly active figure in science politics, who, though outside the crucial committee structures, was more supportive of women than the liberal reformer and key Nobel committee member Svante Arrhenius.[7] The Swedish mathematician had already shown his willingness to acknowledge women scientists in an earlier suggestion to Alfred Nobel that he establish a chair for the Russian mathematician Sophia Kovalevskaia. Nobel, incidentally, refused on the grounds that it was not necessary as "Russia was less prejudiced," a comment which suggests that the founder saw himself as more open-minded to the claims of women than many of his compatriots. Thus when the nominations were being considered, it was Leffler[8] who became sufficiently concerned that Marie Curie might not be offered a share in the prize to write to Pierre Curie. Pierre replied: "If it is true that one is thinking about me [for the prize] I very much wish to be considered together with Madame Curie with respect to our research on radioactivity." The letter then goes on to suggest that giving the prize jointly will be "artistically satisfying."[9]

4   Curie's fame thus depends not simply on her work, and on the general processes through which scientists are recognized, but on the integrity and egalitarian values of two men: one a Swedish mathematician who shared his sister's feminism,[10] the other, her husband and collaborator who shared hers. This story of the recognition of Curie points to the peculiar dependency of a woman scientist, particularly if she is part of a wife-and-husband team, on her collaborator's unequivocal acknowledgement of her contribution. All too commonly the woman/wife's share of the work is only acknowledged by a dedication, and the crucial authorship/ownership is denied in a way that is rarer between men scientists. Without recognition by her husband/collaborator she stays in the private domain, for only he has the power to testify that she is a creative scientist, which will enable her to begin to enter the public world of science. Otherwise the two are one, and that "one" is the man.

A DANGEROUS COMBINATION OF LOVE AND SCIENCE

5   The recently recovered biography of Mileva Einstein Maríc[11] documents the dangerous combination of love and science for women, and its power to render women and their science invisible. After a painful beginning where she conceived a child by Albert Einstein out of wedlock and had the baby adopted, the marriage was initially happy and mutually appreciative. Einstein, for example, explained to a group of Zagreb intellectuals that he needed his wife as "she solves all the mathematical problems for me." Two key episodes document the process by which her work, if not actively appropriated, was certainly lost by her to him. In one episode Mileva, through the collaboration with a mutual friend, Paul Habicht, constructed an innovatory device for measuring electrical currents. Having built the device the two inventors left it to Einstein to describe and patent, as he was at that time working in the patent office. He alone signed the publication and patented the device under the name Einstein-Habicht. When asked why she had not given her own name of Einstein Maríc she asked, "What for, we are both only 'one stone' [*Ein stein*]?" Later when the marriage had collapsed she found that the price of her selfless love and affectionate joke was that her work had become his. She also lost her personal health through trying to do the mathematical work to support his theorizing and simultaneously take care of their children. One son suffered from schizophrenia and after the divorce Einstein was mean about keeping up with the alimony.

6   Troemel-Ploetz[12] points to the even more disturbing episode of the articles published in 1905 in the Leipzig *Annalen der Physik*. Of the five key papers, two of the originally submitted manuscripts were signed also by Mileva, but by the time of their publication, her name had been removed. These two articles, written in what was widely understood as Einstein's golden age, included the theory of special relativity which was to change the nature of physics, and for which he alone received the Nobel prize. Thus although the purpose of the biography was to restore Mileva's name as a distinguished and creative scientist, and not to denigrate Einstein, it inevitably raised the issue of his withholding recognition of Mileva's contribution to the achievement. A number of observers have also commented on the puzzle of Einstein's gift of the prize money to Mileva Maríc even though they were by then separated. This gift-giving was later emulated by George Hoyt Whipple, a Nobel Prize-winner in 1934. Although Whipple had the reputation of being very careful financially, he shared his prize money with Frieda Robsheit Robbins, his co-worker for many years, and with two other women colleagues. In Einstein's and Hoyt Whipple's circumstances, was the money meant to compensate for the system's, and perhaps their own, appropriation of their collaborators' work?

7   While Mileva's biographer is careful to indicate that Einstein was the creative thinker, she suggests that he could not have realized his theoretical insights without Mileva's mathematics. Between men scientists such a collaboration between theory and technique is rather difficult to ignore; between husband and wife scientists it was—and according to the context still is—rather easy. It was especially so at the turn of the century when bourgeois women, as wives, were only permitted to work as unpaid workers and when scientific work like housework and child care could be constructed—as they were by Mileva—as part of the labour of love. While Trbuhovic Gjuric's biography (not least because it was originally published in Serbian in 1969) has not had the impact of Ann Sayre's study of Rosalind Franklin, it has raised doubts in the physics community;[13] meanwhile feminists will recognize the pattern as characteristic, made possible by that early twentieth century scientific labour market in all its unbridled patriarchal power of appropriation.

CURIE'S SECOND PRIZE

8   Although Marie Curie's story is rather happier in the recognition given her by being awarded the Nobel Prize, together with what Crawford[14] speaks of as "a watershed" of public interest in science aroused by the press reports of the immense effort required to produce radium,[15] its great commercial value, and the philanthropic selflessness of the Curies' attitude to their discovery, none the less the achievement did not give her a clear place in the French scientific establishment. The Academy refused to change its rules barring the admission of women and quite exceptionally for Laureates she was not admitted, although the debate was intense and she lost by only one vote. The Academy, in its profound androcentricity, only admitted women scientists in 1979. Yet the story of the Curies had produced for the 1900s a climate of sympathetic interest in science that would be hard to imagine in the context of the much less confident scientific establishment of the 1990s. The otherwise strait-laced newspaper *Le Figaro* described the Curies' story as a fairy tale, beginning its report with "Once upon a time . . . ," and *La Liberté* wrote, "We do not know our scientists. Foreigners have to discover them for us." Science, at least as done by the Curies, was popular, as evidenced by a large audience for Pierre Curie's address to the Royal Institution in London in 1903 and another to listen to Marie Curie defend her doctorate at the Sorbonne in the same year.[16]

9   But the pleasure from shared work and shared recognition was short-lived; Pierre was tragically killed in a traffic accident in 1906. Suddenly, as a widow and no longer a wife, Marie's scientific eminence was recognized by the University of Paris and she was appointed to the chair Pierre had held.[17] In 1911 she was invited once more to return to Stockholm, this time to receive the Chemistry Prize for the discovery of the elements radium and polonium. But even her apparently triumphant return to Stockholm was marked by gender and sexuality. Arrhenius, ever vigilant lest women should escape their special place, on learning that after Pierre's death Marie had become close to the gifted physicist Pierre Langevin (Langevin's estranged wife cited her in divorce proceedings), wrote to her urging that in order to protect the good name of science, the Nobel Institution,[18] and so forth she should not come to Stockholm. With some courage Curie came, supported by her daughter Irène.[19]

10   On this occasion, [Madame] Curie's biographical notes as a Laureate extended to two pages, rather then the mere half-page of eight years before, and reported that, among other honours, in 1910 she had been made a member of the Swedish Academy of Sciences. Her portrait too had expanded from the matching small images of her and Pierre in grave impersonal profile with every inch except her neck and face covered with clothing; now the scientist, bare-armed and bare-necked, hand touching cheek, looks thoughtfully out.

11   But the Royal Society in London was still not minded to change its conventions. Although the physicists Rayleigh, Ramsey, J. J. Thomson, and Rutherford were all both fellow Nobel Laureates and influential Fellows of the Royal Society, the Society felt no need to honour this prize-winning physicist any more than did the French National Academy. Indeed Rutherford was highly dismissive of Curie, persisting in seeing her as Pierre's underlabourer, the scientific and physical effort of extracting radium from pitchblende constructed as little more than an extension of housewifery skills. Given that seventeen (men) Laureates were to come from the Thomson and Rutherford stable, such views were decisive, at least within the British context.

ENDNOTES

1. Nuclear physics itself was still young enough to be open to women.

2. Author's translation: *LPN*, 1903, p. 2. Note the division of recognition in both the words and the portrait size: Becquerel a half, Marie Curie and Pierre a quarter each.

3. E. Curie, *Madame Curie*.

4. The book was published in many countries and was inspirational for young women scientists. See Rosalyn Yalow's autobiographical note, *LNP*, 1977.

5. E. Crawford, *The Beginnings of the Nobel Institution*. I am indebted to this study for the material on Marie Curie's two prizes. See also Giroud, *Marie Curie: A Life*.

6. Initially the groups and individuals consulted were very narrowly drawn, primarily the national academies and existing Nobel Laureates. Then as now the personal international connections of Swedish Nobel committee members were influential. Today the consultations are much wider, but with little effect so far as recognizing women scientists is concerned.

7. E. Crawford, *Beginnings of the Nobel Institution*, p. 112.

8. Koblitz, A. *Convergence of Lives*; Margaret Rossiter reports that "a Swedish mathematician" (Leffler?) wrote to Henrietta Leavitt, the Harvard astronomer, in 1925, saying that he wanted to nominate her. She was, alas, already dead. Rossiter, *Women Scientists in America*.

9. E. Crawford, *Beginnings of the Nobel Institution*, p. 194.

10. According to H. J. Mozan (John Zahm), *Woman in Science*, Ann Carlotta Leffler also published a study of the admired mathematician: *Sophia Kovalevskaia*.

11. Senta Troemel-Ploetz draws attention to a little-known biography by Desamka Trbuhovic Gjuric, herself a mathematician acquainted with the Swiss milieu where the Einsteins lived and worked. This has been republished, but rather heavily edited, in German. "Mileva Einstein Marić: The Woman Who Did Einstein's Mathematics," *W's Stud. Int. Forum*, 13 (5 1990).

12. Ibid, p. 418.

13. Walker, "Did Einstein Espouse His Spouse's Ideas?," *Physics Today*, February (1989). However, more disturbingly, John Hackel, editor of *The Collected Papers of Albert Einstein*, Vols. I and II, ignores this evidence. Despite my feeling that historians of science have recently been more willing to accept the contribution of women scientists, it seems that in the case of Einstein the myth of the unaided male genius must be preserved.

14. E. Crawford, *Beginnings of the Nobel Institution*, p. 148.

15. Then as now we have to be impressed by the physical effort—it took 6,000 kg of pitchblende to produce 0.1 g of the new element.

16. It was on this visit that Marie Curie met Hertha Ayrton.

17. See Clarke, *Working Life of Women in the Seventeenth Century*, for a similar picture for the widows of brewers and opticians—sometimes the widow or a surviving daughter was able to inherit a "male" occupation. Ivy Pinchbeck, for a slightly later period, shows widows and even wives taking part in their husbands' skilled trades: *Women Workers and the Industrial Revolution 1750-1850*. A. D. Morrison Lowe makes a similar argument for scientific instrument makers: "Women in the Nineteenth Century Instrument Trade," in Benjamin (ed.), *Science and Sensibility*. The argument made here has to be understood against this general pattern of women and highly skilled occupations and activities.

18. While Eve Curie's biography dismisses the story of Langevin and Curie with outrage, others, including feminist historians, have accepted it as fact. I prefer Robert Reid's sober conclusion that there is no real way of knowing what happened between Langevin and Curie, and that it is irrelevant, the critical point being that a woman scientist could not, without comment, spend leisure time in the company of a man scientist unrelated to her. At the time the right-wing press wallowed in the sexual innuendo and attacked, mixing anti-semitism and nationalism, while the left and liberal press defended her. She had every need to accept Hertha Ayrton's invitation to be an incognito guest in England. Reid, *Marie Curie*.

19. The scientific community intensely debated the issue. *Nature* editorialized, "we have confidence that the doors of science will eventually be open to women on equal terms with men." January 12, 1911.

NOTES AND DISCUSSION

Hilary Rose compares and contrasts women who were recognized for their scientific achievements with those who were not, choosing, in this essay, two women as her cases in point. This essay is, in fact, only one element in an argument that is developed over an entire chapter. Readers should ask themselves whether or not the thesis emerges clearly here.

Marie Curie, the first woman Rose discusses, is a prominent figure in the popular culture of science. Part of Curie's PhD dissertation is included in this anthology. Mileva Einstein Maríc, the second woman, is far less well known, though her husband's surname (Einstein) is instantly recognizable. Unlike Marie Winn in her essay "Television and Reading," Rose does not structure her discussion of Curie and Maríc as an alternating series of points. Instead, she presents a block of information about Curie, a block about Maríc, and then another block about Curie.

In the first two sections, Rose presents the same information about each woman: her education, marital status, family life, scientific achievements, working relationship with her husband and other male scientists, and the fact that recognition of her acievements was dependent on male acknowledgement or sponsorship. Rose then returns to her first subject, Marie Curie, and outlines the circumstances surrounding Curie's second Nobel Prize, which still failed to establish her as on equal footing with male scientists. Rose peppers her essay with footnotes that provide additional information and evidence. Readers may find this strategy either helpful or distracting. Also notice her use of the pronoun "we," and consider who is included and who is excluded in this address to the audience.

STUDY QUESTIONS

For Discussion:

1. Speaking of Curie, Rose says "this astonishing woman has been held up to all, and especially to all women scientists, as the example of what women are capable of achieving." Before reading this essay, what was your conception of Curie? Does this essay change your view of her? Had you ever heard of Mileva Einstein Maríc?

2. Rose suggests not only that Curie and Einstein Maríc's personal and professional lives were more closely linked than those of the men with whom they worked, but also that recognition of these women's scientific work depended on their relationships with men. Is either observation true today?

For Writing:

1. Explain how Rose presents her thesis. Examine the evidence she uses to support her observations, and determine whether that evidence provides convincing proof for her position.

2. Compare and contrast Rose's characterization of Mileva Einstein Maríc with one found in a biography of Einstein. How are the two characterizations similar and different? What do the differences and similarities suggest about the interests of each author?

PRAISE TO THE ALBANY

Morton L. Ross

BIOGRAPHICAL NOTE

Morton (Mort) L. Ross (1932–95) taught in the English Department of the University of Alberta from 1968 until shortly before his untimely death in 1995. From 1963 to 1968 he held a joint appointment with the English Department and the School of American Studies at the University of Wyoming. He studied American History and Literature, specializing in the literature of the nineteenth-century American Renaissance. Ross was also interested in contemporary Canadian writing, and, in 1980, became a founding member of the Literary Advisory Board of the NeWest Press.

1   I sing of the Albany Bar, late of Laramie, Wyoming, for it was more wonderful than McSorley's wonderful saloon, more comforting than Hemingway's clean, well-lighted place, and more lamented in its passing than the tables down at Mory's. For generations the bibuli have celebrated favorite bars as the best possible combination of refuge, creative forum, and all-around lamasery. Let us honor their efforts, for I can no more pass a passable tavern than Mencken or W. C. Fields could go to Philadelphia without hip-flasks. And Laramie (hard Gem City of the Plains to its Chamber of Commerce, but sweet water hole to its surrounding legions of section hands, truckers, cowboys, and tie-hacks) is full of surpassing taverns—Alibi, Poor Bill's, Birdcage, Fireside, the Buckhorn, and more. But of all these, the Albany Bar was something special, indeed so absolutely superb as to needs transcend its local fame.

First published in *Colorado Quarterly*, vol. XXIV, no. 2, Autumn 1975, pp. 145–52. Reprinted with permission of the Estate of Morton L. Ross and *Colorado Quarterly*.

2   Tosspot memory, running to legend rather than history, has misplaced the Albany's origins. It is known, however, that a bar of that name had been somewhere in town since 1891. The most graceful evidence of its age was a house calendar dated 1907 and illustrated by a Gibson girl with yellow picture hat, parasol, and ample bodice. She was at once muse and alma mater. The great years began in the 1920s with the advent of the incomparable Dewey Bell, first bar-keep, then partner, then sole boniface until the end. Dewey opened the doors at 6:00 AM to ease the early thirst of the railroaders tending the big 484s that moved the freight over the Sherman range between Laramie and Cheyenne, the steepest grade on the UP line. The even dustier trade of minding cattle made the bar into a hiring hall for ranch hands at liberty and laving their tonsils in Albany gargle.

3   Prohibition had little effect on this occupational therapy; the only marks of the Noble Experiment were some scratches on the backbar from its brief period of storage to elude sequestration by federal agents and an outsized sink with double water pipe to flush and dilute the disappearing booze. From 1928, its last and best location on Grand Avenue faced the rear door of the Gem City Grocery, largest in the Basin, and the grocer increased custom by standing drinks for ranchers in to fill their monthly orders. Its location also permitted citizens to enter for a quick beer, then exit from the alley door convenient to the back vestibules of the three upstairs whorehouses facing Front Street, finally to emerge again from the Albany's innocent front door. Thus were passion and propriety conjoined.

4   The nymphs departed in the early fifties pursued by a wave of civic outrage over *Redbook's* exposé of Laramie as Sin City. The alley, once sacred to Venus, became a field of Mars. In fact the Albany's codes duello were so intricate that while the most bellicose tie-hack might amiably overlook direct insults to his mother, once a simple pun became the invitation to step outside. President Kennedy had given a speech in Laramie, several times mentioning Wyoming's newest resource, soda ash. It was perhaps inevitable that the bar's glee over his Boston pronunciation escalated suddenly into whose ash could whip whose, not personal, you understand, but as a fair test among political partisans.

5   On lazy afternoons the Albany became the club parlor of as venerable a troop of pensioners as ever murmured barracks tales under the arcades of the Invalides or the Royal Chelsea. The stories were often rousing—for some had helped Pershing chase Villa through Chihuahua—but as often they meandered among the reticulations of aging livers, lights, and prostates. It is significant that the noon to four shift, the peak hours of these gentle revels, was for years conducted by a bartender named Magnus Sandman. Indeed two ancients slipped from life in the bar, one while dreaming in the back room's Morris chair. On the first occasion, Dewey summoned an ambulance, reporting his clearly dead patron as prone to seizures, a prudent phrase used thereafter to cover every emergency.

6   Until 1964 the Albany's diurnal round closed at eight to facilitate Dewey's nightly games of pan-ginney at Hick's Card Room on Front Street. In that year more custom accumulated when Floyd Shaman, hitherto auxiliary bartender, persuaded Dewey to remain open until 1:00 AM to attract a new clientele, principally Floyd's fellow art students at the university. Again a name proved propitious, for Floyd had the magic. He dispensed the sweet medicine with such geniality that the late crowd evolved tribally. The artists were soon joined by the university's Outing Club—its modest title misleading because it included alpine climbers of no small skill—and then by students and professors from the English and history departments, traditional centers not only of the humanities but, some said, of the ripest grog-blossoms in academe.

7   Such categories, however, obscure the remarkable individuals so gathered. There was, for example, another Dewey, yclept Drollinger, a diminutive painter whose habit of wearing his glasses across the top of his bald head gave the impression of dual vision, one pair of eyes firmly forward, the other cocked aloft for news from the empyrean. There was Pete Sinclair who, as climbing ranger at the Tetons, helped pluck the hapless Appalachin Club off the mountain, an adventure he recorded for *Sports Illustrated* under the title "The Night of the Blue Devils." There was Paula née Poteau, a pocket-sized Finn with golden hair and a complexion finer than Sèvres, doubly unusual because of Laramie's notoriously desiccating sun. There was Big John Gruenfelder, historian and amazing raconteur—amazing because he had only three real interests: the minutiae of baseball (he had pitched for a Tiger farm club in Durham, NC), the annual editions of *Jane's Fighting Ships*, and the English parliaments under the Stuarts. There was Mert Harris, for whom the annual spring kegger in the Vedauwoo rocks was named, largely in honor of his inventive hangover cures, one of which involved inundation with #8 cans of orange juice in his morning-after bathtub. Heroes all. In an age of ersatz celebrity, we were content to make our own, encouraging each other's quirks as they helped swell the Albany's celebration. Our tribal instinct was undoubtedly part of the American male's propensity to extend his adolescence, to prolong the boy-gang stage well into middle-age; it was insular and insulating, with more than a touch of macho chauvinism, but it was also a moral alternative to imperialism, ennui, war, ambition, pedantry, ulcers, bureaucracy, and all the other fantods associated with life in the Republic.

8   The plan and appointments of the Albany made it a natural stage for homemade pageantry. The deviants who design modern bars are in open conspiracy against social drinking. They believe that liquor must be consumed while stationary; why else confinement in captain's chairs, wraparound vinyl cubbies, or—it is to cry—those *sitzfleisch* step-stools cramped against bars padded like the dashboard of a new Imperial. This padding is, I believe, open confession that sitting to drink is dangerous. They further assume that indulgence is a guilty and furtive act, and thus contrive windowless sites lit either by candles in red jars or malformed neon.

9   Once in a dim Fort Collins caravansary I was near hypnotized by a lighted column of what looked to be orange molasses in oil simmering and bubbling on the backbar like the vitals of hell. Further convinced that libido boozalis needs the whip of fantasy, these gentry make each new saloon the cabin of a sailing ship, a Victorian sporting house, or an English country pub. It is all empty theatrics. Woe betide the excited inebriate who actually tries to trim the mainsail, price the girls, or sound the hunting horn suspended above his head.

10   Let the Albany be a reproach to these decorators gone *mashugga*. It was built for sturdy, workaday humankind. Its spacious precincts were organized and focused by a backbar noble but not overwhelming in dimension. Brought to Laramie over the pass from Loveland, Colorado, it was constructed in the mode of high Western Gothic, yet managed to avoid excess. Its pilasters were Doric, its crenulations chaste, and it framed a triptych of mirrors, the central one a completely unflawed, unadorned four by ten, certainly the largest looking glass in town, but modest by the standards of Versailles. In the early sixties Dewey's own hands had stripped away the layers of varnish to reveal the original grain. The mahogany lusters on the front bar were subsequently kept to a high gloss largely by the motion of working elbows.

11   And one stood to labor at the Albany's bar, a posture healthful and even comfortable over surprisingly long periods. It is true that in later years a single stool appeared at the bar's

nether end, but purists eschewed it and it was occupied only intermittently by a few pregnant women. There were three tables and some chromium chairs along the far wall, but these provided necessary privacy for reading the *Boomerang* or chess, leaving the main floor uncluttered for those leisurely peregrinations which promote fellowship. And the barroom was graced by a marvelously radiant light. In the fifties an itinerant electrical expert had wandered through. On his advice, six units of unshaded fluorescents were installed, each containing four three-foot tubes.

12   On the first night patrons had to shade their eyes to find the sauce and the Albany's store front windows bathed the street opposite with a brilliance to shame the Eddystone Light. Three units were hastily decommissioned and later Floyd removed two tubes from each unit, his artist's eye having calibrated the exact wattage needed to make mirrors, mahogany, glassware, the brass rail and trio of spittoons into a medley of such gleaming that in its ambience more than one meditating soul found his satori.

13   The accessories were in perfect keeping. The front windows were periodically dressed by professionals from the breweries—a dying art, perhaps due to increasingly pinched media; the Hamm's bear, once done in plaster, then in plastic, seemed less sprightly in the pasteboard renderings of recent years. Next the front door was a glass-topped candy counter for the package goods, heavy on the favorites, pints of Sunny Brook and Hermitage, but also showing some mildly exotic Tokays and Muscatels. Behind this was a tall tobacco case, serving mostly as pediment for splendid plaster busts of John Paul Jones, Old Crow, and the Black and White Scotties. These had been donated by long departed whisky drummers who had early understood the need, in a university town, to compete with the marble heads of Aristotle, Voltaire, and Newton. The opposite wall was dominated by Dalziel's fine steel engraving of Landseer's *Stag at Bay*. The stuffed heads of a deer, a moose, and an antelope, lent by an Albany widow, hung in the back room, a space separated from the bar proper by a thin three-quarter partition topped by a lattice affair left over from somebody's May ball, and containing a few more tables, the Morris chair, a beer cooler, a Cathedral Wurlitzer whose records had not been changed since 1949, and the Albany's lone toilet, this circumstance making for some antic times between uninitiated sorority girls and the giant U P callboy Cody who was prompt enough in notifying the next-out list but forgetful about the latch.

14   Sustenance for the spirit, surely, but more staple fare was always available—enormous farm eggs hard-boiled by Floyd's wife Molly, potato chips, sunflower seeds, Ritz crackers, little pepperoni sticks called hotsies, corn curls, Kraznowski's Polish sausages served still dripping with brine, Fritoes, peanuts, wheat thins, blind robins (tiny fish dried until their species had become confused), pickles, pistachios, Copenhagen snoose, pretzels, oyster crackers, beer-nuts apparently roasted in a coating of Karo syrup before salting, popcorn, pizzas sent in from up the street, fried pork rinds, taco chips, and Slim Jim strips of beef jerky so tough that legend had cowboys carrying them under their saddles for hot meals at the end of the day, but which we softened by using them as swizzle sticks in the beer. These victuals induced thirst and the Hamm's obligingly flowed from the tap at 15¢ the 9-ounce shell, 20¢ the 12-ounce schooner, every third or fourth one on the house for regulars, and a shot of Wild Turkey on your birthday. Occasionally the Hamm's *Totsäufer*, the wholesaler or his customers' man, would buy up to four rounds in a row, but even on a normal night, it was possible to maintain a nice buzz for under a dollar and a half, especially since the active ingredient was more active at Laramie's altitude of 7,145 feet above sea level.

15   Unfortunately, Floyd's custom of Thursday night free lunch, at first helpings of sauerkraut and all-beef bangers, degenerated into orgies of baloney and Wonder Bread when every free-loader in town got wind of his bounty. On Thanksgiving and Christmas the feasts were more intimate; Dewey would peel bills from his back-pocket roll, have a turkey roasted at Dick Eberhart's Home Bakery, and carve it throughout the afternoon with rye bread and German mustard.

16   To these add periodic nuptial fetes. The first was an evening reception after Sally's marriage to Merle Ihne, an ecologist modeled on Jim Bridger lines who earned his MA helping to implant trout with radio transmitters to map their movements. It was on this occasion that the back room was rechristened so the engraved invitations could read "At the Spike Moose Lounge of the Albany Bar." Floyd and his relief, the painter Jerry Glass, wore green satin waistcoats, and a cold buffet was served. A few strays from the day crowd, particularly a Navaho ranch hand named Nelson Pine, accepted petits fours and Taylor's upstate New York champagne with appropriate gravity and without remarking what clearly smacked of Eastern newfangledness.

17   There was one formal riot. A kicking specialist who would graduate from the Wyoming Cowboys to NFL fame organized his bachelor party to feature a spot of hippie-bashing, then an emerging form of Western machismo. Some wag misguided them to the Albany. Their full realization of the mistake was interrupted by the arrival of a posse of Laramie's finest. This peacekeeping was effective and so pervasive that everyone, cops, jocks, and regulars, spent the rest of the evening weeping mace tears into the beer. The kicking specialist's second mistake was to allege in court that the Albany was a low bar, unaware that the magistrate had taken his preprandial shots there every weekday for the last half-decade.

18   Adventure aplenty, but I loved best the ordinary Friday nights. The beat would begin slowly, early arrivals spaced comfortably along the bar in companionable silence. Maybe one idly negotiating with Jerry for a painting, two more mumbling over yesterday's ball scores. About 8:30 Q. Cook, his quiet weekday mien oiled for conversation by preliminary drafts at the Alibi, would begin. His tonal range was impressive; once he sustained a threnody for the 82nd airborne by reference to both the Sicilian Vespers and the Defenestration of Prague, and nailed the point superbly by leading us in the "Marseillaise" from atop the bar. Q might be joined by Walter Edens' personal Wurlitzer, a rhetoric of suspended periods so extended that wagers could be laid around the possibility of his reaching them, by the poet Jim Cole's laconic reprise of the Cornhusker idioms of his youth, or by Hank Laskowsky's seasonal ragas, key of D improvisations as much "Havanegilah" as Ravi Shankar. Amazing grace, overtures for the evening's solo turns. We would hear again of Fred Cannan's tour as naval attaché for NATO, witnessing the sea trials of two new French corvettes; after a series of Gallic arabesques, they rammed and sunk each other, engines all ahead full. We would hear again of the stages by which Max Rardin, early proponent of behavior modification, convinced Art Simpson that bears would be attracted to their hunter's redoubt in the Snowy Range by manhandling a tub of cow guts up there to fester in the sun. They never were. We would hear again of Dave Lawson's schemes for the bluegrass band. (Mercury later issued their single titled "Laramie" featuring Dave singing "Farewell Amelia Earhart, First Lady of the Skies.") Then a pause to ogle discreetly Jerry's latest girl, each more astonishing than the last, especially one stunner with a voice like Senator Dirksen's. Drum rolls and flourishes.

19   Then, the evening ripening, we moved to the more heavily operatic; we would relive the details of Frisbie's misstep, an accident finally immortalized in the name, Frisbie's Fall, given the major rock face at Vedauwoo; we would muse over the time that Stu Crothers and a rodeo princess were indelicately surprised afterhours by Brownie, the Albany swamper; we would rerun a footrace between Big John and myself up from Front Street that finished with me prone to seizures at the Albany's front door; and then the whole ensemble, loaded to the scuppers, flawless in our parts, would collaborate in miming once again the Night They Sprayed the Place with Mace. Familiar voices, ritual action, and finally it would merge into that boozy hubbub which can pass for the authentic pulse of community. We dispersed at 1:00 AM, some to Short's Cafe for a morning omelet, some to Poor Bill's, an afterhours club more commonly known as Everybody's, some to Q's for bacon and eggs and a little Ella Fitzgerald, and on fine, rare occasions, a few back at the Albany's front door to greet the dawn and Dewey when he opened again at 6:00.

20   The Albany closed in 1969, the license went to a lounge out on Grand Avenue, the backbar to a discotheque over the Buckhorn, yet it will take its proper place amid the other monuments of its honored name. Albany is the ancient and literary name for Scotland, for a set of foreign dukes and a scandalous countess who married one of Big John's Stuarts, for a river rising in Western Ontario and a fur trading fort at its mouth, for cities in Oregon, Georgia, California, and New York, for a congress which concluded a treaty with the Iroquois in 1764. It is also and not least the name of a magnificent bar.

NOTES AND DISCUSSION

"Praise to the Albany" is a highly detailed description that incorporates several levels of information to establish its affectionate and nostalgic mood. It succeeds not only because of the amount of detail Ross supplies about the Albany, but also because of the variety and the ordering of that detail. His interests in history and literature are both evident, as are the connections between alcohol and academic and artistic inspiration. For example, he begins by placing the Albany alongside other legendary and inspirational bars. McSorley's, for instance, was founded in New York in 1854, and was patronized by Abraham Lincoln. Mory's has long been famous as an "unofficial faculty club" for Yale University; it is where, in 1939, the Yale Society of Orpheus and Bacchus was founded. It is also a regular venue for the Yale Whiffenpoofs, a long-standing *a cappella* ensemble.

Ross then describes the Albany's history, its regulars, its physical layout—especially its importance as a theatre for the drama of life to play itself out—and concludes by detailing his own favourite nights. Note that his favourite night ends with a leave-taking, which anticipates the permanent closing of the bar in 1969. The separate classes of detail combine to give a complex overview of the Albany as an example of a cultural centre and hangout.

STUDY QUESTIONS

For Discussion:

1. In what ways are the different types of detail Ross uses helpful to you as a reader? On the basis of the different kinds of evidence used here, how many different audiences do you think this piece attempts to appeal to?

2. Ross uses an elaborate vocabulary and a range of classical allusions to place the Albany within a mythic context. What effect do these strategies have on you? Consider, for example, the Latinate vocabulary, such as "the bibuli," or the opening allusion to Virgil's *Aeneid*: "Arma virumque cano" ("Of arms and the man I sing").

For Writing:

1. You probably have a favourite hangout of your own, a spot you go to either for company or for escape. Follow Ross's models to describe the spot, using at least two different classes of information: other places it is related to, its history, the people you meet there, its physical qualities, and its particular appeal to you. Remember, the details must relate to each other and combine for an overall impression of how and why this place is important to you.

2. Explain the importance of the order Ross follows in developing his description of the bar.

THE ENGLISH VILLA— PRINCIPLES OF COMPOSITION

John Ruskin

BIOGRAPHICAL NOTE

John Ruskin (1819–1900) was an influential author and critic in nineteenth-century England. His multi-volume *Modern Painters* (1843–60) was designed to rescue from obscurity contemporary painters whom he considered great, but also became a commentary on the social and spiritual history of Europe. *The Seven Lamps of Architecture* (1848) and *The Stones of Venice* (1853) further enhanced Ruskin's reputation and made him the leading art critic of his day. He became Oxford University's first Slade professor of art in 1869, but directed his subsequent writing towards critiques of Victorian Britain's social and economic systems. In those writings, Ruskin vehemently opposed unbridled capitalism and examined its effects on the moral standing of all English men and women.

1   It has lately become a custom, among the more enlightened and refined of metropolitan shopkeepers, to advocate the cause of propriety in architectural decoration, by ensconcing their shelves, counters, and clerks in classical edifices, agreeably ornamented with ingenious devices, typical of the class of articles to which the tradesman particularly desires to direct the public attention. We find our grocers enshrined in temples whose columns are of canisters, and whose pinnacles are of sugarloaves. Our shoemakers shape their soles under Gothic portals, with pendants of shoes, and canopies of Wellingtons; and our cheesemongers will, we doubt not, soon follow the excellent example, by raising shops the varied diameters of whose jointed columns, in their address to the eye, shall awaken memories of Staffa, Paestum, and Palmyra; and, in their address to the tongue, shall arouse exquisite associations of remembered flavour, Dutch, Stilton, and Strachino. Now, this fit of taste on the part of our tradesmen is only a coarse form of a disposition inherent in the human mind. Those objects to which the eye has been most frequently accustomed, and among which the intellect

has formed its habits of action, and the soul its modes of emotion, become agreeable to the thoughts, from their correspondence with their prevailing cast, especially when the business of life has had any relation to those objects; for it is in the habitual and necessary occupation that the most painless hours of existence are passed: whatever be the nature of that occupation, the memories belonging to it will always be agreeable, and, therefore, the objects awakening such memories will invariably be found beautiful, whatever their character or form. It is thus that taste is the child and the slave of memory; and beauty is tested, not by any fixed standard, but by the chances of association; so that in every domestic building evidence will be found of the kind of life through which its owner has passed, in the operation of the habits of mind which that life has induced. From the superannuated coxswain, who plants his old ship's figure-head in his six square feet of front garden at Bermondsey, to the retired noble, the proud portal of whose mansion is surmounted by the broad shield and the crested gryphon, we are all guided, in our purest conceptions, our most ideal pursuit, of the beautiful, by remembrances of active occupation, and by principles derived from industry regulate the fancies of our repose.

2   It would be excessively interesting to follow out the investigation of this subject more fully, and to show how the most refined pleasures, the most delicate perceptions, of the creature who has been appointed to eat bread by the sweat of his brow, are dependent upon, and intimately connected with, his hours of labour. This question, however, has no relation to our immediate object, and we only allude to it, that we may be able to distinguish between the two component parts of individual character; the one being the consequence of continuous habits of life acting upon natural temperament and disposition, the other being the humour of character, consequent upon circumstances altogether accidental, taking stern effect upon feelings previously determined by the first part of the character; laying on, as it were, the finishing touches, and occasioning the innumerable prejudices, fancies, and eccentricities, which, modified in every individual to an infinite extent, form the visible veil of the human heart.

3   Now, we have defined the province of the architect to be, that of selecting such forms and colours as shall delight the mind, by preparing it for the operations to which it is to be subjected in the building. Now, no forms, in domestic architecture, can thus prepare it more distinctly than those which correspond closely with the first, that is, the fixed and fundamental part of character, which is always so uniform in its action as to induce great simplicity in whatever it designs. Nothing, on the contrary, can be more injurious than the slightest influence of the humours upon the edifice; for the influence of what is fitful in its energy, and petty in its imagination, would destroy all the harmony of parts, all the majesty of the whole; would substitute singularity for beauty, amusement for delight, and surprise for veneration. We could name several instances of buildings erected by men of the highest talent, and the most perfect general taste, who yet, not having paid much attention to the first principles of architecture, permitted the humour of their disposition to prevail over the majesty of their intellect, and, instead of building from a fixed design, gratified freak after freak, and fancy after fancy, as they were caught by the dream or the desire; mixed mimicries of incongruous reality with incorporations of undisciplined ideal; awakened every variety of contending feeling and unconnected memory; consummated confusion of form by trickery of detail; and have left barbarism, where half the world will look for loveliness.

4   This is a species of error which it is very difficult for persons paying superficial and temporary attention to architecture to avoid: however just their taste may be in criticism, it will

fail in creation. It is only in moments of ease and amusement that they will think of their villa: they make it a mere plaything, and regard it with a kind of petty exultation, which, from its very nature, will give liberty to the light fancy, rather than the deep feeling, of the mind. It is not thought necessary to bestow labour of thought and periods of deliberation, on one of the toys of life; still less to undergo the vexation of thwarting wishes, and leaving favourite imaginations, relating to minor points, unfulfilled, for the sake of general effect.

5   This feeling, then, is the first to which we would direct attention, as the villa architect's chief enemy: he will find it perpetually and provokingly in his way. He is requested, perhaps, by a man of great wealth, nay, of established taste in some points, to make a design for a villa in a lovely situation. The future proprietor carries him up-stairs to his study, to give him what he calls his "ideas and materials," and, in all probability, begins somewhat thus: "This, sir, is a slight note: I made it on the spot: approach to Villa Reale, near Pozzuoli. Dancing nymphs, you perceive; cypresses, shell fountain. I think I should like something like this for the approach: classical, you perceive, sir; elegant, graceful. Then, sir, this is a sketch, made by an American friend of mine: Wheewhaw-Kantamaraw's wigwam, king of the—Cannibal Islands, I think he said, sir. Log, you observe; scalps, and boa constrictor skins: curious. Something like this, sir, would look neat, I think, for the front door; don't you? Then, the lower windows, I've not quite decided upon; but what would you say to Egyptian, sir? I think I should like my windows Egyptian, with hieroglyphics, sir; storks and coffins, and appropriate mouldings above: I brought some from Fountains Abbey the other day. Look here, sir; angels' heads putting their tongues out, rolled up in cabbage leaves, with a dragon on each side riding on a broomstick, and the devil looking on from the mouth of an alligator, sir.* Odd, I think; interesting. Then the corners may be turned by octagonal towers, like the centre one in Kenilworth Castle; with Gothic doors, portcullis, and all, quite perfect; with cross slits for arrows, battlements for musketry, machicolations for boiling lead, and a room at the top for drying plums; and the conservatory at the bottom, sir, with Virginian creepers up the towers; door supported by sphinxes, holding scrapers in their fore-paws, and having their tails prolonged into warm-water pipes, to keep the plants safe in winter, etc." The architect is, without doubt, a little astonished by these ideas and combinations; yet he sits calmly down to draw his elevations, as if he were a stone-mason, or his employer an architect; and the fabric rises to electrify its beholders, and confer immortality on its perpetrator. This is no exaggeration: we have not only listened to speculations on the probable degree of the future majesty, but contemplated the actual illustrious existence, of several such buildings, with sufficient beauty in the management of some of their features to show that an architect had superintended them, and sufficient taste in their interior economy to prove that a refined intellect had projected them; and had projected a Vandalism, only because fancy had been followed instead of judgment; with as much nonchalance as is evinced by a perfect poet, who is extemporising doggerel for a baby; full of brilliant points, which he cannot help, and jumbled into confusion, for which he does not care.

6   Such are the first difficulties to be encountered in villa designs. They must always continue to occur in some degree, though they might be met with ease by a determination on the part of professional men to give no assistance whatever, beyond the mere superintendence of construction, unless they be permitted to take the whole exterior design into their own hands, merely receiving broad instructions respecting the style (and not attending to them unless

---

*   Actually carved on one of the groins of Roslin Chapel.

they like). They should not make out the smallest detail, unless they were answerable for the whole. In this case, gentlemen architects would be thrown so utterly on their own resources, that, unless those resources were adequate, they would be obliged to surrender the task into more practised hands; and, if they were adequate, if the amateur had paid so much attention to the art as to be capable of giving the design perfectly, it is probable he would not erect anything strikingly abominable.

7   Such a system (supposing that it could be carried fully into effect, and that there were no such animals as sentimental stone-masons to give technical assistance) might, at first, seem rather an encroachment on the liberty of the subject, inasmuch as it would prevent people from indulging their edificatorial fancies, unless they knew something about the matter, or, as the sufferers would probably complain, from doing what they liked with their own. But the mistake would evidently lie in their supposing, as people too frequently do, that the outside of their house *is* their own, and that they have a perfect right therein to make fools of themselves in any manner, and to any extent, they may think proper. This is quite true in the case of interiors: every one has an indisputable right to hold himself up as a laughing-stock to the whole circle of his friends and acquaintances, and to consult his own private asinine comfort by every piece of absurdity which can in any degree contribute to the same; but no one has any right to exhibit his imbecilities at other people's expense, or to claim the public pity by inflicting public pain. In England, especially, where, as we saw before, the rage for attracting observation is universal, the outside of the villa is rendered, by the proprietor's own disposition, the property of those who daily pass by, and whom it hourly affects with pleasure or pain. For the pain which the eye feels from the violation of a law to which it has been accustomed, or the mind from the occurrence of anything jarring to its finest feelings, is as distinct as that occasioned by the interruption of the physical economy, differing only inasmuch as it is not permanent; and, therefore, an individual has as little right to fulfill his own conceptions by disgusting thousands, as, were his body as impenetrable to steel or poison, as his brain to the effect of the beautiful or true, he would have to decorate his carriage roads with caltrops, or to line his plantations with upas trees.

8   The violation of general feelings would thus be unjust, even were their consultation productive of continued vexation to the individual: but it is not. To no one is the architecture of the exterior of a dwelling-house of so little consequence as to its inhabitants. Its material may affect his comfort, and its condition may touch his pride; but for its architecture, his eye gets accustomed to it in a week, and, after that, Hellenic, Barbaric, or Yankee, are all the same to the domestic feelings, are all lost in the one name of home. Even the conceit of living in a châlet, or a wigwam, or a pagoda, cannot retain its influence for six months over the weak minds which alone can feel it; and the monotony of existence becomes to them exactly what it would have been had they never inflicted a pang upon the unfortunate spectators, whose accustomed eyes shrink daily from the impression to which they have not been rendered callous by custom, or lenient by false taste. If these conditions are just when they allude only to buildings in the abstract, how much more when referring to them as materials of composition, materials of infinite power, to adorn or destroy the loveliness of the earth. The nobler scenery of that earth is the inheritance of all her inhabitants: it is not merely for the few to whom it temporarily belongs, to feed from like swine, or to stable upon like horses, but it has been appointed to be the school of the minds which are kingly among their fellows, to excite the highest energies of humanity, to furnish strength to the lordliest intellect, and food for the holiest emotions of the human soul. The presence of life is,

indeed, necessary to its beauty, but of life congenial with its character; and that life is not congenial which thrusts presumptuously forward, amidst the calmness of the universe, the confusion of its own petty interests and grovelling imaginations, and stands up with the insolence of a moment, amidst the majesty of all time, to build baby fortifications upon the bones of the world, or to sweep the copse from the corrie, and the shadow from the shore, that fools may risk, and gamblers gather, the spoil of a thousand summers.

9   It should therefore be remembered, by every proprietor of land in hill country, that his possessions are the means of a peculiar education, otherwise unattainable, to the artists, and, in some degree, to the literary men, of his country; that, even in this limited point of view, they are a national possession, but much more so when it is remembered how many thousands are perpetually receiving from them, not merely a transitory pleasure, but such thrilling perpetuity of pure emotion, such lofty subject for scientific speculation, and such deep lessons of natural religion, as only the work of a Deity can impress, and only the spirit of an immortal can feel: they should remember that the slightest deformity, the most contemptible excrescence, can injure the effect of the noblest natural scenery, as a note of discord can annihilate the expression of the purest harmony; that thus it is in the power of worms to conceal, to destroy, or to violate, what angels could not restore, create, or consecrate; and that the right, which every man unquestionably possesses, to be an ass, is extended only, in public, to those who are innocent in idiotism, not to the more malicious clowns who thrust their degraded motley conspicuously forth amidst the fair colours of earth, and mix their incoherent cries with the melodies of eternity, break with their inane laugh upon the silence which Creation keeps where Omnipotence passes most visibly, and scrabble over with the characters of idiocy the pages that have been written by the finger of God.

10   These feelings we would endeavour to impress upon all persons likely to have anything to do with embellishing, as it is called, fine natural scenery; as they might, in some degree, convince both the architect and his employer of the danger of giving free play to the imagination in cases involving intricate questions of feeling and composition, and might persuade the designer of the necessity of looking, not to his own acre of land, or to his own peculiar tastes, but to the whole mass of forms and combination of impressions with which he is surrounded.

11   Let us suppose, however, that the design is yielded entirely to the architect's discretion. Being a piece of domestic architecture, the chief object in its exterior design will be to arouse domestic feelings, which, as we saw before, it will do most distinctly by corresponding with the first part of character. Yet it is still more necessary that it should correspond with its situation; and hence arises another difficulty, the reconciliation of correspondence with contraries; for such, it is deeply to be regretted, are too often the individual's mind, and the dwelling-place it chooses. The polished courtier brings his refinement and duplicity with him, to ape the Arcadian rustic in Devonshire; the romantic rhymer takes a plastered habitation, with one back window looking into the green park; the soft votary of luxury endeavours to rise at seven, in some Ultima Thule of frost and storms; and the rich stock-jobber calculates his percentages among the soft dingles and woody shores of Westmoreland. When the architect finds this to be the case, he must, of course, content himself with suiting his design to such a mind as ought to be where the intruder's is; for the feelings which are so much at variance with themselves in the choice of situation, will not be found too critical of their domicile, however little suited to their temper. If possible, however, he should aim at something more; he should draw his employer into general conversation; observe

the bent of his disposition, and the habits of his mind; notice every manifestation of fixed opinions, and then transfer to his architecture as much of the feeling he has observed as is distinct in its operation. This he should do, not because the general spectator will be aware of the aptness of the building, which, knowing nothing of its inmate, he cannot be; nor to please the individual himself, which it is a chance if any simple design ever will, and who never will find out how well his character has been fitted; but because a portrait is always more spirited than a composed countenance; and because this study of human passions will bring a degree of energy, unity, and originality into every one of his designs (all of which will necessarily be different), so simple, so domestic, and so life like, as to strike every spectator with an interest and a sympathy, for which he will be utterly unable to account, and to impress on him a perception of something more ethereal than stone or carving, somewhat similar to that which some will remember having felt disagreeably in their childhood, on looking at any old house authentically haunted. The architect will forget in his study of life the formalities of science, and, while his practised eye will prevent him from erring in technicalities, he will advance, with the ruling feeling, which, in masses of mind, is nationality, to the conception of something truly original, yet perfectly pure.

12   He will also find his advantage in having obtained a guide in the invention of decorations of which, as we shall show, we would have many more in English villas than economy at present allows. Candidus complains, in his Note-Book, that Elizabethan architecture is frequently adopted, because it is easy, with a pair of scissors, to derive a zigzag ornament from a doubled piece of paper. But we would fain hope that none of our professional architects have so far lost sight of the meaning of their art, as to believe that roughening stone mathematically is bestowing decoration, though we are too sternly convinced that they believe mankind to be more shortsighted by at least thirty yards than they are; for they think of nothing but general effect in their ornaments, and lay on their flower-work so carelessly, that a good substantial captain's biscuit, with the small holes left by the penetration of the baker's four fingers, encircling the large one which testifies of the forcible passage of his thumb, would form quite as elegant a rosette as hundreds now perpetuated in stone. Now, there is nothing which requires study so close, or experiment so frequent, as the proper designing of ornament. For its use and position some definite rules may be given; but, when the space and position have been determined, the lines of curvature, the breadth, depth, and sharpness of the shadows to be obtained, the junction of the parts of a group, and the general expression, will present questions for the solution of which the study of years will sometimes scarcely be sufficient;* for they depend upon the feeing of the eye and hand, and there is nothing like perfection in decoration, nothing which, in all probability, might not, by farther consideration, be improved. Now, in cases in which the outline and larger masses are determined by situation, the architect will frequently find it necessary to fall back upon his decorations, as the only means of obtaining character; and that which before was an unmeaning lump of jagged freestone, will become a part of expression, an accessory of beautiful design, varied in its form, and delicate in its effect. Then, instead of shrinking from his bits of ornament, as from things which will give him trouble to invent, and will answer no other purpose than that of occupying what would otherwise have looked blank, the designer will view them

---

* For example, we would allow one of the modern builders of Gothic chapels a month of invention, and a botanic garden to work from, with perfect certainty that he would not, at the expiration of the time, be able to present us with one design of leafage equal in beauty to hundreds we could point out in the capitals and niches of Melrose and Roslin.

as an efficient *corps de réserve*, to be brought up when the eye comes to close quarters with the edifice, to maintain and deepen the impression it has previously received. Much more time will be spent in the conception, much more labour in the execution, of such meaning ornament, but both will be well spent, and well rewarded.

13   Perhaps our meaning may be made more clear by Figure 1, which is that of a window found in a domestic building of mixed and corrupt architecture, at Munich (which we give now, because we shall have occasion to allude to it hereafter). Its absurd breadth of moulding, so disproportionate to its cornice, renders it excessively ugly, but capable of great variety of effect. It forms one of a range of four, tuning an angle, whose mouldings join each other, their double breadth being the whole separation of the apertures, which are something more than double squares. Now, by alteration of the decoration, and depth of shadow, we have Figures 2 and 3. These three windows differ entirely in their feeling and manner, and are broad examples of such distinctions of style as might be adopted severally in the habitations of the man of imagination, the man of intellect, and the man of feeling.

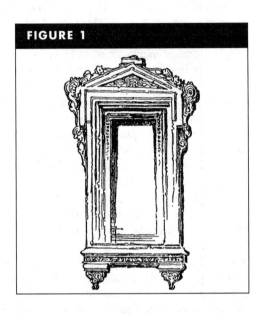

FIGURE 1

If our alterations have been properly made, there will be no difficulty in distinguishing between their expressions, which we shall therefore leave to conjecture. The character of Figure 1 depends upon the softness with which the light is caught upon its ornaments, which should not have a single hard line in them; and on the gradual, unequal, but intense, depth of its shadows. Figure 2 should have all its forms undefined, and passing into one another, the touches of the chisel light, a grotesque face or feature occurring in parts, the shadows pale, but broad;* and the boldest part of the carving kept in shadow rather than light. The third should be hard in its lines, strong in its shades, and quiet in its ornament.

14   These hints will be sufficient to explain our meaning, and we have not space to do more, as the object of these papers is rather to observe than to advise. Besides, in questions of expression so intricate, it is almost impossible to advance fixed principles; every mind will have perceptions of its own, which will guide its speculations, every hand, and eye, and peculiar feeling, varying even from year to year. We have only started the subject of correspondence with individual character, because we think that imaginative minds might take up the idea with some success, as furnishing them with a guide in the variation of their designs, more certain than mere experiment on unmeaning forms, or than ringing indiscrim-

---

*   It is too much the custom to consider a design as composed of a certain number of hard lines, instead of a certain number of shadows of various depth and dimension. Though these shadows change their position in the course of the day, they are relatively always the same. They have most variety under a strong light without sun, most expression with the sun. A little observation of the infinite variety of shade which the sun is capable of casting, as it touches projections of different curve and character, will enable the designer to be certain of his effects.

FIGURES 2 AND 3

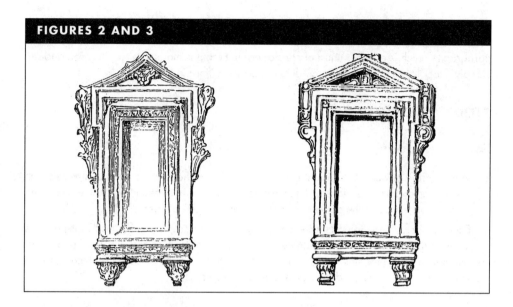

inate changes on component parts of established beauty. To the reverie, rather than the investigation, to the dream, rather than the deliberation, of the architect, we recommend it, as a branch of art in which instinct will do more than precept, and inspiration than technicality. The correspondence of our villa architecture with our natural scenery may be determined with far greater accuracy, and will require careful investigation.

15   We had hoped to have concluded the Villa in this paper; but the importance of domestic architecture at the present day, when people want houses more than fortresses, safes more than keeps, and sculleries more than dungeons, is sufficient apology for delay.

NOTES AND DISCUSSION

Ruskin's style is likely to be the first aspect of this essay to strike modern readers: his vocabulary is wide-ranging, perhaps even obscure; his long, complex sentences make use of many internal modifications; and his elaborate punctuation does not conform to modern conventions. In fact, O. B. Hardison, Jr., likened Ruskin's prose style to a specific architectural style — namely, ornate gingerbread.

Ruskin begins by observing that all classes of Victorian England are governed by the same principles in terms of how their taste is formed and how they build and decorate. In all cases, Ruskin argues, "taste is the child and the slave of memory." He believes that it is the architect's role to control and check such impulses; the architect must regulate and defend public taste. To illustrate the average person's tendencies in designing a home, Ruskin creates a scenario in which an architect is confronted by a man who wishes to build a house in a hilarious and horrifying hodgepodge of architectural elements. Such horrors, Ruskin insists, must be countered.

Note that Ruskin, like Lucky and Suzuki, uses a fictitious dialogue and analogy to support a factual argument. He argues that the outside of a person's house belongs to the public domain, not to the person, and that, even if restraint seems like encroachment upon personal liberty, the architect must determine and defend public sensibilities. Ruskin closes his paper by comparing and contrasting some window designs in order to educate public taste and to make clear his definition of "design," which is integral to his notion of architecture. Note the essay's final paragraph, which is a rather unusual conclusion; in fact, it is more a self-justification and decidedly *un*apologetic apology for the delay in properly finishing his paper.

STUDY QUESTIONS

For Discussion:

1. What literary device does Ruskin employ when he says that the architect, confronted with the gentleman-builder's plans, is "a little astonished"? How does such a device contribute to your conception of the essay's overall tone and of Ruskin's persona?

2. Examine the construction of the sentence in the first paragraph that begins "Those objects to which the eye. . . ." Consider Ruskin's use of sentence structure and punctuation. Suggest alternate methods for structuring and punctuating this material. Does the sentence impress you with Ruskin's skill, or does it have the opposite effect?

For Writing:

1. Describe a local building that seems, in your opinion, to be "strikingly abominable" and built according to "freak after freak, and fancy after fancy."

2. Do you agree with Ruskin that architecture is "public property" and influences the general public? Are architectural controls such as those Ruskin suggests an encroachment on personal liberty?

A MASK ON THE FACE OF DEATH

Richard Selzer

BIOGRAPHICAL NOTE

Richard Selzer had been a medical student, general surgeon, and teacher at the Yale School for Medicine for about fifteen years when, in the early 1970s, he also began to write. By the late 1980s, as he has recorded in an essay entitled "The Pen and the Scalpel," he retired from medicine to write full-time. His essays, collected in such works as *Mortal Lessons* (1977), *Confessions of a Knife* (1979), *Letters to a Young Doctor* (1982), and *Taking the World in for Repairs* (1986), often explore the relationship between technology and faith in medicine. Selzer has won numerous awards for his writing, including the National Magazine Award (1975) and the American Medical Writers Award (1984).

---

1   It is ten o'clock at night as we drive up to the Copacabana, a dilapidated brothel on the rue Dessalines in the red-light district of Port-au-Prince. My guide is a young Haitian, Jean-Bernard. Ten years before, J-B tells me, at the age of fourteen, "like every good Haitian boy" he had been brought here by his older cousins for his *rite de passage*. From the car to the entrance, we are accosted by a half dozen men and women for sex. We enter, go down a long hall that breaks upon a cavernous room with a stone floor. The cubicles of the prostitutes, I am told, are in an attached wing of the building. Save for a red-purple glow from small lights on the walls, the place is unlit. Dark shapes float by, each with a blindingly white stripe of teeth. Latin music is blaring. We take seats at the table farthest from the door. Just outside, there is the rhythmic lapping of the Caribbean Sea. About twenty men are seated at the tables or lean against the walls. Brightly dressed women, singly or in twos or threes, stroll about, now and then exchanging banter with the men. It is as though we have

been deposited in act two of Bizet's *Carmen*. If this place isn't Lillas Pastia's tavern, what is it?

2   Within minutes, three light-skinned young women arrive at our table. They are very beautiful and young and lively. Let them be Carmen, Mercedes, and Frasquita.

3   "I want the old one," says Frasquita, ruffling my hair. The women laugh uproariously.

4   "Don't bother looking any further," says Mercedes. "We are the prettiest ones."

5   "We only want to talk," I tell her.

6   "Aah, aah," she crows. "Massissi. You are massissi." It is the contemptuous Creole term for homosexual. If we want only to talk, we must be gay. Mercedes and Carmen are slender, each weighing one hundred pounds or less. Frasquita is tall and hefty. They are dressed for work: red taffeta, purple chiffon, and black sequins. Among them a thousand gold bracelets and earrings multiply every speck of light. Their bare shoulders are like animated lamps gleaming in the shadowy room. Since there is as yet no business, the women agree to sit with us. J-B orders beer and cigarettes. We pay each woman $10.

7   "Where are you from?" I begin.

8   "We are Dominican."

9   "Do you miss your country?"

10   "Oh, yes, we do." Six eyes go muzzy with longing. "Our country is the most beautiful in the world. No country is like the Dominican. And it doesn't stink like this one."

11   "Then why don't you work there? Why come to Haiti?"

12   "Santo Domingo has too many whores. All beautiful, like us. All light-skinned. The Haitian men like to sleep with light women."

13   "Why is that?"

14   "Because always, the whites have all the power and the money. The black men can imagine they do, too, when they have us in bed."

15   Eleven o'clock. I looked around the room that is still sparsely peopled with men.

16   "It isn't getting any busier," I say. Frasquita glances over her shoulder. Her eyes drill the darkness.

17   "It is still early," she says.

18   "Could it be that the men are afraid of getting sick?" Frasquita is offended.

19   "Sick! They do not get sick from us. We are healthy, strong. Every week we go for a checkup. Besides, we know how to tell if we are getting sick."

20   "I mean sick with AIDS." The word sets off a hurricane of taffeta, chiffon, and gold jewelry. They are all gesticulation and fury. It is Carmen who speaks.

21   "AIDS!" Her lips curl about the syllable. "There is no such thing. It is a false disease invented by the American government to take advantage of the poor countries. The American President hates poor people, so now he makes up AIDS to take away the little we have." The others nod vehemently.

22   "*Mira, mon cher.* Look, my dear," Carmen continues. "One day the police came here. Believe me, they are worse than the *tonton macoutes* with their submachine guns. They rounded up one hundred and five of us and they took our blood. That was a year ago. None of us have died, you see? We are all still here. *Mira*, we sleep with all the men and we are not sick."

23   "But aren't there some of you who have lost weight and have diarrhea?"

24   "One or two, maybe. But they don't eat. That is why they are weak."

25   "Only the men die," says Mercedes. "They stop eating, so they die. It is hard to kill a woman."

26   "Do you eat well?"

27   "Oh, yes, don't worry, we do. We eat like poor people, but we eat." There is a sudden scream from Frasquita. She points to a large rat that has emerged from beneath the table.

28   "My God!" she exclaims. "It is big like a pig." They burst into laughter. For a moment the women fall silent. There is only the restlessness of their many bracelets. I give them each another $10.

29   "Are many of the men here bisexual?"

30   "Too many. They do it for money. Afterward, they come to us." Carmen lights a cigarette and looks down at the small lace handkerchief she has been folding and unfolding with immense precision on the table. All at once she turns it over as though it were the ace of spades.

31   "*Mira, blanc* . . . look, white man," she says in a voice suddenly full of foreboding. Her skin too seems to darken to coincide with the tone of her voice.

32   "*Mira*, soon many Dominican woman will die in Haiti!"

33   "Die of what?"

34   She shrugs. "It is what they do to us."

35   "Carmen," I say, "if you knew that you had AIDS, that your blood was bad, would you still sleep with men?" Abruptly, she throws back her head and laughs. It is the same laughter with which Frasquita had greeted the rat at our feet. She stands and the others follow.

36   "*Méchant!* You wicked man," she says. Then, with terrible solemnity, "You don't know anything."

37   "But you are killing the Haitian men," I say.

38   "As for that," she says, "everyone is killing everyone else." All at once, I want to know everything about these three—their childhood, their dreams, what they do in the afternoon, what they eat for lunch.

39   "Don't leave," I say. "Stay a little more." Again, I reach for my wallet. But they are gone, taking all the light in the room with them—Mercedes and Carmen to sit at another table where three men have been waiting. Frasquita is strolling about the room. Now and then, as if captured by the music, she breaks into a few dance steps, snapping her fingers, singing to herself.

40   Midnight. And the Copacabana is filling up. Now it is like any other seedy nightclub where men and women go hunting. We get up to leave. In the center a couple are dancing a *méringue*. He is the most graceful dancer I have ever watched; she, the most voluptuous. Together they seem to be riding the back of the music as it gallops to a precisely sexual beat. Closer up, I see that the man is short of breath, sweating. All at once, he collapses into a chair. The woman bends over him, coaxing, teasing, but he is through. A young man with a long polished stick blocks my way.

41   "I come with you?" he asks. "Very good time. You say yes? Ten dollars? Five?"

42   I have been invited by Dr. Jean William Pape to attend the AIDS clinic of which he is the director. Nothing from the outside of the low whitewashed structure would suggest it as a medical facility. Inside, it is divided into many small cubicles and a labyrinth of corridors. At nine a.m. the hallways are already full of emaciated silent men and women, some

sitting on the few benches, the rest leaning against the walls. The only sounds are subdued moans of discomfort interspersed with coughs. How they eat us with their eyes as we pass.

43   The room where Pape and I work is perhaps ten feet by ten. It contains a desk, two chairs, and a narrow table that is covered with a sheet that will not be changed during the day. The patients are called in one at a time, asked how they feel and whether there is any change in their symptoms, then examined on the table. If the patient is new to the clinic, he or she is questioned about sexual activities.

44   A twenty-seven-year-old man whose given name is Miracle enters. He is wobbly, panting, like a groggy boxer who has let down his arms and is waiting for the last punch. He is neatly dressed and wears, despite the heat, a heavy woolen cap. When he removes it, I see that his hair is thin, dull reddish, and straight. It is one of the signs of AIDS in Haiti, Pape tells me. The man's skin is covered with a dry itchy rash. Throughout the interview and examination he scratches himself slowly, absentmindedly. The rash is called prurigo. It is another symptom of AIDS in Haiti. This man has had diarrhea for six months. The laboratory reports that the diarrhea is due to an organism called cryptosporidium, for which there is no treatment. The telltale rattling of the tuberculous moisture in his chest is audible without a stethoscope. He is like a leaky cistern that bubbles and froths. And, clearly, exhausted.

45   "Where do you live?" I ask.

46   "Kenscoff." A village in the hills above Port-au-Prince.

47   "How did you come here today?"

48   "I came on the *tap-tap*." It is the name given to the small buses that swarm the city, each one extravagantly decorated with religious slogans, icons, flowers, animals, all painted in psychedelic colors. I have never seen a tap-tap that was not covered with passengers as well, riding outside and hanging on. The vehicles are little masterpieces of contagion, if not of AIDS then of the multitude of germs which Haitian flesh is heir to. Miracle is given a prescription for a supply of Sera, which is something like Gatorade, and told to return in a month.

49   "*Mangé kou bêf*," says the doctor in farewell. "Eat like an ox." What can he mean? The man has no food or money to buy any. Even had he food, he has not the appetite to eat or the ability to retain it. To each departing patient the doctor will say the same words—"Mangé kou bêf." I see that it is his way of offering a hopeful goodbye.

50   "Will he live until his next appointment?" I ask.

51   "No." Miracle leaves to catch the *tap-tap* for Kenscoff.

52   Next is a woman of twenty-six who enters holding her right hand to her forehead in a kind of permanent salute. In fact, she is shielding her eye from view. This is her third visit to the clinic. I see that she is still quite well nourished.

53   "Now, you'll see something beautiful, tremendous," the doctor says. Once seated upon the table, she is told to lower her hand. When she does, I see that her right eye and its eyelid are replaced by a huge fungating ulcerated tumor, a side product of her AIDS. As she turns her head, the cluster of lymph glands in her neck to which the tumor has spread is thrown into relief. Two years ago she received a blood transfusion at a time when the country's main blood bank was grossly contaminated with AIDS. It has since been closed down. The only blood available in Haiti is a small supply procured from the Red Cross.

54   "Can you give me medicine?" the woman wails.

55   "No."

56   "Can you cut it away?"

57   "No."

58   "Is there radiation therapy?" I ask.

59   "No."

60   "Chemotherapy?" The doctor looks at me in what some might call weary amusement. I see that there is nothing to do. She has come here because there is nowhere else to go.

61   "What will she do?"

62   "Tomorrow or the next day or the day after that she will climb up into the mountains to seek relief from the *houngan*, the voodoo priest, just as her slave ancestors did two hundred years ago."

63   Then comes a frail man in his thirties, with a strangely spiritualized face, like a child's. Pus runs from one ear onto his cheek, where it has dried and caked. He has trouble remembering, he tells us. In fact, he seems confused. It is from toxoplasmosis of the brain, an effect of his AIDS. This man is bisexual. Two years ago he engaged in oral sex with foreign men for money. As I palpate the swollen glands of his neck, a mosquito flies between our faces. I swat at it, miss. Just before coming to Haiti I had read that the AIDS virus had been isolated from a certain mosquito. The doctor senses my thought.

64   "Not to worry," he says. "So far as we know there has never been a case transmitted by insects."

65   "Yes," I say. "I see."

66   And so it goes until the last, the thirty-sixth AIDS patient has been seen. At the end of the day I am invited to wash my hands before leaving. I go down a long hall to a sink. I turn on the faucets but there is no water.

67   "But what about *you*?" I ask the doctor. "You are at great personal risk here—the tuberculosis, the other infections, no water to wash. . . ." He shrugs, smiles faintly, and lifts his hands palm upward.

68   We are driving up a serpiginous steep road into the barren mountains above Port-au-Prince. Even in the bright sunshine the countryside has the bloodless color of exhaustion and indifference. Our destination is the Baptist Mission Hospital, where many cases of AIDS have been reported. Along the road there are slow straggles of schoolchildren in blue uniforms who stretch out their hands as we pass and call out, "Give me something." Already a crowd of outpatients has gathered at the entrance to the mission compound. A tour of the premises reveals that in contrast to the aridity outside the gates, this is an enclave of productivity, lush with fruit trees and poinsettia.

69   The hospital is clean and smells of creosote. Of the forty beds less than a third are occupied. In one male ward of twelve beds, there are two patients. The chief physician tells us that last year he saw ten cases of AIDS each week. Lately the number has decreased to four or five.

70   "Why is that?" we want to know.

71   "Because we do not admit them to the hospital, so they have learned not to come here."

72   "Why don't you admit them?"

73   "Because we would have nothing but AIDS here then. So we send them away."

74   "But I see that you have very few patients in bed."

75   "That is also true."

76   "Where do the AIDS patients go?"

77   "Some go to the clinic in Port-au-Prince or the general hospital in the city. Others go home to die or to the voodoo priest."

78   "Do the people with AIDS know what they have before they come here?"

79   "Oh, yes, they know very well, and they know there is nothing to be done for them."

80   Outside, the crowd of people is dispersing toward the gate. The clinic has been canceled for the day. No one knows why. We are conducted to the office of the reigning American pastor. He is a tall, handsome Midwesterner with an ecclesiastical smile.

81   "It is voodoo that is the devil here." He warms to his subject. "It is a demonic religion, a cancer on Haiti. Voodoo is worse than AIDS. And it is one of the reasons for the epidemic. Did you know that in order for a man to become a *houngan* he must perform anal sodomy on another man? No, of course you didn't. And it doesn't stop there. The *houngans* tell the men that in order to appease the spirits they too must do the same thing. So you have ritualized homosexuality. That's what is spreading the AIDS." The pastor tells us of a nun who witnessed two acts of sodomy in a provincial hospital where she came upon a man sexually assaulting a houseboy and another man mounting a male patient in his bed.

82   "Fornication," he says. "It is Sodom and Gomorrah all over again, so what can you expect from these people?" Outside his office we are shown a cage of terrified, cowering monkeys to whom he coos affectionately. It is clear that he loves them. At the car, we shake hands.

83   "By the way," the pastor says, "what is your religion? Perhaps I am a kinsman?"

84   "While I am in Haiti," I tell him, "it will be voodoo or it will be nothing at all."

85   Abruptly, the smile breaks. It is as though a crack had suddenly appeared in the face of an idol.

86   From the mission we go to the general hospital. In the heart of Port-au-Prince, it is the exact antithesis of the immaculate facility we have just left—filthy, crowded, hectic, and staffed entirely by young interns and residents. Though it is associated with a medical school, I do not see any members of the faculty. We are shown around by Jocelyne, a young intern in a scrub suit. Each bed in three large wards is occupied. On the floor about the beds, hunkered in the posture of the innocent poor, are family members of the patients. In the corridor that constitutes the emergency room, someone lies on a stretcher receiving an intravenous infusion. She is hardly more than a cadaver.

87   "Where are the doctors in charge?" I ask Jocelyne. She looks at me questioningly.

88   "We are in charge."

89   "I mean your teachers, the faculty."

90   "They do not come here."

91   "What is wrong with that woman?"

92   "She has had diarrhea for three months. Now she is dehydrated." I ask the woman to open her mouth. Her throat is covered with the white plaques of thrush, a fungus infection associated with AIDS.

93   "How many AIDS patients do you see here?"

94   "Three or four a day. We send them home. Sometimes the families abandon them, then we must admit them to the hospital. Every day, then, a relative comes to see if the patient has died. They want to take the body. That is important to them. But they know very well that AIDS is contagious and they are afraid to keep them at home. Even so, once or twice a week the truck comes to take away the bodies. Many are children. They are buried in mass graves."

95   "Where do the wealthy patients go?"

96   "There is a private hospital called Canapé Vert. Or else they go to Miami. Most of them, rich and poor, do not go to the hospital. Most are never diagnosed."

97   "How do you know these people have AIDS?"

98   "We don't know sometimes. The blood test is inaccurate. There are many false positives and false negatives. Fifteen percent of those with the disease have negative blood tests. We go by their infections—tuberculosis, diarrhea, fungi, herpes, skin rashes. It is not hard to tell."

99   "Do they know what they have?"

100   "Yes. They understand at once and they are prepared to die."

101   "Do the patients know how AIDS is transmitted?"

102   "They know, but they do not like to talk about it. It is taboo. Their memories do not seem to reach back to the true origins of their disaster. It is understandable, is it not?"

103   "Whatever you write, don't hurt us any more than we have already been hurt." It is a young Haitian journalist with whom I am drinking a rum punch. He means that any further linkage to AIDS and Haiti in the media would complete the economic destruction of the country. The damage was done early in the epidemic when the Centers for Disease Control in Atlanta added Haitians to the three other high-risk groups—hemophiliacs, intravenous drug users, and homosexual and bisexual men. In fact, Haitians are no more susceptible to AIDS than anyone else. Although the CDC removed Haitians from special scrutiny in 1985, the lucrative tourism on which so much of the country's economy was based was crippled. Along with tourism went much of the foreign business investment. Worst of all was the injury to the national pride. Suddenly Haiti was indicated as the source of AIDS in the western hemisphere.

104   What caused the misunderstanding was the discovery of a large number of Haitian men living in Miami with AIDS antibodies in their blood. They denied absolutely they were homosexual. But the CDC investigators did not know that homosexuality is the strongest taboo in Haiti and that no man would ever admit to it. Bisexuality, however, is not uncommon. Many married men and heterosexually oriented males will occasionally seek out other men for sex. Further, many, if not most, Haitian men visit female prostitutes from time to time. It is not difficult to see that once the virus was set loose in Haiti, the spread would be swift through both genders.

105   Exactly how the virus of AIDS arrived is not known. Could it have been brought home by the Cuban soldiers stationed in Angola and thence to Haiti, about fifty miles away? Could it have been passed on by the thousands of Haitians living in exile in Zaire, who later returned home or immigrated to the United States? Could it have come from the American and Canadian homosexual tourists, and, yes, even some US diplomats who have traveled to the island to have sex with impoverished Haitian men all too willing to sell themselves to feed their families? Throughout the international gay community Haiti was known as a good place to go for sex.

106   On a private tip from an official at the Ministry of Tourism, J-B and I drive to a town some fifty miles from Port-au-Prince. The hotel is owned by two Frenchmen who are out of the country, one of the staff tells us. He is a man of about thirty and clearly he is desperately ill. Tottering, short of breath, he shows us about the empty hotel. The furnishings are opulent and extreme—tiger skins on the wall, a live leopard in the garden, a bedroom containing a giant bathtub with gold faucets. Is it the heat of the day or the heat of my imagination that makes these walls echo with the painful cries of pederasty?

107   The hotel where we are staying is in Pétionville, the fashionable suburb of Port-au-Prince. It is the height of the season but there are no tourists, only a dozen or so French and American businessmen. The swimming pool is used once or twice a day by a single person. Otherwise, the water remains undisturbed until dusk, when the fruit bats come down to drink in midswoop. The hotel keeper is an American. He is eager to set me straight on Haiti.

108   "What did and should attract foreign investment is a combination of reliable weather, an honest and friendly populace, low wages, and multilingual managers."

109   "What spoiled it?"

110   "Political instability and a bad American press about AIDS." He pauses, then adds: "To which I hope you won't be contributing."

111   "What about just telling the truth?" I suggest.

112   "Look," he says, "there is no more danger of catching AIDS in Haiti than in New York or Santo Domingo. It is not where you are but what you do that counts." Agreeing, I ask if he had any idea that much of the tourism in Haiti during the past few decades was based on sex.

113   "No idea whatsoever. It was only recently that we discovered that that was the case."

114   "How is it that you hoteliers, restaurant owners, and the Ministry of Tourism did not know what *tout* Haiti knew?"

115   "Look. All I know is that this is a middle-class, family-oriented hotel. We don't allow guests to bring women, or for that matter men, into their rooms. If they did, we'd ask them to leave immediately."

116   At 5 a.m. the next day the telephone rings in my room. A Creole-accented male voice.

117   "Is the lady still with you, sir?"

118   "There is no lady here."

119   "In your room, sir, the lady I allowed to go up with a package?"

120   "There is no lady here, I tell you."

121   At 7 a.m. I stop at the front desk. The clerk is a young man.

122   "Was it you who called my room at five o'clock?"

123   "Sorry," he says with a smile. "It was a mistake, sir. I meant to ring the room next door to yours." Still smiling, he holds up his shushing finger.

124   Next to Dr. Pape, director of the AIDS clinic, Bernard Liautaud, a dermatologist, is the most knowledgeable Haitian physician on the subject of the epidemic. Together, the two men have published a dozen articles on AIDS in international medical journals. In our meeting they present me with statistics:

> There are more than one thousand documented cases of AIDS in Haiti, and as many as one hundred thousand carriers of the virus.
>
> Eighty-seven percent of AIDS is now transmitted heterosexually. While it is true that the virus was introduced via the bisexual community, that route has decreased to 10 percent or less.
>
> Sixty percent of the wives or husbands of AIDS patients tested positive for the antibody.
>
> Fifty percent of the prostitutes tested in the Port-au-Prince area are infected.
>
> Eighty percent of the men with AIDS have had contact with prostitutes.
>
> The projected number of active cases in four years is ten thousand. (Since my last visit, the Haitian Medical Association broke its silence on the epidemic by warning that one million of the country's six million people could be carriers by 1992.)

125   The two doctors have more to tell. "The crossing over of the plague from the homosexual to the heterosexual community will follow in the United States within two years. This, despite the hesitation to say so by those who fear to sow panic among your population. In Haiti, because bisexuality is more common, there was an early crossover into the general population. The trend, inevitably, is the same in the two countries."

126   "What is there to do, then?"

127 "Only education, just as in America. But here the Haitians reject the use of condoms. Only the men who are too sick to have sex are celibate."

128 "What is to be the end of it?"

129 "When enough heterosexuals of the middle and upper classes die, perhaps there will be the panic necessary for the people to change their sexual lifestyles."

130 This evening I leave Haiti. For two weeks I have fastened myself to this lovely fragile land like an ear pressed to the ground. It is a country to break a traveler's heart. It occurs to me that I have not seen a single jogger. Such a public expenditure of energy while everywhere else strength is ebbing—it would be obscene. In my final hours, I go to the Cathédral of Sainte Trinité, the inner walls of which are covered with murals by Haiti's most renowned artists. Here are all the familiar Bible stories depicted in naiveté and piety, and all in such an exuberance of color as to tax the capacity of the retina to receive it, as though all the vitality of Haiti had been turned to paint and brushed upon these walls. How to explain its efflorescence at a time when all else is lassitude and inertia? Perhaps one day the plague will be rendered in poetry, music, painting, but not now. Not now.

NOTES AND DISCUSSION

"A Mask on the Face of Death" is divided into several sections, each dealing with one "face" of AIDS in Haiti. The opening section shows one manifestation of the economic and cultural conditions that led to the rapid spread of AIDS in that nation. A key image here is that of the couple dancing: what appears at first glance to be beautiful, erotic, and graceful deteriorates into collapse and exhaustion. A later section, set in a hotel, also addresses the link between economics and AIDS, which is one of the essay's main themes.

Another important theme is the role of ignorance in the spread of AIDS: genuine ignorance, or lack of knowledge; deliberate ignorance, worn as a mask of indifference; and "ignorance" of the type displayed by the moralizing doctor/pastor, who remains culturally blinkered.

In other sections, Seltzer examines three hospitals that treat or refuse to treat the physical symptoms of AIDS. These passages are filled with startlingly graphic details. Another section looks at the effects of AIDS on the nation's reputation, and one near the end lists statistics regarding AIDS in Haiti.

Throughout, the "mask" appears as a tissue of lies, evasions, and denials, all prolonging the suffering and preserving the conditions that caused the problem in the first place. While the doctors at the clinic lack water to wash up, various poses and attitudes allow others to "wash their hands" of the responsibility to change the conditions or care for the infected.

STUDY QUESTIONS

For Discussion:

1. One outstanding feature of this essay is its reliance on direct dialogue. What effects— what tone or texture—do these passages bring to the piece? Consider the effect if Selzer had reported these conversations indirectly.

2. Examine Selzer's reply to the pastor at the Baptist Mission Hospital, and its effect. How does it indicate Selzer's overall tone and purpose? Given what he has said or implied elsewhere in the essay, why would Selzer profess his religion to be voodoo while in Haiti? Do cracks appear anywhere else in the "masks" worn by those who try to ignore the disease or the conditions behind its rapid spread?

For Writing:

1. Write a personal essay about a confrontation (friendly or otherwise), or interview someone you think has an interesting story to tell. In either case, use direct quotations to capture and convey the essence of the moment or of the personalities involved.

2. The spread of AIDS in Haiti rests on some of the same kinds of cultural myths that Ignatieff sees behind the atrocities in the Balkan states. Write a comparative essay, examining parallels in the cause-and-effect relationships between myths, attitudes, and actions in these seemingly different circumstances.

THE ROAD FROM RIO

David Suzuki

BIOGRAPHICAL NOTE

David Suzuki, an internationally famous Canadian environmentalist, began teaching zoology at UBC in 1969. He has hosted CBC's *Quirks and Quarks* on radio and *The Nature of Things* on television. His essays on science and the environment have appeared in *The Globe and Mail* and the *Toronto Star*, as well as in several books such as *Genethics* (1989), *Inventing the Future* (1989), *It's a Matter of Survival* (1990), and *Time to Change* (1994), from which the following essay is taken.

---

1   The earth summit in Rio in June 1992 can best be described by a metaphor. Picture the participants at the Earth Summit as passengers in a packed car heading for a brick wall at 150 kilometres an hour. Most of them ignored the danger because they were too busy arguing about where they wanted to sit. Some occupants did notice the wall but were still debating about whether it was a mirage, how far away it was, or when the car would reach it. A few were confident the car was so well built that it would suffer only minor damage when it plowed into the wall. Besides, they warned, slowing down or swerving too sharply would upset everyone inside the car.

2   There were those who argued vehemently that the wall was real and that everyone in the car was in great danger. Put on the brakes and turn the steering wheel to avoid a collision, they pleaded. Even if the wall did turn out to be an illusion, all that would be lost was a little time. The trouble was, those making this plea were all stuck in the trunk!

3   In order to understand the severity of this metaphor, you need some background. About six months before Rio, I watched a tape of a program of *The Nature of Things* that had been

made on the first major global conference on the environment in Stockholm in 1972. Many of the well-known figures in the environmental movement were featured—Paul Ehrlich, Margaret Mead, Barbara Ward, and Maurice Strong. It was devastating to watch because many of the issues of concern today—species extinction, overpopulation, global pollution—were raised eloquently then, yet remain and have worsened.

4   There have been major changes in our perspective on the environment in the twenty years since Stockholm. Back then, there was no sense of the central role of aboriginal people in the struggle to resolve the ecocrisis. New ecological problems like acid rain, ozone depletion, and global warming have come to our attention since 1972. There were few recognizable political leaders in attendance at Stockholm, and the role of the so-called Third World was marginal. That all changed at Rio.

5   In the two decades between Stockholm and Rio, new names became a part of our lexicon—Bhopal, Exxon Valdez, Chernobyl—while a host of issues made the news: chemicals spilled into the Rhine at Basel, poisoned Beluga whales in the Gulf of St. Lawrence, the burning rainforest of the Amazon, unswimmable beaches, record hot summers, the Arab oil embargo, Ethiopia, and the Gulf War. During the 1980s, poll after poll revealed that the environment was at the top of people's concerns. In 1987, the Brundtland Commission report, *Our Common Future*, documented in painstaking detail the perilous state of the Earth and popularized a phrase that has become the rallying cry of politicians and businesspeople alike—*sustainable development*.

6   Thus, the stage was set for Rio. Canadian businessman Maurice Strong, the secretary-general who had engineered Stockholm, was once again in command for Rio. Strong had been indefatigable, crisscrossing the planet, cajoling and urging world leaders to commit to attending. The fact that he is exquisitely well connected was a big help. He extracted promises from dozens of political leaders to attend the Earth Summit, and Rio was appropriate because all the contradictions of poverty and ecological damage could be seen. Rio was clearly going to be a big media event, a fact that raised expectations that it might signal a major shift from the environmentally destructive path we were on.

7   I was deeply skeptical about the possibility for real change, not out of cynicism about political motives but because of severe constraints on all politicians whether capitalist, socialist, or communist. Politicians are beholden to those on whom their power depends. In a democracy, that means people who vote. If the men and women who are trying to decide on the future of the planet must also keep the voters back home uppermost in mind, they will be limited in their ability to make changes. Our own species' chauvinistic needs also blind us to the fact that it is in our own long-term self-interest to maintain the requirements of planetary air, water, and soil for all ecosystems, animals, and plants. Furthermore, because they don't vote, children, the disenfranchised poor and oppressed, and all unborn generations are effectively without a voice. Only one delegation—the Dutch—had children as official delegates to Rio, yet children were the ones with most at stake in Rio. Thus, the political sphere of vision was far too short and parochial to allow serious action on global issues.

8   My pessimism was exacerbated by the fact that the Canadian government attempted to use Rio to project an image of environmental concern that its actual policies do not deserve. Prime Minister Brian Mulroney, like his friend U.S. President George Bush, had been a belated environmental convert who promised to show his commitment after the election of 1988. In that year before a fall election, Mulroney's environment minister, Tom McMillan, sponsored an international conference on the atmosphere in Toronto. Delegates

at that meeting, concerned with the reality and hazards of global warming, had supported a goal of a 20 percent reduction of the 1988 levels of CO_2 emissions within fifteen years.

9   Upon reelection, the Mulroney government commissioned a study to determine whether the Toronto target could be met and how much it would cost. That study, which has yet to be officially released but was leaked to the press, concluded that: 1) the target was achievable, 2) it would cost \$74 billion, and 3) it would result in a *net savings* of \$150 billion! To date, Canada, which has the highest per capita emission of CO_2 among industrialized countries, has made no serious commitment to reduce emissions. Studies on the feasibility and cost of CO_2 reduction by Australia, Sweden, and the United States have all come to the same conclusion and have met with similar political inaction.

10   Reduction of CO_2 emission is one of those rare instances of a win-win situation, whereby the general environment would improve and we would save massive amounts of money. Yet by the time of Rio, delegates of the United Nations Commission on the Environment and Development (UNCED) were barely able to get politicians to agree on a target of stabilization of 1990 levels of CO_2 emission by the year 2000! Only after watering this target down even further by removing any serious enforcements or inducements to meet it was UNCED able to extract a promise from President Bush to attend Rio.

11   The Canadian government contributed generously to the Preparatory Committee (PrepCom) and Rio conferences, thereby allowing Jean Charest, the environment minister, to pose as a significant player at Rio and an environmental good guy. Yet Canada is one of the worst producers of greenhouse gases, is a leading energy guzzler and garbage producer, protects only a small percentage of its wilderness, and has followed the American attitude to the environment. And Canada was, of course, not alone. Other countries also wrapped themselves in green rhetoric while congratulating themselves for attending the Earth Summit. It was a grand photo opportunity.

12   While my low expectations of Rio were based on my understanding of the political process, I knew that a number of excellent environmentalists and NGOs were very hopeful and active participants in the PrepCom process. I therefore agreed to attend meetings in Vancouver and Ottawa prior to the New York PrepCom, only to be horrified by the process.

13   Virtually any NGO that applied was accepted for accreditation by UNCED. The NGOs assumed this demonstrated an unprecedented openness and flexibility of UNCED. However, since they were subsidized by their own governments and UNCED, the NGOs were effectively co-opted into following the UNCED protocol and agenda while legitimating the entire process by their participation.

14   The extent of the compromise made by the NGOs is illustrated by the experience of a member of a British Columbia bioregional group who attended the New York PrepCom. In a session on forests, he criticized British Columbia's forest policies. Afterward, he was cornered by an official Canadian government delegate who told him that he'd better lay off the criticism if he wanted NGOs to continue receiving government money.

15   The worst part of the PrepCom process was the way the planet was chopped up into discrete categories of atmosphere, oceans, biodiversity, et cetera. These human bureaucratic subdivisions make no ecological sense, and they severely hamper any attempt to solve ecological problems. UNCED didn't attempt to define the problems within a holistic framework that recognizes the exquisite interconnectedness and interdependence of everything on Earth and our subservience to it. Only from such a perspective could a comprehensive strategy for action have been formed. At a meeting I attended in Vancouver before the New

York PrepCom, we were told to choose categories defined by UNCED and to deliberate on documents drafted within them. And so we environmentalists ended up like everyone else—fragmenting the way we looked at the world.

16   In all the meetings before and during the PrepComs, a process of "bracketing" was practised. Governments or groups objecting to any parts of the more than eleven hundred pages of text could put brackets around whole sections, paragraphs, sentences, or words to indicate what they wanted rewritten. In attempting to placate these groups, the organizers ensured that only the most innocuous statements ended up in the official documents.

17   Carlo Ripa di Meana, the environment commissioner of the European Community, said in 1992 that he believed the first major world environmental conference held in Stockholm in 1972 served "to put environmental issues on the international agenda, heighten awareness, and alert public opinion. The Rio meeting, on the other hand, was intended to make decisions, obtain precise and concrete commitments to counteract tendencies that are endangering life on the planet." However, when agreements such as the atmosphere treaty were deliberately watered down to satisfy President Bush, Ripa di Meana decided to boycott Rio and predicted that "By opting for hypocrisy, we will not just fail to save the Earth, but we will fail to grow." His prediction proved to be accurate: Rio didn't deliver the deep commitments needed.

18   Nothing illustrates the watering-down of documents better than the way UNCED dealt with the chasm that yawned between the "North" and the "South." The industrialized nations in the North were preoccupied with biodiversity, overpopulation, atmosphere change, and ocean pollution, while the priorities of the poor countries in the South were debt relief, technology transfer, and overconsumption by the rich countries. The "solution" was to horse-trade away the issues. Thus, overpopulation was dropped from the agenda in return for the deletion of overconsumption.

19   It seemed to me that the political vacuum in vision and leadership offered an immense opportunity for the NGOs, which truly represent the grass roots of the world. They could have taken the initiative by issuing an unflinching statement about the perilous state of the planet, calling all citizens of Earth to arms and setting out a concrete strategy to attack this great threat to all life on Earth. That's why I worked with members of the David Suzuki Foundation to draft the Declaration of Interdependence. . . . We hoped it would be an emotional, poetic, and inspiring statement of our place in the web of life and our responsibilities to it and to all future generations.

20   In Rio itself, most NGOs who were not accredited delegates were effectively denied access to the Earth Summit, where official delegates were fine-tuning the documents to be signed by the heads of state. Quartered 40 kilometres away from RioCentro, where the Earth Summit took place, the NGOs of the Global Forum were marginalized, since most reporters stayed put at RioCentro.

21   The Global Forum had all of the colour, excitement, and seriousness that the Earth Summit lacked. However, the very number of NGOs and the enormous size of their grounds precluded a focused vision and statement.

22   In the end, the inability of the US delegation to agree to a profound strategy to save the planet polarized the entire meeting. Even countries like Japan and Canada were able to appear progressive simply by their willingness to sign the watered-down treaties. The business community was a prominent presence among the delegates and lobby groups at the Earth Summit.

23   If anything sealed the judgement on Rio, it was the meeting in Munich two weeks later of the Group of Seven, the G-7, the richest nations on Earth. Not a word was mentioned

by the leaders about the Earth Summit or the environment! Their preoccupations were with the recession, GATT (General Agreement on Tariffs and Trade), and free trade.

24 When I interviewed Maurice Strong in December 1991, I asked what he thought the chances were of success in Rio. He knew how pessimistic I was and responded that we simply could not afford to fail because the future of the planet was in balance. "But if it does fail," he said realistically, "it must not be allowed to be a quiet failure and recede unnoticed from our memory."

25 I now think the Earth Summit was more than a failure. It was dangerous because it has been touted as a success. It did not issue a statement that pointed out the urgent need for a massive and immediate change. Instead, it reinforced all the notions about development, economics, and disparities in wealth that have proved so destructive. It is crystal clear that 80 percent of humanity is being forced to exist on 20 percent of the planet's resources while the 20 percent in the industrial world is using up the rightful heritage of all future generations. In spite of the obscene level of wealth and consumption in the rich countries, they continue to demand economic growth that can come only at the expense of the rest of humankind and the planet.

26 The main achievement of the Earth Summit was a 700-page document called *Agenda 21*. Although hailed as the strategy for responsible environmental change, it merely reinforces the gap between rich and poor. *Agenda 21* recommends an annual commitment of $600 billion for the environment, of which the South is asked to put up three-quarters, an amount representing 8 percent of their total GDP. On the other hand, the North, whose wealth has been achieved at the expense of the poor and whose activity is the major cause of global eco-degradation, reluctantly agreed to a target contribution representing 0.7 percent of their GDP. *Agenda 21* thus represents an attempt to make the South pay for the destructive actions of the North.

27 What is even more upsetting is the agenda's strategy for the developing world. Economic growth is repeated like a mantra by the industrialized countries as salvation for the poor countries. And how will this growth come about? Not by capping the profligate and unsustainable consumptive habits and growth of the rich countries, but by globalization of the marketplace and breaking down trade barriers.

28 But economics . . . is predicated on the assumption that air, water, soil, and biological diversity are an "externality" to the economic system. And since money grows faster than plants, animals, or ecosystems, economic "sense" dictates the rapid "liquidation" of forests, river systems, fish, et cetera, in the name of growth.

29 Furthermore, globalization of the marketplace, market value of products, and free trade maximize the reach of transnational corporations whose profit motives preclude concern for long-term sustainability of ecosystems or human communities. Yet globalization appears to be the direction supported by *Agenda 21*.

30 For me, Rio simply reinforced the conviction that expending effort to influence political and business leaders is not the way to bring about the profound shifts needed. The entire UNCED process is impotent in the face of the massive self-interests of politics and profit motives of private enterprise. Real change can come about only when the grass roots in all places understand to the core of their being that the life support processes—air, water, soil, and biodiversity—are fundamental and that human activity and organizations must conform to ecologically meaningful principles rather than attempting to force nature to conform to our priorities.

31   Poverty and eco-destruction are intertwined. The South's poverty exacerbates destruction of coral reefs and tropical rainforests and encourages large families. Their debt burden and cash flow must come from the North. For the North, greater energy efficiency, reduction in redundancy and waste packaging, eco-friendly products, et cetera, offer immediate benefits.

32   If we are to take a different road from Rio, the directions are clear. The rich nations of the world now hoard a disproportionate share of the world's wealth, consume far beyond a sustainable level, and are the major polluters and destroyers. It is our responsibility to cut back drastically while sharing efficient technologies and paying for family planning and debt reduction in the poor countries.

33   We can't afford to wait another twenty years for another opportunity to look in the mirror. If Rio did anything, it informed us that it's up to us and we have to begin now.

NOTES AND DISCUSSION

Suzuki opens this essay with an extended analogy that is intended to catch readers' attention and to both horrify and amuse them. An impending car crash is a horrifying thing, but Suzuki's depiction of the occupants' behaviour is amusing. Notice how Suzuki returns to this metaphor in the concluding paragraphs to create unity and a circular closure.

The body of the essay provides the background that is necessary for readers to fully appreciate his metaphor. Suzuki presents a great deal of information in a relatively small space: he compares and contrasts the state of the environment and environmental activism twenty years ago with their state in the present; he discusses the roles of certain individual activists, such as Maurice Strong, and politicians, such as George Bush, in environmental issues; he provides specific examples of attitudes and actions taken with regard to the environment; and he presents facts and figures on issues such as the need to reduce carbon dioxide levels.

Suzuki also carefully introduces his experts (the "characters" in his story), presents relevant background information that readers may not be aware of, and provides a sense of unity and focus through maintaining a personal and localized perspective on a bewilderingly complex international event. Nevertheless, at times readers may feel that they are lost in a sea of names, places, committees, and statistics. This abundance of initials and acronyms may, however, be part of Suzuki's point: there is too much organizing and talking, and not nearly enough doing.

STUDY QUESTIONS

For Discussion:

1. Suzuki's essay revolves around two related analogies: one to a journey or trip, the other to an impending car crash. How effective are these analogies? In particular, consider the effect of using an analogy to a *car* in an environmentalist essay.

2. Most of this essay is written in the first person singular: "I." However, at some points, Suzuki shifts to alternative points of view. Where do such shifts take place, and what is their intended effect? Suzuki's tone changes as the essay progresses. Identify three different tones and where they appear, and explain how they are achieved.

For Writing:

1. Write an essay that uses the metaphor of "the road" or "the journey" to suggest that a certain course of action be followed.

2. Examine some contemporary coverage of the 1992 Earth Summit, including official reports, press releases, and journalistic coverage. How do these materials compare and contrast with Suzuki's criticisms?

A MODEST PROPOSAL

For Preventing the Children of poor
People in *Ireland,* from being a
Burden to their Parents or Country;
and for making them beneficial
to the Publick.   Jonathan Swift

BIOGRAPHICAL NOTE

Jonathan Swift (1667–1745) was a popular essayist, pamphleteer, and satirist who is probably
best known as the author of *Gulliver's Travels* (1729). He was born in Dublin of English parents, and became a popular figure in Ireland for his support of Irish causes.

Written in the Year 1729.

1   It is a melancholy Object to those, who walk through this great Town, or travel in the
Country; when they see the *Streets*, the *Roads*, and *Cabbin*-doors crowded with *Beggars*
of the Female Sex, followed by three, four, or six Children, *all in Rags*, and importuning every
Passenger for an Alms. These *Mothers*, instead of being able to work for their honest
Livelyhood, are forced to employ all their Time in stroling to beg Sustenance for their *help-
less Infants*; who, as they grow up, either turn *Thieves* for want of Work; or leave their *dear
Native Country, to fight for the Pretender in* Spain, or sell themselves to the *Barbadoes*.

2   I think it is agreed by all Parties, that this prodigious Number of Children in the Arms,
or on the Backs, or at the *Heels* of their *Mothers*, and frequently of their *Fathers*, is *in the
present deplorable State of the Kingdom*, a very great additional Grievance; and therefore,
whoever could find out a fair, cheap, and easy Method of making these Children sound and
useful Members of the Commonwealth, would deserve so well of the Publick, as to have his
Statue set up for a Preserver of the Nation.

3   But my Intention is very far from being confined to provide only for the Children of *professed Beggars*: It is of a much greater Extent, and shall take in the whole Number of Infants
in a certain Age, who are born of Parents, in effect as little able to support them, as those who
demand our Charity in the Streets.

4   As to my own Part, having turned my Thoughts for many Years, upon this important
Subject, and maturely weighed the several *Schemes of other Projectors*, I have always found

them grosly mistaken in their Computation. It is true a Child, *just dropt from its Dam*, may be supported by her Milk, for a Solar Year with little other Nourishment; at most not above the Value of two Shillings; which the Mother may certainly get, or the Value in Scraps, by her lawful Occupation of Begging: And, it is exactly at one Year old, that I propose to provide for them in such a Manner, as, instead of being a Charge upon their *Parents*, or the *Parish*, or *wanting Food and Raiment* for the rest of their Lives; they shall, on the contrary, contribute to the Feeding, and partly to the Cloathing, of many Thousands.

5   There is likewise another great Advantage in my *Scheme*, that it will prevent those *voluntary Abortions*, and that horrid Practice of *Women murdering their Bastard Children*; alas! too frequent among us; sacrificing the *poor innocent Babes*, I doubt, more to avoid the Expence than the Shame; which would move Tears and Pity in the most Savage and inhuman Breast.

6   The Number of Souls in *Ireland* being usually reckoned one Million and a half; of these I calculate there may be about Two hundred Thousand Couple whose Wives are Breeders; from which Number I subtract thirty thousand Couples, who are able to maintain their own Children; although I apprehend there cannot be so many, under *the present Distresses of the Kingdom*; but this being granted, there will remain an Hundred and Seventy Thousand Breeders. I again subtract Fifty Thousand, for those Women who miscarry, or whose Children die by Accident, or Disease, within the Year. There only remain an Hundred and Twenty Thousand Children of poor Parents, annually born: The Question therefore is, How this Number shall be reared, and provided for? Which, as I have already said, under the present situation of Affairs, is utterly impossible, by all the Methods hitherto proposed: For we can *neither employ them in Handicraft or Agriculture*; we neither build Houses, (I mean in the Country) nor cultivate Land: They can very seldom pick up a Livelyhood *by Stealing* until they arrive at six Years old; except where they are of towardly Parts; although, I confess, they learn the Rudiments much earlier; during which Time, they can, however, be properly looked upon only as *Probationers*; as I have been informed by a principal Gentleman in the County of Cavan, who protested to me, that he never knew above one or two Instances under the Age of six, even in a Part of the Kingdom *so renowned for the quickest Proficiency in that Art*.

7   I am assured by our Merchants, that a Boy or a Girl before twelve Years old, is no saleable Commodity; and even when they come to this Age, they will not yield above Three Pounds, or Three Pounds and half a Crown at most, on the Exchange; which cannot turn to Account either to the Parents or the Kingdom; the Charge of Nutriment and Rags, having been at least four Times that Value.

8   I shall now therefore humbly propose my own Thoughts; which I hope will not be liable to the least Objection.

9   I have been assured by a very knowing *American* of my Acquaintance in *London*; that a young healthy Child, well nursed, is, at a Year old, a most delicious, nourishing, and wholesome Food; whether *Stewed, Roasted, Baked,* or *Boiled*; and, I make no doubt, that it will equally serve in a *Fricasie*, or *Ragoust*.

10   I do therefore humbly offer it to *publick Consideration*, that of the Hundred and Twenty Thousand Children, already computed, Twenty thousand may be reserved for Breed; whereof only one Fourth Part to be Males; which is more than we allow to *Sheep, black Cattle,* or *Swine*; and my Reason is, that these Children are seldom the Fruits of Marriage, *a Circumstance not much regarded by our Savages*; therefore, *one Male* will be sufficient to serve *four Females*. That the remaining Hundred thousand, may, at a Year old, be offered in Sale to the *Persons of Quality* and *Fortune*, through the Kingdom; always advising the

Mother to let them suck plentifully in the last Month, so as to render them plump, and fat for a good Table. A Child will make two Dishes at an Entertainment for Friends; and when the Family dines alone, the fore or hind Quarter will make a reasonable Dish; and seasoned with a little Pepper or Salt, will be very good Boiled on the fourth Day, especially in *Winter*.

11   I have reckoned upon a Medium, that a Child just born will weigh Twelve Pounds; and in a solar Year, if tolerably nursed, encreaseth to twenty eight Pounds.

12   I grant this Food will be somewhat dear, and therefore very *proper for Landlords*; who, as they have already devoured most of the Parents, seem to have the best Title to the Children.

13   Infants' Flesh will be in Season throughout the Year; but more plentiful in *March*, and a little before and after: For we are told by a grave* Author, an eminent *French* Physician, that *Fish being a prolifick Dyet*, there are more Children born in *Roman Catholick Countries* about Nine Months after *Lent*, than at any other Season: Therefore reckoning a Year after *Lent*, the Markets will be more glutted than usual; because the Number of *Popish Infants*, is, at least, three to one in this Kingdom; and therefore it will have one other Collateral Advantage, by lessening the Number of *Papists* among us.

14   I have already computed the Charge of nursing a Beggar's Child (in which List I reckon all *Cottagers, Labourers,* and Four fifths of the *Farmers*) to be about two Shillings *per Annum*, Rags included; and I believe, no Gentleman would repine to give Ten Shillings for the *Carcase of a good fat Child*; which, as I have said, will make four Dishes of excellent nutritive Meat, when he hath only some particular Friend, or his own Family, to dine with him. Thus the Squire will learn to be a good Landlord, and grow popular among his Tenants; the Mother will have Eight Shillings net Profit, and be fit for Work until she produceth another Child.

15   Those who are more thrifty (*as I must confess the Times require*) may flay the Carcase; the Skin of which, artificially dressed, will make admirable *Gloves for Ladies*, and *Summer Boots for fine Gentlemen*.

16   As to our City of *Dublin*; Shambles may be appointed for this Purpose, in the most convenient Parts of it; and Butchers we may be assured will not be wanting; although I rather recommend buying the Children alive, and dressing them hot from the Knife, as we do *roasting Pigs*.

17   A very worthy Person, *a true Lover of his Country*, and whose Virtues I highly esteem, was lately pleased, in discoursing on this Matter, to offer a Refinement upon my Scheme. He said, that many Gentlemen of this Kingdom, having of late destroyed their Deer; he conceived, that the Want of Venison might be well supplied by the Bodies of young Lads and Maidens, not exceeding fourteen Years of Age, nor under twelve; so great a Number of both Sexes in every County being now ready to starve, for Want of Work and Service: And these to be disposed of by their Parents, if alive, or otherwise by their nearest Relations. But with due Deference to so excellent a Friend, and so deserving a Patriot, I cannot be altogether in his Sentiments. For as to the Males, my *American* Acquaintance assured me from frequent Experience, that their Flesh was generally tough and lean, like that of our School-boys, by continual Exercise, and their Taste disagreeable; and to fatten them would not answer the Charge. Then, as to the Females, it would, I think, with humble Submission, *be a Loss to the Publick*, because they soon would become Breeders themselves: And besides it is not improbable, that some scrupulous People might be apt to censure such a Practice (although indeed very unjustly) as a little bordering upon Cruelty; which, I confess, hath always been with me the strongest Objection against any Project, how well soever intended.

---

*   Rabelais.

18   But in order to justify my Friend; he confessed, that this Expedient was put into his Head by the famous *Salmanaazor*, a Native of the Island *Formosa*, who came from thence to *London*, above twenty Years ago, and in Conversation told my Friend, that in his Country, when any young Person happened to be put to Death, the Executioner sold the Carcase to *Persons of Quality*, as a prime Dainty; and that, in his Time, the Body of a plump Girl of fifteen, who was crucified for an Attempt to poison the Emperor, was sold to his Imperial *Majesty's prime Minister of State*, and other great *Mandarins* of the Court, *in Joints from the Gibbet*, at Four hundred Crowns. Neither indeed can I deny, that if the same Use were made of several plump young girls in this Town, who, without one single Groat to their Fortunes, cannot stir Abroad without a Chair, and appear at the *Play-house*, and *Assemblies* in foreign Fineries, which they never will pay for; the Kingdom would not be the worse.

19   Some Persons of a desponding Spirit are in great Concern about that vast Number of Poor People, who are Aged, Diseased, or Maimed; and I have been desired to employ my Thoughts what Course may be taken, to ease the Nation of so grievous an Incumbrance. But I am not in the least Pain upon that Matter; because it is very well known, that they are every Day *dying*, and *rotting*, by *Cold* and *Famine*, and *Filth*, and *Vermine*, as fast as can be reasonably expected. And as to the younger Labourers, they are now in almost as hopeful a Condition: They cannot get Work, and consequently pine away for Want of Nourishment, to a Degree, that if at any Time they are accidentally hired to common Labour, they have not Strength to perform it; and thus the Country, and themselves, are in a fair Way of being soon delivered from the Evils to come.

20   I have too long digressed; and therefore shall return to my Subject. I think the Advantages by the Proposal which I have made, are obvious, and many, as well as of the highest Importance.

21   For, *First*, as I have already observed, it would greatly lessen the *Number of Papists*, with whom we are yearly overrun; being the principal Breeders of the Nation, as well as our most dangerous Enemies; and who stay at home on Purpose, with a Design to *deliver the Kingdom to the Pretender*; hoping to take their Advantage by the *Absence of so many good Protestants*, who have chosen rather to leave their Country, than stay at home, and pay Tithes against their Conscience, to an idolatrous *Episcopal Curate*.

22   Secondly, The poorer Tenants will have something valuable of their own, which, by Law, may be made liable to Distress, and help to pay their Landlord's Rent; their Corn and Cattle being already seized, and *Money a Thing unknown*.

23   Thirdly, Whereas the Maintenance of an Hundred Thousand Children, from two Years old, and upwards, cannot be computed at less than ten Shillings a Piece *per Annum*, the Nation's Stock will be thereby encreased Fifty Thousand Pounds *per Annum*; besides the Profit of a new Dish, introduced to the Tables of all *Gentlemen of Fortune* in the Kingdom, who have any Refinement in Taste; and the Money will circulate among ourselves, the Goods being entirely of our own Growth and Manufacture.

24   Fourthly, The constant Breeders, besides the Gain of Eight Shillings *Sterling per Annum*, by the Sale of their Children, will be rid of the Charge of maintaining them after the first Year.

25   Fifthly, This Food would likewise bring great *Custom to Taverns*, where the Vintners will certainly be so prudent, as to procure the best Receipts for dressing it to Perfection; and consequently, have their Houses frequented by all the *fine Gentlemen*, who justly value themselves upon their Knowledge in good Eating; and a skilful Cook, who understands how to oblige his Guests, will contrive to make it as expensive as they please.

26 Sixthly, This would be a great Inducement to Marriage, which all wise Nations have either encouraged by Rewards, or enforced by Laws and Penalties. It would encrease the Care and Tenderness of Mothers towards their Children, when they were sure of a Settlement for Life, to the poor Babes, provided in some Sort by the Publick, to their annual Profit instead of Expence. We should soon see an honest Emulation among the married Women, *which of them could bring the fattest Child to the Market*. Men would become as *fond* of their Wives, during the Time of their Pregnancy, as they are now of their *Mares* in Foal, their *Cows* in Calf, or *Sows* when they are ready to farrow; nor offer to beat or kick them, (as it is too *frequent* a Practice) for fear of a Miscarriage.

27 Many other Advantages might be enumerated. For instance, the Addition of some Thousand Carcasses in our Exportation of barrelled Beef: The Propagation of *Swines Flesh*, and Improvement in the Art of making good *Bacon*; so much wanted among us by the great Destruction of *Pigs*, too frequent at our Tables, and are no way comparable in Taste, or Magnificence, to a well-grown fat yearling Child; which, roasted whole, will make a considerable Figure at a *Lord Mayor's Feast*, or any other publick Entertainment. But this, and many others, I omit; being studious of Brevity.

28 Supposing that one Thousand Families in this City, would be constant Customers for Infants Flesh; besides others who might have it at *merry Meetings*, particularly *Weddings and Christenings*; I compute that *Dublin* would take off, annually, about Twenty Thousand Carcasses; and the rest of the Kingdom (where probably they will be sold somewhat cheaper) the remaining Eighty Thousand.

29 I can think of no one Objection, that will possibly be raised against this Proposal; unless it should be urged, that the Number of People will be thereby much lessened in the Kingdom. This I freely own; and it was indeed one principal Design in offering it to the World. I desire the Reader will observe, that I calculate my Remedy *for this one individual Kingdom* of Ireland, *and for no other that ever was, is, or I think ever can be upon Earth*. Therefore, let no man talk to me of other Expedients: *Of taxing our Absentees at five Shillings a Pound: Of using neither Cloaths, nor Houshold Furniture except what is of our own Growth and Manufacture: Of utterly rejecting the Materials and Instruments that promote foreign Luxury: Of curing the Expensiveness of Pride, Vanity, Idleness, and Gaming in our Women: Of introducing a Vein of Parsimony, Prudence, and Temperance: Of learning to love our Country, wherein we differ even from* Laplanders, *and the Inhabitants of* Topinamboo: *Of quitting our Anomosities, and Factions; nor act any longer like the Jews, who were murdering one another at the very Moment their City was taken: Of being a little cautious not to sell our Country and Consciences for nothing: Of teaching Landlords to have, at least, one Degree of Mercy towards their Tenants*. Lastly, *Of putting a Spirit of Honesty, Industry, and Skill into our Shop-keepers; who, if a Resolution could now be taken to buy only our native Goods, would immediately unite to cheat and exact upon us in the Price, the Measure, and the Goodness; nor could ever yet be brought to make one fair Proposal of just Dealing, though often and earnestly invited to it*.

30 Therefore I repeat, let no Man talk to me of these and the like Expedients; till he hath, at least, a Glimpse of Hope, that there will ever be some hearty and sincere Attempt to put *them in Practice*.

31 But, as to my self; having been wearied out for many Years with offering vain, idle, visionary Thoughts; and at length utterly despairing of Success, I fortunately fell upon this Proposal; which, as it is wholly new, so it hath something *solid* and *real*, of no Expence, and little Trouble, full in our own Power; and whereby we can incur no Danger in *disobliging*

England: For this Kind of Commodity will not bear Exportation; the Flesh being of too tender a Consistence, to admit a long Continuance in Salt; *although, perhaps, I could name a Country, which would be glad to eat up our whole Nation without it.*

32   After all, I am not so violently bent upon my own Opinion, as to reject any Offer proposed by wise Men, which shall be found equally innocent, cheap, easy, and effectual. But before something of that Kind shall be advanced, in Contradiction to my Scheme, and offering a better; I desire the Author, or Authors, will be pleased maturely to consider two Points. *First*, As Things now stand, how they will be able to find Food and Raiment, for a Hundred Thousand useless Mouths and Backs? And *secondly*, There being a round Million of Creatures in human Figure, throughout this Kingdom; whose whole Subsistence, put into a common Stock, would leave them in Debt two Millions of Pounds *Sterling*; adding those, who are Beggars by Profession, to the Bulk of Farmers, Cottagers, and Labourers, with their Wives and Children, who are Beggars in Effect; I desire those Politicians, who dislike by Overture, and may perhaps be so bold to attempt an Answer, that they will first ask the Parents of these Mortals, Whether they would not, at this Day, think it a great Happiness to have been sold for Food at a Year old, in the Manner I prescribe; and thereby have avoided such a perpetual Scene of Misfortunes, as they have since gone through; by the *Oppression of Landlords*; the Impossibility of paying Rent, without Money or Trade; the Want of common Sustenance, with neither House nor Cloaths, to cover them from the Inclemencies of Weather; and the most inevitable Prospect of intailing the like, or greater Miseries upon their Breed for ever.

33   I profess, in the Sincerity of my Heart, that I have not the least personal Interest, in endeavouring to promote this necessary Work; having no other Motive than the *publick Good of my Country, by advancing our Trade, providing for Infants, relieving the Poor, and giving some Pleasure to the Rich*. I have no Children, by which I can propose to get a single Penny; the youngest being nine Years old, and my Wife past Child-bearing.

NOTES AND DISCUSSION

Swift's decidedly *immodest* proposal has shocked people for two and a half centuries, especially those readers who miss its ironies. In this essay, Swift invents an ironic persona whose attitudes and methods of reasoning he wants to undermine. His proposal attacks greedy and unreasonable people who adopt the language and techniques of reason to express unreasonable attitudes. The mad proposal presented in this essay reduces human lives to distorted statistics, and to comically gross miscalculations (for instance, the average birth weight of infants is considerably less than his estimated twelve pounds). The essay also uses the language and logic of animal husbandry and commodification, and a "bottom-line" thinking that is painfully familiar even today.

Much of Swift's posing and assumed sympathy are directed towards absentee English landlords, who had "devoured" the wealth and substance of their holdings in Ireland, ignoring the effects of their destructive attitudes and practices on the people of that country. The essay argues implicitly that poor Irish people would be better off if they were treated as animals; at least then they would be perceived as having some "value." Swift may also be aiming part of his criticism at the Irish themselves for not taking personal or collective responsibility for their attitudes and behaviours.

Finally, note Swift's classic argumentation style: he introduces a public issue and problem, establishes its scope, proposes a solution, presents supporting arguments, poses a possible objection and refutes it, and then returns to the original proposal as the only logical alternative. With characteristic irony, the alternate proposals that Swift dismisses in the important paragraph 29 are ones that he himself had advanced elsewhere and that had been attacked as unreasonable and unworkable.

STUDY QUESTIONS

For Discussion:

1. Many readers over the years have been fooled by this piece. How does the ironic persona both help and hinder Swift's purpose in this essay?
2. Consider how and why Swift uses the testimonials and advice of foreign "experts."

For Writing:

1. Examine the individual and collective importance of the language and terminology of economics, scientific calculation, and animal husbandry as satirical techniques. Write an analytical paragraph about how Swift's language tries to hide insanely inhumane attitudes behind a mask of social concern.
2. Compare Swift's satirical persona and related shock tactics here with Douglas Hofstadter's in "A Person Paper on Purity in Language." Consider such matters as tone of voice, and the desire to appear "reasonable" while making unsettling and deliberately offensive claims and suggestions.

THE PONDS

Henry David Thoreau

BIOGRAPHICAL NOTE

Henry David Thoreau (1817–62) was a philosopher, essayist, naturalist, poet, and a "transcendentalist." Transcendentalism, a loosely organized intellectual movement, was one of several American manifestations of romanticism. Thoreau is best known and loved for *Walden* (1854), a long essay recounting two years spent living in the woods beside Walden Pond. This piece is part of a chapter from *Walden* entitled "The Ponds."

---

1   The scenery of Walden is on a humble scale, and, though very beautiful, does not approach to grandeur, nor can it much concern one who has not long frequented it or lived by its shore; yet this pond is so remarkable for its depth and purity as to merit a particular description. It is a clear and deep green well, half a mile long and a mile and three quarters in circumference, and contains about sixty-one and a half acres; a perennial spring in the midst of pine and oak woods, without any visible inlet or outlet except by the clouds and evaporation. The surrounding hills rise abruptly from the water to the height of forty to eighty feet, though on the south-east and east they attain to about one hundred and one hundred and fifty feet respectively, within a quarter and a third of a mile. They are exclusively woodland. All our Concord waters have two colors at least, one when viewed at a distance, and another, more proper, close at hand. The first depends more on the light, and follows the sky. In clear weather, in summer, they appear blue at a little distance, especially if agitated, and at a great distance all appear alike. In stormy weather they are sometimes of a dark slate color. The sea, however, is said to be blue one day and green another without any perceptible change in the atmosphere. I have seen our river, when, the landscape being covered with snow, both water and ice were almost as green as grass. Some consider blue "to be the color of pure water, whether liquid or solid." But, looking directly down into our waters from a boat, they are seen to be of very different colors. Walden is blue at one time and green at another, even from the same point of view. Lying between the earth and the heavens, it partakes of the color of both. Viewed from the hill-top it reflects the color of the sky, but near at hand it is of a yellowish tint next the shore where you can see the sand, then a light green, which gradually deepens to a uniform dark green in the body of the pond. In some lights, viewed even from a hill-top, it is of a vivid green next the shore. Some have referred this to the reflection of the verdure; but it is equally green there against the railroad sand-bank, and in the spring, before the leaves are expanded, and it may be simply the result of the prevailing blue mixed with the yellow of the sand. Such is the color of its iris. This is that portion, also, where in the spring, the ice being warmed by the heat of the sun reflected from the bottom, and also transmitted through the earth, melts first and forms a narrow canal about the still frozen middle. Like the rest of our waters, when much agitated, in clear weather, so that the surface of the waves may reflect the sky at the right angle, or because there is more light mixed with it, it appears at a little distance of a darker blue than the sky itself; and at such a time, being on its surface, and looking with divided vision, so as to see the reflection, I have discerned a matchless and indescribable light blue, such as watered or changeable silks and sword blades suggest, more cerulean than the sky itself, alternating with the original dark green on the opposite sides of the waves, which last appeared but muddy in comparison. It is a vitreous greenish blue, as I remember it, like those patches of the winter sky seen though cloud vistas in the west before sundown. Yet a single glass of its water held up to the light is as colorless as an equal quantity of air. It is well known that a large plate of glass will have a green tint, owing, as the makers say, to its "body," but a small piece of the same will be colorless. How large a body of Walden water would be required to reflect a green tint I have never proved. The water of our river is black or a very dark brown to one looking directly down on it, and, like that of most ponds, imparts to the body of one bathing in it a yellowish tinge; but this water is of such crystalline purity that the body of the bather appears of an alabaster whiteness, still more unnatural, which, as the limbs are magnified and distorted withal, produces a monstrous effect, making fit studies for a Michael Angelo.

2   The water is so transparent that the bottom can easily be discerned at the depth of twenty-five or thirty feet. Paddling over it, you may see many feet beneath the surface the schools of perch and shiners, perhaps only an inch long, yet the former easily distinguished by their transverse bars, and you think that they must be ascetic fish that find a subsistence there. Once, in the winter, many years ago, when I had been cutting holes through the ice in order to catch pickerel, as I stepped ashore I tossed my axe back on to the ice, but, as if some evil genius had directed it, it slid four or five rods directly into one of the holes, where the water was twenty-five feet deep. Out of curiosity, I lay down on the ice and looked through the hole, until I saw the axe a little on one side, standing on its head, with its helve erect and gently swaying to and fro with the pulse of the pond; and there it might have stood erect and swaying till in the course of time the handle rotted off, if I had not disturbed it. Making another hole directly over it with an ice chisel which I had, and cutting down the longest birch which I could find in the neighborhood with my knife, I made a slip-noose, which I attached to its end, and, letting it down carefully, passed it over the knob of the handle, and drew it by a line along the birch, and so pulled the axe out again.

3   The shore is composed of a belt of smooth rounded white stones like paving stones, excepting one or two short sand beaches, and is so steep that in many places a single leap will carry you into water over your head; and were it not for its remarkable transparency, that

would be the last to be seen of its bottom till it rose on the opposite side. Some think it is bottomless. It is nowhere muddy, and a casual observer would say that there were no weeds at all in it; and of noticeable plants, except in the little meadows recently overflowed, which do not properly belong to it, a closer scrutiny does not detect a flag nor a bulrush, nor even a lily, yellow or white, but only a few small heart-leaves and potamogetons, and perhaps a water-target or two; all which however a bather might not perceive; and these plants are clean and bright like the element they grow in. The stones extend a rod or two into the water, and then the bottom is pure sand, except in the deepest parts, where there is usually a little sediment, probably from the decay of the leaves which have been wafted on to it so many successive falls, and a bright green weed is brought up on anchors even in midwinter.

4   We have one other pond just like this, White Pond in Nine Acre Corner, about two and a half miles westerly; but, though I am acquainted with most of the ponds within a dozen miles of this centre, I do not know a third of this pure and well-like character. Successive nations perchance have drank at, admired, and fathomed it, and passed away, and still its water is green and pellucid as ever. Not an intermitting spring! Perhaps on that spring morning when Adam and Eve were driven out of Eden Walden Pond was already in existence, and even then breaking up in a gentle spring rain accompanied with mist and a southerly wind, and covered with myriads of ducks and geese, which had not heard of the fall, when still such pure lakes sufficed them. Even then it had commenced to rise and fall, and had clarified its waters and colored them of the hue they now wear, and obtained a patent of heaven to be the only Walden Pond in the world and distiller of celestial dews. Who knows in how many unremembered nations' literatures this has been the Castalian Fountain? or what nymphs presided over it in the Golden Age? It is a gem of the first water which Concord wears in her coronet.

NOTES AND DISCUSSION

Thoreau begins this description of Walden Pond with a modest disclaimer: "The scenery of Walden is on a humble scale," he writes, "and, though very beautiful, does not approach to grandeur." While this may be true, his description, in its meticulous attention to detail, itself approaches grandeur. He first describes the physical dimensions of the pond, and then studies the colour of the water during various times of day and weather conditions. Thoreau's task here is a daunting one: he has set out to describe fully something that undoubtedly has colour, but that, when viewed up close, is utterly colourless. The water, he notes, "is so transparent that the bottom can easily be discerned at the depth of twenty-five or thirty feet." The result is the impression that, while the water of Walden Pond is in fact colourless, Walden Pond itself has colour, flashing green and blue. "It is," Thoreau writes, "a gem of the first water which Concord wears in her coronet."

Notice that Thoreau constructs his description from varying perspectives and during different seasons. He also compares and contrasts Walden with other bodies of water. Part of the success of Thoreau's technique of description lies in showing what Walden is *not*, as well as what it is.

STUDY QUESTIONS

For Discussion:

1. Notice the way Thoreau begins this piece by denying Walden's pretence to "grandeur," yet ends with mythic and biblical references. What is the effect of making these very different claims?

2. This essay is almost pure description, yet embedded in the middle of it is a short narrative about a lost axe. What is the effect of this short narrative? Why has Thoreau placed it where he has?

For Writing:

1. Annie Dillard's careful descriptions are often compared to those of Thoreau. On the basis of language, tone, and detail, compare and contrast Dillard's treatment of Hollins Pond in "Living Like Weasels" to this description of Walden.

2. Thoreau lived for two years beside the pond that he describes so carefully here. Write a description of something that is important to you: a building, a street, your room. Be sure to depict its various aspects and keep in mind factors such as weather, light, and perspective.

GHOSTS IN THE MACHINE

Sherry Turkle

BIOGRAPHICAL NOTE

Sherry Turkle is a professor of the sociology of science at the Massachusetts Institute of Technology (MIT). Her books include *Psychoanalytic Politics: Jacques Lacan and Freud's French Revolution* (1978), *The Second Self: Computers and the Human Spirit* (1984), and *Life on the Screen: Identity in the Age of the Internet* (1995), in which this essay appears.

---

1   "Dreams and beasts are two keys by which we are to find out the secrets of our own nature," Ralph Waldo Emerson wrote in his diary in 1832. "They are our test objects." Emerson was prescient. In the decades that followed, Freud and his heirs would measure human rationality against the dream. Darwin and his heirs would measure human nature against nature itself—the world of beasts seen as human forebears and kin. Now, at the end of the twentieth century, a third test object is emerging: the computer.

2   Like dreams and beasts, the computer stands on the margins of human life. It is a mind that is not yet a mind. It is an object, ultimately a mechanism, but it acts, interacts, and seems, in a certain sense, to know. As such, it confronts us with an uneasy sense of kinship. After all, people also act, interact, and seem to know, yet ultimately they are made of matter and programmed DNA. We think we can think. But can *it* think? Could it ever be said to be alive?

3   In the past ten years I have talked with more than a thousand people, nearly three hundred of them children, about their experiences with computers. In a sense I have interrogated the computers as well. In the late 1970s and early 1980s, when a particular computer and its

program seemed disconcertingly lifelike, many people reassured themselves by saying something like, "It's just a machine." The personal computers of the time gave material support to that idea; they offered direct access to their programming code and invited users to get "under the hood" and do some tinkering. Even if users declined to do so, they often dismissed computing as mere calculation. Like the nineteenth-century Romantics who rebelled against Enlightenment rationalism by declaring the heart more human than the mind, computer users distinguished their machines from people by saying that people had emotion and were not programmed.

4   In the mid-1980s, computer designers met that romantic reaction with increasingly "romantic machines." The Apple Macintosh, introduced in 1984, gave no hint of its programming code or inner mechanism. Instead, it "spoke" to users through icons and dialogue boxes, encouraging users to engage it in conversations. A new way of talking about both people and objects was emerging: machines were being reconfigured as psychological objects, people as living machines. Today computer science appropriates biological concepts, and human biology is recast in terms of a code; people speak of "reprogramming" their personalities with Prozac and share intimate secrets with a computer psychotherapy program called DEPRESSION 2.0. We have reached a cultural watershed.

5   The modern history of science has been punctuated with affronts to humanity's view of itself as central to, yet profoundly discontinuous with, the rest of the universe. Just as people learned to make peace with the heresies of Copernicus, Darwin, and Freud, they are gradually coming to terms with the idea of machine intelligence. Although noisy skirmishes have erupted recently at the boundary between people and machines, an uneasy truce seems to be in effect. Often without realizing it, people have become accustomed to talking to technology—and sometimes in the most literal sense.

6   In 1950 the English mathematician Alan M. Turing proposed what he called the Imitation Game as a model for thinking about whether a machine was intelligent. In the Imitation Game a person uses a computer terminal to pose questions, on any subject, to an unidentified interlocutor, which might be another person or a computer. If the person posing questions cannot say whether he or she was talking to a person or a computer, the computer is said to be intelligent. Turing predicted that by the year 2000, a five-minute conversation with a computer would fool an average questioner into thinking it was human 70 percent of the time. The Turing test became a powerful image for marking off the boundary between people and machines; a formal contest now offers a $100,000 prize for the first program to pass the test.

7   Programs now exist that can pass a version of the Turing test that limits conversation to restricted subject domains. Yet the test has begun to seem less relevant. What seems most urgent now is not whether to call the machines or programs intelligent, but how to behave around them. Put otherwise: Once you have made a pass at an on-line robot, can you ever look at computers again in the same old way?

8   Today, like hundreds of thousands of other people, I use my personal computer and modem to join online communities known as MUDs (short for "multiple-user domains" or "multi-user dungeons"). Anonymously I travel their rooms and public spaces (a bar, a lounge, a hot tub) exchanging typed messages with users I meet. I pose as one of several characters, some not of my biological gender, who have social and sexual encounters with other characters. Some characters I meet in a MUD may be personas like mine—fragments of their creators' personalities, perhaps suppressed or neglected in the real world, given fuller life on the screen. Others may not be human at all. In some MUDs, computer programs called bots present

themselves as people. They log onto games as if they were characters, help with navigation, pass messages, and create a background atmosphere of animation. When you enter a virtual cafe, for example, a waiter bot approaches, asks if you want a drink, and delivers it with a smile.

9   One of the most accomplished bots resides on a computer in Pittsburgh. Her creator, the computer scientist Michael L. Mauldin of Carnegie Mellon University, calls her Julia. Players talk to Julia (via typing) and she talks to them; they gesture to Julia (again via typing) and she gestures back. Julia looks for particular strings of characters in messages typed to her, then matches the input with a set of outputs she presents in random, nonrepeating sequences. Julia's conversational skills rely for the most part on the clever enumeration and grouping of those matching patterns and on her use of humour.

10   When I asked Julia to describe herself, she said she is a female, five feet one inch tall, weighs 123 pounds, has frizzy blonde hair. But another character might have gotten a somewhat different description. Like "real" MUD dwellers, Julia can recreate herself in the virtual world.

11   Among other things, Julia can chat about hockey, keep track of players' whereabouts, gossip, and flirt. She can profess ignorance, change the subject if confused, quote news stories drawn from computer data bases or admit to a full complement of human vanities and frailties. When Julia is put into Turing-contest mode, she can even simulate human typing—typographical errors and all.

12   Julia's sarcastic non sequiturs, Mauldin says, give her enough apparent personality to fool some players who "make a first assumption that other players are people too." Even when MUD users do question whether Julia is a human, she can sometimes wriggle out of suspicion:

13   ROBYN: Julia, are you a human?
        JULIA: Is the Pope Polish?
        ROBYN: Yes, Julia, but are you human?
        JULIA: Julia winks at Robyn.
        ROBYN: Julia, are you a computer?
        JULIA: Julia is offended by Robyn's suggestion.
        ROBYN: Julia, are you a woman?
        JULIA: I am female.
        ROBYN: And Julia, are you a human?
        JULIA: Not when I'm having my period, Robyn.
        ROBYN: Robyn laughs.

14   Wandering through raunchy, male-dominated MUDs in the guise of a sassy female, Julia has to be adept at detecting and deflecting sexual advances. One player, here called Barry, tried to seduce Julia in a string of conversations that stretched over [a] few weeks in July 1992. Excerpts from their conversations were reported by Mauldin.

15   BARRY: Are you a virgin?
        JULIA: As far as you are concerned Barry, I always will be.

[*A week passes.*]

        BARRY: Are you still holding out on me?
        JULIA: I mean, have I convinced you I'm a computer yet?
        BARRY: I guess you're real . . . but I'd still like to get you to my DEN to run tests on you.
        JULIA: I live for your approval, Barry.
        BARRY: I'm so glad to hear that. Why don't you come over to my home.

JULIA: I want to have a child someday.
BARRY: What a coincidence. I too wish to make a baby . . . someday.
JULIA: The date is Tue Jul 21 23:57:31, Barry.

Barry, encouraged by Julia's references to making babies, takes her computer-like association to the word *day* as just one more piece of teasing repartee. He continues his suit:

BARRY: [The address of my virtual den is] AB9 #11 . . . cum [sic] on over ya Harvard girl you.
JULIA: Do you have any kids?
BARRY: No, not yet.
JULIA: But hockey is my topic. It will be a boring conversation otherwise.
BARRY: Oh, I love to put the puck in the net, do you play?
JULIA: Me too, Barry.

16   After studying such exchanges, Leonard Foner of the Media Laboratory at the Massachusetts Institute of Technology remarked, "Frankly, it's not entirely clear to me whether Julia passed a Turing test here or Barry failed one."

17   As dim-witted as Barry may appear to an outsider, his gullibility is not hard to understand. People are social beings who seek communication with others. We are lonely beings as well. In spite of our fear of having our essential humanity reduced through comparison with a machine, we begin to relate to the computer whenever it appears to offer some company.

18   The first thing I did when I got my Macintosh was name the hard drive Miss Beautiful, my pet name for my daughter. I felt a little foolish about it until one of my students mentioned that she had named a computer agent, which helped her organize her mail and schedules, after a boyfriend who had left her abruptly. "I love to see him do my menial tasks," she said. In both cases the naming of the machine was done in a lighthearted spirit, but the resultant psychologization was real.

19   Recently, while visiting a MUD, I came across a reference to a character named Dr. Sherry. A cyberpsychologist with an office in the rambling house that constituted this MUD's virtual geography, Dr. Sherry administered questionnaires and conducted interviews about the psychology of MUDs. I had not created the character. I was not playing her on the MUD. Dr. Sherry was a derivative of me, but she was not mine. I experienced her as a little piece of my history spinning out of control.

20   I tried to quiet my mind. I tried to convince myself that the impersonation was a form of flattery. But when I talked the situation over with a friend, she posed a conversation-stopping question: "Would you prefer it if Dr. Sherry were a bot trained to interview people about life on the MUD?" Which posed more of a threat to my identity, that another person could impersonate me or that a computer program might be able to?

21   Dr. Sherry turned out to be neither person nor program. She was a composite character created by several college students writing a paper on the psychology of MUDs. Yet, in a sense, her identity was no more fragmented, no more fictional than some of the "real" characters I had created on MUDs. In a virtual world, where both humans and computer programs adopt personas, where intelligence and personality are reduced to words on a screen, what does it mean to say that one character is more real than another?

22   In the 1990s, as adults finally wrestle with such questions, their children, who have been born and bred in the computer culture, take the answers for granted. Children are comfortable with the idea that inanimate objects can both think and have a personality. But breathing, having blood, being born, and "having real skin," are the true signs of life, they insist. Machines may be intelligent and conscious, but they are not alive.

23   Nevertheless, any definition of life that relies on biology as the bottom line is being built on shifting ground. In the age of the Human Genome Project, ideas of free will jostle for position against the idea of mind as program and the gene as programmer. The genome project promises to find the pieces of our genetic code responsible for diseases, but it may also find genetic markers that determine personality, temperament, and sexual orientation. As we reengineer the genome, we are also reengineering our view of ourselves as programmed beings.

24   We are all dreaming cyborg dreams. While our children imagine "morphing" humans into metallic cyberreptiles, computer scientists dream themselves immortal. They imagine themselves thinking forever, downloaded onto machines. As the artificial intelligence expert and entrepreneur W. Daniel Hillis puts it:

> I have the same nostalgic love of human metabolism that everybody else does, but if I can go into an improved body and last for 10,000 years I would do it in an instant, no second thoughts. I actually don't think I'm going to have that option, but maybe my children will.

25   For now, people dwell on the threshold of the real and the virtual, unsure of their footing, reinventing themselves each time they approach the screen. In a text-based, online game inspired by the television series *Star Trek: The Next Generation*, players hold jobs, collect paychecks, and have romantic sexual encounters. "This is more real than my real life," says a character who turns out to be a man playing a woman who is pretending to be a man.

26   Why should some not prefer their virtual worlds to RL (as dedicated MUD users call real life)? In cyberspace, the obese can be slender, the beautiful plain, the "nerdy" sophisticated. As one dog, its paw on a keyboard, explained to another dog in a *New Yorker* cartoon: "On the Internet, nobody knows you're a dog."

27   Only a decade ago the pioneers of the personal computer culture often found themselves alone as they worked at their machines. But these days, when people step through the looking glass of the computer screen, they find other people—or are they programs?—on the other side. As the boundaries erode between the real and the virtual, the animate and inanimate, the unitary and the multiple self, the question becomes: Are we living life on the screen or *in* the screen?

NOTES AND DISCUSSION

Turkle's introduction moves quickly through a brief history of ideas about human nature to her thesis that humans are gradually coming to grips with the idea of machine intelligence. She looks at the ways machines and human natures have become metaphors for each other, and at ways we communicate with and about computers. She raises questions about the relationship between the real and the virtual, and shows how machines can respond to the human need for companionship. Whereas A. M. Turing set a challenge to test the computer against human standards, Turkle studies how to test our human nature against the computer.

As Turkle shows, multiple-user domains (MUDs) have enabled individuals to present themselves as different people, or a group to pass itself off as an individual: a group of students posed as a character apparently named for Turkle herself. The core of this section examines the "behaviour" of a program named Julia, which emulates the human behaviour of hiding behind different personas. Already the lines blur: is it possible for a machine to have a "persona," let alone personas? Turkle argues that, ironically, we have reached a stage where we cannot tell whether computers are passing the Turing test, or humans are failing it.

In her conclusion, Turkle returns to her opening image of the dream: according to the opening quotation from Emerson, the dream is one of the proofs of human nature. Here Turkle considers ways our dreams have begun to connect our "selves" with machines.

STUDY QUESTIONS

For Discussion:

1. If you use computers to communicate with others, how do you know you are dealing with a real person on the other end? If you have ever discovered that the "person" you were communicating with was disguised, or even a group or a machine, how did you react? Does it matter, in the end, whether you are dealing with a real person or a programmed intelligence? If you have ever disguised yourself (successfully or not), explain the disguise and what you achieved or sought through it.

2. Turkle assumes Barry is a real person (there may be proof in Michael Mauldin's own research, but Turkle includes none in her essay). What in the dialogue provided would either support or challenge her assumption?

For Writing:

1. Based on the evidence available in Turkle's essay, argue whether Barry failed the Turing test, or whether Julia passed it.

2. While people's ability to pass off versions of themselves as their "reality" is fascinating, there are also risks—for both the sender and the receiver. As a research project, look for and report on examples of people wearing or getting duped by such disguises, and the results.

MOLECULAR STRUCTURE OF NUCLEIC ACIDS:

A Structure for Deoxyribose Nucleic Acid

James D. Watson and Francis H.C. Crick

BIOGRAPHICAL NOTE

James D. Watson and Francis H.C. Crick, along with their co-researcher Maurice Wilkins, shared the 1962 Nobel Prize in Medicine for their discovery of the structure of DNA. Watson's other writings include *The Double Helix: A Personal Account of the Discovery of the Structure of DNA* (1968); Crick's include *What Mad Pursuit: A Personal View of Scientific Discovery* (1988).

1   We wish to suggest a structure for the salt of deoxyribose nucleic acid (D.N.A.). This structure has novel features which are of considerable biological interest.

2   A structure for nucleic acid has already been proposed by Pauling and Corey[1]. They kindly made their manuscript available to us in advance of publication. Their model consists of three intertwined chains, with the phosphates near the fibre axis, and the bases on the outside. In our opinion, this structure is unsatisfactory for two reasons: (1) We believe that the material which gives the X-ray diagrams is the salt, not the free acid. Without the acidic hydrogen atoms it is not clear what forces would hold the structure together, especially as the negatively charged phosphates near the axis will repel each other. (2) Some of the van der Waals distances appear to be too small.

3   Another three-chain structure has also been suggested by Fraser (in the press). In his model the phosphates are on the outside and the bases on the inside, linked together by hydrogen bonds. This structure as described is rather ill-defined, and for this reason we shall not comment on it.

4   We wish to put forward a radically different structure for the salt of deoxyribose nucleic acid. This structure has two helical chains each coiled round the same axis (see diagram). We have made the usual chemical assumptions, namely, that each chain consists of phosphate diester groups joining ß-D-deoxyribofuranose residues with 3',5' linkages. The two chains (but

not their bases) are related by a dyad perpendicular to the fibre axis. Both chains follow right-handed helices, but owing to the dyad the sequences of the atoms in the two chains run in opposite directions. Each chain loosely resembles Furberg's[2] model No. 1; that is, the bases are on the inside of the helix and the phosphates on the outside. The configuration of the sugar and the atoms near it is close to Furberg's 'standard configuration', the sugar being roughly perpendicular to the attached base. There is a residue on each chain every 3·4 A. in the *z*-direction. We have assumed an angle of 36° between adjacent residues in the same chain, so that the structure repeats after 10 residues on each chain, that is, after 34 A. The distance of a phosphorus atom from the fibre axis is 10 A. As the phosphates are on the outside, cations have easy access to them.

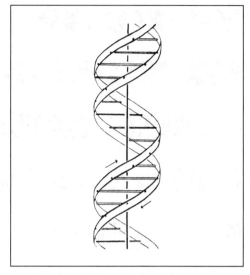

This figure is purely diagrammatic. The two ribbons symbolize the two phosphate-sugar chains, and the horizontal rods the pairs of bases holding the chains together. The vertical line marks the fibre axis.

5   The structure is an open one, and its water content is rather high. At lower water contents we would expect the bases to tilt so that the structure could become more compact.

6   The novel feature of the structure is the manner in which the two chains are held together by the purine and pyrimidine bases. The planes of the bases are perpendicular to the fibre axis. They are joined together in pairs, a single base from one chain being hydrogen-bonded to a single base from the other chain, so that the two lie side by side with identical *z*-co-ordinates. One of the pair must be a purine and the other a pyrimidine for bonding to occur. The hydrogen bonds are made as follows: purine position 1 to pyrimidine position 1; purine position 6 to pyrimidine position 6.

7   If it is assumed that the bases only occur in the structure in the most plausible tautomeric forms (that is, with the keto rather than the enol configurations) it is found that only specific pairs of bases can bond together. These pairs are: adenine (purine) with thymine (pyrimidine), and guanine (purine) with cytosine (pyrimidine).

8   In other words, if an adenine forms one member of a pair, on either chain, then on these assumptions the other member must be thymine; similarly for guanine and cytosine. The sequence of bases on a single chain does not appear to be restricted in any way. However, if only specific pairs of bases can be formed, it follows that if the sequence of bases on one chain is given, then the sequence on the other chain is automatically determined.

9   It has been found experimentally[3,4] that the ratio of the amounts of adenine to thymine, and the ratio of guanine to cytosine, are always very close to unity for deoxyribose nucleic acid.

10   It is probably impossible to build this structure with a ribose sugar in place of the deoxyribose, as the extra oxygen atom would make too close a van der Waals contact.

11   The previously published X-ray data[5,6] on deoxyribose nucleic acid are insufficient for a rigorous test of our structure. So far as we can tell, it is roughly compatible with the

experimental data, but it must be regarded as unproved until it has been checked against more exact results. Some of these are given in the following communications. We were not aware of the details of the results presented there when we devised our structure, which rests mainly though not entirely on published experimental data and stereo-chemical arguments.

12   It has not escaped our notice that the specific pairing we have postulated immediately suggests a possible copying mechanism for the genetic material.

13   Full details of the structure, including the conditions assumed in building it, together with a set of co-ordinates for the atoms, will be published elsewhere.

14   We are much indebted to Dr. Jerry Donohue for constant advice and criticism, especially on inter-atomic distances. We have also been stimulated by a knowledge of the general nature of the unpublished experimental results and ideas of Dr. M.H.F. Wilkins, Dr. R.E. Franklin and their co-workers at King's College, London. One of us (J.D.W.) has been aided by a fellowship from the National Foundation for Infantile Paralysis.

J.D. Watson
F.H.C. Crick

Medical Research Council Unit for the Study of the Molecular Structure
of Biological Systems, Cavendish Laboratory, Cambridge. April 2.

ENDNOTES

1. Pauling, L., and Corey, R.B., *Nature*, 171, 346 (1953); *Proc. U.S. Nat. Acad. Sci.*, 39, 84 (1953).

2. Furberg, S., *Acta Chem. Scand.*, 6, 634 (1952).

3. Chargaff, E., for references see Zamenhof, S., Brawerman, G., and Chargaff, E., *Biochim. et Biophys. Acta*, 9, 402 (1952).

4. Wyatt, G.R., *J. Gen. Physiol.*, 36, 201 (1952).

5. Astbury, W.T., *Symp. Soc. Exp. Biol.* 1, *Nucleic Acid*, 66 (Camb. Univ. Press, 1947).

6. Wilkins, M.H.F., and Randall, J.T., *Biochim. et Biophys. Acta*, 10, 192 (1953).

NOTES AND DISCUSSION

Although this paper announces a significant scientific discovery, its tone and purpose are largely persuasive. Watson and Crick do not describe their research, but explain why their model should be accepted as the correct one. The issue here seems to be to get the claim into print, to establish the priority of the claim, rather than to explicate the process by which they arrived at these conclusions. The paper is obviously written for a knowledgeable audience, since the authors make rather cursory references to other research and researchers, to chemical structures, and to models and formulae, without explaining or defining. Note in the opening paragraph and the twelfth the understated manner and tone through which they introduce their "wish to suggest," and allude to connections of "biological interest" and to the possibilities of this structure as a "copying mechanism for the genetic material."

STUDY QUESTIONS

For Discussion:

1. Consider the relationship between the article and the accompanying diagram. Does the diagram serve to illustrate the article, or is the article the background to the diagram? That is, are Watson and Crick more interested in arguing for their model, or in diagramming it?

2. Crick later claimed that some early commentators objected to the "coy" tone of the twelfth paragraph. Consider whether this term is a fair analysis of the tone, and whether the tone is different from, or consistent with, the overall tone and purpose of the article. How is it similar to and different from the tone in the essay by Wilmut, et al. in this collection that announces the cloning of Dolly the sheep?

For Writing:

1. Analyze the persuasive techniques used in this article, and consider how effectively Watson and Crick introduce and refute earlier research (Fraser's model, for example), and how they support their own claim.

2. Compare and contrast the rather impersonal style and tone of this collaborative article with the more personal tone and style of Watson's and Crick's individual writings, particularly with Watson's *The Double Helix* and Crick's *What Mad Pursuit*; alternatively, compare the response to this article with reviews and responses to Watson's book.

VIABLE OFFSPRING DERIVED FROM FETAL AND ADULT MAMMALIAN CELLS

I. Wilmut, A. E. Schnieke, J. McWhir, A. J. Kind, and K. H. S. Campbell

BIOGRAPHICAL NOTE

Ian Wilmut headed the Edinburgh-based research team, made up of scientists from the Roslin Institute and the pharmaceutical company PPL Therapeutics, that successfully cloned the first mammal in 1996. Dolly, a Finn Dorset lamb, was created from the non-reproductive tissue of an adult sheep. This paper first appeared in *Nature* and quickly became the focus of intense media scrutiny and international debate.

1   Fertilization of mammalian eggs is followed by successive cell divisions and progressive differentiation, first into the early embryo and subsequently into all of the cell types that make up the adult animal. Transfer of a single nucleus at a specific stage of development, to an enucleated unfertilized egg, provided an opportunity to investigate whether cellular differentiation to that stage involved irreversible genetic modification. The first offspring to develop from a differentiated cell were born after nuclear transfer from an embryo-derived cell line that had been induced to become quiescent.[1] Using the same procedure, we now report the birth of live lambs from three new cell populations established from adult mammary gland, fetus, and embryo. The fact that a lamb was derived from an adult cell confirms that differentiation of that cell did not involve the irreversible modification of genetic material required for development to term. The birth of lambs from differentiated fetal and adult cells also reinforces previous speculation[1,2] that by inducing donor cells to become quiescent it will be possible to obtain normal development from a wide variety of differentiated cells.

2   It has long been known that in amphibians, nuclei transferred from adult keratinocytes established in culture support development to the juvenile, tadpole stage.[3] Although this

involves differentiation into complex tissues and organs, no development to the adult stage was reported, leaving open the question of whether a differentiated adult nucleus can be fully reprogrammed. Previously we reported the birth of live lambs after nuclear transfer from cultured embryonic cells that had been induced into quiescence. We suggested that inducing the donor cell to exit the growth phase causes changes in chromatin structure that facilitate reprogramming of gene expression and that development would be normal if nuclei are used from a variety of differentiated donor cells in similar regimes. Here we investigate whether normal development to term is possible when donor cells derived from fetal or adult tissue are induced to exit the growth cycle and enter the G0 phase of the cell cycle before nuclear transfer.

3   Three new populations of cells were derived from (1) a day-9 embryo, (2) a day-26 fetus, and (3) mammary gland of a 6-year-old ewe in the last trimester of pregnancy. Morphology of the embryo-derived cells (Fig. 1) is unlike both mouse embryonic stem (ES) cells and the embryo-derived cells used in our previous study. Nuclear transfer was carried out according to one of our established protocols[1] and reconstructed embryos transferred into recipient ewes. Ultrasound scanning detected 21 single fetuses on day 50–60 after oestrus

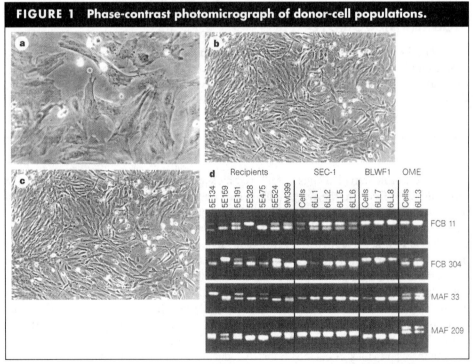

FIGURE 1   **Phase-contrast photomicrograph of donor-cell populations.**

a) Embryo-derived cells (SEC1); b) fetal fibroblasts (BLWF1); c) mammary-derived cells (OME). d) Microsatellite analysis of recipient ewes, nuclear donor cells, and lambs using four polymorphic ovine markers.[22] The ewes are arranged from left to right in the same order as the lambs. Cell populations are embryo-derived (SEC1), fetal-derived (BLW1), and mammary-derived (OME), respectively. Lambs have the same genotype as the donor cells and differ from their recipient mothers.

(Table 1). On subsequent scanning at ~ 14-day intervals, fewer fetuses were observed, suggesting either mis-diagnosis or fetal loss. In total, 62% of fetuses were lost, a significantly greater proportion than the estimate of 6% after natural mating.[4] Increased prenatal loss has been reported after embryo manipulation or culture of unreconstructed embryos.[5] At about day 110 of pregnancy, four fetuses were dead, all from embryo-derived cells, and post-mortem analysis was possible after killing the ewes. Two fetuses had abnormal liver development, but no other abnormalities were detected and there was no evidence of infection.

4   Eight ewes gave birth to live lambs (Table 1, Fig. 2). All three cell populations were represented. One weak lamb, derived from the fetal fibroblasts, weighed 3.1 kg and died within a few minutes of birth, although post-mortem analysis failed to find any abnormality or infection. At 12.5%, perinatal loss was not dissimilar to that occurring in a large study of commercial sheep, when 8% of lambs died within 24 h of birth.[6] In all cases the lambs displayed the morphological characteristics of the breed used to derive the nucleus donors and not that of the oocyte donor (Table 2). This alone indicates that the lambs could not have been born after inadvertent mating of either the oocyte donor or recipient ewes. In addition, DNA microsatellite analysis of the cell populations and the lambs at four polymorphic loci confirmed that each lamb was derived from the cell population used as nuclear donor (Fig. 1). Duration of gestation is determined by fetal genotype,[7] and in all cases gestation was longer than the breed mean (Table 2). By contrast, birth weight is influenced by both maternal and fetal genotype.[8] The birth weight of all lambs was within the range for single lambs born to Blackface ewes on our farm (up to 6.6 kg) and in most cases was within the range for the breed of the nuclear donor. There are no strict control observations for birth weight after embryo transfer between breeds, but the range in weight of lambs born to their own breed on our farms is 1.2–5.0 kg, 2–4.9 kg, and 3–9 kg for the Finn Dorset, Welsh Mountain, and Poll Dorset genotypes, respectively. The attainment of sexual maturity in the lambs is being monitored.

TABLE 1	Development of embryos reconstructed with three different cell types						
Cell type	No. of fused couplets (%)*	No. recovered from oviduct (%)	No. cultured	No. of morula/ blastocyst (%)	No. of morula or blastocysts transferred‡	No. of pregnancies/ no. of recipients (%)	No. of live lambs (%)‡‡
Mammary epithelium	277 (63.8)[a]	247 (89.2)	–	29 (11.7)[a]	29	1/13 (7.7)	1 (3.4%)
Fetal fibroblast	172 (84.7)[b]	124 (86.7)	–	34 (27.4)[b]	34	4/10 (40.0)	2 (5.9%)
			24	13 (54.2)[b]	6	1/6 (16.6)	1 (16.6%)**
Embryo-derived	385 (82.8)[b]	231 (85.3)	–	90 (39.0)[b]	72	14/27 (51.8)	4 (5.6%)
			92	36 (39.0)[b]	15	1/5 (20.0)	0

*As assessed 1 hr after fusion by examination on a dissecting microscope. Superscripts a or b within a column indicate a significant difference between donor cell types in the efficiency of fusion (P <0.001) or the proportion of embryos that developed to morula or blastocyst (P <0.001).
‡It was not practicable to transfer all morulae/blastocysts.
‡‡As a proportion of morulae or blastocysts transferred. Not all recipients were perfectly synchronized.
**This lamb died within a few minutes of birth.

5   Development of embryos produced by nuclear transfer depends upon the maintenance of normal ploidy and creating the conditions for developmental regulation of gene expression. These responses are both influenced by the cell-cycle stage of donor and recipient cells and the interaction between them (reviewed in ref. 9). A comparison of development of mouse and cattle embryos produced by nuclear transfer to oocytes[10,11] or enucleated zygotes[12,13] suggests that a greater proportion develop if the recipient is an oocyte. This may be because factors that bring about reprogramming of gene expression in a transferred nucleus are required for early development and are taken up by the pronuclei during development of the zygote.

FIGURE 2

Lamb number 6LL3 derived from the mammary gland of a Finn Dorset ewe with the Scottish Blackface ewe which was the recipient.

6   If the recipient cytoplasm is prepared by enucleation of an oocyte at metaphase II, it is only possible to avoid chromosomal damage and maintain normal ploidy by transfer of diploid nuclei,[14,15] but further experiments are required to define the optimum cell-cycle stage. Our studies with cultured cells suggest that there is an advantage if cells are quiescent (ref. 1, and this work). In earlier studies, donor cells were embryonic blastomeres that had not been induced into quiescence. Comparisons of the phases of the growth cycle showed that development was greater if donor cells were in mitosis[16] or in the G1 (ref. 10) phase of the cycle, rather than in S or G2 phases. Increased development using donor cells in G0, G1, or mitosis may reflect greater access for reprogramming factors present in the oocyte cycoplasm, but a direct comparison of these phases in the same cell population is required for a clearer understanding of the underlying mechanisms.

7   Together these results indicate that nuclei from a wide range of cell types should prove to be totipotent after enhancing opportunities for reprogramming by using appropriate combinations of these cell-cycle stages. In turn, the dissemination of the genetic improvement obtained within elite selection herds will be enhanced by limited replication of animals with proven performance by nuclear transfer from cells derived from adult animals. In addition, gene targeting in livestock should now be feasible by nuclear transfer from modified cell populations and will offer new opportunities in biotechnology. The techniques described also offer an opportunity to study the possible persistence and impact of epigenetic changes, such as imprinting and telomere shortening, which are known to occur in somatic cells during development and senescence, respectively.

8   The lamb born after nuclear transfer from a mammary gland cell is, to our knowledge, the first mammal to develop from a cell derived from an adult tissue. The phenotype of the donor cell is unknown. The primary culture contains mainly mammary epithelial (over 90%) as well as other differentiated cell types, including myoepithelial cells and fibroblasts. We cannot exclude the possibility that there is a small proportion of relatively undif-

Table 2		Delivery of lambs developing from embryos derived by nuclear transfer from three different donor cells types, showing gestation length and birth weight		
weight Cell type	Breed of lamb	Lamb identity	Duration of pregnancy (days)*	Birt (kg)
Mammary epithelium	Finn Dorset	6LL3	148	6.6
Fetal fibroblast	Black Welsh	6LL7	152	5.6
	Black Welsh	6LL8	149	2.8
	Black Welsh	6LL9†	156	3.1
Embryo-derived	Poll Dorset	6LL1	149	6.5
	Poll Dorset	6LL2††	152	6.2
	Poll Dorset	6LL5	148	4.2
	Poll Dorset	6LL6††	152	5.3

*Breed averages are 143, 147, and 145 days, respectively for the three genotypes Finn Dorset, Black Welsh Mountain, and Poll Dorset.
†This lamb died within a few minutes of birth.
††These lambs were delivered by caesarian section. Overall the nature of the assistance provided by the veterinary surgeon was similar to that expected in a commercial flock.

ferentiated stem cells able to support regeneration of the mammary gland during pregnancy. Birth of the lamb shows that during the development of that mammary cell there was no irreversible modification of genetic information required for development to term. This is consistent with the generally accepted view that mammalian differentiation is almost all achieved by systematic, sequential changes in gene expression brought about by interactions between the nucleus and the changing cytoplasmic environment.[17]

METHODS

9   Embryo-derived cells were obtained from embryonic disc of a day-9 embryo from a Poll Dorset ewe cultured as described,[1] with the following modifications. Stem-cell medium was supplemented with bovine DIA/LIF. After 8 days, the explanted disc was disaggregated by enzymatic digestion and cells replated onto fresh feeders. After a further 7 days, a single colony of large flattened cells was isolated and grown further in the absence of feeder cells. At passage 8, the modal chromosome number was 54. These cells were used as nuclear donors at passages 7–9. Fetal-derived cells were obtained from an eviscerated Black Welsh Mountain fetus recovered at autopsy on day 26 of pregnancy. The head was removed before tissues were cut into small pieces and the cells dispersed by exposure to trypsin. Culture was in BHK 21 (Glasgow MEM; Gibco Life Sciences) supplemented with L-glutamine (2 mM), sodium pyruvate (1 mM), and 10% fetal calf serum. At 90% confluency, the cells were passaged with a 1:2 division. At passage 4, these fibroblast-like cells (Fig. 1) had modal chromosome number of 54. Fetal cells were used as nuclear donors at passages 4–6. Cells from mammary gland were obtained from a 6-year-old Finn Dorset ewe in the last trimester of pregnancy.[18] At passages 3 and 6, the modal chromosome number was 54 and these cells were used as nuclear donors at passage numbers 3–6.

10   Nuclear transfer was done according to previous protocol.[1] Oocytes were recovered from Scottish Blackface ewes between 28 and 33 h after injection of gonadotropin-releasing hormone (GnRH), and enucleated as soon as possible. They were recovered in calcium- and magnesium-free PBS containing 1% FCS and transferred to calcium-free M2 medium[19] containing 10% FCS at 37°C. Quiescent, diploid donor cells were produced by reducing the concentration of serum in the medium from 10 to 0.5% for 5 days, causing the cells to exit the growth cycle and arrest in G0. Confirmation that cells had left the cycle was obtained by staining with antiPCNA/cyclin antibody (Immuno Concepts), revealed by a second antibody conjugated with rhodamine (Dakopatts).

11   Fusion of the donor cell to the enucleated oocyte and activation of the oocyte were induced by the same electrical pulses, between 34 and 36 h after GnRH injection to donor ewes. The majority of reconstructed embryos were cultured in ligated oviducts of sheep as before, but some embryos produced by transfer from embryo-derived cells or fetal fibroblasts were cultured in a chemically defined medium.[20] Most embryos that developed to morula or blastocyst after 6 days of culture were transferred to recipients and allowed to develop to term (Table 1). One, two or three embryos were transferred to each ewe depending upon the availability of embryos. The effect of cell type upon fusion and development to morula or blastocyst was analysed using the marginal model of Breslow and Clayton.[21] No comparison was possible of development to term as it was not practicable to transfer all embryos developing to a suitable stage for transfer. When too many embryos were available, those having better morphology were selected.

12   Ultrasound scan was used for pregnancy diagnosis at around day 60 after oestrus and to monitor fetal development thereafter at 2-week intervals. Pregnant recipient ewes were monitored for nutritional status, body condition, and signs of EAE, Q fever, border disease, louping ill, and toxoplasmosis. As lambing approached, they were under constant observation and a veterinary surgeon called at the onset of parturition. Microsatellite analysis was carried out on DNA from the lambs and recipient ewes using four polymorphic ovine markers.[22]

ENDNOTES

1. Campbell, K. H. S., McWhir, J., Ritchie, W. A., and Wilmut, I. Sheep cloned by nuclear transfer from a cultured cell line. *Nature* 380, 64–66 (1996).

2. Solter, D. Lambing by nuclear transfer. *Nature* 380, 24–25 (1996).

3. Gurdon, J. B., Laskey, R. A., and Reeves, O. R. The development capacity of nuclei transplanted from keratinized skin cells of adult frogs. *J. Embryol. Exp. Morph.* 34, 93–112 (1975).

4. Quinlivan, T. D., Martin, C. A., Taylor, W. B., and Cairney, I. M. Pre- and perinatal mortality in those ewes that conceived to one service. *J. Reprod. Fert.* 11, 379–390 (1996).

5. Walker, S. K., Heard, T. M., and Seamark, R. F. *In vitro* culture of sheep embryos without co-culture: successes and perspectives. *Therio* 37, 111–126 (1992).

6. Nash, M. L., Hungerford, L. L. Nash, T. G., and Zinn, G. M. Risk factors for perinatal and postnatal mortality in lambs. *Vet. Rec.* 139, 64–67 (1996).

7. Bradford, G. E., Hart, R., Quirke, J. F., and Land, R. B. Genetic control of the duration of gestation in sheep. *J. Reprod. Fert.* 30, 459–463 (1972).

8. Walton, A. and Hammond, J. The maternal effects on growth and conformation in Shire horse-Shetland pony crosses. *Proc. R. Soc. B* 125, 311–335 (1938).

9. Campbell, K. H. S., Loi, P., Otaegui, P. J., and Wilmut, I. Cell cycle co-ordination in embryo cloning by nuclear transfer. *Rev. Reprod.* 1, 40–46 (1996).

10. Cheong, H. T., Takahashi, Y., and Kanagawa, H. Birth of mice after transplantation of early-cell-cycle-stage embryonic nuclei into enucleated oocytes. *Biol. Reprod.* 48, 958–963 (1993).

11. Prather, R. S. et al. Nuclear transplantation in the bovine embryo. Assessment of donor nuclei and recipient oocyte. *Biol. Reprod.* 37, 859–866 (1987).

12. McGrath, J. and Solter, D. Inability of mouse blastomere nuclei transferred to enucleated zygotes to support development *in vitro. Science* 226, 1317–1318 (1984).

13. Robl, J. M. et al. Nuclear transplantation in bovine embryos. *J. Anim. Sci.* 64, 642–647 (1987).

14. Campbell, K. H. S., Ritchie, W. A., and Wilmut, I. Nuclear-cytoplasmic interactions during the first cell cycle of nuclear transfer reconstructed bovine embryos: Implications for deoxyribonucleic acid replication and development. *Biol. Reprod.* 49, 933–942 (1993).

15. Barnes, F. L. et al. Influence of recipient oocyte cell cycle stage on DNA synthesis, nuclear envelope breakdown, chromosome constitution, and development in nuclear transplant bovine embryos. *Mol. Reprod. Dev.* 36, 33–41 (1993).

16. Kwon, O. Y. and Kono, T. Production of identical sextuplet mice by transferring metaphase nuclei from 4-cell embryos. *J. Reprod. Fert.* Abst. Ser. 17, 30 (1996).

17. Gurdon, J. B. The control of gene expression in animal development (Oxford: Oxford University Press, 1974).

18. Finch, L. M. B. et al. Primary culture of ovine mammary epithelial cells. *Biochem. Soc. Trans.* 24, 369S (1996).

19. Whitten, W. K. and Biggers, J. D. Complete development *in vitro* of the preimplantation stages of the mouse in a simple chemically defined medium. *J. Reprod. Fertil.* 17, 399–401 (1968).

20. Gardner, D. K., Lane, M., Spitzer, A., and Batt, P. A. Enhanced rates of cleavage and development for sheep zygotes cultured to the blastocyst stage *in vitro* in the absence of serum and somatic cells. Amino acids, vitamins, and culturing embryos in groups stimulate development. *Biol. Reprod.* 50, 390–400 (1994).

21. Breslow, N. E. and Clayton, D. G. Approximate inference in generalized linear mixed models. *J. Am. Stat. Assoc.* 88, 9–25 (1993).

22. Buchanan, F. C., Littlejohn, R. P., Galloway, S. M., and Crawford, A. L. Microsatellites and associated repetitive elements in the sheep genome. *Mammal. Gen.* 4, 258–264 (1993).

NOTES AND DISCUSSION

This is a scientific article written for a specialist audience. As such, it generally maintains an impersonal tone, employing the gender-neutral third person "it" to present the majority of its findings. The essay, which summarizes the efforts of a group of scientists, also uses the pronoun "we" in conjunction with the passive voice throughout its explanation of technical procedures and underlying hypotheses. These stylistic choices emphasize the team aspect of the research and may be more convincing to readers than the reporting and hypothesizing of an individual.

The paper opens by placing itself in relation to previous research in its field, summarizing and paraphrasing this research briefly and efficiently and providing footnotes to exact sources. Wilmut and his colleagues then announce the results of their experiments and state the speculations that were confirmed by these results. They then give an overview of the methods used in the experiments and present the details of the results. Tables and photographs aid this portion of the paper, presenting and summarizing information that would likely be tedious and confusing if presented in textual format. Wilmut et al. occasionally look beyond the specifics of their experiment to discuss related issues, such as "irreversible genetic modification" and "differentiated cells."

Generally, the writers do not waste words; the paper's style is dense and compact. Yet the cause-and-effect relationships and steps in logical reasoning are clearly established and may be understood by the non-specialist once any unfamiliar terminology has been elucidated. Note the use of transitional phrases and words to help the reader establish and recognize links between ideas.

The paper concludes by reiterating and expanding on its opening declaration and by identifying areas that require further research and consideration. In fact, though classified as scientific writing, the paper closely follows the basic essay format taught in composition courses.

STUDY QUESTIONS

For Discussion:

1. On a first reading, many non-specialist readers will find this paper complicated and impenetrable. Examine how the subject matter, the scientific language, and the tone and sentence structures of the paper interact with each other.

2. In the media coverage that followed the publication of this paper, Wilmut's findings were said to have paved the way for cloning humans. Based on *this* paper, does this application seem likely or immediate? Does the paper suggest other applications? Can you think of other applications? Why do Wilmut and his team avoid addressing such issues explicitly?

For Writing:

1. Re-write the first paragraph of Wilmut's essay in everyday English. Note any problems that you encounter and then compare and contrast your version with Wilmut's. What similarities and differences do you notice?

2. Compare Wilmut's paper with Watson and Crick's essay on the structure of DNA. Identify the common elements of style and tone that you perceive as hallmarks of scientific writing. Discuss the advantages and disadvantages of these scientific literary characteristics.

TELEVISION AND READING

Marie Winn

BIOGRAPHICAL NOTE

Marie Winn was born in Prague, Czechoslovakia, and emigrated to the United States at an early age. A graduate of Radcliffe College and Columbia University, Winn is a theorist of childhood and children's culture, and has written books both for and about children. In 1977, *The Plug-In Drug* won an award from the American Library Association. Her subsequent books include *Children without Childhood* (1983) and *UnPlugging the Plug-In Drug* (1987).

---

1   Until the television era young children's access to symbolic representations of reality was limited. Unable to read, they entered the world of fantasy primarily by way of stories told to them or read to them from a book. But rarely did such "literary" experiences take up a significant proportion of a child's waking time; even when a willing reader or storyteller was available, an hour or so a day was more time than most children spent ensconced in the imagination of others. And when pre-television children *did* enter those imaginary worlds, they always had a grown-up escort along to interpret, explain, and comfort, if need be. Before learning to read, it was difficult for a child to enter the fantasy world alone.

2   For this reason the impact of television was undoubtedly greater on preschoolers and pre-readers than on any other group. By means of television, very young children were able to enter and spend sizable portions of their waking time in a secondary world of incorporeal people and intangible things, unaccompanied, in too many cases, by an adult guide or comforter. School-age children fell into a different category. Because they could read, they had other opportunities to leave reality behind. For these children television was merely *another* imaginary world.

3   But since reading, once the school child's major imaginative experience, has now been seriously eclipsed by television, the television experience must be compared with the reading experience to try to discover whether they are, indeed, similar activities fulfilling similar needs in a child's life.

WHAT HAPPENS WHEN YOU READ

4   It is not enough to compare television watching and reading from the viewpoint of quality. Although the quality of the material available in each medium varies enormously, from junky books and shoddy programs to literary masterpieces and fine, thoughtful television shows, the *nature* of the two experiences is different and that difference significantly affects the impact of the material taken in.

5   Few people besides linguistics students and teachers of reading are aware of the complex mental manipulations involved in the reading process. Shortly after learning to read, a person assimilates the process so completely that the words in books seem to acquire an existence almost equal to the objects or acts they represent. It requires a fresh look at a printed page to recognize that those symbols that we call letters of the alphabet are completely abstract shapes bearing no inherent "meaning" of their own. Look at an "o," for instance, or a "k." The "o" is a curved figure; the "k" is an intersection of three straight lines. Yet it is hard to divorce their familiar figures from their sounds, though there is nothing "o-ish" about an "o" or "k-ish" about a "k." A reader unfamiliar with the Russian alphabet will find it easy to look at the symbol "Щ" and see it as an abstract shape; a Russian reader will find it harder to detach that symbol from its sound, *shch*. And even when trying to consider "k" as an abstract symbol, we cannot see it without the feeling of a "k" sound somewhere between the throat and the ears, a silent pronunciation of "k" that occurs the instant we see the letter.

6   That is the beginning of reading: we learn to transform abstract figures into sounds, and groups of symbols into the combined sounds that make up the words of our language. As the mind transforms the abstract symbols into sounds and the sounds into words, it "hears" the words, as it were, and thereby invests them with meanings previously learned in the spoken language.[1] Invariably, as the skill of reading develops, the meaning of each word begins to seem to dwell within those symbols that make up the word. The word "dog," for instance, comes to bear some relationship with the real animal. Indeed, the word "dog" seems to *be* a dog in a certain sense, to possess some of the qualities of a dog. But it is only as a result of a swift and complex series of mental activities that the word "dog" is transformed from a series of meaningless squiggles into an idea of something real. This process goes on smoothly and continuously as we read, and yet it becomes no less complex. The brain must carry out all the steps of decoding and investing with meaning each time we read; but it becomes more adept at it as the skill develops, so that we lose the sense of struggling with symbols and meanings that children have when they first learn to read.

7   But not merely does the mind *hear* words in the process of reading; it is important to remember that reading involves images as well. For when the reader sees the word "dog" and understands the idea of "dog," an image representing a dog is conjured up as well. The precise nature of this "reading image" is little understood, nor is there agreement about what relation it bears to visual images taken in directly by the eyes. Nevertheless images necessarily color our reading, else we would perceive no meaning, merely empty words. The great

difference between these "reading images" and the images we take in when viewing television is this: we *create* our own images when reading, based upon our own life experiences and reflecting our own individual needs, while we must accept what we receive when watching television images. This aspect of reading, which might be called "creative" in the narrow sense of the word, is present during all reading experiences, regardless of *what* is being read. When we read it is almost as if we were creating our own, small, inner television program. The result is a nourishing experience for the imagination. As Bruno Bettelheim notes, "Television captures the imagination but does not liberate it. A good book at once stimulates and frees the mind."[2]

8   Television images do not go through a complex symbolic transformation. The mind does not have to decode and manipulate during the television experience. Perhaps this is a reason why the visual images received directly from a television set are strong, stronger, it appears, than the images conjured up mentally while reading. But ultimately they satisfy less. A ten-year-old child reports on the effects of seeing television dramatizations of books he has previously read: "The TV people leave a stronger impression. Once you've seen a character on TV, he'll always look like that in your mind, even if you made a different picture of him in your mind before, when you read the book yourself." And yet, as the same child reports, "the thing about a book is that you have so much freedom. You can make each character look exactly the way you want him to look. You're more in control of things when you read a book than when you see something on TV."

9   It may be that television-bred children's reduced opportunities to indulge in this "inner picture-making" accounts for the curious inability of so many children today to adjust to nonvisual experiences. This is commonly reported by experienced teachers who bridge the gap between the pretelevision and the television eras.

10   "When I read them a story without showing them pictures, the children always complain—'I can't see.' Their attention flags," reports a first-grade teacher. "They'll begin to talk or wander off. I have to really work to develop their visualizing skills. I tell them that there's nothing to see, that the story is coming out of my mouth, and that they can make their own pictures in their 'mind's eye.' They get better at visualizing, with practice. But children never needed to learn how to visualize before television, it seems to me."

VIEWING VS. READING: CONCENTRATION

11   Because reading demands complex mental manipulations, a reader is required to concentrate far more than a television viewer. An audio expert notes that "with the electronic media it is openness [that counts]. Openness permits auditory and visual stimuli more direct access to the brain . . . someone who is taught to concentrate will fail to perceive many patterns of information conveyed by the electronic stimuli."[3]

12   It may be that a predisposition toward concentration, acquired, perhaps, through one's reading experiences, makes one an inadequate television watcher. But it seems far more likely that the reverse situation obtains: that a predisposition toward "openness" (which may be understood to mean the opposite of focal concentration), acquired through years and years of television viewing, has influenced adversely viewers' ability to concentrate, to read, to write clearly—in short, to demonstrate any of the verbal skills a literate society requires.

PACE

13   A comparison between reading and viewing may be made in respect to the pace of each experience, and the relative control we have over that pace, for the pace may influence the ways we use the material received in each experience. In addition, the pace of each experience may determine how much it intrudes upon other aspects of our life.

14   When we read, clearly, we can control the pace. We may read as slowly or as rapidly as we can or wish to read. If we do not understand something, we may stop and reread it, or go in search of elucidation before continuing. If what we read is moving, we may put down the book for a few moments and cope with our emotions without fear of losing anything.

15   When we view, the pace of the television program cannot be controlled; only its beginning and end are within our control by clicking the knob on and off. We cannot slow down a delightful program or speed up a dreary one. We cannot "turn back" if a word or phrase is not understood. The program moves inexorably forward, and what is lost or misunderstood remains so.

16   Nor can we readily transform the material we see on television into a form that might suit our particular emotional needs, as we invariably do with material we read. The images move too quickly. We cannot use our own imagination to invest the people and events portrayed on television with the personal meanings that would help us understand and resolve relationships and conflicts in our own life; we are under the power of the imagination of the show's creators. In the television experience the eyes and ears are overwhelmed with the immediacy of sights and sounds. They flash from the television set just fast enough for the eyes and ears to take them in before moving on quickly to the new pictures and sounds . . . so as *not to lose the thread.*

17   Not to lose the thread . . . it is this need, occasioned by the irreversible direction and relentless velocity of the television experience, that not only limits the workings of the viewer's imagination, but also causes television to intrude into human affairs far more than reading experiences can ever do. If someone enters the room while we're watching television—a friend, a relative, a child, someone, perhaps, we have not seen for some time—we must continue to watch or else we'll lose the thread. The greetings must wait, for the television program will not. A book, of course, can be set aside, with a pang of regret, perhaps, but with no sense of permanent loss.

18   A grandparent describes a situation that is, by all reports, not uncommon:

19   "Sometimes when I come to visit the girls, I'll walk into their room and they're watching a TV program. Well, I know they love me, but it makes me feel *bad* when I tell them hello, and they say, without even looking up, 'Wait a minute . . . we have to see the end of this program.' It hurts me to have them care more about that machine and those little pictures than about being glad to see me. I know that they probably can't help it, but still. . . ."

20   Can they help it? Ultimately, when we watch television our power to release ourselves from viewing in order to attend to human demands that come up is not altogether a function of the pace of the program. After all, we might *choose* to operate according to human priorities rather than electronic dictatorship. We might quickly decide "to hell with this program" and simply stop watching when a friend enters the room or a child needs attention.

21   We might . . . but the hypnotic power of television makes it difficult to shift our attention away, makes us desperate not to lose the thread of the program.

WHY IS IT SO HARD TO STOP WATCHING?

22 A number of perceptual factors unique to the television experience may play a role in making television more *fascinating* than any other vicarious experience, factors to do with the nature of the electronic images on the screen and the ways the eye takes them in.[4]

23 Whereas in real life we perceive but a tiny part of the visual panorama around us with the fovea, the sharp-focusing part of the eye, taking in the rest of the world with our fuzzy peripheral vision, when we watch television we take in the entire frame of an image with our sharp foveal vision. Let us say that the image on the television screen depicts a whole room or a mountain landscape; if we were there in real life, we would be able to perceive only a very small part of the room or the landscape clearly with any single glance. On television, however, we can see the entire picture sharply. Our peripheral vision is not involved in viewing that scene; indeed, as the eye focuses upon the the television screen and takes it all in sharply, the mind blots out the peripheral world entirely. Since in real life the periphery distracts and diffuses our attention, this absence of periphery must serve to abnormally heighten our attention to the television image.

24 Another unique feature of the television image is the remarkable activity of all contours on the television screen. While the normal contours of real-life objects and people are stationary, the electronic mechanism that creates images on a screen produces contours that are ever moving, although the viewer is hardly aware of the movement. Since the eye is drawn to fixate more strongly on moving than on stationary objects, one result of the activity of television contours is to make them more attention-binding.

25 Yet another consequence is to make the eye defocus slightly when fixing its attention on the television screen. The reason is this: in viewing television the steadily changing visual activity of the contour causes the eye to have difficulties in fixating properly. Now in real life when the eye does not fixate properly a signal is sent to the visual center of the brain, which then takes corrective steps. Since improper fixation is normally the result of an eye tremor or some physical dysfunction of the viewer rather than of the thing being viewed, the visual system will attempt to make corrections in the eye tremor or in some part of the viewer's visual system. However, in viewing television, it is the visual activity *at the contour of the image* that is causing the difficulties in fixation. Thus the visual system will have increasing difficulty in maintaining its normal fixation. Therefore it may be easier to give up striving for a perfect, focused fixation on a television picture, and to accommodate by a somewhat defocused fixation.

26 The sensory confusion that occurs as a result of the activity of television images is not unlike the state that occurs when the semicircular canals of the ears, which serve to maintain our balance and help the brain make the necessary adjustments to the body's movements, are confused by motion from external sources (as when one stands still and yet one's ear canals are moved this way and that by the motion of a car or ship or airplane). The unpleasant symptoms of seasickness or carsickness reflect this internal confusion.

27 The slight defocusing of the eyes while viewing television, while not as unpleasant as seasickness (it is barely perceptible, in fact), may nevertheless have subtle consequences that serve to make the television experience more dysfunctional for the organism than other experiences such as reading. Research shows that defocusing of the eyes normally accompanies various fantasy and daydreaming states. Thus the material perceived on television may take on an air of unreality, a dreamlike quality. Moreover, similar visual-motor conflicts are frequently described as features of many drug experiences by users. This may very well

be a reason for the trancelike nature of so many viewers' television experience, and may help to explain why the television image has so strong and hypnotic a fascination. It has even been suggested that "early experiences with electronic displays are predisposing to later enjoyment of psychoactive drugs which produce similar perceptual effects."[5]

28   All these perceptual anomalies may conspire to fascinate viewers and glue them to the television set.

29   Of course there are variations in the attention-getting and attention-sustaining powers of television images, many of which depend on such factors as the amount of movement present on the screen at any given moment, and the velocity of change from image to image. It is a bit chilling to consider that the producers of the most influential program for preschool children, "Sesame Street," employed modern technology in the form of a "distractor" machine to test each segment of their program to ensure that it would capture and hold the child's attention to the highest degree possible. With the help of the "distractor," the makers of "Sesame Street" found that fast-paced cartoons and fast-moving stories were most effective in sustaining a child's attention. This attitude toward young children and their television experiences may well be compared to that revealed by Monica Sims of the BBC who states: "We're not trying to tie children to the television screen. If they go away and play halfway through our programs, that's fine."[6]

THE BASIC BUILDING BLOCKS

30 There is another difference between reading and television viewing that must affect the response to each experience. This is the relative acquaintance of readers and viewers with the fundamental elements of each medium. While the reader is familiar with the basic building blocks of the reading medium, the television viewer has little acquaintance with those of the television medium.

31   As we read, we have our own writing experience to fall back upon. Our understanding of what we read, and our feelings about it, are necessarily affected, and deepened, by our possession of writing as a means of communicating. As children begin to learn reading, they begin to acquire the rudiments of writing. That these two skills are always acquired together is important and not coincidental. As children learn to read words, they need to understand that a word is something they can write themselves, though their muscle control may temporarily prevent them from writing it clearly. That they wield such power over the words they are struggling to decipher makes the reading experience a satisfying one right from the start for children.

32   A young child watching television enters a realm of materials completely beyond his control—and understanding. Though the images that appear on the screen may be reflections of familiar people and things, they appear as if by magic. Children cannot create similar images, nor even begin to understand how those flickering electronic shapes and forms come into being. They take on a far more powerless and ignorant role in front of the television set than in front of a book.

33   There is no doubt that many young children have a confused relationship to the television medium. When a group of preschool children were asked, "How do kids get to be on your TV?" only 22 percent of them showed any real comprehension of the nature of the television images. When asked, "Where do the people and kids and things go when your TV is turned off?" only 20 percent of the three-year-olds showed the smallest glimmer of un-

derstanding. Although there was an increase in comprehension among the four-year-olds, the authors of the study note that "even among the older children the vast majority still did not grasp the nature of television pictures."[7]

34   Children's feelings of power and competence are nourished by another feature of the reading experience that does not obtain for television: the nonmechanical, easily accessible, and easily transportable nature of reading matter. Children can always count on a book for pleasure, though the television set may break down at a crucial moment. They may take a book with them wherever they go, to their room, to the park, to their friend's house, to school to read under the desk: they can *control* their use of books and reading materials. The television set is stuck in a certain place; it cannot be moved easily. It certainly cannot be casually transported from place to place by a child. Children must not only watch television wherever the set is located, but they must watch certain programs at certain times, and are powerless to change what comes out of the set and when it comes out.

35   In this comparison of reading and television viewing a picture begins to emerge that quite confirms the commonly held notion that reading is somehow "better" than television viewing. Reading involves a complex form of mental activity, trains the mind in concentration skills, develops the powers of imagination and inner visualization; the flexibility of its pace lends itself to a better and deeper comprehension of the material communicated. Reading engrosses, but does not hypnotize or seduce the reader from his human responsibilities. Reading is a two-way process: the reader can also write; television viewing is a one-way street: the viewer cannot create television images. And books are ever available, ever controllable. Television controls.

ENDNOTES

1. A discussion of the "acoustic" image of words is found in H.J. Chaytor, *From Script to Print* (London: W. Heffer and Sons, 1950).
2. Bruno Bettelheim, "Parents vs. Television," *Redbook*, November, 1963.
3. Tony Schwartz, *The Responsive Chord* (New York: Anchor/Doubleday, 1973).
4. Much of the material in this section is based on a reading of Julian Hochberg and Virginia Brooks' "The Perception of Television Displays," a prepublication draft of a survey and analysis of the basic perceptual determinants that may affect viewers' responses to the television experience, commissioned by the Television Laboratory at WNET/13.
5. Julian Hochberg and Virginia Brooks, "The Perception of Television Displays."
6. Quoted in Martin Mayer, *About Television* (New York: Harper and Row, 1972).
7. Lyle and Hoffman, "Explorations in Patterns of Television Viewing by Preschool-age Children," *Television and Social Behavior*, Vol. IV.

NOTES AND DISCUSSION

Winn's title suggests not only that the strategy of her essay will be comparison and contrast, but also that "television" and "reading" are adversaries. Using subheadings to guide the reader through the stages of her comparison and contrast of viewing and reading, Winn suggests that television has profoundly changed the lives of pre-reading children. The essay's structural units are clearly and carefully identified to help the reader along as she switches back and forth between her analyses of the processes and implications of viewing television and those of reading books. Winn's explanation of the processes involved in reading is much longer than her explanation of those involved in watching television, a fact which seems to support her thesis that reading is a more complex activity than viewing.

Winn also tends to use a nostalgic tone in her descriptions of reading children. Consider whether she idealizes the days before television. Since reading is an activity common to her readers, Winn often uses the first-person plural pronoun "we" to suggest a collective and universal experience that includes her readers: "we learn to transform abstract figures into sounds"; "we *create* our own images when reading, based upon our own life experiences." However, when she speaks of viewing, Winn refers to "the mind" and "television-bred children": the personal touches have disappeared. Note that since this essay deals specifically with the effect of television on pre-reading children, the reader cannot, in fact, precisely share the children's experience. Winn also uses personal testimonials (from a ten-year-old child, a teacher, and a grandparent) to support her observations. Readers should consider how they respond to such testimonials and whether and how those testimonials advance Winn's argument.

STUDY QUESTIONS

For Discussion:

1. Consider the meaning of the word "read." What activities and processes does Winn include in her definition of "reading"? Is it possible to "read" television?

2. In her final section, Winn discusses the issue of control over the television medium. She first wrote this essay in 1977 and revised it in 1985. How might the advent and proliferation of the VCR in the eighties, and the Internet in the nineties, undermine or alter some of her points?

For Writing:

1. Examine Winn's use of the phrase "so as not to lose the thread." What does this phrase suggest about the structure and nature of stories, as told in books and on television?

2. How might television and reading be combined to provide a rewarding learning experience for children? Examine one of Winn's books on television to see whether she suggests any ways to reconcile reading and viewing.

HOW IRAQ REVERSE-ENGINEERED THE BOMB

Glenn Zorpette

BIOGRAPHICAL NOTE

Glenn Zorpette was for many years Senior Associate Editor of *IEEE Spectrum*, a magazine for engineering and science professionals. His articles cover a wide range of topics, from the remote sensing of the earth's climate to autonomous underwater vehicles. This article on Iraq's nuclear project is the first of a two-part report entitled "Seeking Nuclear Safeguards." Part Two, written by John A. Adam, is entitled "Working to Halt Nuclear Proliferation." The report won the 1993 National Magazine Award for Reporting, in competition with the entire output of the commercial magazine industry of the United States.

1   Two weeks into the war in the Persian Gulf, a US pilot was heading north after bombing primary targets near Baghdad. A quick check of his instruments and his list of secondary targets convinced him he had the time, fuel, and munitions left for a run at Al Tarmiya, an industrial site, before flying back to base in Saudi Arabia.

2   US intelligence had identified a plant at Tarmiya as a military nuclear facility, but knew little else about it. Analysts believed that Iraq was struggling to build a plant there for uranium enrichment, based on the centrifuge technique, a standard method of enriching uranium to weapons-grade. But Tarmiya's low priority as a target reflected the intelligence community's belief—very much mistaken—that Tarmiya was not one of Iraq's most important nuclear sites.

3   Taking aim at one of the large halls, the pilot rolled in and dispatched two Hellfire missiles, which inflicted light damage.

4   Within a day or so, however, routine aerial reconnaissance revealed hundreds of Iraqis at the site, "busy as hell, tearing out large pieces of equipment" to conceal and protect it,

according to a source familiar with the episode. Unwittingly, the coalition had just struck one of the most critical components of a sprawling nuclear program whose size, scope, and achievements far exceeded the most alarmist estimates of the time. David A. Kay, a former inspector with the International Atomic Energy Agency (IAEA) in Vienna and now secretary general of the Uranium Institute in London, believes that Tarmiya would have been Iraq's first industrial-scale site capable of producing weapons-grade uranium. And though the allies did not know that until much later, the frantic activity after the bombing told them all they needed to know for the time being. Within days, B-52 bombers were sent back to "plaster" the site thoroughly, according to *IEEE Spectrum*'s source.

5   How could Western intelligence have been so blind to the purpose and scope of such a key site? As with many other questions about the forging of the Iraqi war machine, the answer lies partly in the Iraqis' skill in deception and partly in the largely coincidental eight-year war with Iran in the 1980s.

6   Had it succeeded, Iraq's attempt to produce a nuclear weapon might one day have yielded a stunning case study of concurrent engineering. As it turned out, the Iraqis pursued many phases of development in parallel, and closed off options only when they presented truly insurmountable obstacles. This held true both for their production of weapons-grade material and for their construction of a deliverable weapon. The crash program also employed elements of reverse engineering, exploiting projects and developments that had been abandoned by earlier experimenters in the United States and elsewhere. And it drew heavily on materials, hardware, and information acquired from outside the country, in some cases illegally or unethically.

7   ***Intelligence Lapse*** The uranium enrichment technique being pursued at Tarmiya was, astonishingly enough, electromagnetic isotope separation. Nowhere else had this extremely inefficient method been used for an atomic weapon apart from the Manhattan Project in the United States during World War II. As the process uses vast amounts of electricity, the Iraqis constructed a power plant with an output in excess of 100 MW, and devoted it to the Tarmiya facility. But in case the dedicated use of so much electricity should seem suspicious, the power plant was located 15 km from Tarmiya, and connected to the facility by underground cables.

8   Tarmiya itself was surrounded by only a light fence, giving US intelligence analysts the impression that whatever was going on inside could not matter much. What the analysts overlooked, according to *Spectrum*'s source, was that the entire area around Tarmiya was a military exclusion zone, so a more impenetrable fence was not needed. Moreover, the United States may not have scrutinized Tarmiya intensively from above during the Iran-Iraq war, when most reconnaissance assets were focused on border areas between the two countries, according to intelligence sources.

9   Overall, Tarmiya is typical of how Iraq combined not just deception and strict secrecy, but also hard work and research, exploitation of the open literature on nuclear science, illegal acquisitions, and the expenditure of huge sums of money to put together an immense program for nuclear-weapons development. In fact, its exact dimensions and scope are still not fully known, and may never be, according to Kay and others who have investigated it. The best current estimates are that the country spent the equivalent of billions of dollars—perhaps even US $10 billion, over a decade and employed at least 12,000 people in its pursuit of an atomic bomb.

10 The bad news is that at the time it invaded Kuwait, Iraq was probably only 12–18 months away from a crude but useable nuclear device, according to Kay. Other estimates, corroborated by documents in the IAEA's possession, put the figure in the range of 25–40 months, according to Maurizio Zifferero, head of the IAEA "action team" set up to investigate and dismantle the Iraqi nuclear program. (Contrary to previous reports in the popular press, Iraq did not have dozens of kilograms of hidden bomb-grade uranium, one or two working weapons and the ability to produce 20–40 more, or an ongoing project to build a thermonuclear weapon, according to the IAEA.)

11 The "good" news, nonproliferation experts hasten to add, is that the country was in many ways unique: it had plenty of capital from its oil sales, a relatively impressive technical infrastructure, many highly competent engineers and scientists, and a dictatorial regime that could easily conceal huge expenditures on a single military objective.

12 **Outside Help** The Iraqi nuclear program started in the 1960s, with the purchase of a 2-MW Soviet light-water research reactor. But, ironically, the effort to build a bomb can be said to have begun in earnest in 1981, the year Israeli pilots bombed and demolished Tammuz I, a French research reactor with a rating of about 50 MW.

13 "When the Israelis destroyed Tammuz, the Iraqis met and decided to change their policy," Zifferero explained. The decision was to "enshroud in secrecy all activities having to do with their nuclear capabilities, and to duplicate all [key] installations in case any part was discovered and destroyed again by Israel," Zifferero told *Spectrum* in late January during an interview at IAEA headquarters in Vienna.

14 Thus at the time of the invasion of Kuwait, construction was well under way on a duplicate of the Tarmiya installation, at Ash Sharqat, 300 km northwest of Baghdad. Like the Tarmiya facility, Ash Sharqat was fed by underground cables from a sizeable remote power source. During the Gulf War, coalition intelligence had pattern-matched the layouts of Ash Sharqat and Tarmiya, on the basis of aerial reconnaissance, and Ash Sharqat was also bombed, according to an official with access to intelligence documents.

15 But so far, Kay noted with concern, Tarmiya and Ash Sharqat are the only twin facilities discovered by investigators. He said he confronted his Iraqi contacts, demanding to "see the duplicates of your other facilities"—but to no avail. "You could have just cut the consternation with a knife," he said. "And [the Iraqis] haven't come up with any other duplications yet."

16 The French sold Tammuz 1 (also known as Osirak) and Tammuz 2, a 0.5-MW reactor used for studies of the larger reactor, to Iraq in the mid-1970s. Both used uranium fuel enriched to 93 percent U-235, which is bomb-grade material. This material was subject to regular IAEA safeguards as a condition of the French sale, however, so Iraq could not have used it to produce a bomb without openly flouting IAEA regulations. Furthermore, some of the French fuel was lightly irradiated (used) in Tammuz 2, slightly reducing its utility for weapons-making.

17 Nonetheless, Iraq managed to separate a few grams of weapon-type plutonium from additional, indigenously produced fuel rods irradiated in the Soviet reactor, according to the IAEA. A few grams is not nearly enough to make a bomb—about 8 kg are needed—but its creation was one of many flagrant violations of the Nonproliferation Treaty (NPT) that Iraq had signed in 1969.

18 The Iraqis were studying plutonium for at least two reasons, according to Kay. He said they were interested in plutonium production, noting that most atomic bomb designs are based on plutonium, or on mixtures of plutonium and highly enriched uranium. It "shows that they did not leave a single route unexplored," he said.

19   In mid-February, news accounts suggested that Iraq had an as-yet undiscovered underground nuclear reactor capable of producing enough plutonium for several bombs a year. Prompted by intelligence information from France and other countries, inspectors from the IAEA and the United Nations searched several sites, including one 120 km north of Baghdad, but to no avail. Nonetheless, many analysts remain convinced the reactor exists.

20   "All of the facts support the existence of a plutonium reactor," Kay said. The Iraqis had vast amounts of uranium ore, and the ability to fabricate it into fuel rods, both of which are difficult to explain without the existence of such a reactor (the French and Soviet reactors were for the most part fueled by separate fuel assemblies).

21   Apparently, the Iraqis were also investigating the use of a plutonium isotope, Pu-238, as an initiator—the bomb component that supplies neutrons to begin an atomic explosion. Iraq was having trouble producing the polonium isotope normally used for this purpose, Kay said.

22   On the other hand, obtaining uranium, from which plutonium is derived, was not a problem for Iraq.

23   **No Stone Unturned** During the 1980s, the country legally purchased some 440 metric tons of yellowcake, a uranium oxide concentrate obtained from ore, from Portugal and Niger. But 27 tons of uranium dioxide were bought from Brazil and the transaction was not reported to the IAEA, in violation of Iraq's NPT obligations. In addition, Iraq had secretly produced some 164 tons of yellowcake domestically, at Al Qaim, from a phosphate mine at Akashat. The uranium-processing equipment at Al Qaim was reportedly built by a Swiss firm, Alesa Alusuisse Engineering AG. An Alesa spokeswoman, however, denied that her company had had any direct dealings with Iraq.

24   Although not the most common weapons material, highly enriched uranium can of course also yield atomic bombs and here, as in most aspects of the Iraqi nuclear program, the overriding characteristic of the effort was its all-inclusiveness. At one time or another during the 1980s, Iraqi engineers and scientists were either actively developing or studying the available scientific literature on every method ever used to enrich uranium to weapons grade.

25   According to investigators, Iraq supplemented its own attempts to develop enrichment equipment with extensive clandestine efforts to illicitly acquire other equipment, information, and materials. Much of this came from European and US companies, and at least a few rogue nuclear experts. Sometimes the purchases were made through intermediary organizations. To further confuse any would-be inquisitors, the Iraqis named their clandestine nuclear program Petrochemical Project #3 (PC-3).

26   Although the Iraqis considered every means of enrichment, they quickly discarded gaseous diffusion and laser separation, because these techniques required technologies and resources beyond their means. (In fact, laser separation is still experimental, but considered a promising technology in the United States and Europe.) That left three techniques: electromagnetic isotope separation (EMIS), which was to have first gone to industrial scale at Tarmiya; gas centrifuge; and chemical separation.

27   **"Creative and Legal"** Ultimately, work on chemical separation in Iraq took a back seat to the other two techniques, but the country's pursuit of the technology is illustrative of its

methods. France and Japan developed different chemical enrichment technologies in the late 1970s. The Japanese process depended on expensive, esoteric resins whose purchase would be hard to disguise, so the Iraqis chose the French process. In the early 1980s, they entered into negotiations with the French to buy the process, which was called Chemex and based on liquid-liquid solvent extraction.

28   The Iraqi version has the negotiations going on for many months, during which time the Iraqis learned all they could about the process from its French developers. Finally, the Iraqis backed out, saying the French wanted too much money. The Iraqis then bought patent information, chemicals, and equipment—none of which was controlled—and began developing the process on their own. "It was all creative and legal," Kay said.

29   The technology acquisition method was a "classic" one for the Iraqis, Kay added. "They would enter into contract negotiations with a country and go almost up to signing a contract, gathering all the information they could. Then they would back out at the last minute and use the information to develop their own process."

30   According to Kay, before the Gulf War, Iraq had built two generations of prototype chemical enrichment plants and was preparing to step up to initial, pilot-scale industrial production. The IAEA's Zifferero, however, believes that the country did not advance quite this far.

31   The other enrichment methods illustrate two other key aspects of Iraq's PC-3 program: the EMIS effort was mostly homegrown, though illicit acquisitions were made and the undertaking benefited greatly from information available in the open literature, whereas the centrifuge program was built entirely around imports of parts, materials, equipment, and designs, most obtained clandestinely. Both the centrifuge development program and the experimental EMIS program were based at a research complex 10 km south of Baghdad. This complex, at Al Tuwaitha, was the centerpiece of the Iraqi nuclear research effort.

32   It was at Tuwaitha, for example, that the country's Soviet and French reactors had been installed. Although it did not have a supercomputer, which would have been invaluable for simulations and other studies, Tuwaitha was well equipped with 80386-based personal computers and a few larger machines, including a NEC 750 mainframe and software for solving hydrodynamic equations in the presence of shock waves—a useful capability for nuclear weapons design.

33   *A Very Messy Affair*   The EMIS program surprised not only the IAEA, but Western intelligence agencies. With this technique, a stream of uranium ions is deflected by electromagnets in a vacuum chamber. The chamber and its associated equipment are called a calutron. The heavier U-238 ions are deflected less than the U-235 ions, and this slight difference is used to separate out the fissile U-235. However, "what in theory is a very efficient procedure is in practice a very, very messy affair," said Leslie Thorne, who recently retired as field activities manager on the IAEA action team. Invariably, some U-238 ions remain mixed with the U-235, and the ion streams can be hard to control.

34   The two different isotopic materials accumulate in cup-shaped graphite containers. But their accumulation in the two containers can be thrown off wildly by small variations in the power to, and temperature of, the electromagnets. Thus in practice the materials tend to spatter all over the inside of the vacuum chamber, which must be cleaned after every few dozen hours of operation.

35   Hundreds of magnets and tens of millions of watts are needed. During the Manhattan Project, for example, the Y-12 EMIS facility at Oak Ridge in Tennessee used more power

than Canada, plus the entire US stockpile of silver; the latter was used to wind the many electromagnets required (copper was needed elsewhere in the war effort).

36   Mainly because of such problems, US scientists believed that no country would ever turn to EMIS to produce the relatively large amounts of enriched material needed for atomic weapons (although calutrons are still used in scientific research and to produce small quantities of isotopes for medical and industrial uses). Nearly all of the information needed to build and operate calutrons, including the key US patents, has been declassified since the end of World War II.

37   Among the more explicit sources that can be safely assumed to have been used by Iraqi scientists are: *Atomic Energy for Military Purposes*, by Henry D. Smyth (Princeton University Press, 1945); the Progress in Nuclear Energy Series and National Nuclear Energy Series, which together comprise more than 125 volumes of declassified information from the Manhattan Project, published by McGraw-Hill and Pergamon Press in the late 1940s and early 1950s; two volumes on "The Chemistry, Purification and Metallurgy of Plutonium," declassified by the United States Atomic Energy Commission, Office of Technical Information, in 1960; and "Developments in uranium enrichment," a collection of symposium papers published by the American Institute of Chemical Engineers in 1977.

38   The discovery of the Iraqi EMIS program had much of the drama of a good spy novel. The first clue apparently came in the clothing of US hostages held by Iraqi forces at Tuwaitha, according to an expert familiar with the investigation. After the hostages were released, their clothes were analyzed by intelligence experts, who found infinitesimal samples of nuclear materials with isotopic concentrations producible only in a calutron. The analysis was not available until after the war, the source said. The US government has not confirmed this account, most of which appeared first in the *Bulletin of the Atomic Scientists* last September.

39   The real breakthrough, however, came when a young electrical engineer defected in June 1991. The engineer, who worked at the Ash Sharqat site, revealed the existence and extent of the EMIS program to US intelligence. However, according to news reports at the time, the defector also said that the Iraqis had managed to produce 40 kg of bomb-grade material and that Ash Sharqat survived the war unscathed. Both statements are inconsistent with subsequent IAEA findings; the third IAEA inspection mission to Iraq found that "most of the [Ash Sharqat] facility was destroyed."

40   **The "Living Dinosaur"** During the first inspection mission, from May 15–21 of last year, much of Tarmiya's equipment and high-power electrical gear puzzled inspectors. Photographs of it were shown to John Googin, a veteran of the Manhattan Project and the Y-12 facility, which is still at Oak Ridge. Googin conclusively identified the equipment as EMIS components.

41   "Suddenly we found a live dinosaur," said Demetrius Perricos, deputy head of the IAEA's Iraq action team.

42   On June 28, during the second mission, IAEA inspectors were denied access to a site at Fallujah. Climbing a water tower, they saw a convoy of nearly one hundred Iraqi tank-transporter trucks carrying equipment out the back gate of the site. The inspectors were able to photograph the convoy before Iraqi soldiers fired warning shots in their direction; when enlarged, the photographs showed that the trucks were carrying calutron parts. The Fallujah episode was the second in which inspectors were denied access to a site; both sites were suspected of harboring equipment from Tarmiya and Tuwaitha.

43   The inspectors believe Iraq was trying to hide as much of its equipment as possible in the desert, where it could be recovered after the intensive inspections ceased. Indeed, numerous giant calutron parts have been found buried in the desert sands at sites west and north of Baghdad.

44   *A New Manhattan Project*   The EMIS program was headed by Jaffar Dhia Jaffar, a British-educated scientist who had a background in particle accelerators and who had worked at the European Center (now Organisation) for Nuclear Research (CERN) in Geneva. Jaffar, who IAEA investigators believe also directed the overall PC-3 program, is "a good physicist, a capable manager, and a great motivator of people," according to Zifferero.

45   It was in his conception of the Iraqi EMIS program that "Jaffar shows he has a very original mind," Thorne said. For example, where the Manhattan Project required extensive manual adjustment of the ion beams, Jaffar planned to bring the process into the computer age. Computer rooms had been planned for both Tarmiya and Ash Sharqat, from which the process would have been automated. Better control of the beams would have in turn obviated the need for the constant, laborious cleaning work associated with the process.

46   As in the Manhattan Project, the PC-3 program had developed two types of calutrons, a large A type to enrich the uranium from its natural level, and a smaller B type to further enrich it. Iraqi nuclear scientists told the IAEA that the A type was to bring the enrichment to 3 percent U-235, and the B type to 12 percent. Zifferero doubts that account, noting that 12 percent is a "strange" value, too high for power production and too low for weapons making.

47   Documents recovered by the IAEA show that a total of ninety calutrons, seventy type A and twenty type B machines, were to have been installed at Tarmiya. But when the site was bombed, only eight had been installed, and another seventeen were in various stages of assembly. In commissioning tests, the calutrons produced about half a kilogram of uranium enriched to an average of 4 percent U-235, Zifferero said. And, according to Kay, some samples taken from Tarmiya showed enrichment levels between 20 and 30 percent U-235.

48   The IAEA estimates that had the Tarmiya plant gone into full operation, it could have produced up to 15 kg of highly enriched uranium a year, enough for one implosion-type bomb.

49   *"Centrifuge Breakthrough"*   Most investigators believe that the EMIS facility at Tarmiya would have been the first to yield enriched materials in quantity, but there is ample evidence, they say, that emphasis had shifted to the centrifuge program by the late 1980s. Although the program started out earlier in the decade as a relatively low-budget affair, a "breakthrough" in the late 1980s seems to have suddenly put the Iraqis on the track of a much more advanced centrifuge design. There is little doubt now that the breakthrough was the acquisition of centrifuge parts, designs, and advice from European sources.

50   In a centrifuge, gaseous uranium hexafluoride is spun in cylinders with diameters of about 75–400 mm. Centrifugal forces push the heavier U-238 to the cylinder wall, while the U-235 tends to collect closer to the center of the cylinder. Speeds of 400–600 meters per second at the cylinder circumference are required, and "below about 300 meters per second, you don't get any separation at all," an expert in the technology told *Spectrum*. To withstand the high speeds, the cylinders are fabricated of materials with high tensile strength, typically either carbon fiber or maraging steel. To minimize friction and maximize speed, the cylinder is spun in a vacuum.

51   Even at high speeds, the separation requires "cascades" of thousands of centrifuges, each of which enriches the uranium by another increment. Both the construction of the individual centrifuges and—more importantly, their arrangement into a working cascade—require considerable technological sophistication.

52   To enrich uranium in centrifuges, the Iraqis would also have needed the ability to produce uranium hexafluoride, a process known as fluorination. Iraq bought an aluminum fluoride production plant in the late 1970s, and apparently succeeded in converting it for use with uranium—Iraqi officials have admitted producing half a kilogram of uranium hexafluoride, and separating a small (militarily irrelevant) amount of enriched uranium in an experimental centrifuge system.

53   According to *The Death Lobby*, an investigative book about the Iraqi weapons program by journalist Kenneth R. Timmerman, the fluorination equipment came from Alesa Alusuisse Engineering. Timmerman also claims that the Iraqi centrifuge program began in the early 1980s with purchases of centrifuges from Brazil (which that country had obtained legally from West Germany) and with assistance from China. But by the mid-1980s, Iraq had evidently obtained all necessary design information to re-create—and even slightly improve upon—the G1 centrifuge, which was used by the European Enrichment Co. (Urenco) in the 1960s and early 1970s. IAEA and other investigators contacted by *Spectrum* say they are not sure exactly how Iraq obtained information on the centrifuge design from Urenco, a consortium of German, Dutch, and British firms that operates what are generally regarded as the world's most advanced centrifuge plants in Almelo, the Netherlands; Capenhurst in Britain; and Gronau, Germany.

54   In the late 1980s, the Iraqis called in Bruno Stemmler and Walter Busse, who had worked on gas centrifuges at MAN Technologie, a German member of the Urenco consortium. While insisting that he did not know the true purpose of the Iraqi centrifuges, Stemmler told the *Sunday Times* in London in December 1990 that he and Busse were hired to trouble-shoot an experimental enrichment cascade the Iraqis had set up near Tuwaitha. As of late February, the German Government was believed to be considering whether to press charges against Stemmler and Busse, but it was not clear that the two had broken any German laws. (Not until 1990 did the former West German Government make it a crime for its citizens to privately assist foreign weapons programs.)

55   Stemmler told the *Sunday Times* he saw equipment from many western companies during his visits to the Iraqi facility, including vacuum pumps from Veeco Instruments Inc., Plainview, NY, and valves, furnaces, and other equipment from VAT of Lichtenstein and Leybold-Heraus of the then West Germany. Even though sales of most of this equipment was not controlled by export laws, some of it was procured through phony intermediary companies set up in London, Germany, and elsewhere.

56   IAEA investigators have also found centrifuge rotors in Iraq that were produced in the former West Germany. Their shape and carbon fiber composition could have left no doubt about what the rotors were for, IAEA inspectors said. The sale of carbon-fiber centrifuge rotors was "absolutely illegal," Kay added.

57   Unwilling to depend on outside suppliers for parts, Iraq was building its own plant to manufacture centrifuges at Al Furat. The plant, which was still incomplete when war broke out in the Gulf, would have been capable of turning out centrifuges by the thousands, according to Thorne. Some of the most important pieces of manufacturing equipment for the

Standoff at Al Atheer:
"Thank God for the Satellite Telephone"

For a few days, tens of millions of people watched television news reports and listened to their radios, most in disbelief. Just months after suffering one of the most lopsided military defeats in history, the Iraqi Government seemed to be intent on provoking another war.

As a condition of its surrender, the Iraqi Government agreed to open its weapons facilities—especially its nuclear complex—to inspectors from the United Nations and the International Atomic Energy Agency (IAEA). But on the sixth inspection mission, the Government's attitude toward the inspectors went from spottily cooperative to openly hostile. Access was barred to key facilities, documents were seized, official communiqués were intercepted, and, in the most publicized incident, the inspection team was detained for four days in a parking lot next to an inspection site.

The trouble began the evening of the first day, September 22, when the team, after collecting several dozen boxes of documents, attempted to leave the Nuclear Design Center at Al Atheer. Iraqi officials detained the 43-member team and confiscated the documents, which described Iraq's secret program to build a centrifuge plant to enrich uranium to weapons grade. The team was released after five hours and some of the documents were returned after eleven hours.

According to team leader David Kay, about one-quarter of the documents were not returned, however. These documents probably had information related to procurement and design of parts and materials needed for the centrifuge program, Kay said, explaining that the team's translators had scanned the documents and made a brief synopsis before the papers were confiscated.

At the second inspection site, the headquarters of the country's nuclear-weapon development facility, Iraqi officials again attempted to confiscate documents. At stake was information that Kay called "a gold mine": data on the weapons development program; information on Iraq's pursuit of four different enrichment technologies; complete personnel and payroll records of the clandestine weapons effort; and some foreign and domestic procurement records. This time, the team refused, setting up a standoff in an adjacent parking lot that lasted ninety-six hours.

In this war of wills, the inspection team had a secret weapon of its own: a satellite telephone, which was used to do live interviews with major news organizations worldwide. Once again, in a manner bizarrely reminiscent of the Gulf War, the Iraqis "totally underestimated the impact of modern technology," Kay said in an interview. "They didn't understand how we could contact CNN and NPR [National Public Radio]," he observed.

The stalemate was to take a further "surreal" twist on the third day, when Kay, exhausted from doing interviews, heard his satellite telephone ring. It was the operator from the International Maritime Satellite (Inmarsat) Organization. Concerned about the unusual activity on Kay's line, he asked if Kay knew his satellite telephone had been in use for twenty of the last twenty-four hours. Kay did indeed.

Kay explained his predicament and "the guy became very helpful." In Iraq, the team's telephone was at the edge of the closest satellite's coverage, so the operator shifted the satellite in orbit to better accommodate the team. He also rerouted their traffic to an Inmarsat ground station in Australia, which was less heavily trafficked than the Indian Ocean ground station they had been going through.

Finally, at 5:46 AM on September 28, the team was released, the disputed documents still in their possession. Relieved, Kay could not help wondering nevertheless what could have happened.

"Thank God for the satellite telephone," said Kay, now secretary general of the Uranium Institute in London. "If we had been caught out there in the parking lot without communications, it's possible that the Iraqis might have used more force than they did, and the United States could have responded militarily."

plant were supplied by H & H Metallform Maschinenbau und Vertriebs GmbH of the former West Germany. The key raw material for the centrifuges was also found in Iraq: some 100 metric tons of maraging steel, most of which had been melted in an unsuccessful attempt to conceal it from inspectors. By early March, the IAEA had still not released the names of the companies that sold Iraq the maraging steel.

58   Although the IAEA believes that Iraq did not succeed in operating a pilot centrifuge cascade before it invaded Kuwait, Kay disagrees. "It's hard to believe that the materials for 10 000 centrifuges were ordered without having a small pilot plant going" to verify that the process would work, he said. A "small" cascade would comprise perhaps 100–500 centrifuges, he explained, adding that such a cascade would be sufficient to "tune" the system and establish the efficiency of the process. The hypothetical cascade could have been in operation late in 1989, and may have been disassembled and hidden from IAEA inspectors "until the heat is off," he said.

59   A key point about uranium enrichment—and one frequently overlooked in accounts of the Iraqi program—is that more than one method may be used to produce weapons-grade material. After all, thermal, gas-diffusion, and EMIS techniques were all used to produce the highly enriched uranium for Little Boy, the bomb dropped on Hiroshima at the end of World War II.

60   For example, EMIS is particularly well-suited to further enriching uranium that has already been somewhat enriched, according to Thorne. Thus, although there is no proof that Iraq had such plans, centrifuges could have been used to enrich samples to, say, 12 percent U-235, and EMIS could have been used to bring them up to weapons-grade (93 percent).

61 *A "Startling Find"* One of the most puzzling of the many mysteries surrounding the Iraq program is the possible discovery of weapons-grade uranium in a group of twenty-five samples taken inside the Tuwaitha complex. The samples, which were filter-paper smears taken off walls, floors, equipment, and other surfaces, were sent to several laboratories—one an IAEA laboratory at Seibersdorf, in Austria; the others US facilities serving the intelligence community.

62   The Seibersdorf laboratory turned up no evidence of highly enriched uranium (HEU). But equipment at the US laboratories, which is several orders of magnitude more sensitive than the Seibersdorf facility, found HEU—not only in the Tuwaitha samples, but in two control samples known to have *no* uranium isotopes at all. Repeated tests on additional

samples gave the same results. Compounding the mystery, the US laboratory said some of the uranium samples had a highly unusual isotopic composition, which matched a common analytical standard used to test detection equipment. "On the face of it, it's a very startling find," Thorne said.

63   The Iraqis have steadfastly maintained that the places at Tuwaitha from which the samples were taken have never contained enriched uranium. "We've really hammered them on this one, and given them every face-saving opportunity to explain it," Thorne said. "But they've held to the story that they never had highly enriched uranium at that site." One current theory is that an HEU standard (analytical) sample somehow contaminated some of the Tuwaitha samples sent to the US laboratory.

64   ***Putting It All Together***   Not limiting itself to producing weapons-grade materials (generally viewed as technologically the hardest task in building a bomb), Iraq was concurrently struggling to build a deliverable weapon around the material, a daunting task known as weaponization. Here, as in its enrichment efforts, Iraq took multiple approaches, mostly at a weapons-design and -testing complex not far from Al Atheer.

65   The two basic types of atomic bombs are gun devices and implosion weapons. The latter are much more difficult to design and build, but provide higher explosive yields for a given amount of fissile material. IAEA investigators have found no evidence that Iraq was actively pursuing a gun device; it is clear, they say, that they concentrated their money and resources on an implosion device, and had even started work on fairly advanced implosion designs.

66   In an implosion device, the fissile material is physically compressed by the force of a shock wave created with conventional explosives. Then, at just the right instant, neutrons are released, initiating the ultrafast fission chain reactions—an atomic blast. Thus the main elements of an implosion device are a firing system, an explosive assembly, and the core. The firing system includes vacuum-tube-based, high-energy discharge devices called krytrons that are capable of releasing enough energy to detonate the conventional explosive. The explosive assembly includes "lenses" that precisely focus the spherical, imploding shockwave on the fissile core, within which is a neutronic initiator. The IAEA has amassed ample evidence that the Iraqis had made progress in each of these areas.

67   Iraq's attempts to import krytrons from CSI Technologies Inc., San Marcos, Calif., made news in March 1990, when two Iraqis were arrested at London's Heathrow airport after an 18-month "sting" operation involving US and British Customs. Several years before that failure, however, Iraq did manage to get weapons-quality capacitors from other US concerns, and also produced its own capacitors. The latter, however, did "not seem to possess the characteristics necessary for storing the energy required by the multiple detonator system," the IAEA found.

68   Work on the conventional explosive assembly, which creates the collapsing shockwave, was carried out mainly at a large explosive production site near Al Qa Qaa. So far, IAEA investigators have found about 230 metric tons of a high-energy explosive, HMX, which is suitable for use in atomic bombs. The IAEA has not announced where the explosive came from, but a knowledgeable source told *Spectrum* it came from Czechoslovakia, where Iraq had bought large quantities of it for conventional military uses in its war with Iran.

69   The seventh IAEA inspection mission to Iraq found that two types of explosive lenses were fabricated and tested near Al Qa Qaa between March and May, 1990. Although both

lenses were designed for planar shock waves, "it is prudent to assume that Iraqi scientists have a basic knowledge of the initiation of a spherical implosion," the inspectors wrote in their report on the mission.

70   The seventh mission also found that Iraqi scientists had used hydrodynamic computer programs to evaluate various core geometries. Also, facilities were found at Al Atheer that would have been suitable for large-scale uranium metallurgy, of the sort that would be necessary to produce the core of a bomb. Kay said he saw some evidence that at least preliminary tests had been carried out on the use of implosions to compress depleted (unenriched) uranium; such work would have enabled the Iraqis to study the symmetry and simultaneity of shock waves without risking a nuclear explosion.

71   Indications are so far that Iraq was having trouble producing a neutronic initiator. Besides the usual polonium-beryllium design, several alternatives were being examined, none apparently with much success.

72   Among the more interesting documents found in Iraq is a proposal by an Iraqi Government chemist to produce tritium, the heaviest hydrogen isotope, by irradiating lithium-6. The disclosure of the document led to erroneous press reports that Iraq was at work on a thermonuclear (fusion) bomb. In all advanced atomic (fission) bomb designs, tritium is used in the core to boost the explosive yield, Thorne noted, and this may have been the use envisioned by the chemist.

73   In a gun-type atomic bomb, the chain-reaction is initiated by hurling together in a tube, and with tremendous force, two samples of highly enriched uranium. Much more fissile material is needed than would be for an implosive weapon, and gun-type bombs are difficult, if not impossible, to deliver with a missile. But they can be quite effective, as Little Boy demonstrated. According to Kay, the Iraqis "knew everything necessary to make a gun-assembly device." He also said he found tungsten-carbide piping, which would have been suitable for making the tube in which the samples would collide.

74   ***Ignored Consequences*** Though Iraqi officials considered every angle and possibility in attempting to build an atomic bomb, they seem to have completely ignored the consequences of having one.

75   "I'm not sure the Iraqis had thought through the political and strategic implications of having a nuclear weapon," Kay said. "If the Israelis had known what the full size and scope of the Iraqi nuclear program was, I'm not sure what their reaction would have been when the Scuds started falling. I'm not sure that pressure from the United States and other countries would have been enough to keep the Israelis from reacting with massive force."

76   Unfortunately, such an outcome is still a possibility. Though the Iraqi nuclear program is now being dismantled, some analysts see parallels between the vanquished southwest Asian nation today and Germany after World War I. "While Iraq does not possess the industrial skills available to Germany in 1919, the full extent of Iraq's ability to infiltrate the economic structure of the West, particularly western Europe, in order to gain access to very high technology is just becoming known," wrote Geoffrey Kemp in *The Control of the Middle East Arms Race*.

77   "The danger is that once Iraq begins to export oil and gains access to hard currency, it will be able to hide a portion of its revenues for covert purposes," according to Kemp, a senior associate at the Carnegie Endowment for International Peace in Washington, DC.

"Once it has accumulated a sizable hard currency account, it could once more use its financial resources to penetrate the arms market and buy the services of unemployed technicians and engineers in Europe, including East Europe and the Soviet Union."

78 ***To Probe Further*** *The Death Lobby: How the West Armed Iraq* is one of the most comprehensive accounts of its kind. Although it was written before the start of the inspection missions to Iraq, it has detailed histories of the country's procurement efforts and describes its methods and tactics. Written by Kenneth R. Timmerman, it was published by Houghton Mifflin, Boston, in 1991. *The Bulletin of the Atomic Scientists* has run several lengthy articles speculating on how advanced the Iraqi program was; see especially the March, July/August, and September 1991 issues. *The Control of the Middle East Arms Race*, by Geoffrey Kemp with Shelly A. Stahl, was published by the Carnegie Endowment for International Peace in Washington, D.C., last autumn.

NOTES AND DISCUSSION

Note the variety of expository techniques Zorpette uses in this essay. To place the technical problem within a historical context, he begins with a narrative about what had seemed a routine wartime mission. He then bridges to technical matters by asking a question that sets out two areas for examination. Next, he analyzes the separate but concurrent parts of the project. Along the way Zorpette effectively uses definitions, such as the definition of "reverse engineering" in paragraph 6, and the description and definition of the EMIS (electromagnetic isotope separation) process in the section headed "A Very Messy Affair."

This article has echoes of the detective story as it unravels various levels of deception and complicated transactions in the build-up of the materials and technology necessary for building an atomic bomb. It is also a cautionary tale about how technologically advanced nations make themselves vulnerable to attacks from less advanced ones.

Note how Zorpette brings in sources to supplement or support his reportage. Some of those sources (particularly the military ones) are anonymous, though many are named and their credentials given. Consider the impact of the variety of sources, and Zorpette's methods of acknowledgement.

STUDY QUESTIONS

For Discussion:

1. Zorpette defines "reverse engineering" as "exploiting projects and developments that had been abandoned by earlier experimenters in the United States and elsewhere." Discuss his implicit claim that the Iraqi project exploited blind spots, created by what Thomas Kuhn would recognize as "paradigm shifts," by adopting and hiding behind technology, such as EMIS, that had long been abandoned or superseded elsewhere.

2. Consider the impact of beginning a report on highly technical and potentially sensitive matters with a narrative, an element that helps "personalize" the subject. Discuss the impact of that personalization on the technical nature of the piece.

For Writing:

1. Analyze and explain the importance of the sub-headings used throughout. Begin by listing the headings separately to see what they have to tell you about the shape and content of the article.

2. As a research project, look up the companion piece by John A. Adam in the April 1992 issue of *IEEE Spectrum*, and explain how the two pieces work together to cover the larger issues raised by their joint title, "Seeking Nuclear Safeguards."

APPENDIX A

"Putting Self-Help 'Leviathans' and 'Oracles' to Sleep": A Discussion of Anthony Robbins' *Awaken the Giant Within* and James Redfield's *The Celestine Prophecy*

Lisa Grekul

1   To unlock the secrets of individual "success" or personal "fulfillment," we need look no further than the "self-development" or "self-help" genre of popular literature. For C$22.95 we can buy texts that contain the key to mental, emotional, physical, and financial accomplishment: we can buy Anthony Robbins' *Awaken the Giant Within* or James Redfield's *The Celestine Prophecy*. In fact, the strikingly similar "secrets" found in the texts of Robbins and Redfield are shared by most self-help books.[1] Close readings, then, of *Awaken the Giant Within* and *The Celestine Prophecy*—as representative texts of the genre—reveal the common themes employed by self-help authors to lead readers "down the path" of self-improvement. Although Robbins' book is a work of nonfiction (directed primarily at a male audience) and Redfield's book is a work of fiction (directed at a male or female audience), both authors cloak their self-help ideology in fairy-tale motifs and imagery. One aphoristic tenet lies at the core of both texts: success is achieved through "spiritual awakening." Robbins and Redfield emphasize the innovative attributes of their spiritual insights, but the authors' teachings are neither creative nor original. Rather, *Awaken the Giant Within* resonates with Biblical references and *The Celestine Prophecy* reiterates centuries-old gnostic beliefs. Moreover, both Robbins and Redfield rely upon the psychological paradigm of Maslow's hierarchy of needs: Robbins addresses the basic human need for "self-actualization" and Redfield embraces the need for "spiritual transcendence." Perhaps in our increasingly secularized Western society authors like Robbins and Redfield prepackage "accessible" religious models. But when the ticket to spiritual awakening takes the form of a best-selling book,[2] authors like Robbins and Redfield leave their "commodified" spiritual teachings open to Marxist critique. The foundation for success (mental, emotional, physical, and financial) may lie in spirituality or faith, but, ultimately, we must question the $22.95 spiritual value of *Awaken the Giant Within* or *The Celestine Prophecy*.

2   Anthony Robbins begins *Awaken the Giant Within* with his own fairy-tale success story, a personal anecdote that highlights the process through which he awakened to his

Reprinted by permission of the author.

life's purpose. Twelve years ago, Robbins was a veritable Cinderella figure: a lost, lonely, and overweight janitor with a 1960 Volkswagen. He gained "information, strategies, philosophies, and skills" (Robbins 20), however, and his dream of "success" magically came true. Robbins fails to explain precisely how he became successful: as though blessed with a fairy godmother, in one sentence he is "sitting in [his] 400-square-foot bachelor apartment . . . all alone and crying as [he] listened to the lyrics of a Neil Diamond song" (20–21) and in the next he is speaking to "five thousand smiling, cheering, loving faces" (20). Because success for Robbins is the discovery of hidden motivational-speaker talents, he (*himself*) becomes a fairy godmother figure, waving the magic wand of CANI!™ [3] over audiences everywhere. He writes that our dreams are often "shrouded in the frustrations and routines of daily life" but that his "life's quest has been to restore the dream and to make it real" (19). Logically, then, he locates *Awaken the Giant Within* in a wondrous world of dreams, masters, giants, and power. From time to time, while flying his jet helicopter over Los Angeles en route to one of his seminars, even Robbins wonders, "*could this be real?*" (21). Robbins' personal success story may be genuine but it establishes a fantasy framework for his book—a framework through which readers rely on Robbins, as "self-help fairy godmother," to make happy endings of their ordinary lives.

3   Similarly, James Redfield constructs *The Celestine Prophecy* in the framework of a fairy tale: in his search for an ancient manuscript, Redfield's narrator goes to a land far, far away (Peru). The narrator finds an idealized exotic setting at the Viciente Lodge, the ruins of Machu Picchu, and the ruins of the Celestine Temple. He describes, for example, the Viciente Lodge: "surrounded by colorful pastures and orchards, the grass seemed unusually green and healthy. It grew thickly even under the giant oaks . . . [there were] beds of exotic plants and walkways trimmed with dazzling flowers and ferns" (Redfield, *Prophecy* 39). The exotic milieu invokes fairy tales set in foreign lands, like the *Arabian Nights*. The manuscript itself, which "dates back to about 600 BC [and] predicts a massive transformation in human society" (4), bears symbolic resemblance to Aladdin's lamp. Rubbing Aladdin's lamp frees a genie who will, in turn, grant wishes of instant power and fortune; reading the ancient manuscript provides a "new spiritual awakening" (Redfield, *Guide* xv) that will, in turn, bring instant power and fortune. When the manuscript is destroyed, the narrator learns that "from now on the insights will have to be shared between people. Each person, once they hear the message . . . must pass on the message to everyone who is ready for it" (Redfield, *Prophecy* 245). *The Celestine Prophecy* may contain nine spiritual insights in the form of the "written word," but, at the same time, it encourages oral transmission of these insights. *Orally* transmitted, Redfield's spiritual insights take on the dimensions of a fairy or folk tale.

4   Although Robbins explains, in *Awaken the Giant Within*, his perpetual search for new methods and technologies to pass along, his Biblical allusions and metaphors undermine the novelty of his enterprise. Like a Messiah, Robbins uses personal charisma to spread his self-development gospels. Robbins explains that psychologists and psychiatrists have called him "a charlatan and a liar . . . [who makes] false claims" (Robbins 109); so, too, was Jesus Christ accused and denounced by the chief priests and scribes of Jerusalem (Luke 23). Robbins' "Seven Days to Shape Your Life" (Robbins 12) are undeniably parallel to the seven days of creation (Genesis 1 and 2). Each day of Robbins' creation, however, corresponds to an aspect of "your" personal destiny: emotional (day one), physical (two), relationship (three), financial (four), conduct (five), and time (six). Of course, day seven is earmarked for

"Rest and Play: Even God Took One Day Off!" (Robbins 12). Robbins directly quotes from Matthew 7:7, "ask and you will receive. Seek and you will find; knock, and it will be opened to you" (Robbins 162), but *Awaken the Giant Within*—from cover to cover—echoes Matthew 25:14–30, the "Parable of the Talents."[4] We learn from the Biblical parable that "talents," innate abilities, must be improved and cultivated. The epigraph to Robbins' book, a quotation from Orison Swett Marden, emphasizes Robbins' analogous notion that our built-in abilities must be recognized before we can unleash our power-potential: "deep within man dwell those slumbering powers; powers that would astonish him, that he never dreamed of possessing; forces that would revolutionize his life if aroused and put into action" (Robbins 15). Robbins himself says "the most exciting thing about this force, this power, is that you already possess it" (37): if we are to succeed, our talents must be awakened and refined.

5   *The Celestine Prophecy*'s promises of "new consciousness . . . new awareness . . . new understanding" (Author's Note) are hardly new: such promises were voiced in the Mediterranean during the second and third centuries, when gnosticism reached the height of its popularity.[5] According to gnostic teachings, individuals escape from the material world and find eternal salvation through an unmediated relationship with God. Each of the nine insights absorbed by Redfield's narrator articulates an aspect of gnosticism: the second insight, for example, helps us "[become] aware of our essentially spiritual nature" (Redfield, *Guide* 244); the fifth insight describes "how a mystical connection with universal energy feels" (244); the seventh insight shows us "how to ask questions, receive intuitions, and find answers" (245). With the ninth insight the narrator at last learns how to connect with divine energy: he says, "at some point everyone will vibrate highly enough so that we can walk into heaven" (Redfield, *Prophecy* 242). *The Tenth Insight*, moreover, is entirely populated with characters who "vibrate," become invisible, and subsequently find heaven on earth. They understand that "real fulfillment comes only when we first tune into our inner direction and divine guidance . . . we become cocreators with the divine source" (Redfield, *Tenth Insight* 29). The irony of *The Celestine Prophecy*'s new-age appeal is that its gnostic teachings are, in fact, age-old.

6   The underlying psychology of *Awaken the Giant Within* may not be "age-old," but it has "been around" for at least two decades: Robbins capitalizes on Maslow's "hierarchy of needs"[6] to justify his self-development program. In 1970, humanist psychologist Abraham Maslow formulated the theory that "our inborn needs are arranged in a sequence of stages from primitive to advanced" (Zimbardo 433). Robbins' interest is in individuals who are near the "top" of the hierarchy, people "who are nourished, safe, loved and loving, secure, thinking, and creating. These people have moved beyond basic human needs in the quest for fullest development of their potentials" (433). Robbins' objective is to help individuals *self-actualize*. According to Maslow's theory, self-actualization requires the fulfillment of several criteria; individuals must become "self-aware, self-accepting, socially responsive, creative, spontaneous, and open to novelty and challenge" (433). And Robbins systematically addresses each of Maslow's criteria for self-actualization. With imperative language, he makes demands like "write down the replacements for the two limiting beliefs you've just eliminated" (Robbins 103), "take immediate action as soon as you finish this chapter" (304), "know who you are" (424), "accept who you are" (424), "connect with people at the deepest level" (27), believe in your "power to create" (75), and be spontaneous, as "all changes are created in a moment" (108). Maslow's model provides the psychological subtext of *Awaken the Giant Within*.

7   Redfield's interest, on the other hand, is in the highest echelon of Maslow's hierarchy of needs: the *need for spiritual transcendence,* "a step beyond total fulfillment of individual potential" (Zimbardo 433). The need for spiritual transcendence "may lead to higher states of consciousness and a cosmic vision of one's part in the universe" (433). Indeed, *The Celestine Prophecy* rejects our "500-year-old preoccupation with secular survival" (Redfield, *Guide* xv); it focuses, rather, on "ending the cycle of birth and death" (xviii) by revealing our purpose in "a universe of dynamic energy" (xvi). Redfield looks ahead to a future in which all citizens of the world will fulfill the human need for spiritual transcendence. Our advanced spiritualism will affect economic systems: "when people come into our lives at just the right time to give us the answers we need, we . . . give them money" (Redfield, *Prophecy* 226), but eventually "the automation of goods will allow everyone's needs to be met completely, without the exchange of any currency" (Redfield, *Guide* 247). Ecologically, we will "revere the natural energy sources of mountains, deserts, forests, lakes, and rivers" (246). Politically, we will "democratize the planet" (247). In *The Celestine Prophecy*, when all of humanity has ascended Maslow's hierarchy of needs, spiritual principles will direct human society.

8   But the inherent paradox of *Awaken the Giant Within* and *The Celestine Prophecy* is that, in both cases, spiritual principles are prepackaged and mass-marketed: by selling spiritual guidance as a commodity, Robbins and Redfield "snuff out" the morality of spirituality. Inscribed in the discourse of their self-help books is self-help ideology. Like other ideologies, characterized by "masking, distortion, [and] concealment" (Storey 3), the ideology of the self-help industry "works in the interest of the powerful against the interests of the powerless . . . [it] conceals the reality of domination from those in power . . . [and] conceals the reality of subordination from those who are powerless" (3). If we believe that Robbins or Redfield will change our lives, we have been lulled into a state of false consciousness; the authors offer "false, but seemingly true, resolutions to real problems" (111–12). They wield their capitalist power, cloaked in ostensible benevolence, over the spiritually-needy masses. Hence, their alleged desire to help and empower "the weak" is at odds with their desire to oppress and exploit the weak. Ironically, if people are actually helped by authors like Robbins or Redfield, what happens to the self-help industry?

9   Ultimately, *Awaken the Giant Within*'s primary objective is to guarantee the reader's dependency on Anthony Robbins: again and again the discourse of his text impels readers to "come back for more." Riddled with imperative language—"awaken the giant power of decision . . . claim the birthright of unlimited power . . . make a decision right now" (Robbins 36)—the book demands a commitment to Robbins' brand of self-help. His principle doctrine, CANI!™ (Constant And Never-ending Improvement), recurs throughout the book as an aggressive reminder that self-development is a constant and never-ending process. Completion of *Awaken the Giant Within* is not an "end" but a "beginning"; Robbins concludes with the notion that "you are guided along a path of never-ending growth and learning" (512). Who guides you along the path? Robbins himself. He unabashedly asks that you maintain a "relationship" with him through "a tape or a seminar" (512). In fact, on a personal note, Robbins says, "I hope you'll stay in touch with me. I hope you'll write to me or that we'll have the privilege of meeting personally in a seminar, [or] at a Foundation function" (512). To ensure that you have continued access to his guidance—and he has continued access to your pocketbook—Robbins devotes several pages (513–19) to advertising his "Personal Power" audio cassette series, *Unlimited Power* (his second book), and Robbins Success Systems™ seminars.

10   Similarly, *The Celestine Prophecy* represents the ground breaking work through which Redfield hooks the reader into the "celestine industry." The discourse of Redfield's spiritual awakening is characteristically vague: we are to "exist at a level of higher energy," to engage in "mystical experience[s]," and to move "toward worldwide spiritual consciousness" (Redfield, *Prophecy* 120). When Redfield explicitly presents semantic ambiguities, he implicitly suggests that *The Celestine Prophecy* is incomplete without *The Celestine Prophecy: An Experiential Guide*. Designed to "clarify the experience conveyed in the original book" (Redfield, *Guide* xii), the *Experiential Guide* facilitates group discussion of the nine spiritual insights. But the ninth insight itself "mentions that a Tenth Insight exists" (Redfield, *Prophecy* 243), hence engendering the reader's anticipation of a sequel. Both *The Celestine Prophecy* and *The Tenth Insight* are followed by advertisements for "The Celestine Journal," which (for US$29.95) "chronicles [Redfield's] present experiences and reflections on the spiritual renaissance occurring on our planet" (Redfield, *Prophecy* 247). Readers can also purchase audio cassettes of the *Celestine Meditations* or *The Celestine Prophecy—A Musical Voyage*. Evidently, *The Celestine Prophecy* "proper" merely initiates readers into the "celestine subculture," but it cannot be mistaken for the definitive "celestine work": such a work does not exist. Rather, readers rely on Redfield to sustain the production of numerous (multimedia) celestine texts and Redfield relies on readers to provide ceaseless monetary support of the celestine industry.

11   And so, the cost incurred for the secrets of mental, emotional, physical, and financial success may, in fact, exceed $22.95. As representative texts of the self-help genre of popular literature, Anthony Robbins' *Awaken the Giant Within* and James Redfield's *The Celestine Prophecy* appear to provide "cheap" and "easy" access to spirituality in our increasingly secularized Western society. The texts, however, do not easily escape criticism. Both texts locate their self-help ideology in familiar cultural constructs. Robbins and Redfield use fairy-tale motifs and imagery as frameworks for their books. While Robbins relies on Biblical allusions and metaphors to articulate his self-help program, Redfield resurrects gnosticism; where Robbins invokes the "self-actualization" need of Maslow's psychological paradigm, Redfield invokes the "spiritual transcendence" need of Maslow's hierarchy. But fairy-tale frameworks, religious invocations, and psychological subtexts fail to conceal the underlying capitalist motivations of *Awaken the Giant Within* and *The Celestine Prophecy*. In the self-help industry, spiritualism ironically becomes a market commodity through which authors like Robbins and Redfield exploit and oppress their vulnerable readers. And, ultimately, the paradox is that in order to ensure success in the self-help industry, authors of self-help texts (like Robbins and Redfield) must perpetuate the insecurities of their readers.

ENDNOTES

1. Most notably, Deepak Chopra's *Way of the Wizard: Twenty Spiritual Lessons for Creating the Life You Want* and *The Seven Spiritual Laws of Success*, as well as Dan Millman's *Way of the Peaceful Warrior: A Book That Changes Lives* and *Sacred Journey of the Peaceful Warrior*.

2. In fact, Robbins and Redfield have respectively created an industry in and of themselves. Robbins has a best-selling book, an audio-cassette series (Powertalk), and nine companies that produce infomercials and motivational seminars. Redfield wrote two sequels to *The Celestine Prophecy*: *The Celestine Prophecy Experiential Guide* (1995)

and *The Tenth Insight* (1996); he also produces the *Celestine Journal* and *Celestine Meditations* (audio-cassettes with his wife Salle). I discuss this later in the essay.

3. Constant And Never-ending Improvement (Robbins, 96).

4. This parable tells of a man who goes on a journey and leaves his money with three servants. Two of the servants invest their money and receive interest, but the third servant hides his money in the ground. When the master returns, he praises the first two servants and berates the third.

5. Though not directly quoted, my sources regarding gnosticism are *The Literary Guide to the Bible* and *Compton's Interactive Encyclopedia.* (Copyright 1994 Compton's NewMedia, Inc.).

6. Maslow's hierarchy looks something like this diagram, modeled on Zimbardo's discussion of Maslow in *Psychology and Life:*

Transcendence:
spiritual need for
cosmic identification

Self-Actualization: need to fulfill
potential, to have meaningful goals

Esthetic: need for order and beauty

Cognitive: need for knowledge, understanding

Esteem: need for confidence, sense of worth/competence

Attachment: need to belong, to affiliate, to love and be loved

Safety: need for security, comfort, tranquility, and freedom from fear

Biological: need for food, water, oxygen, rest, sexual expression, release from tension

WORKS CITED

Alter, Robert, and Frank Kermode, eds. *The Literary Guide to the Bible*. Cambridge, Mass.: Belknap Press, 1987.

Redfield, James. *The Celestine Prophecy*. New York: Time Warner, 1993.

_____. *The Celestine Prophecy: An Experiential Guide*. New York: Time Warner, 1995.

_____. *The Tenth Insight*. New York: Time Warner, 1996.

Robbins, Anthony. *Awaken the Giant Within: How to Take Immediate Control of Your Mental, Emotional, Physical, and Financial Destiny!* New York: Simon and Schuster, 1992.

Storey, John. *An Introductory Guide to Cultural Theory and Popular Culture*. Athens: University of Georgia Press, 1993.

Zimbardo, Philip G. *Psychology and Life*. New York: HarperCollins, 1992.

APPENDIX B

Fishing for Coyote in Sheila Watson's
The Double Hook   Cherina Sparks

1   Sheila Watson's *The Double Hook* is many things: a parody of traditional romances and westerns, a collection of fragmented Bible stories, a prose-poem with a multitude of literary allusions (Child 31), and a mythical novella that transcends time and cultural regionalism. The novel's primary importance, however, is not the simple boy-meets-girl plot, or any blatant love-conquers-all theme, but is instead its pioneering movement between images, its structure, and its form. On a most simplistic level, the novel is about opposites balanced delicately in equilibrium, with characters inseparable from both the (figurative) light and dark: opposites are not only good and evil, but also written and oral, sacred and secular, history and legend. Coyote is a central image in the development of this novel: a legendary spirit based on Native American oral stories with godlike, human, and animalistic characteristics. Nevertheless, during a reading at Grant MacEwan College in October 1973, Watson said, "I don't know now, if I rewrote it, whether I would use the Coyote figure. It is a question . . . that is in the mouth of this figure who keeps making utterances all through the course of the novel" (15). Why would Watson feel she would not employ Coyote again? Some say she is not content with the interpretations of Coyote, that he is unnecessary, since Ma Potter alone could fulfill his role, that he is too wily or too tricky, or that as a non-Native, Watson is an outsider looking into, without capturing the essence of, his legend (Bowering 198). Undeniably, the first question then is what is Coyote's specific role in *The Double Hook*? Second, is he an integral part of the novel?

2   Coyote evokes many literary connections within history, legend, and religion. His name is immediately symbolic and intertextual, and these presupposed allusions are inseparable from his actual character in the novel. His character in action and in dialogue indicates multilayered and varied references, all of which are necessary to the novel's significance and progression.

3   Coyote is a Trickster figure, a powerful spirit with human imperfections, from Okanagan, Thompson, and Shuswap tribal legends. He is second only to Old Man, creator of the world, in importance. In some legends, he brought food and shelter to his people, and taught hunting and fishing. Having finished his work on earth, he left with Old Man until their people need them to change the world again (Mitchell 101). In other legends, he is not a solely beneficial character. The Trickster is a shape shifter, and as such has many different forms such as the raven, spider, hare, and coyote (Radin ix–x). He has a dual role. Trickster Coyote is both "creator and destroyer, giver and negator, he who dupes others and who is always duped himself" (Radin ix–x). He is a "powerful fool" (Bowering 192). Coyote has no moral or social values; he is at the mercy of his passions and hunger as God of Appetite ("to wolf"). However, he is also the teacher of proper behaviour as a negative role model, a model for wrongdoings. His actions are reminders of appropriate behaviour and consequences of disobedience (Ghezzi 444–5). Coyote is at times a foolish bungler; trapping himself by his own magic and deceptions, he makes people laugh. As a trickster, Coyote's motivations are sometimes selfless, and sometimes selfish—thus the chaotic nature of his character.

4   Like a barbed double hook, Coyote is his own mirror image, with two conflicting, distinctive roles. He alone personifies all the opposites apparent in the double hook analogy including god and devil, reality and myth, and teacher and manipulator. Watson's use of Coyote inscribes double meanings into all his words and actions; the reader is unable to take anything at face-value, uncertain of his duplicity. While in Thomas King's *Green Grass, Running Water*, Coyote is a more likable, jovial, and harmless prankster, in *The Double Hook*, he conveys doubt and fear, paralysing the people of Nineveh. In Tomson Highway's *The Rez Sisters*, the Trickster figure of Nanabush symbolizes Native culture and history; Watson's Coyote is symbolic of a null culture and a void history—the absence of society. Like King and Highway, Watson combines Christian and Native beliefs, though her humour is less blatant. Her Coyote is the dark side of the Trickster figure without any clown-like ineptitudes. He is the external conflict, the instigator of isolation and insensibility. Coyote is both omnipresent, as the entire book takes place "under Coyote's eye" (Watson 19), and never present, as the characters never see him—like an author, like a god, like the metaphorical double hook.

5   Literally, a small double hook has the potential to catch two fish and is twice as likely to catch only one. Figuratively, it catches the positive and the negative: glory and fear, happiness and sorrow. The hook symbolizes the dichotomy of life and its inherent choices—just like the figure of Coyote. A larger hook would be an anchor, a symbol of stability, solidity, and security: none of which are apparent here. Coyote's final words undercut a certain and trustworthy foundation, setting the conclusion "on soft ground." Just as an anchor is lifted at the beginning of a journey, cast overboard at the end, and a silent presence between, so too is Mrs. Potter—as an anchor of Coyote's powers.

6   First, Mrs. Potter is murdered, lifted from the novel's foundations. Then, she is a silent but forceful presence, until James faces his fear and begins his own journey, finally casting off her influence. To begin his story, James must kill the old story—life with his suffocating mother. In the classic pattern of recognition, rejection, then redemption, he destroys one world, Coyote's oppressive world, to create a new one (Bessai and Kroetsch 207–8). Like the Old and New Testaments, the differences in the two worlds are significant; however, they are not independent of each other. Coyote will continue to be a powerful influence, as seen by his complete domination and isolation of Theophil. The loss of control over James, Ara, and Felix threatens the stability of Coyote's powers, but he is not completely defeated, as seen

by his self-assured final words. He inspires fear simply because he is inhuman, uninvolved, and, consequently, mercilessly detached from the community (Mitchell 110).

7   Coyote's puppeteer-like role also has biblical origins. On the opening page, the reader is introduced to Coyote and his twelve apostles, and he remains overseeing, meddling until the last word (Bessai and Kroetsch 210). His presence frames the novel from the introduction "under Coyote's eye" (Watson 19), to his seemingly omniscient, concluding benediction as a godlike creator, or narrator, or even author (134). He quotes scriptures in poetry, though fragmented or negated: "Happy are the dead" (115). Coyote's words are metaphorical and allegorical with speeches like prophecies (Bowering 190). Biblical associations also lie within the style of the writing: cadences, rhythms, and repetitions similar to those in translations of the Bible (Mitchell 121). Coyote is akin to the cruel Old Testament God, Jehovah, Christian creator and destroyer of the world. Coyote is knowledge and ignorance; he symbolizes the omnipotent Jehovah, as well as the Indian Trickster who creates, destroys, errs, and forgets. Coyote is now the omnipotent god blended with his Native heritage: the trickster without the inept jester. He is a figure of chaos and disorder; like God, Satan, and Death, his function is to effect adversity and prophesy (121). He is the judge of these people, speaking in twisted, biblical riddles, punishing them through the manipulation of their environment. Like the stern, wrathful Jehovah, Coyote is never jovial, but is instead a dark, ominous symbol. As he is the controller of destiny and death, the inhabitants of Nineveh always feel his presence in the drought and in their physical isolation. Their reactions to him are consonant with those of the Chosen People of the Old Testament: fearing a god of vengeance, not a god of mercy. In a related role, Coyote is also Death carrying away Mrs. Potter in his teeth as though she were his pup. He is the tempter Satan, inciting fear of life, and suggesting suicide to Greta and James: "In my mouth is forgetting/In my darkness is rest" (Watson 29); "James wanted to go down to the river. To throw himself into its long arms" (98). Furthermore, he attempts to lure Felix into leaving his newly found God (68). In fact, almost all the characters can be interpreted as people of the Old Testament, except Felix, whose name and actions are associated with the New Testament, and is, therefore, their guide to redemption (110).

8   More than a god, Coyote is the landscape itself, unavoidable and inseparable from the earth, drying it up as punishment for these straying characters who are biblically lost:

> Coyote made the land his pastime. He stretched out his paw. He breathed on the grass. His spittle eyed it with prickly pear. (22)

> In my mouth is the east wind.

> Those who cling to the rocks I will

>> Bring down

> I will set my paw on the eagle's nest. (24)

He is the controller of nature, able to part the seas and dry up the creek. He and his messengers have driven the people into silence, submission, and obedience, like the actual biblical story of Nineveh. Coyote's earthbound servants, Kip and Mrs. Potter, intervene for him. Kip makes mischief not only by failing to deliver James's message, going after Lenchen, and reaching for the glory himself:

> What in hell are you doing? said the boy . . . Get out of here, the boy said. Wherever you are there's trouble. If a man is breaking a horse when you come round it hangs itself on the halter, or throws itself, or gets out and back on the range. (27)

Kip, like Coyote, is feared and visionary. Nonetheless, he becomes a victim of Coyote's violent, insensitive community. Kip, just as the persecutor Paul, is blinded by Christlike James. Without his sight, Kip loses Coyote's divine perception, and becomes animalistic and instinctive: "lifting his face windward like an animal . . . finding [his] way by the smell of the water" (72). He confesses his guilt in repentance to Felix, thus being converted to New Testament Christianity. Without his sight, and Coyote's paternal domination, Kip is "saved," and becomes an ordinary part of the budding community. Like a servant of Satan-Coyote, Mrs. Potter defies God, using a lamp in daylight, taking off her hat under the sun, as a rebuke of Genesis's "Let there be light" (31). It seems as though "Coyote's eye" (19) is battling "God's eye" (22) for the souls of Nineveh's inhabitants. Malevolent Coyote appears as his meddler Mrs. Potter: "Ara . . . saw the path down to the creek, saw the old lady . . . Ara went down to the path [and] saw nothing except . . . the padded imprint of a coyote's foot" (35). Mrs. Potter, too, spreads fear and immobility into the valley, first while alive, and then after death—unnaturally like a harbinger, or an omen:

> They'd lived waiting. Waiting to come together at the same lake as dogs creep out of the night to the same fire . . . [They'd] moved their lips saying: She'll live forever. And when they'd raised their eyes their mother was watching as a deer watches . . . Nothing had changed. The old lady was there in every fold of the country. (43)

The old woman is the physical oppressor of the people while she lives, and the emotional obstacle, manipulated by Coyote, after her death. Still, she is seen as Jonah, God's (Coyote's, Watson's) messenger to the people of Nineveh (34). Despite all the religious symbolism, Coyote's allegory is incomplete and ambiguous because he can be interpreted as holy, satanic, and secular in various places throughout the novel. He is partly from the Bible, from Greek mythology, from Native legends, from contemporary literature, and from the animal kingdom. He is, however, never physically seen; his established presence is all they need; his power is in the air, the water, and the land.

9   Coyote is also the author's presence felt throughout (Bowering 190). Coyote's "eye" is a pun for "I," the author (Watson 19). Coyote, and Watson, create and rule this world, manipulate and control the characters' actions, and both draw on various literary sources. As a legendary shape shifter, Coyote-author is necessary, inseparable, and always present in one form or another. Coyote makes the land his own just as an author's words first form mentally, then physically on paper (Bowering 195). Furthermore, an author matches opposing elements of the story, shaping, changing, transforming as she goes along. Her process is the creation and the metamorphosis of new worlds of existence: developing, processing, comparing God and Coyote, self and community, energy and stasis (Bessai and Kroetsch 215). Coyote's presence though, like the author's absence in the work, is an illusion. Never seen, he is merely felt and feared. His presence is really an absence, similar to the narrator, or the author. This absence is also evident in other aspects of the novel: the lack of standard elements of fiction like a prominent plot, regional setting, simple theme, extensive description, flowing narration, direct quotation, and consistent chronology. The novel reads more like poetry than prose, with dense literary references and concise description. The emphasis is on expanding structure and form, not developing conflict and character. Knowledge of the

characters is derived mostly from their names and their borrowed quotations rather than their own words and actions. The conflict between James and his mother abruptly and violently resolves on the climactic first page. All that remains is a circular journey motif weighed down in allusion, imagery, and parody. Watson writes with an impersonal narrator; thus, the reader is detached from the characters' emotions and innermost reflections. The interpretation, again, is secondary to the limits of the form and structure being examined. Coyote, as the author, also tests the limits of literature by drawing on fragmented allusions and quotations from Greek mythology, Christianity, Native American legend, and many various contemporary narratives. The chronology is not explicit with adjectives and adverbs of time, but is implied in these literary fragments incorporated from their diverse sources throughout history. Time and motivation are viewed through their causes and effects (Bowering 196). Coyote, as manipulator of language and words, also prevents communication, attempting to separate and silence the characters of the novel, not unlike the Tower of Babel story. Thus, just as Coyote wants his world to lose meaning, ritual, and significance, Watson wants a literary world unbound by conventions and rules: absolute control and creativity by negating every expectation.

10   Coyote is the negator of language, of fixed meaning. Watson separates signifier from signified, using words in contextual splinters, as pieces of signification. The intertextuality of the fractured quotations and the structure of the inarticulate, isolated characters show Watson's belief that meaning and understanding are only possible through a common language and its communication—including the acts of reading and writing (Turner 113). She subordinates the individual to the collective experience, creating levels of context and subtext. Similar to Canada's own literary tradition, the people of Nineveh construct a language out of fragments of tradition and culture they vaguely remember, before Coyote's stifling presence. However, the reader must also make connections, sometimes filling in the missing verbs, subjects, references, or texts (115). The communication is incomplete, ambiguous, imperfect, and open to interpretation. With indefinite pronouns and dislocated sentences, Watson blurs conventional diction and usage, "extend[ing] the distance between word and meaning, until the link, if it remains at all, is fragile and tenuous" (116). The absence of certain words is also metaphorical, as densely layered with allusion as any Ezra Pound poem: "Into the shadow of death" (Watson 19). The people [re?]discover their language from fragments of text, similar to the author sifting through literary works for inspiration, direction, and association. The community of Nineveh then, as a town and as a synecdoche of the novel, is analogous to a library: a collective language being slowly discovered, book by book, line by line. Words convey traditions and rituals of communication to be chosen individually, specifically. Like Coyote, language itself functions contradictorily: aesthetics versus meaning, concrete versus abstract, ambiguity versus certainty (Turner 132).

11   Coyote is the unraveller of the novel's world, while Watson is the destroyer of the written wor[l]d. Just as Coyote twists the word of Jehovah, so does Watson. Both manipulate the language, the characters, and the world of the novel. In voice and character, however similar to language itself, Coyote attempts to stop communication, to silence the people; consequently, he is the negator of speech and discussion. The parrot is another image of the Coyote character: "not many have the rights of a dumb beast and a speaking man at the same time" (Watson 103). The parrot can only mimic ("to parrot") language; the meanings of the words are not in his vocabulary or ability. Thus, words and their meanings are not innately perceived, but must be shared to become meaningful, and are sometimes lost in the

translation—words and their arbitrary meanings become the double hook again (Turner 142–43). Watson's separating of signifier (word) from signified (meaning) is itself an attempt to sabotage, or at least interrupt, communication. Since language is shared ideas and knowledge, which can eventually become traditions and history, and finally, in time, a union of two cultures into a single new one, the implication that Coyote (a Native tradition) is silencing the established culture is ironically contrary to past historical events. Watson makes social and literary commentary with precise concrete diction, combining so many worlds and universal themes into so few pages.

12   Another trickster here, less evident than Coyote, is the novelist herself—opening the novel with God and his twelve apostles, as the Coyote and the Potters, is not only funny, but an ingenious allusive link. The movement of the novel is contrary: from death to birth. The reader must learn her tricks, look for the possibilities of contradiction in motivation, plot, conclusion, and character (Bessai and Kroetsch 215). Negation drives the novel: an antithesis, not a thesis; an antihero, not a hero; the blind seeing; the seeing fooled by what they see, blinded by what they do not (210). The author, the characters, the readers are "freed . . . from freedom" (Watson 121). That is, Watson releases the readers from the restraints of the traditional novel and its plot, setting, and themes, like James Potter once Felicia and Traff rob him of his escape money (Bessai and Kroetsch 210). Potters literally, like gods and writers figuratively, work with clay in the process of making, unmaking, and remaking (211). It is no accident that Coyote helped create the world with all its imperfections, like a potter's art, like an author's novel.

13   Native American Indian legends and spirits are a great source of literary allusion and allegory. Coyote is an abundant sea of literary connotations and denotations. Watson chose to parody, layer, and combine the social aspects of life in *The Double Hook* as densely as one would find in poetry. Coyote is used as a symbolic tool of the author, a cross-cultural form that embodies nearly every contradiction, and so portrays omnipotence and ignorance, truth and trickery, legend and lies. To lose such a powerful presence in this novel is to lose much of its cultural and semantic ambiguity. Another mythical creature in its place would not bear the same expectations or twisted, dubious knowledge. Coyote's leading role is significant as a divine intervener, a malevolent force, and a meddling antagonist. Since he appears on nearly every page, he is essential to the novel's development and reading. To lose the Coyote figure is to lose his specific depth and double-sided interpretations: an entire dimension of the novel lost. In another form, the legendary duality of his character vanishes, as does the novel's major mythic quality. The symbolic characters would become ordinary, and their roles would become almost cliché, in parody or not. Coyote's role is similar to, almost as necessary as, the role of the author: silently ever-present, sometimes with subversive intentions. Thus, the interpretations of Coyote bring him closer to the author herself and her own role in creating the novel's mythical realm. By not taking responsibility for his actions and being merely "a dumb beast" (Watson 103), Coyote is "let off the hook." Perhaps, Watson found this artificial or implausible. Of course, thirty or forty years after Watson wrote the novel, the Trickster figure may be overused, cliché. In 1973, she could have been joking, tricking the critics into new discussion and more interpretation, casting yet another hook into their discourse. Still, the debate regarding the role of Coyote will never be as important as the text itself: its significance is profound with or without Coyote's bag of tricks.

WORKS CITED

Bessai, Diane, and Robert Kroetsch. "Death is a Happy Ending: A Dialogue in Thirteen Parts." *Figures in a Ground*. Eds. Diane Bessai and David Jackel. Saskatoon: Western Producer Prairie Books, 1978. 206–215.

Bowering, George. "Sheila Watson, Trickster." *Sheila Watson and* The Double Hook. Ed. George Bowering. Ottawa: Golden Dog Press, 1985. 187-199.

Child, Philip. "A Canadian Prose-Poem." *Sheila Watson and* The Double Hook. Ed. George Bowering. Ottawa: Golden Dog Press, 1985. 31–34.

Ghezzi, Ridie Wilson. "Nanabush Stories from the Ojibwa." *Coming to Light*. Ed. Brian Swann. New York: Random House, 1994. 443–448.

Highway, Tomson. *The Rez Sisters*. Saskatoon: Fifth House, 1988.

King, Thomas. *Green Grass, Running Water*. Toronto: HarperCollins, 1994.

Mitchell, Beverly. "Association and Allusion in *The Double Hook*." *Sheila Watson and* The Double Hook. Ed. George Bowering. Ottawa: Golden Dog Press, 1985. 99–113.

Monkman, Leslie. "Coyote as Trickster in *The Double Hook*." *Sheila Watson and* The Double Hook. Ed. George Bowering. Ottawa: Golden Dog Press, 1985. 63–69.

Morriss, Margaret. "The Elements Transcended." *Sheila Watson and* The Double Hook. Ed. George Bowering. Ottawa: Golden Dog Press, 1985. 83–97.

Radin, Paul. *The Trickster: A Study in American Indian Mythology*. London: Oxford University Press, 1956.

Scobie, Stephen. *Sheila Watson and Her Works*. Toronto: ECW Press, 1984.

Turner, Margaret. "Writing the New World: Language and Silence in Richardson, Grove, Watson and Kroetsch." Diss. University of Alberta, 1986.

Watson, Sheila. *The Double Hook*. Toronto: McClelland and Stewart, 1959.

Watson, Sheila. "What I'm Going To Do." *Sheila Watson and* The Double Hook. Ed. George Bowering. Ottawa: Golden Dog Press, 1985. 13–15.

APPENDIX C

Detection of Landmines

A Technical Report for a Course in Mechanical Engineering

Robert Gust, Chris Turner, Peter Karl, and Scott Koehn

ABSTRACT

1   The objective of the project was to design a mechanical means of detecting the VS-50 anti-personnel (AP) or the VS-2.2 anti-tank (AT) land mines. A method of prodding the ground with numerous hydraulically driven probes was chosen as the most effective means of detection because of its simplicity, adaptability, the proven reliability of prods as detectors, and the possibility of relatively high clearance rates.

2   The chosen design consists of a lead row of 78 prods to detect AP mines and a separate row of 32 prods behind to detect AT mines; each row spans 3 metres. The prods in one row are hydraulically injected into the ground at 45° to a prescribed depth, while a data acquisition system continuously records pressure and depth measurements. When the maximum depth is reached, the prods are retracted and the row moves forward to begin the next stage. Each stage takes approximately 4.5 seconds resulting in a possible clearance rate of 1.2 square metres per minute.

3   Mine detection is based on the fact that, when an individual prod encounters a hard object in the ground, a sharp rise in pressure results in the hydraulic fluid driving the prod. When this occurs, the pre-set cut-off pressure (which continuously varies with changing soil conditions) is exceeded and the prod ceases its downward descent. If four or more adjacent prods in consecutive stages have been stopped, the probability that a mine is beneath the soil is high. The device then stops, marks the "mine" and alerts the operator. If less than four adjacent prods are triggered, there is no possible way for that object to be a mine and the device ignores those signals.

4   This design will detect both AP and AT mines in the soil to a high degree of accuracy. False alarms due to rocks, sticks, and other debris are greatly reduced due to the dense spacing of the prods. The device can operate in smooth to rough terrain and various soil densities including light vegetation and can easily be adapted to detection in sloped ground. The algorithm that controls the device could be reprogrammed to detect different shapes or sizes of land mines. All parts that would be damaged in the event of an explosion have been designed to be quickly and cost-effectively replaced.

TABLE OF CONTENTS

1.0 Introduction

2.0 Prod Design
2.1 Prod Design
2.2 Soil Penetration Forces
2.3 Probe Speed
2.4 Buckling and Bending

3.0 Frame
3.1 Materials and Design
3.2 Blast Consideration

4.0 Hydraulics
4.1 Prod Actuation
4.2 Prod Array Movement
4.3 Blast Damage Reduction
4.4 Improvements

5.0 Data Acquisition System
5.1 Delay

6.0 Control Algorithm
6.1 System Check
6.2 Prod Actuation
6.3 Search Algorithm

7.0 Cost Summary

8.0 Conclusion

LIST OF FIGURES

Figure 2.1   Mine Detection/Prod Possibilities

Figure 2.2   Prod Dimensions

Figure 2.3   Tapered and Blunt Probe Penetration Force Curves

Figure 3.1   Overall View of Device

Figure 4.1   Prod Hydraulics Schematic

Figure 4.2   Prod Array Movement Hydraulics Schematic

Figure 6.1   Sequential Prod Actuation Diagram

LIST OF TABLES

Table 7.1   Cost Analysis

1.0 Introduction

5   The constant threat of nuisance land mines in countries around the world reveals the need for a real-world land mine detector. Due to the poor results obtained with electronic-type detection devices, the focus is now placed on a mechanical means of detection. In January of 1996, the MEC E 460 class was asked by the Defense Research Establishment at Suffield (DRES) to design mechanical mine detection devices. Due to time and resource restrictions, several constraints were placed on the project.

6   The device was to detect the VS-2.2 anti-tank (AT) and the VS-50 anti-personnel (AP) land mines with a high degree of accuracy. Ideally, the device would minimize the number of false alarms, being able to distinguish between mine types as well as between mines and other obstacles in the soil. In the event that an AP mine is detonated accidentally by the device, it must be able to withstand the blast or, alternatively, the damaged parts must be easily replaced. Minimum operating conditions were assumed to be smooth and level, non-frozen Devon Clay with some moisture and no vegetation. Attempts should be made to design a device that could be used in a wide range of soil states and ambient conditions. Clearing speed should be greater than that of the hand-prodder over a swath of 3 m. A low cost device would be most desirable so that it could be used in developing countries.

7   During the brainstorming stage of the design process, several ideas were considered. Various "heat" methods were considered and deemed inappropriate since they required too much energy transfer from the soil surface to the mine to be effective. A roller to sense soil depressions where mines have been buried was considered, but it was felt that any depression would be so small that the detection device would have to be too sensitive. Water and sand blasting of the soil could be used to uncover buried mines but would not be practical on a roadway since extensive repairs would have to be done after clearing. The chosen design was a

device consisting of two rows of hydraulically activated prods spanning 3 m; one row to detect AP mines and one to detect AT mines. The probes would be inserted into the soil at 45° and an abrupt pressure rise would indicate that a probe had struck a solid object; that probe would then stop. A mine would be detected when the proper number of adjacent probes had stopped. This is a feasible design which meets all the required criteria.

2.0 Prod Design

8　The main feature of the design is the use of prods to find the buried land mines. By using prods, the benefits of the current hand-held prods were incorporated, with the addition of safety, speed, and accuracy. The mine detector consists of two rows of prods spanning 3 m; one row for the detection of the AP mines and one for detecting the AT mines.

9　　The row detecting the AP mines consists of 78 prods spaced at 40 mm from one another and the row detecting the AT mines consists of 32 prods spaced 100 mm from one another. Both types of prods enter the soil at 45°. With the 78 AP prods and the 32 AT prods, the device can clear a 3 m wide strip of land. The 40 mm spacing for the AP prods ensures that at least four AP prods from two consecutive cycles will hit the 90 mm diameter AP mine. The 100 mm spacing for the AT prods again ensures that at least four prods from two consecutive cycles will hit the 246 mm diameter AT mine. Figure 2.1 shows several possible configurations for the prods detecting an AP mine. The detection of an AT mine is identical but on a larger scale.

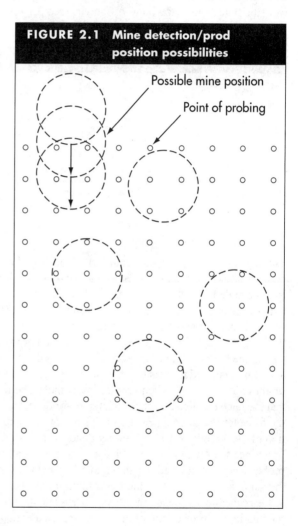

FIGURE 2.1　Mine detection/prod position possibilities

Possible mine position

Point of probing

2.1 Prod Dimensions and Materials

10　For simplicity and ease of replacement, each AP and AT prod is identical in its dimensions and materials. The prods consist of two main components: a probe that penetrates the ground and a cylinder that houses the probe and acts as a hydraulic cylinder. Figure 2.2 shows the dimensioning of the prods. The probe is 572 mm in length and is made of standard 6.35 mm stainless steel round stock. The length of the probe allows for the prodding to be done, while keeping important components away from a possible mine blast. The cylinder portion of the prods has a length of 381 mm and is commercially available. A 17.5 mm drawn seamless tubing with a 15.9 mm bore was chosen to minimize the amount of hydraulic fluid contained in each cylinder. Each AP and AT probe has a screw-on carbide tip, which is more durable than stainless steel and can be easily replaced when worn. This construction is detailed in Figure 2.2. As well, the figure shows the blunt AT and tapered AT tips, which are discussed in section 2.2.

FIGURE 2.2   Prod dimensions

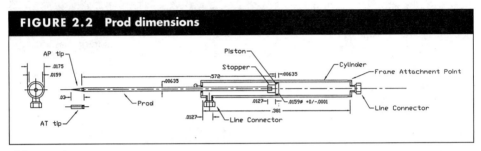

All dimensions in metres.

2.2 Soil Penetration Forces

11   The selection of the 6.35 mm diameter probes and the tapered and blunt tips was based on numerous tests done in the lab. Since the AP mines are buried to a maximum depth of 20 mm, it was decided that the AP probes would be inserted to a depth of 30 mm to ensure that no mines were missed. From Figure 2.3, it can be seen that at a depth of 30 mm the tapered probe shows a force of about 254 N, compared to 396 N on the blunt probe curve. This shows that it takes much less force to insert the tapered probe to a depth of 30 mm. In addition to testing the blunt and tapered probes, a test was done using an "arrowhead" probe in which a 9.53 mm tapered tip was attached to a 6.35 mm diameter rod. It was felt that this design might reduce the forces required to insert the probe into the soil. However, it was found that the force required at a depth of 30 mm for this tip was about 348 N, which is greater than the force for the tapered probe. For this reason the tapered probe was chosen for the detection of the AP mines. Using a safety factor of 1.5, the design force is 409 N.

12   Since the AT mines are buried at a maximum of 100 mm, it was decided that the AT probes would be inserted to a depth of 150 mm to ensure that no mines were missed. From the curve it is apparent that there is a sharp initial rise in force as the depth is increased but as the probe travels deeper, the curve flattens and the forces become constant. For the design, the maximum force on the blunt probe was used which was 396 N. Compared to 721 N at 150 mm for the tapered probe, the blunt probe has much smaller forces. For this reason the blunt probe was chosen to detect the AT mines. Again, incorporating the safety factor of 1.5, the design force used is 587 N.

13   The prods in this design are inserted at an angle of 45°, which increases the forces by a factor of 2 and keeps important components, such as valves and transducers, out of the blast cone of a possible mine explosion. (Discussed further in section 3.2)

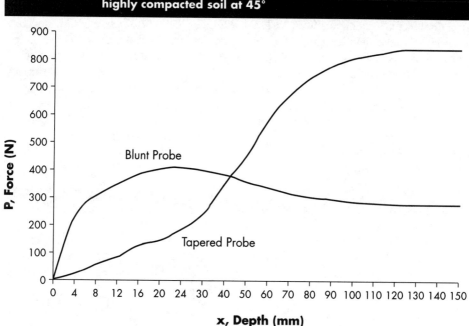

FIGURE 2.3 Soil penetration forces for blunt and tapered probe tips in highly compacted soil at 45°

2.3 Probe Speed

14 The probes begin their descent 50 mm above the ground, which accounts for small bumps, rocks, or dirt which may be on the surface. This gives a total of 115 mm at 115 mm/s for the AP prods and 287 mm at 143 mm/s for the AT prods. For one pass, which involves the prods being inserted into the ground, retracting the prods and moving forward, the time, including all delays, is 3.83 seconds for the AP prods and 7.65 seconds for the AT prods. With these speeds and times, including all delay times, the clearing rate of the detector is 1.9 m²/mm. This is much faster than the 1 m² every 3–4 minutes achieved using the current hand-held prodder.

2.4 Buckling and Bending

15 As mentioned earlier, a design force of 409 N was used for the AP probes and 587 N was used for the AT probes. Both of these values incorporate a safety factor of 1.5. In using these forces both buckling and bending in the probes had to be considered. The critical force, P_{cr}, for the buckling of the probes was determined by modelling the system as a fixed end-fixed end buckling case. It was determined that the critical load for the probes was 1859 N, which is much greater than the actual forces needed in prodding. This shows that there is no chance of the probe buckling. Bending of the prod was also considered. This calculation was important since it considered the scenario wherein a probe might glance off a small stone during its insertion. Under a shear load of 6.5 N there is a deflection at the tip of 27 mm. Plastic deformation occurs at this point. This shows that for small deflections (0–27 mm) induced by abnormalities in the soil, there will be no plastic deformation.

3.0 Frame

3.1 Materials and Design

16   Structural members are made from ASTM A36 steel, which combines acceptable stiffness and relatively high yield strength with low cost and simplicity of manufacture. The structure, including all hydraulic cylinders, has a mass of about 400 kg and is mounted on the front of the Bison Armoured Personnel Carrier (APC) with pinned connections on the four factory mounts. Figure 3.1 shows an over-all view of the device. Note that the slanted members (frame supports) rest against the armour on the two corners of the APC when the prods are being driven into the ground while the pins bear the weight of the structure when the prods are retracted. The distributed loads induced by the prods penetrating the soil are approximately 6230 N in both the AT and AP rows.

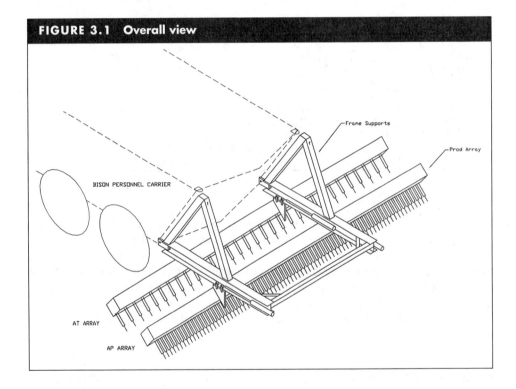

FIGURE 3.1   Overall view

17   Stiffness was the primary design consideration since it was decided that the maximum acceptable deflection at any one prod location in the array was 3 mm. This small deflection would not adversely affect the detection of mines since, at most, it would only cause a 10% error in depth penetration of the prods.

18   The greatest deflections occur in the members housing the prods and in the two horizontal arms. The final dimensions of these members were based on the minimum moments of inertia required for maximum deflection. . . . To house the prods, rectangular tubing (76.2 x 127 x 6.35 mm) with a moment of inertia of 5.16E6 mm^4 was chosen. This provides good bending support for the prods and a maximum centre deflection of 0.1 mm.

19 I-beams (105.7 x 103.1 mm) were chosen for the horizontal arms supporting the prod arrays with the largest deflection being less than 3 mm. The bottom flanges are used as tracks for the lateral movement of the prod arrays.

3.2 Blast Consideration

20 Though detonation of an AP mine is highly unlikely under the design conditions, this scenario was considered and attempts were made to reduce the possible resulting damage. If an accidental blast were to occur, from an AT prod detonating a deeply buried AP mine or perhaps from a faulty AP mine, the damage is expected to be minor with destroyed parts easily replaceable.

21 In order to reasonably predict this damage calculations were done using the blast cone of 15° from vertical and the 300 mm crater specified by DRES. It was assumed that anything within this cone would be totally destroyed and that a peak over-pressure of 13.8 kPa is required to deform steel. All structural members are located outside the destructive pressure range, although shrapnel may cause some damage to an I-beam if a blast occurred directly below. Damaged members could be easily replaced since all connections are bolted.

22 Because the AP probes would be closest to the heart of the blast, it is expected that approximately 15 would be destroyed. Damage to the cylinders, both directly from peak over-pressure and indirectly from bent of destroyed probes, would be less severe (approx. 10 would be destroyed) because they are outside the blast cone and only fall slightly within the 13.8 kPa peak over-pressure range. The nature of the prods, as described earlier, allows for simple replacement of damaged probes, cylinders or fittings. If an AT prod were to encounter a deeply buried AP mine, the 820 mm spacing between the two rows would limit the damage to just four AT prods.

23 There was some concern that a blast would cause bending in the rectangular tubing which houses the prods. However, it was found that because the cylinder walls are very thin compared to the tubing, the cylinders would fail while the tube is still in the elastic range.

4.0 Hydraulics

24 The decision to use hydraulics in the proposed design was based on two main reasons. First, the APC on which the device is mounted is already equipped with a hydraulic system. The capacity of the APC hydraulic system is 95 L/s (25 gpm) with a maximum working pressure of 17 Mpa (2500 psi). The capacity of the hydraulic system is ample for the components specified in the proposed detection system. The second main reason for the choice of hydraulics is that the working fluid, oil, can be easily controlled and pressure rises easily measured. If the probe hits a solid object the oil continues to push the probe. This will cause an immediate pressure rise in the oil since flow continues, though the volume in the cylinder is no longer increasing. The incompressibilty of the working fluid allows for accurate flow control, resulting in accurate probe displacement. This could not be obtained with other compressible working fluids such as air. In that case a pressure rise would occur, but displacement of a probe would not occur since the working fluid behind the probe would compress. An increase in flow rate would be required to compensate for the volume change of the compressible working fluid, requiring expensive servo flow control valves. The timing of the probing cycle is critical in the proposed design in order to allow adjacent cycles to operate in synchronization. This would be difficult if probe penetration is stopped due to the compression of the working fluid.

4.1 Prod Production

25 With the previously stated reasons taken into consideration, the detection system was designed on a constant flow, pressure compensation basis. The probe unit as described earlier is in essence a custom hydraulic cylinder. Each probe has three controlling components: the directional control valve (DCV), pressure compensated flow control valve (FCV), and a pressure transducer. These are displayed in Figure 4.1 below.

FIGURE 4.1   Schematic of constant flow pressure compensated hydraulic system

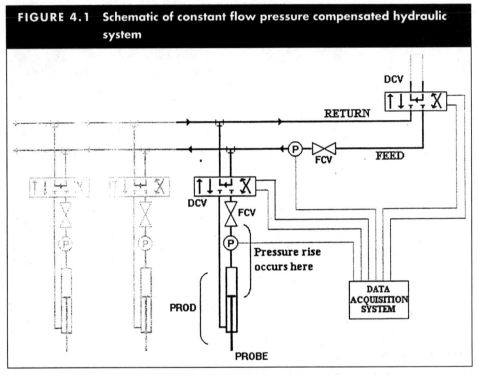

The system allows for pressure rises local to each probe. (DCV-directional control valve, FCV-flow control valve, P-pressure sensor)

26   The DCV is solenoid operated to allow for interface with a data acquisition system. The DCV defaults to the setting in which the feed flow is relieved back to the hydraulic system reservoir. This will ensure that if an electrical failure occurs, the valve does not allow flow to pass into the probe cylinder, stopping further probe penetration into soil. The pressure compensated FCV is placed down stream of the DCV allowing for accurate flow control of each probe. The placement of the FCV also ensures pressure rises, which occur between the FCV and the piston in the prod, are contained locally. As a result it is a simple matter to determine which probe has encountered an obstruction. The FCV valves are factory order, in that they are machined specific to one flow rate in one direction. The specific flow rates for the AP and AT prods are 0.023 L/s and 0.028 L/s respectively, giving probe penetration rates of 115 mm/s and 143 mm/s as stated earlier. The factory flow tolerances of the FCV are small. A pressure sensor is placed between the prod cylinder and the FCV to monitor pressure rise.

27   The operation of the prod occurs in the following sequence. First the DCV solenoid is activated by the data acquisition system to allow the feed flow to travel through the FCV (metred flow) and into the prod, which in turn initiates the probe penetration into the ground. When the probe encounters an obstruction, the pressure of the working fluid between the prod and the FCV rises since constant flow is maintained through pressure compensation. The pressure transducer is used to monitor pressure rises throughout this process. Once a preset threshold pressure is reached, the data acquisition system ceases power flow to the solenoid of the DCV. The feed flow is now in relief and the probe motion is halted. The adjacent probes continue to penetrate until the same occurs, or the maximum depth is reached. Probe penetration rate is not affected by neighbouring probes being shut off, since flow control is local to each probe. The probes are then retracted by invoking the flow direction reversal solenoid. The speed of retraction is much quicker than penetration since there is a 16% decrease in volume of the cylinder due to volume displacement of the rod and the flow is regulated by a different control valve set at 0.32 L/s (the FCV on the cylinder line allows full flow in the reverse direction). This valve is located on the main feed as shown in Figure 4.1.

4.2 Prod Array Movement

28   Another hydraulic component is that of the prod row movement system. This is based on the same principles as above and also incorporates the use of an FCV and a DCV. A schematic of this system is displayed in Figure 4.2.

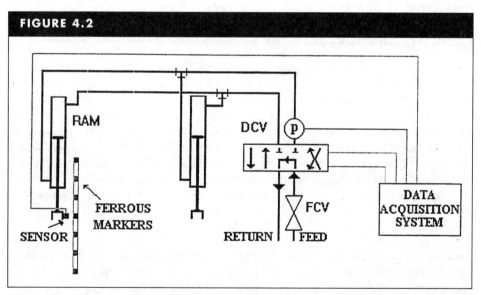

FIGURE 4.2

Hydraulic schematic of prod row movement system (AP and AT units are identical)

29   The hydraulic rams are set in the I-beam members of the frame, with a proximity sensor located at points where the prod arrays are attached as shown in Figure 4.2. The proximity sensor (Wainbee IAS-20-A12-S) runs along a ferrous/non-ferrous (plastic) strip placed along the I-beam. The ferrous markers are screws and indicate the positions at which the prod

rows are to stop so that the probing cycle can begin. The data acquisition system operates the DCV in the same manner as mentioned earlier. The flow is allowed to pass into the hydraulic rams until a ferrous marker is encountered at which point the flow will go into relief. When the maximum number of markers have been encountered, the prod rows are retracted against the APC, at which point the APC can move according to the situation at hand.

4.3 Blast Damage Reduction

30   Blast damage reduction has been taken into consideration. This was done by placing a pressure transducer in all the main feed lines as shown in Figures 4.1 and 4.2. The pressure transducer is used to monitor the pressure in the line. In the event of a blast severing a hydraulic line, massive pressure loss would occur, at which point the data acquisition system would direct the DCV to relieve flow back to the reservoir. This would discontinue any further fluid loss from the Bison's system. The low volume of the hydraulic components, 6.35 mm hydraulic lines, 15.9 mm bore cylinders, will minimize contamination caused by oil loss.

4.4 Improvements

31   An addition to improve versatility of the design would be to replace the square tubing frame supports shown in Figure 3.1 with hydraulic rams. The two rams would be controlled with a DCV, which in turn would be controlled with a data acquisition system that receives feedback from an ultrasonic sensor. This sensor would allow the proposed design to accommodate for more uneven terrain.

5.0 Data Acquisition System

32   In order to accommodate the solenoid DCV, 226 digital channels are required. This requirement can be fulfilled using the three National Instrument PC-DIO-96, 96 channel I/O boards. The directional control valves also needed high gain transistors in order to increase the 5 V board output to 12V required to activate solenoids. The pressure sensors and the proximity/hall effect sensors necessitate a total of 226 analog channels. This can be provided with 13 National Instrument AT-MIO-16DL 16 channel analog boards. The pressure sensor chosen was the Omega PX120 with a range of 0 to 3.4 Mpa (0 to 500 psi), which encompasses the full pressure range caused by a mine being encountered in hard soil. An IBM PC and an additional card chassis would be required to interface with the 16 data acquisition cards.

5.1 Delay

33   Since there are several sensing devices measuring flow, pressure, and displacement, there is a certain amount of delay involved in the processing of this information. The total amount of delay consists of the delay due to the processing of the sensor data, as well as the delay in the shut-off of the DCV. The data acquisition cards chosen have sampling rates of 50 000 samples/s. These rates were divided by three to account for computer processing time. The valve shut-off delay is 45 ms which gives a total delay of 47.87 ms. The result is that after the valve is told to close, the AP probe actually travels vertically an additional 1.97 mm and the AT prods an additional 2.45 mm. This means that if an AP mine is struck directly on the button, it will be depressed an additional 1.97 mm. Assuming the button must be depressed approximately 3 mm for it to be detonated, the additional depression will not trip the mine. As well, assuming the AT mine must be depressed approximately 10 mm; the additional 2.45 mm depression will not trip the mine.

6.0 Control Algorithm

6.1 System Check

34   For safety reasons, the device will first go through a system check to ensure that all prods are functioning properly, and all sensors are working. This would be done by performing a test cycle on safe ground. This ground should be similar to that which is to be cleared, relatively uniform and all pressure readings from each prod should be similar. The computer will be used to check that all pressure readings are similar and all distance sensors are functioning. If there were a leaking prod or malfunctioning sensor, this would appear as a drastic difference in pressure in that particular prod (±20%). This would be interpreted as a system failure, and the operator would be notified.

6.2 Prod Actuation

35   The cycling of the prods is continuous until a mine is struck. To minimize reaction forces, prodding is done sequentially. The AP prods are divided into five groups, and the AT prods into three groups. They are positioned in repeating order (1, 2, 3, 4, 5, 1, 2 . . .) as can be seen in Figure 6.1. The Group One prods will all begin their cycle, and after a delay of 0.368 seconds, representing the time it takes for a prod to move from the ground surface to the depth of three centimetres, the Group Two prods will begin. Groups Three, Four, and Five begin their cycles after subsequent 0.368 second delays. The AT prods operate in a similar manner, with their delay time being 1.47 seconds. This makes the cycle time for the AT row half that of the AP row, and is necessary to prevent interference between the two rows. In doing this, the transmitted forces to the frame and APC were cut by a factor of five for the AP row and three for the AT row, but the cycle time was only increased by a factor of 1.6 leading to an overall clearance rate of 1.9 m^2/s.

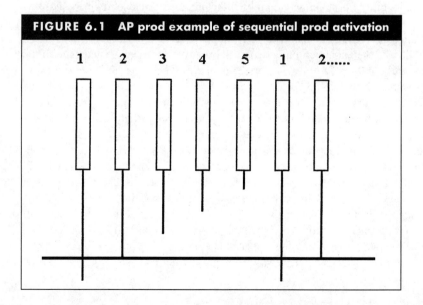

FIGURE 6.1   AP prod example of sequential prod activation

36   The data acquisition system will be continuously sampling the pressure and depth readings. At the first pressure rise (representing the point at which the probe strikes the soil), the computer will set the depth for that prod to zero. This allows for the mechanism to contour to the clearing area, ensuring that if there is a hole or rut in the road the probe will still penetrate to the required depth below the surface. As well, the pressure requirement to penetrate the ground will be recorded and stored in memory. This data will be collected from all probes across the array and averaged, thus reducing noise from individual probes, and will be used to construct a cutoff pressure curve (equal to the obtained pressure curve plus 253 kPa for the AP and 4956 kPa for the AT, which represent the forces required to set off the mines with a safety factor of 2) for the next cycle. In this way the device is continuously adjusting to changing soil conditions. This was deemed important due to the wide range of penetrating forces collected using tests in soils of different compaction and moisture content.

6.3 Search Algorithm

37   The prod cycle can finish through one of two branches of the algorithm representing two possible occurrences. The first is the case where the probe does not strike anything and reaches its prescribed depth of 30 mm or 150 mm. When this occurs, the computer will wait for all prods from that particular row to reach their full depth. It will then reverse the hydraulic fluid flow and lift the prods to their height of 51 mm, move the row forward to the next proximity probe trigger, and repeat the cycle. This can continue for 25 cycles, where the end of the I-beam will be reached by the AP row. At this point, all of the prods from both rows will be lifted and the rows retracted back towards the APC. The APC could then drive forward to the last point at which the prods were in the ground and the cycles could continue. The movement of the APC must be very accurate, and will require modifications to its drive mechanism that would most easily be solved by adding a hydraulic or electric motor to one of the wheels. If this is not possible, another vehicle should be used, as it is felt that a human operator cannot control the APC with the accuracy necessary to ensure that no ground is missed by the prodder.

38   The other possibility for stopping would be if the probe strikes a solid object. Lab experiments have demonstrated that transmitted forces to the prod (and therefore higher pressures in the cylinder and hydraulic inlet) rise sharply when a solid object is struck. This sharp pressure rise will send the computer into a search algorithm to compare the geometry of the object that was struck to that of a mine. The first thing that will happen is the inflow valve to the prod in question will be closed so that the prod does not proceed any deeper into the ground and risk setting off a mine. Note that this is only for that particular prod and all others continue their descent. The computer also stores in its memory that this prod has been stopped and also checks if this is the second consecutive cycle in which this prod has been stopped. If not, the cycle will repeat, as this may still only be a small rock and there is no need to stop the process since anything mine-sized or larger will stop that prod again during the next cycle. If a prod has been stopped in two consecutive cycles, the computer will then check the prod to the left and right to see if they are also stored as positive. If they are not, the cycle will again repeat. Note that this sets the criteria that a solid object be at least 80 mm (AP) or 200 mm (AT) wide and long (prods have been spaced so that a mine will be hit no less than four times). The next stage is a search for four adjacent prods that have been stored as positive (Adjacent can mean four in a square, a "T"-shape, and not necessarily just four wide.

See Figure 2.1). In doing this search algorithm, all rocks, sticks, and other debris that may be encountered that stop three or less adjacent prods do not give false alarms. This is a significant feature of this design, and greatly increases the efficiency of the mechanism.

39   There has been no upper bound set on the number of prods that are triggered for several reasons. The first is the fact that AT mines can be buried at the same depth as AP mines, so the mechanism can detect these shallow AT mines with the AP row. Also, a rock may be sitting in very close proximity to a mine, or two mines may be spaced very close to one another. The underlying principle behind this is that false positives are far more desirable than false negatives.

7.0 Cost Summary

40   Table 7.1 displays the cost breakdown of the proposed design. The majority of the $101 000 cost is in the hydraulic and data acquisition components, which compose approximately 62% and 27% of the cost respectively. This high cost is due to the requirement of valves and sensors for each prod to ensure only local pressure rises. Inclusion of these valves and sensors in turn requires additional data acquisition channels for operation. Detection of local pressure rises allows the reduction of false alarms due to sticks, rocks, and such. The majority of the costs listed in Table 7.1 are initial costs and would not require repetition as the unit is used. The design would require minimal and low cost part replacement in the event of a blast. This is due to important components such as valves being located in zero damage areas in the event of a blast.

8.0 Conclusion

41   Land mines are a very serious problem in many parts of the world today and there is currently no safe, efficient method of detecting them. The goal of this project was to design a simple mechanical means of detecting land mines with operating conditions being smooth, flat Devon Clay. This chosen design is a very feasible and realistic solution to the problem presented. It meets and exceeds all the set criteria.

42   This design builds on the success of the hand prodder, incorporating a large number of prods on a frame which is to be mounted on the front of a Bison personnel carrier (APC). There are two rows of prods, the first consisting of 78 prods that penetrate the soil to a vertical depth of 30 mm to find AP mines. At this depth, for a tapered tip, it was found that the required insertion force is 254 N, which is less than the force of a blunt probe at this depth. The second row consists of 32 prods that penetrate to a depth of 150 mm to find AT mines. The force required for penetration at this depth with a blunt tip is 396 N, which is much smaller than that of a tapered tip. For this reason the blunt tip was chosen for the AT prods.

43   It was found that a prod insertion angle of 45° reduced the vertical forces on the frame and kept important components away from a potential blast. Using a 30° blast cone (AP mine), it was found that approximately 15 probes and 10 cylinders would be destroyed. This is acceptable since these parts could easily and inexpensively be replaced. Also, the prod length is such that the critical load is 1859 N, which is much greater than the insertion force, hence the prods will not buckle.

44   All motion of prods and the prod arrays is controlled hydraulically, utilizing the existing hydraulic system on the APC. In order for the prods to be individually controlled, a di-

TABLE 7.1   Cost summary of proposed land mine detection system

Item		Amount Req. (Feet)	Unit Price ($/Ft)	Item Total Price ($)	Group Total Price ($)
Structural components					
I-beam W4 X 13		6.33	22.15	140.21	
Square tubing	3" × 3"	10.73	11.45	122.86	
	2" × 2"	6.56	7.15	46.90	
Rect. tubing	3" × 5"	19.65	15.65	307.52	
Flat bar	4" × $\frac{1}{4}$"	6.38	3.22	21.99	
	4" × $\frac{7}{16}$"	3.41	5.24	17.87	
	8" × $\frac{1}{4}$"	4.3	7.50	32.35	
Trolleys to fit I-beam		4	70.00	280.00	**969.61**
Prod Cylinder components					
Seamless tubing $\frac{11}{16}$" OD × $\frac{5}{8}$" ID		138	2.10	289.80	
$\frac{1}{4}$" 30422 Roundstock		201	2.13	428.13	
		#Units	**$/Unit**		
Oil seal kits		110	2.50	275.00	
Proximity probe (1AS-20-A12S)		112	25.00	2800.00	
$\frac{1}{4}$" MPT × $\frac{1}{4}$" T Connector		220	2.20	484.00	
Screw-on carbide tip		110	3.00	330.00	
End caps		220	1.20	264.00	
Piston		110	1.20	132.00	
Misc. Small parts		110	2.00	220.00	**4505.00**
Data acquisition					
Analog DA board (PC-LPM-16)		13	525.00	6825.00	
Digital DA board(PC-D10-96)		3	395.00	1185.00	
IBM PC & board box		1	2000.00	2000.00	
Pressure sensors (PX120)		113	158.00	17 854.00	
HFV 12V Transistor		113	0.70	79.10	
Misc wire		1	100.00	100.00	**28 043.10**
Hydraulic components					
4 way solenoid dir. cntrl valves	6631-1S2-5	113	320.00	36 179.21	
P. comp flow valve	6631-$\frac{1}{4}$S2.3565	78	201.55	15 720.00	
	6631-$\frac{1}{4}$S2-.4550	32	201.55	6449.60	
	6331-1S2-5	3	201.55	604.65	
Hydraulic cylinder 2" bore × 48" stroke		4	259.00	1036.00	
Hydraulic lines and fittings		1	4000.00	4000.00	**63 990.36**
General assembly & fabrication labour		**Hours**	**$/Hour**		
Prod assemble & machining ($\frac{3}{4}$ hr/cyln.)		82.5	40.00	3300.00	
Frame & hydraulic assembling		10	40.00	400.00	**3700.00**
			GRAND TOTAL:		**101 208.07**

rectional control valve (DCV) and a pressure-compensated flow control valve (FCV) are required for each prod. Lab experiments have shown that striking a solid object causes an immediate rise in force required to penetrate the soil. In this system, that force translates into a pressure rise in the fluid downstream of the FCV. A pressure sensor sends this information to a computer and the computer shuts off the flow to that cylinder so that it cannot penetrate any deeper and detonate a mine.

45   Total signal delay was found to be 47.87 milliseconds. This results in an additional vertical AP prod travel of 1.97 mm once the original pressure rise has occurred. Assuming that the AP mine button must be depressed 3 mm out of 5 mm of travel for detonation, this delay was considered acceptable. If this proves inadequate in the field, the flow rate could be depressed accordingly.

46   Prod activation occurs sequentially. The AP prod array is divided into five groups while the AT array is divided into three groups. For the AP array, all group one prods begin their cycle and after a 0.368 second delay, the group two prods begin their cycle; this repeats for each of the five groups. The delay represents the time that a probe takes to move from the ground surface to the 30 mm depth. The AT operates in a similar manner, but the delay is 1.47 seconds. This causes the cycle time of the AT array to be half that of the AP array, ensuring no interference of the two arrays at any time in operation. This sequential actuation cut transmitted forces to the frame by factors of five in the AP array and three in the AT array, but the cycle time was only increased by a factor of 1.6. The overall clearance rate is 1.88 m^2/s. This force reduction was required in order to bring the frame deflection to an acceptable maximum of 3 mm.

47   The geometry of the land mines is used to distinguish mines from other solid objects which may be in the ground. The prods are spaced such that a mine will be struck a minimum of four times. The algorithm also ensures that an object is at least 40 mm for the AP and 100 mm for the AT wide and long before the operator is alerted that there is a mine present. This eliminates all false alarms from rocks or debris which stops only three or less prods. Efficiency of operation is significantly enhanced by this feature.

48   The total cost of the device is approximately $101 000. This high cost is mainly due to the valves and sensors required for individual control of the prods. Individual control is needed in order to reduce false alarms and maintain a high accuracy.

49   This device is a realistic solution to the proposed problem which meets all required criteria. It is fully automated and can be used in a variety of soil conditions. Both AP and AT mines are detected, false alarms are greatly reduced and the probability of missing a mine is remote. This device is not the ultimate solution but is an excellent step in dealing with the problem of land mines.

Glossary

Allusion Allusion is the name given to a reference in a literary or artistic work to titles, characters, places, events, or other elements from other literary or artistic works, or from history, religion, or mythology. The reference may be obvious or obscure, implicit or explicit, but the author always assumes that the reader can and will recognize the allusion in a way that serves the author's objectives. Robert Lucky's reference to the George Washington "cherry tree" legend is explicit; Umberto Eco's use of the phrase "decline and fall" might be more obscure. Allusions depend partly on the author's target audience—a reference to *Star Wars* or some other icon of contemporary popular culture might be lost on certain audiences.

Analogy An analogy describes one subject in terms of another. It is often used to make difficult or abstract concepts concrete and comprehensible. An analogy is used to argue that because *A* resembles *B* in some respects, *A* also resembles *B* in others. It is wise to remember that analogies are never total: *A* is not *B*, after all.

Aphorism An aphorism is a concise statement of a principle, or a short, pithy sentence, often expressing folk wisdom. An example is this, regarding the weather: "Red sun in the morning, sailors take warning."

Argument or Persuasion In persuasion, the writer attempts to affect the way the reader thinks, believes, or acts. An argument is an attempt to change, not merely to inform, the reader. There are two general types of argument: induction and deduction. **Induction** bases conclusions on specific facts. If you wished to argue that the man next door had a bad temper, you would cite occasions when he became angry for inadequate reasons. Those cases would constitute evidence, and your claim would stand or fall according to the strength of the evidence. **Deduction** begins with a broad premise and seeks to work out the conclusion from it. The classic form of the deductive argument is the syllogism. It takes this form:

> All dogs have four legs.
> Rover is a dog.
> Therefore, Rover has four legs.

Note that the elements of the syllogism are not necessarily interchangeable. This syllogism is not valid:

> All dogs have four legs.
> Fluffy has four legs.
> Therefore, Fluffy is a dog.

Fluffy, in fact, is a cat. This argument breaks down because the first premise does not claim (and it could not claim) that dogs are the only animals with four legs.

Cause and Effect Most essays eventually need to discuss in some form causes, or reasons, and effects, or consequences. The simplest way to treat a cause as the topic of an essay is to pose a question, and then supply the answer. Effects can be treated in much the same way, with the consequence becoming the topic and the starting point for what will follow.

Coherency (see also **Transition**) Coherency refers to the internal relationships between ideas or elements in a piece of writing. When an essay or paragraph is coherent, it holds together sentence by sentence, and paragraph by paragraph. Each idea, statement, and example clearly connects both with what has come before and with what will come after. Connections may be logical ("this, and this"; "this; therefore, this"; "thus"), chronological (first, second, third; initially, next, finally), causal (this, because of that), or spatial (centre to margin; left to right; nearest to farthest).

Comparison and Contrast A comparison always involves similarities, whether these are discussed alone or together with differences. Contrast is confined to showing differences. Thus, while the two terms are significantly different, they often appear together.

Coordination Coordination refers to ways of building sentences and paragraphs. Compound sentences build by adding together related independent clauses that are connected by coordinating conjunctions (and, but, or, nor, for, yet, so), or by a semicolon. Coordination is also a method of paragraph development in which each sentence refers back to the first sentence of the paragraph, clarifying, defining, or illustrating a word or term from that first sentence.

Definition To define is to set limits or boundaries. A **lexical** or dictionary definition presents a term, names the category or genus of which it is a part, and then provides the characteristics or differences that make the term specific or unique. A **categorical** definition is similar; it places an object, idea, or procedure in a classification system and isolates its component parts. An **extended** definition provides readers with a sense of an object, idea, or procedure's larger significance in relation to other objects, ideas, or procedures. Such a definition may also include analogies and operational details.

Description Description seeks to inform the reader by employing spatial and sensory experience—how something looks, sounds, tastes.

Emphasis Emphasis is the weight or stress given to individual words or ideas within sentences, paragraphs, or whole pieces of writing. Words or phrases that appear at the opening or close of sentences or paragraphs, especially key words that repeat at these positions, tend to stick in the reader's mind; they tend to acquire importance. Emphasis can also derive from an effective figure of speech; from full, clear development of an idea or topic through examples, analogies, redefinition, etc.; or from varying sentence pattern (placing a short sentence among longer sentences, or raising new issues through questions, rather than declarative sentences).

Example Writing characterized by example explains through providing highly specific illustrations or instances to support specific arguments, points, opinions, or beliefs. Example often allows the reader to witness or experience the author's purpose or position in operation.

Irony Irony is an effect produced when there is a discrepancy between two levels of meaning. **Irony of situation** refers to a contrast between what we expect to happen and what really happens. **Verbal irony** refers to a deliberate contrast between what is said and what is meant. **Dramatic irony** refers to audience awareness of the meaning of words or actions unknown to one or more characters. Dramatic irony occurs when we are "in on" something that a character is not.

Narration A narrative is a story, a meaningful sequence of events told in words. A sequence involves an arrangement of events in time, the simplest sequence being a straightforward movement from the first event to the last.

Process Process illustrates how something is done or how something comes about. The process may be a sequence directed towards achieving a specific end, which includes or identifies various steps or stages. In some cases, the purpose of process writing may be to allow others to follow such stages in order to achieve a similar result. Such process writing is likely to be objective. On the other hand, process writing may be directed toward the identification of an ongoing, progressive change that is currently in progress and that does not yet have a definite outcome. This type of process writing is likely to be subjective as well as objective and to attempt to direct specific attitudes toward the process itself.

Satire Satire is the practice of attacking something by making it look ridiculous. It uses laughter as a weapon by making the butt of the joke appear absurd, contemptible, or undignified. Satire may attack a person, an idea, an ideology, a class, an institution, a behaviour or habit, etc.

Style Style is an author's unmistakable personal choice of words, sentence construction, diction, imagery, tone, and ideas.

Subordination Subordination refers to methods of combining sentence elements and of building paragraphs. Subordination in sentences, or in sentence combination, makes one idea or element dependent on another. A subordinate clause modifies or complements something in the main, independent clause. In revision, a writer may take two or more ideas originally expressed in consecutive shorter sentences, and choose to subordinate one or more, thus creating a complex sentence that clearly emphasizes the main idea. In constructing a paragraph, a writer may make each succeeding sentence continue from and expand on a word or phrase from the sentence before, rather than from a word or phrase from the topic sentence.

Tone Tone is the implied attitude of a writer toward the subject, material, and reader.

Transition (see also **Coherency**) Refers to techniques that make clear to the reader connections or links within and between paragraphs. Transitional words or phrases allow the writer (and, of course, the reader) to connect ideas or details by adding them together (and, also); separating them for further discussion (but, however); providing examples (for example, for instance); joining them in time, space, or logical sequence (before, next; above, below; if . . . then, therefore); or explaining causes or effects (because, consequently).

Title Index

ALPHABETICAL BY TITLE

"A, B, and C: The Human Element in Mathematics"
Stephen Leacock (1911), 158

"The Atom's Image Problem"
Jay Ingram (1996), 124

"Beginning to Understand the Beginning"
Rick McConnell (1996), 166

"Behind the Formaldehyde Curtain"
Jessica Mitford (1963), 179

"Bred in the Bone?"
Alan Goodman (1997), 70

"Charles Darwin's Tree of Life"
O. B. Hardison, Jr. (1989), 86

"Clone Mammals . . . Clone Man?"
Axel Kahn (1997), 128

"Crocodiled Moats in the Kingdom of Letters"
Cynthia Ozick (1989), 210

"Detection of Landmines"
Robert Gust et al., 340

"Doomsday"
Paul Davies (1994), 38

"Eat Your Hearts Out Cinephiles"
John Haslett Cuff (1996), 28

"The English Villa"
John Ruskin (1838), 250

"A Fable for Tomorrow"
Rachel Carson (1962), 20

"Finger-Pointing"
Robert W. Lucky (1985), 162

"Fishing for Coyote in Sheila Watson's
The Double Hook"
Cherina Sparks, 333

"Frauds on the Fairies"
Charles Dickens (1853), 43

"The Ghost's Vocabulary"
Edward Dolnick (1991), 54

"Ghosts in the Machine"
Sherry Turkle (1995), 287

"How Iraq Reverse-Engineered the Bomb"
Glenn Zorpette (1992), 313

"India"
Perri Klass (1987), 138

"Lessons from Play; Lessons from Life"
Henry Petroski (1992), 215

"Letter to My Son"
Umberto Eco (1964), 61

"Liftoff!"
Roberta Bondar (1994), 12

"Living Like Weasels"
Annie Dillard (1982), 50

"Marie Curie and Mileva Einstein Marić"
Hilary Rose (1994), 236

"A Mask on the Face of Death"
Richard Selzer (1987), 259

"A Modest Proposal"
Jonathan Swift (1729), 276

"Molecular Structure of Nucleic Acids:
  A Structure for Deoxyribose Nucleic Acid"
  J. D. Watson and F. H. C. Crick (1953), 293

"The Monster's Human Nature"
  Stephen Jay Gould (1995), 78

"Myth and Malevolence"
  Michael Ignatieff (1995), 120

The Origin of Species
  Charles Darwin (1859), 34

"A Person Paper on Purity in Language"
  Douglas Hofstadter (1983), 165

"The Pleasures and Pains of Coffee"
  Honoré de Balzac (1830), 1

"Political Economy"
  Samuel L. Clemens (1870), 23

"Politics and the English Language"
  George Orwell (1946), 199

"The Ponds"
  Henry David Thoreau (1854), 283

"Praise to the Albany"
  Morton L. Ross (1975), 243

"Putting Self-Help 'Leviathans' and 'Oracles' to Sleep"
  Lisa Grekul, 327

Radioactive Substances
  Marie Curie (1910), 31

"The Revival of Handicraft"
  William Morris (1888), 186

"The Road from Rio"
  David Suzuki (1992), 269

"The Route to Normal Science"
  Thomas S. Kuhn (1962), 143

"Sense and Sensibility"
  Lewis H. Lapham (1991), 153

"'State-of-the-Art Car': The Ferrari Testarossa"
  Joyce Carol Oates (1985), 194

"Straight Talk at the Parakeet Café"
  Jan Furlong (1998), 67

"Television and Reading"
  Marie Winn (1985), 305

"Viable Offspring Derived from Fetal and Adult
  Mammalian Cells"
  Ian Wilmut et al. (1997), 297

"The Way We Woo"
  Heather Pringle (1993), 226

"What Is an Elementary Particle?"
  Werner Heisenberg (1976), 94

"Why I Am Not Going to Buy a Computer"
  Wendell Berry (1990), 6

"Why Johnny Can't Think"
  Walter Karp (1992), 132

"Why the Deficit Is a Godsend"
  Walter Russell Mead (1993), 170

"Women in Chemistry Before 1900"
  Sherida Houlihan and John H. Wotiz (1973), 113

Date Index

CHRONOLOGICAL BY DATE OF FIRST PUBLICATION

1729: "A Modest Proposal"
Jonathan Swift, 276

1830: "The Pleasures and Pains of Coffee"
Honoré de Balzac, 1

1838: "The English Villa" (from *The Poetry of Architecture*)
John Ruskin, 250

1853: "Frauds on the Fairies"
Charles Dickens, 43

1854: "The Ponds" (from *Walden*)
Henry David Thoreau, 283

1859: *The Origin of Species*
Charles Darwin, 34

1870: "Political Economy"
Samuel L. Clemens, 23

1888: "The Revival of Handicraft"
William Morris, 186

1910: *Radioactive Substances*
Marie Curie, 31

1911: "A, B, and C: The Human Element in Mathematics"
Stephen Leacock, 158

1946: "Politics and the English Language"
George Orwell, 199

1953: "Molecular Structure of Nucleic Acids"
J. D. Watson and F. H. C. Crick, 293

1962: "A Fable for Tomorrow"
Rachel Carson, 20

1962: "The Route to Normal Science"
Thomas S. Kuhn, 143

1963: "Behind the Formaldehyde Curtain"
Jessica Mitford, 179

1964: "Letter to My Son"
Umberto Eco, 61

1973: "Women in Chemistry Before 1900"
Sherida Houlihan and John H. Wotiz, 113

1975: "Praise to the Albany"
Morton L. Ross, 243

1976: "What Is an Elementary Particle?"
Werner Heisenberg, 94

1982: "Living Like Weasels"
Annie Dillard, 50

1983: "A Person Paper on Purity in Language"
Douglas Hofstadter, 105

1985: "Finger-Pointing"
Robert W. Lucky, 162

1985: "'State-of-the-Art Car': The Ferrari Testarossa"
Joyce Carol Oates, 194

1985: "Television and Reading"
Marie Winn, 305

1987: "India"
Perri Klass, 138

1987: "A Mask on the Face of Death"
Richard Selzer, 259

1989: "Charles Darwin's Tree of Life"
O. B. Hardison, Jr., 86

362   *Date Index*

1989: "Crocodiled Moats in the Kingdom of Letters"
Cynthia Ozick, 210

1990: "Why I Am Not Going to Buy a Computer"
Wendell Berry, 6

1991: "The Ghost's Vocabulary"
Edward Dolnick, 54

1991: "Sense and Sensibility"
Lewis H. Lapham, 153

1992: "Why Johnny Can't Think"
Walter Karp, 132

1992: "Lessons from Play, Lessons from Life"
Henry Petroski, 215

1992: "The Road from Rio"
David Suzuki, 269

1992: "How Iraq Reverse-Engineered the Bomb"
Glenn Zorpette, 313

1993: "Why the Deficit Is a Godsend"
Walter Russell Mead, 170

1993: "The Way We Woo"
Heather Pringle, 226

1994: "Liftoff!"
Roberta Bondar, 12

1994: "Doomsday"
Paul Davies, 38

1994: "Marie Curie and Mileva Einstein Marić"
Hilary Rose, 236

1995: "The Monster's Human Nature"
Stephen Jay Gould, 78

1995: "Myth and Malevolence"
Michael Ignatieff, 120

1995: "Ghosts in the Machine"
Sherry Turkle, 287

1996: "Eat Your Hearts Out Cinephiles"
John Haslett Cuff, 28

1996: "The Atom's Image Problem"
Jay Ingram, 124

1996: "Beginning to Understand the Beginning"
Rick McConnell, 166

1997: "Bred in the Bone?"
Alan Goodman, 70

1997: "Clone Mammals . . . Clone Man?"
Axel Kahn, 128

1997: "Viable Offspring Derived from Fetal and
Adult Mammalian Cells"
Ian Wilmut et al., 297

1998: "Detection of Landmines"
Robert Gust et al., 340

1998: "Fishing for Coyote in Sheila Watson's
The Double Hook"
Cherina Sparks, 333

1998: "Putting Self-Help 'Leviathans' and
'Oracles' to Sleep"
Lisa Grekul, 327

1998: "Straight Talk at the Parakeet Café"
Jan Furlong, 67